Scientometrics

SCIENTOMETRICS

Editors
I.K. Ravichandra Rao
and
A. Neelameghan

Published By

Ess Ess Publications
New Delhi
for

Sarada Ranganathan Endowment for Library Science
Bangalore

Scientometrics

S.R. Ranganathan's
Five Laws of Library Science

Books are for Use
Every Reader his/her Book
Every Book its Reader
Save the Time of the Reader
Library is a Growing Organism

ISBN: 978-81-7000-717-3

₹ 1295/-

First Published 2014

Published by:
Ess Ess Publications
4831/24, Ansari Road,
Darya Ganj,
New Delhi-110 002.
INDIA
Phones: 23260807, 41563444
Fax: 41563334
E-mail: info@essessreference.com
www.essessreference.com

for

Sarada Ranganathan Endowment for Library Science
702, 'Upstairs', 42nd Cross, III Block, Rajajinagar,
Bangalore-560 010
E-mail: srels@dataone.in Phone: 080-23305109

Printed and bound in India at Salasar Imaging Systems.

ACKNOWLEDGEMENT

This work is supported in part by the World Bank / Government of India research grant under the TEQIP programme (subcomponent 1.2.1) to the Centre for Knowledge Analytics and Ontological Engineering (KAnOE) at PES Institute of Technology, Bangalore, India.

I thank Ms. S.K. Lalitha, Project Assistant, Sarada Ranganathan Endowment for Library Science (SRELS), 702, 42nd Cross, III Block, Rajajinagar, Bangalore 560 010, INDIA, for help in preparing the manuscript.

The papers included in this volume have been separately published in the *SRELS Journal of Information Management*, 50(5), October 2013, special issue on Scientometrics.

CONTENTS

FOREWORD

Sarada Ranganathan Endowment for Library Science (SRELS), founded by Dr. S.R. Ranganathan, Renowned Library and Information Scientist in 1961, is registered as a Charitable Endowment with the Government of India (1963). It is also registered with the Government of Karnataka (2006).

The aims and objectives of the Endowment briefly are:

- To improve the library and information services in India;
- To train library and information service personnel;
- To promote the provision of efficient library and information service; and
- To apply research results to library and information studies.

The Endowment is implementing these objectives by publishing books, reports and the periodical *SRELS Journal of Information Management* and by organizing Workshops, Lecture and Seminars. *SRELS Journal of Information Management* has completed ***50 years*** of publication.

Three series of lectures are organized under the auspices of the Endowment are:

1. Sarada Ranganathan Endowment Lectures. (1965-);
2. Dr. S.R. Ranganathan Memorial Lectures. (1973-); and
3. Curzon Co-Seshachalam Endowment Lectures. (2001-).

Scientometrics: A Collection of Papers, edited by I.K. Ravichandra Rao and A. Neelameghan, contains 15 articles on scientometrics and other related areas. These articles discuss several issues related to Scintometrics including Citation analysis, Webometrics, Hierarchy studies, Scientometric profile, Study of acknowledgements in research papers, Research collaboration studies, Mapping of research, etc.

The research papers included in this book indicate that scientometric research in India is centered on the quantitative analysis of the literature by subject and a few by country. The scientometric literature indicates that Indian publications are becoming increasingly more visible.

K.N. Prasad
Executive Officer
Sarada Ranganathan Endowment for Library Science

Introduction

I.K. Ravichandra Rao

Librametry, Bibliometrics, Informetrics and Scientometrics are closely related topics. Its main scope is to evaluate and measure various characteristics of libraries (including the library services), scientific publications and science in general. In practice, much of the research work that falls under these headings mostly centered on various types of citation analysis -- looking at how scholars cite one another in publications. Whether we call the research area (-- application of quantitative methods to library and information science) as librametry or bibliometrics or scientometrics or informetrics, most of the topics we deal with are:

- Quantitative aspects of library and information studies, especially use and user studies, growth of collection, age distribution of documents, circulation statistics, etc.
- Journal productivity (by subject coverage, coverage in databases, by use, by citation, cost-effectiveness measures, impact factor, sources of citations, immediacy of citations, age of sources cited, etc.)
- Measures of author productivity, including studies related to multiple-authorship (number of publications. number of un-cited publications, cost-effectiveness measures, impact factor, h-index, reprints request, photo copies made, sources of citations, immediacy of citations, number of reviews, adoption rates (text books), etc.)
- Obsolescence and growth of literature
- Co-citation, bibliographic coupling, co-word analysis, rank distribution of words, etc.
- Quantitative analyses of science (science indicators -- country-wise, language-wise, subject-wise, all other measures as given inn journal productivity and author productivity, etc.)
- Identifying relationships among various disciplines, structure of subjects, etc.

Acceptance of a single term to define a subject and acceptance of its scope help us in:

- Studying and understanding a subject;
- Designing a syllabus for a teaching programme;

- Getting the research grant from different agencies; and
- Identifying the research groups especially at national and international levels.

In this book, we are using the term scientometrics, instead of librametry or bibliometrics or informetrics. Realizing the importance of scientometrics, since mid-1960s, many research projects were initiated in India in this area. Most of the papers came from DRTC and INSDOC. The Documentation Research and Training Centre organized a seminar on librametry in 1969, as a part of its regular research programme; the papers presented in this seminar were published in the Proceedings of the DRTC Annual Seminar (1969). Since then DRTC continued the research in scientometrics. Again in 2008, DRTC jointly with NISSAT organized a Workshop on Scientometrics and Informetrics. The papers presented in this workshop were also published (-- Workshop on Informetrics and Scientometrics, March 1998, Edited by I K Ravichandra Rao) as one of the DRTC publications.

Sarada Ranganathan Endowment for Library science, as a part of its annual lecture series, organized four following lectures in the area of 'metrics.'

1. 'Measuring Information: Some Problems and Directions for Information Science' by Jean Tague-Sutcliff (1993.);
2. 'Lectures on Informetrics and Scientometrics' by Leo Egghe (2000.);
3. 'Bibliometric Methods in Assessing Productivity and Impact of Research' F.W. Lancater (1991.); and
4. 'Growth of Literature and Measures of Scientific Productivity: Scientometric Models' by I K Ravichandra Rao (2010.)

The DRTC in its regular teaching programme (-- leading to Associateship in Documentation), 'quantitative methods', including the scientometrics, was included as one of the core papers. Based on his experience of teaching in DRTC, Ravichandra Rao published a book on 'quantitative methods for library and information science,' with a detailed chapter on bibliometrics, published first by Wiley-Eastern in 1983.

The Sarada Ranganathan Endowment for Library Science and DRTC together has initiated several academic activities in the area of scientometrics. The SRELS Journal was first published in 1964; then its title was 'Library Science with a slant to Documentation' (1964-1987); since 2000, its title is 'SRELS Journal of Information Management.' Between 1988 and 1999, its title was "Library Science with a slant to

Documentation and Information Studies' In the initial years, the journal mostly published the research papers from Documentation Research and Training Centre; now it has grown beyond the delimited subject and institutional scope and it is now a peer reviewed journal. With the advent of e-publishing, keeping with the trend, an online version of the journal is also available. In 1960s, the journal focused on library classification and library cataloguing; gradually it covered the new areas of interest to library science, like computer applications, library management and information systems. In mid 1970's, special issues of this journal devoted to Information Systems - planning and organization, were brought out. Now the journal covers all facets of library and information science and is moving forward attracting the LIS professionals from India and abroad.

The book consists of 15 articles in scientometrics and related topics. These articles discuss several issues related to scientometrics and these are briefly mentioned below. In one of the articles in this book, Using citation analysis, Stegmann and Kretschmer investigated the presence of S. R. Ranganathan's work in the modern scientific literature. The authors have observed that during the past twenty two years nearly 400 papers cite at least one of Ranganathan's works, significantly, more than in the preceding forty years. There is much evidence for a sustainable pervasion of modern science by Ranganathan's work and ideas. On the basis of citation data, the authors in their paper have shown that work and ideas of Shiyali Ramamrita Ranganathan are enduring parts of the modern scientific discourse. The authors have concluded that further research on all aspects of Ranganathan's work is required; for example, studies involving co-citation and bibliographic coupling analyses could reveal Ranganathan's presence in core papers and research fronts, giving 'important stimuli to the further development of library and information science.'

Ravichandra Rao carried out a survey of scientometric literature of India (based on the LIS database) for the period 2000-12. He observed that most of the articles were published in Annals of Library and Information Science, SRELS Journal Information Management, DESIDOC Bulletin of Information Technology, COLLNET Journal of Scientometrics and Information management and Journal of Scientometrics. These scientometric articles mostly covered the following topics:

- Quantitative aspects of library and information studies;
- Journal productivity;
- Measures of productivity or author productivity, including studies related to multiple- authorship;

- Obsolescence and growth of literature; and
- Quantitative analyses of science (--National mapping of science).

Liu, Guns and Rousseau used a binary tree model for studying hierarchies using Q-measures. All nodes in a binary tree situated at the same height are assumed to form a group. The global and local Q-value, being measures for the extent to which a node plays a bridging function between groups, are determined.

Garg, Kumar and Krishnan Marg analyzed 90,958 papers published by Indian scientists and indexed by *Science Citation Index-Expanded (SCI-E)* during 2010-2011. Their study indicates that

1. Scientific output during 2010-11 increased almost two and half times as compared to 2000-01;
2. Academic institutions published the highest number of papers -- 43% of the output;
3. The highest number of papers was published in the discipline of chemical sciences;
4. Highest impact as judged by the values of Citation per Paper (CPP) and Relative Citation Impact (RCI) was also made by chemical sciences. About 83% papers were published in journals originated from abroad;
5. US journals were the most preferred choice of publishing papers;
6. About half of the papers were published in medium impact factor journals and 66% papers were cited one or more times; and
7. Indian Institute of Science (Bangalore) published the highest number of papers; however, Jawaharlal Nehru Centre for Advanced Scientific Research (Bangalore) made the highest impact.

In another paper on scientometric profile of vector borne diseases, Garg, Sandhya Dwivedi and Kumar analyzed 2,074 papers published on different aspects of Japanese Encephalitis (JE) from 1991 to 2010 and indexed by *Science Citation Index-Expanded*; their study indicates that the output increased many folds since 1991 except a significant dip in 2005. These papers were scattered in 501 journals, originated from 29 different countries. Articles came from 62 countries of which 14 countries contributed 90% of the total output. The highest number of publications came from USA, followed by India. The authors have further observed that

1. Publication activity increased significantly for China, South Korea, France, Austria, Singapore and Germany;
2. Data indicates that about 87% of the total output is concentrated among 15 sub-disciplines and the remaining in other 53 sub-disciplines;

3. Highest output (18%) is in the sub-discipline of virology. Among the prolific institutions, the publication output of institutions from the USA and Taiwan had higher impact. Citation per Paper (CPP) and Relative Citation Impact (RCI) were more than average for USA; and
4. All the Indian institutes listed under prolific institutions had made low impact.

Adarsh Bala and Santosh Kumari analyzed the research performance of National Institutes of Technology (NITs) of India during 2001-2010 on several parameters -- NITs' overall contribution, its growth pattern, citation impact, the share of international collaboration, identification of significant participating countries in NITs' international collaboration, contribution and impact by different subject areas, identification of weak and strong subject areas, productivity and impact of prolific authors, pattern of communication of NITs' output in most productive journals and characteristics of high cited papers of NITs'. The Scopus Citation Database has been used to retrieve the data for 10 years (2001-10). The important findings are:

1. During the survey period, NITs published 8,841 papers (-- 66.41% are articles, 31.09% as conference papers, 1.55% reviews, 0.24% notes, 0.20% editorials, etc;) average number of papers per year is 884; average annual growth rate is 38.45%, 2.14 citations per paper (with total of 18,878 citations);
2. The publication share of individual NIT varied from 0.16% to 12.83% during 2001-2010. NIT-Rourkela scored the 1st rank with its publication share of 12.83%;
3. The NIT's cumulative international collaborative publication output consisted of 905 papers, accounting for 10.24% share in its publication output during 2001-2010, NIT-Tiruchirappallli has published the highest number (223) of international collaborative papers with 24.64% share; USA is the major collaborating partner with NITs with 22.76% international collaborative publication share;
4. Among the broad subject wise contribution of NITs, engineering sciences contributed the highest publication share (81.93%); however, life sciences scored the maximum average citation impact per paper (3.6). Engineering science, computer science, material science, physics & astronomy and chemistry are considered as the five high priority areas of NITs; and
5. The 1,059 (11.98%) research papers were published in top 20 highly productive foreign and Indian journals; results show a decline in publication output from 16.08% share during 2001-05 to 11.22% share. Among the 100

high cited papers, 15 papers involve international collaboration (12 bilateral and 3 multilateral), 41 involve national collaboration and 44 papers have zero collaboration.

Kumbar and Gupta in their study the research contribution of the Mysore University and the Karnatak University in terms of number of papers in science and technology, its growth and citation impact during 2001-10. They identified the strong and weak subject areas of universities research and their citation impact. Their paper also

1. Describes the international collaborative share of research output of the universities at the overall level, indicating the contribution of the major collaborating partner countries;
2. Provides analyses of the national collaborating links of the two universities; with a view to study their collaborating linkages with academic institutions, institutes of national importance, research institutions and industry; and
3. Studies the contribution and citation impact of the top 15 most productive authors and also the productivity of their most productive journals, where the two universities authors have published.

Gupta, Saxena and Visakhi examined the contribution of twenty agricultural universities to the mainstream scientific literature during 2007-2011. Both inter-related dimensions of quantity (-- number of papers, number of international collaborative papers, etc.) and quality of research output (assessed through the citations received) were examined. A number of measures are used for inter-field and inter-university comparisons. Inter-field comparisons are made at the level of 10 macro subject fields. They have observed that:

1. Twenty Indian agricultural universities together have published 9,272 papers, constituting 2.75% of the Indian research output -- increased from 1,701 in 2,007 to 2,112 papers in 2011; the annual average growth rate is 5.71%;
2. Productivity of individual agricultural university varied from 138 to 1,588; the average productivity per organization is 526.95. The average citation per paper is 1.76, and varies from 0.77 to 2.96;
3. There were 1,049 (11.36%) international collaborative papers with 83 countries; decreasing from 13.52% in 2007 to 11.36% in 2011. Of the collaborating countries, the largest share (32.32%) of papers was published with United States, followed by UK (10.39% share), Germany (9.25% share), Australia (7.91% share), China (6.96% share), Canada (6.67% share);

4. The national collaboration links varies from 26.41% to 81.31%. Of the total national collaboration links, the largest share of collaboration links (50.26%) were to academic institutions (varying from 27.27% to 75.86%), followed by research institutions (45.36%)(varying from 26.23% to 62.30%), institutes of national importance (3.80%)(varying from 0.0% to 15.85%), industry (1.32%) (0.0% to 6.80%) and others (0.99%) (0.0% to 6.86%); and
5. In terms of average institutional share of 20 agricultural universities in different subjects , the largest share (68.76%) was in agricultural & biological sciences, followed by veterinary sciences (25.05%), biochemistry, genetics & molecular biology (13.57%), environment science (8.26%), immunology & microbiology (6.31%), engineering (4.61%), medicine (4.59%), , pharmacology, toxicology & pharmaceutics (3.43%), chemistry (3.14%) and energy (1.221%) during 2007-11.

Koley and Sen studied the acknowledgements incorporated in research papers on electronics and related fields appearing during 2008-2012 in *IETE Technical Review*, and *IETE Journal of Research*, official publications of The Institution of Electronics and Telecommunication Engineers (IETE). The authors have observed that 35% of articles contain acknowledgements -- average acknowledgement per articles is 2.2; most of the acknowledgements (51%) relates to financial support. Only 21% of acknowledgements address to the Peer Interactive Communication (PIC), and two persons are acknowledged two times. The number of articles with acknowledgements is higher in *IETE Technical Review* compared to IETE *Journal of Research*. The number of PIC acknowledgements in electronics research is very low compared to other journals. Forty-two percent articles acknowledge one addressee and 1% articles acknowledges up to ten addressees at a time.

Sangam and Shivaranjini attempted to investigate the pattern of authorship, type of collaborated research and the degree of collaboration in the field of Social Sciences, based on the data from social science citation index of ISI Thomson Reuters, for the period of twelve years, 2000-2011. The authors have computed collaborative index (CI) and degree of collaboration (DC) and collaboration coefficient (CC). They have further argued that:

1. The movement towards collaborative innovation is affecting scientific research, bringing scientists from different disciplines together in their pursuit of solutions to today's challenges. In particular, teams that work

collaboratively can obtain greater resources, recognition and reward when facing competition for finite resources; and

2. The collaboration is not limited to individual scientists; it is extended even up to institutions, communities, and nations and so on. The concept of team work is in vogue because of various funding agencies.

Dutta and Rath studied 834 articles (downloaded from Web of Science) on Carbon nanotube research in India for the period 1999-2012. The study analyses literature growth trends, which reveals an initiation of potential growth of research in this area since 2008. The authors have also examined collaborations with different countries worldwide. The authorship pattern, document types involved and active Indian institutions co-coordinating research in this subject area have also been studied. Bradford's law of scattering was employed to identify the core journals and Lotka's law was employed to study the authors' productivity pattern. The authors have observed:

1. Authorship pattern shows dominance of two-authored and three-authored articles. As this research field is experimental one, solo research is almost negligible. Team research is prominent with tiny team size while large teams are hardly involved;
2. The author productivity pattern is not in close proximity with Lotka's law;
3. The core journals in this subject area have been identified by employing Bradford's law of scattering. Almost all core journals are published from USA and possess fairly high impact factor;
4. The subject domain analysis shows that it is an interdisciplinary area with so many subjects overlapped thereon. The subjects like physics, chemistry, material science and nanoscience & nanotechnology are in close proximity with the subject of Carbon nanotube;
5. The analysis of institutional pattern shows that the top three sectors, viz. university, IIT and foreign institutions affiliate nearly two-third (66%) of total number of authors. Also, individually IITs, IISc and JNCASR are top three affiliating institutions. The potential universities in Carbon nanotube research include BHU, DU and MKU, and potential laboratories for the same are NPL, NCL , BARC and IACS; and
6. It can thus be inferred that Carbon nanotube research in India though started in recent past gained thrust importance within few years. It is a budding topic of active interdisciplinary research with high prospects.

Webometrics, a related topic of scientometrics, is the quantitative analysis of web phenomenon. Harinarayana and Vasantha Raju look at the recent developments in webometrics research in light of emergence of social web and big data and their applications in new research fronts and future perspective of webometrics research. Their paper gives an overview of the emerging trends and impact measuring techniques used in webometrics research. They also discuss about the recent developments in research techniques in webometrics such as query splitting and virtual memetics in the social network sites. The authors have observed that the growth of web technologies has possibly posed new challenges for traditional citation databases which have been extensively used so far measuring research impact of universities, institutions or individual researchers. The new trend has shown that impact measures are in the verge of acceptance as new method for measurement of academic and research contributions.

Thirumagal and Sethukumari analyzed the research papers in the area of cloud computing for the period 2008 to 2012. The study is based on the 2,207 records which were downloaded from the Web of Knowledge. These records were analyzed with the Bibexcel tool. The authors have analyzed the growth pattern, authorship pattern and examined the publication type of research, applicability of Lotka's Law, etc. The authors have further observed that

1. Number of papers with single and multiple authors are 363 and 1844 respectively; the Degree of Collaboration is 0.84;
2. Relative Growth Rate has been decreasing from 0.85 in 2008 to 0.43 in 2012. The Doubling Time has increases from 0.80 to 1.58;
3. Astronomy and Astrophysics" Journal has first rank with 93 contributions; and
4. Distribution of papers confirms to Lotka's Law; 5503 authors have contributed to the literature in cloud computing.

Aparna Basu tried to summarize the criteria used by some of these agencies. In particular we note the presence of only a few Indian institutes in these rankings. The need for initiating a systematic ranking of Indian institutes at regular intervals is stressed. She points out that

1. Ranking exercises work with constructs which may not always reflect quality adequately;
2. Some degree of care and calibration is required in the choice and relative weights of factors; and

3. The race to achieve high ranks can also skew the activities in the institutions, according lower priority to important factors of performance which cannot directly be measured.

She observed that only a few Indian institutions feature in the lists that may rank up to 500 institutions (at the global level) although some do feature in the regional lists. She suggests a similar rank list of Indian Institutions by considering almost all factors relevant to India, so that performance of institutions within India may be compared. She suggested that research institutes and primarily teaching institutions such as universities be evaluated on the same footing. She also suggests a slightly different set of factors, as against the global factors, to suit the Indian context, such as the use of the Bhatnagar awards, separate ranking for different disciplines, normalization for the size of the institution, etc. Finally, she argues that there is a need to adopt caution in these exercises so that the results adequately express the accepted notions of quality and do not adversely affect the normal activities of institutions under study.

Asundi attempted to map the subject analytical of this journal's path it has spanned in the last Fifty years. The analysis would serve as a check list for the areas of current and traditional subject interests in the field of LIS. The paper also highlights some noble contributions and special issues brought out on some eventful occasions in the past.

REMARKS

- The research papers which are discussed in the literature review in Ravichandra Rao's paper and the papers of this book certainly indicate that;
- Scientometric research in India is centered on the quantitative analysis of the literature by subject wise and in very few cases, it is country wise. There is very few research papers on theoretical aspects of scientometrics; and
- Science in general is growing in India; the Indian publications are now visible and it is increasing; this is what we could observe from the scientometric literature. There is hardly any scientometric research is being carried out to evaluate and measure research outcome; there is also no evidence that the results of the scientometric research is being used in drafting science policy or in science administration. It is hoped that science administrators may use scientometrics research results may use in their day to day administration of science!

1

Ranganathan Today: A Citation Study

Johannes Stegmann and ***Hildrun Kretschmer***

Using citation analysis we investigated the presence of S. R. Ranganathan's work in the modern scientific literature. We found that during the past twenty two years nearly 400 papers cite at least one piece of Ranganathan's work, significantly more than in the preceding forty years. There is much evidence for a sustainable pervasion of modern science by Ranganathan's work and ideas.

KEYWORD: Citation received, S.R. Ranganathan

1 INTRODUCTION

Nowadays, the term "citation analysis" has a bad reputation due to its overwhelming use - often for economic reasons - in studies aiming at comparative ranking, evaluating, judging, assessing the scientific "quality" of journals, authors, institutions. The primary and distinguished purpose of citation analysis, however, is to track down the origins and dissemination of ideas and concepts, thereby implicitly acknowledging the significance of particular works, persons, and institutions (*Garfield*, 1955).

Certainly, everybody person working or having worked in a library has heard of Ranganathan, even if lacking formal education in librarianship. In 1948, when one of us (J.S.) was born, Ranganathan instituted a master of library science degree at the university of Delhi (*Garfield*, 1984 a). Most of his main works, as *Five Laws of Library Science* (1931), *Classified Catalogue Code* (1934), *Colon Classification* (1933), *Prolegomena to Library Classification* (1937), *Theory of the Library Catalogue* (1938), *Elements of Library Classification* (1945) had appeared, and Ranganathan was already acknowledged as one of the most influential persons in library science.

Screening of the *Web of Science* (WoS) literature mentioning and/or citing Ranganathan, however, revealed an astonishingly low number of papers having used citation analysis to illustrate the influence of Ranganathan's work. *Garfield* (1984b) mentions that Ranganathan's works were cited more than 400 times within twenty years. In addition, *Garfield* (2005) has visualised Ranganathan's work covering citing years up to 2005 using *HistCite*^{TM} (*Garfield* et al., 2006). *HistCite*^{TM} is particularly suitable for tracking individual cited/citing papers within a collection. We will refer to Garfield's Ranganathan-specific *HistCite*^{TM} file where appropriate. *Chung* (1994) found that Ranganathan was one of the core (cited) authors in the literature on classification systems by analysing the "Classification Literature" section of the journal *International Classification* for the years 1981 to 1990. A more comprehensive citation analysis of Ranganathan's influence over the period 1956-1990 was performed by *Lancaster* et al. (1992). We will several times refer to that paper below and compare our results with those of *Lancaster* et al. where appropriate. We think it might be of some interest to find out whether Ranganathan's influence is still present and visible in the more recent literature of library and information science.

2 DATA AND METHODS

The *Web of Science* (WoS) database (*Thomson Reuters* [http://isiknowledge.com/wos]) was searched for the cited author RANGANATHAN SR, including different spellings like RANGANATHAM SR or RANGANATAN SR etc. The cited reference strings retrieved were carefully inspected to eliminate references not pointing to publications of the librarian Ranganathan. Eventually, we retrieved 727 records containing 570 distinct reference strings specific to Ranganathan's work. These records citing Ranganathan were downloaded on June 26, 2013. Using *PERL* (version 5.14.2) scripts the contents of the record fields (e.g. publication year, source, cited references) were extracted. For computation and plotting the software package *R* version 2.14.1 (*R Development Core Team,* 2004) was used. All operations were done on a commercial PC run under *Ubuntu* version 12.04 LTS.

3 RESULTS AND DISCUSSION

Fig. 1&2 display the distributions over time of the number of papers citing Ranganathan's work (Fig. 1) and of the number of cites given to Ranganathan's publications (Fig. 2). The graphs are not identical because many papers cite more than one piece of Ranganathan's work. In total, we found 727 papers (Fig. 1) with 1210 cites given to Ranganathan's work (Fig. 2). The numbers for the periods up to

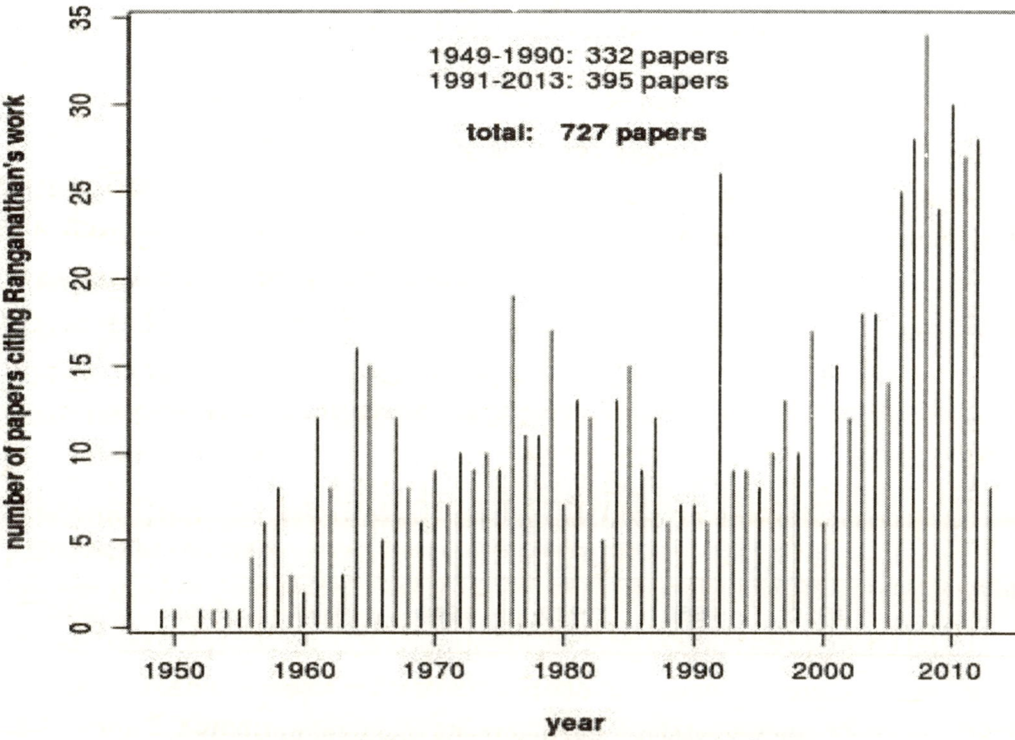

Fig. 1: Distribution over time of papers citing Ranganathan

1990 and 1991 to 2013 are also displayed in Fig. 1&2. *Lancaster* et al. (1992) found 477 citations in the *Social Sciences Citation Index* (SSCI) (1956-1990) and 153 citations in the *Science Citation* Index (1964-1990). According to Figs. 1&2 we found 326 citing papers and 642 Ranganathan-specific citations in the period 1956-1990. We think that our results fairly agree with those of *Lancaster* et al. Our slightly higher citation numbers may be due to papers contained in the *Arts & Humanities Citation Index* (A&HCI) which is part of the WoS with records from 1975 onwards (A&HCI was not searched by *Lancaster* et al.). For the period 1964-1984 we found 423 citations to Ranganathan which is similar to the number mentioned by *Garfield* (1984 b) (*see* Introduction). Up to 2005 we found 523 papers citing at least one of Ranganathan's publication which likewise agrees with the number of 518 nodes displayed in Garfield's Ranganathan-specific *HistCite*^{TM} file (*Garfield*, 2005).

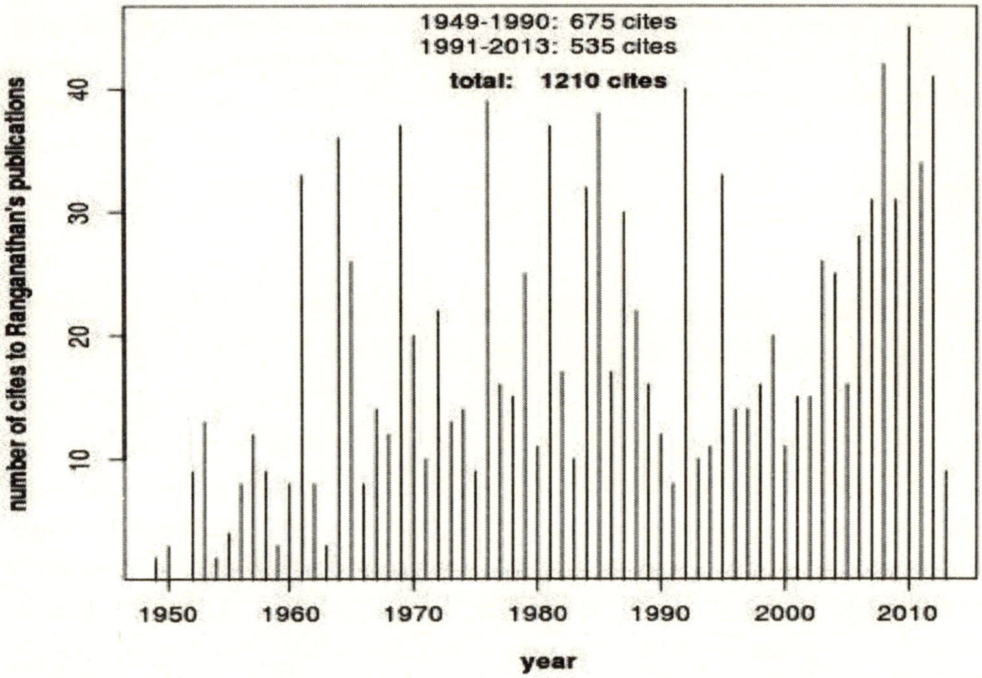

Fig. 2: Distribution over time of cites received by Ranganathan

The diagrams presented in Figs. 1&2 clearly show that Ranganathan's influence is not diminishing with time - a result also reported by *Lancaster* et al. (1992) for the period up to 1990. Quite the contrary, the presence of Ranganathan's work is obviously increasing in the more recent years. The number of papers citing Ranganathan over the years 1991-2013 is even higher than in the preceding 40 years, and the maximum so far (34 papers) is in 2008 (Fig. 1). The number of cites received by Ranganathan's work 1991-2013 is with 44% somewhat lower than in years before, but the citation maximum so far (45 cites) is also in modern times, in 2010 (Fig. 2). *Garfield* (1984 b) mentions that citation numbers would be much higher also for the early years of the citation indexes if coverage of the literature would have been more comprehensive. Thankfully, the WoS now also include book citation indexes although covering the time since 2005 only; yet about 13% of the citing papers 2005-2013 come from theses indexes (data not shown).

To determine the citation distribution of Ranganathan's main works we first had to merge the many different forms of the citing references strings pointing to the same work, e.g. the reference strings "5 LAWS LIB" or "FIVE LAWS LIBRARY" both cite

Five Laws of Library Science, and "PROLEGOMENA LIBRARY" or "PROLEGOMENA LIB" point to *Prolegomena to Library Classification*. Table 1 shows the results for some of the books authored by Ranganathan. These main works received about 55% of all citations in the whole period, and half of them were obtained after 1990, making again evident the ongoing significance of Ranganathan. The "ranking" of the main works up to 1990 is identical with that observed by *Lancaster* et al. (1992) (*see* Table 1). For the newer period this order has changed a bit. Interestingly, Ranganathan's "Five Laws", "Colon Classification", "Prolegomena", and "Elements" are more frequently cited in the more recent years, indicating their fundamental character and importance. Particularly "Five Laws" has gained 78% of the cites from 1991 onwards. This may be due at least in part to the since then upcoming electronic (r)evolution with its massive implementation of online catalogues and internet capable facilities which inevitably forced all librarians and libraries to more open-mindedness and user-friendliness. It is fantastic to see that Ranganathan's now more than 80 years old ideas and suggestions have yielded so many fruits and still are not forgotten.

Table 1: Citation rates of some of Ranganathan's main works*

Work	1949-1990	1991-2013	Total
Five Laws of Library Science (1931)	29	102	131
Colon Classification (1933)	78	92	170
Classified Catalogue Code (1934)	36	1	37
Prolegomena to Library Classification (1937)	111	137	248
Elements of Library Classification (1945)	23	45	68
Headings and Canons (1955)	16	1	17
Sum	**293**	**378**	**671**

*Cites received by different editions of the same work were cumulated.

That Ranganathan's publications are used for research is indicated by the fact that over 70% of the citing papers are research articles; about 7% are proceedings papers, and 6% are reviews (data not shown).

As *Lancaster* et al. (1992) did we analysed the distribution of Ranganathan-specific citations over the citing journals. On top of the period 1991-2013 ranks the journal *Knowledge Organization* which is the successor of *International Classification* being top-ranking for the period up to 1990. The journals *Libri, Library*

Trends, Journal of Documentation are within the top ten in both periods (see also *Lancaster* et al, 1992). Interestingly, the *Journal of the American Society for Information Science (and Technology)* (JASIS, JASIST) is on the 3rd position in 1991-2013 whereas it was on the 11th place according to *Lancaster* et al. (1992) or the 16th one according to our data, indicating that Ranganathan's body of thought now has spread out also to US research (*see also* Figure 3). More interesting may be that we found 62 distinct source titles in the early period, but 177 in the more recent time (data not shown). This is in part certainly due to the overall growth of number of journals and papers but surely also indicates sustained pervasion of the scientific community with Ranganathan's ideas. Next, we analysed the *Subject Categories* (data field SC) to which the citing papers/journals have been assigned. Not surprisingly, the category *Information Science & Library Science* ranks on top in both periods, occurring in 90% of the papers published in 1990, but to a considerably lower percentage (69%) in the papers published after 1990.

On the other hand, the earlier period comprises 16 distinct subject categories, whereas the later period comprises 24 categories, including *Tele-communications, Business & Economics, Operations Research & Management Science* (data not shown), once more demonstrating the effective incorporation of Ranganathan's work into the body of scientific knowledge.

Finally, we looked at the citing countries, i.e. the country affiliation of the authors citing Ranganathan's publications. We restricted this analysis to papers published 1991 or later, because 93% of the records of the later period contain country affiliation data, but almost half of the papers of the earlier period lack this information.

Fig. 3 displays the top-down ranked country distribution, the USA on top with almost three times more papers than the 2nd ranking country, UK. The top five countries each published more than twenty papers, the top eleven countries each published at least nine papers. Thirty two countries published at least two papers, and in total, we found thirty eight distinct countries having published at least one Ranganathan-citing paper since 1991 (Fig. 3).

4 CONCLUSION

On the basis of citation data we have shown that the work and ideas of the great Indian librarian Shiyali Ramamrita Ranganathan are enduring parts of the

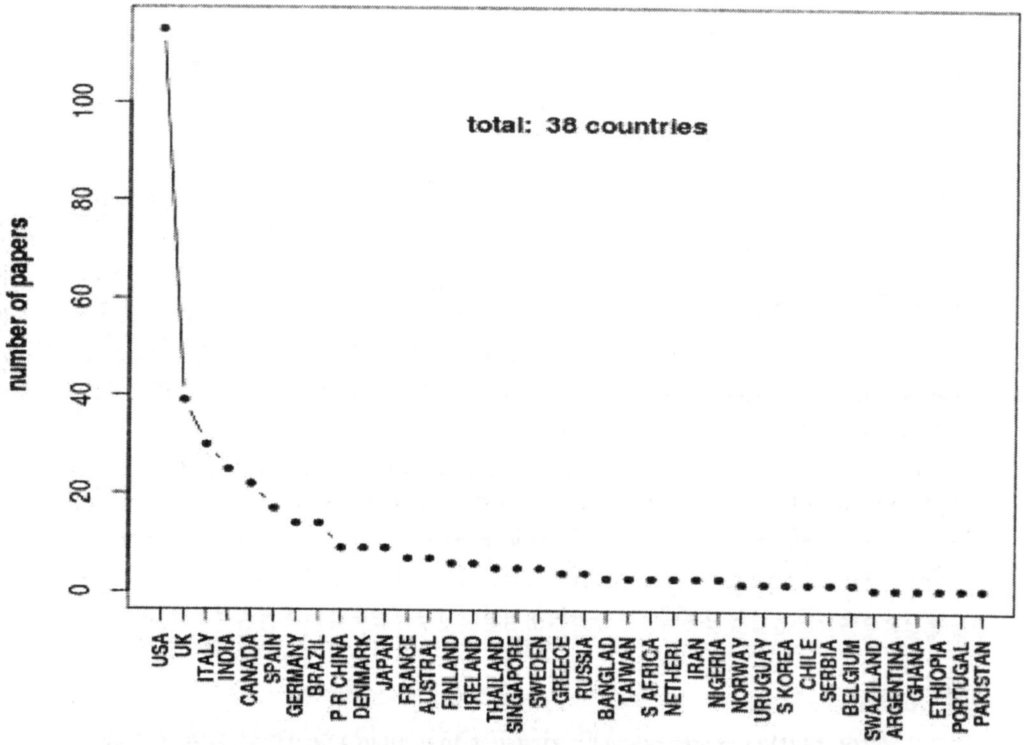

Fig. 3: Distribution over countries of of papers citing Ranganathan (1991-2013)

modern scientific discourse. From the results presented it is a compelling conclusion that further research on all aspects of Ranganathan's work is worthwhile. For example, a detailed analysis of the content of Ranganathan citing papers - as has been performed to some extent by *Lancaster* et al. (1992) for papers published until 1990 - seams reasonable. Studies involving co-citation and bibliographic coupling analyses could reveal Ranganathan's presence in core papers and research fronts, giving important stimuli to the further development of library and information science.

5 REFERENCES

1 Chung, Y.K. (1995) Bradford Distribution and Core Authors in Classification Systems Literature. *Scientometrics*, 29(2): 253-269.

2 Garfield, E. (1955) Citation Indexes for Science: A new dimension in documentation through association of ideas. *Science,* 122: 108-111.

3 Garfield, E. (1984a). A Tribute to S. R. Ranganathan, the father of Indian Library Science. Part 1. Life and Works. *Current Contents*, 7: 37-44.

4 Garfield, E. (1984b) A Tribute to S. R. Ranganathan, the father of Indian Library Science. Part 2. Contribution to Indian and International Library Science. *Current Contents*, 7: 45-49.

5 Garfield, E. (2005) Publications by S.R. Ranganathan and the papers citing S.R. Ranganathan. Available http://garfield.library.upenn.edu/ histcomp/ranganathan-sr_w-citing/.

6 Garfield, E.; Paris, S. and Stock, W.G. (2006) HistCite™: A software tool for informetric analysis of citation linkage. *Information Wissenschaft & Praxis*, 57(8): 391-400.

7 Lancaster, F.W.; Zeter, M.J. and Metler, L. (1992) Ranganathan's Influence examined bibliometrically. *Libri*, 43(3): 268-281.

8 R Development Core Team (2004). R: A language and environment for statistical computing, *R Foundation for Statistical Computing*, Vienna.

2

From Librametry to Webometric Research in India with Emphasis on the Work Done Since 2001[1]

I. K. Ravichandra Rao

A survey of scientometric literature of India for the period 2000-12 was carried out to study and understand scientometric research in India. The data were collected from LISA; 175 documents are covered in this survey. most of which were published in *Annals of Library and Information Science, SRELS Journal of Information Management, DESIDOC Bulletin of Information Technology, COLLNET Journal of Scientometrics and Information management and Journal of Scientometrics.* Discussions in the reviewed papers relate to several topics in scientometrics - India's contribution to world literature, growth of Indian literature, proportion of collaborative research, etc. This review indicates that the Indian publications are now visible and it is increasing, There is hardly any research being done to evaluate and measure research outcome; there is also no evidence that the results of the scientometric research is being used in drafting science policy or in science administration.

KEYWORDS: Librametry, Scientometrics, Research, India, Review

Note: Meaning of the abbreviations is given in Appendix.

1 INTRODUCTION

In recent years, there have been significant changes in science research in India and it is growing. In 1990s, NISSAT made several attempts to study and understand science research activities; as a part of their programmes, NISSAT had undertaken several projects to analyze various international databases, with an objective to draw science map of India. Ravichandra Rao and Suma (1997, [1]), Dhawan and Arunachalam (1998, [2]) analyzed different databases and the results were published as NISSAT reports. These two reports are only examples. Basu and Nagpaul (1998, [3]) also attempted to map S&T publications in 1997;

---

1 The paper has been revised and developed based on the presentation (talk) I gave at the Dinner meeting, arranged for the participants of pre-COLLNET Conference Training Programme, organized by the Estonia Research Council held at Tartu, Estonia on 13th August 2013

that study was based on SCI database; the results were published in one of the NISTADS reports.

Thomson Reuters in 2012 [4] submitted an "Evidence" report to the Department of Science and Technology, New Delhi. The purpose of this project was to gather evidence for changes, if any, in scientific publication outputs originating from India. This report mentions the following:

- The analysis of changing trends in outputs of scientific publications, based on the 5-year moving averages, indicate a growth rate of about 66% between 2006-10 relative to 2001-05 period. That is, on an average, publications grow at the rate of 13% per year!
- Chemistry, Physics, Materials Science, Engineering and Clinical medicine are the active areas of research outputs
- The current level of un-cited papers is about 48%; there is a plan to reduce this to 30% by various interactions.
- Citation impact of Indian papers has increased from 0.35 in 1981-85 to 0.68 in 2006-10. Thus it requires significant efforts to improve the impact of Indian research outputs.
- There is an 81% increase in the number of publications in top 1% high impact factor journals, during 2006-10 relative to 2001-05 periods.

In another study, Gupta and Gupta (2011, [5]) analyzed the Indian S&T outputs and the International Collaborative strength for the period 2004-09. In their study they noted:

- India's global publications share in 15 broad subjects (in S & T) varied from 1.84% (medicine, 9th rank) to 5.45% (in Chemistry, 5th rank)
- India's annual average growth rate is 12.64%; it is much higher than some of the advanced countries, such as Germany (4.25%)
- The average annual growth rate in 15 broad subjects ranged from 5.61% to 44.61% (computer science); energy (32.24%), Pharmacology and related topics (23.18%), mathematics (19.63%) and engineering (19.26%). Does this indicate India's priorities?
- The top 50 Indian Science organizations have contributed 128,955 articles; however, the average number of citations per paper, published by the top 50 Indian organizations is only 3.47.

Arora and Trivedi (2012, [6]) prepared a profile of 50 selected Universities with an objective to measure research output and its impact, using Bibliometric Indicators; the second objective of the study is to generate awareness about research performance of these Universities. They have computed several indicators; one of them is the h-index; the Delhi University has the highest h-index of 97. The third objective was to study the impact of library consortia, provided by the INFLIBNET -- measuring download and other activities. In an article on 'scientific productivity, impact and collaboration of the top Asian countries in Scopus during 1996-2010' Erfanmanesh and others [2013, [7]) mentioned that:

- Number of publications by India is 533,006 (India ranked 3, the first two countries being China and Japan);
- Citations Received are 3,211,864 (Citations per Publication: 6.03); and
- Self Citations are 1,102,820 (Self Citations per Publication: 2.06).

1.1 Historical Development

Ranganathan suggested as early as 1948 at the ASLIB Conference in Lamington Spa that it is necessary for librarians to develop 'librametry' on the lines of biometry, econometry and psychometry, since 'many of the matters connected with library work and services involve large numbers' (ASLIB Proceedings, 1948, [8]). In spite of his early attempt to define the scope of librametry, the subject hardly developed until early 1970s. Ranganathan (1969, [9]) in a paper submitted at the seventh Annual Seminar of the Documentation research and Training Centre (DRTC), illustrated a few examples of the applications of statistics to library science. On the basis of this paper and investigations carried out at DRTC, Neelameghan (1969, [10]) outlined the applicability of librametry.

In another paper Ravichandra Rao and Neelameghan (1972, [11]) traced the development of the application of quantitative methods in library and information science, from librametry to informetrics. They discussed briefly the contributions of S R Ranganathan to quantification in library work and service; some of the applications appear to be intuitive with a view to improving information services to users, making the services more user friendly and enhancing efficiency of library and information management.

Although the term librametry was well defined, the term was hardly known among the professionals in library and information field! For instance, Brookes

(1990, [12]) in his address at the 2nd International Conference on Informetrics held in Canada, said that "had I known of Ranganathan's term in time, I would have adopted "librametry" for information studies and "bibliometrics" for information science; librametry and bibliometrics show that librametry primarily aims at the quantitative analysis of the management of libraries and bibliometrics is limited to recorded knowledge. The publication in both the fields suggests that in librametry and bibliometrics, one examines the statistical distributions of the processes relating to the utilization of documents, library staff, and library users, to establish a theory for the structural aspects of library. Bibliometrics and librametry may therefore be commonly defined as areas in which one studies 'information processes and information handling in libraries and information centers by quantitatively analyzing the characteristics and behavior of documents, library staff, and library users.' (Ravichandra Rao, 1981, [13])

In the 1960s, particularly in Eastern Europe, the term "scientometrics" was used to denote "measurement of informatics process." In another development, Otto Nacke of West Germany in 1979 proposed the term "informetrics." (Brookes, 1990, [12])

In fact acceptance of a single term to define a subject and its scope is necessary for any scientist. Otherwise, it is difficult to include it in a syllabus. It is also difficult to get research grant from different agencies. It helps us in identifying the research groups especially at national and international levels. At present, the term 'scientometrics' is used as a synonym to both 'bibliometrics' and 'informetrics'.

1.2 Objectives

The main objective of this review is to survey the research publications (since 2000) in Scientometrics and related topics in India. For this review, the data were collected from the LISA database; all the records in LISA were searched using the terms based on the scope and definition of scientometrics. Searches then were narrowed down to those journal articles which were published during 2000-12. We were able to identify 167 relevant articles. 110 articles were summarized and presented in different groups; the distribution of papers in different groups is as follows:

- Library and Information Science (14 articles);
- Mathematics, Physical Sciences, Engineering, Technology, etc. (28 articles);

- Chemical Sciences (12 articles);
- Biological Sciences, Agricultural science, Crop Studies, etc. (32 articles);
- Health Sciences (13 articles); and
- Humanities and Social Sciences (including, management, economics, industrial research, patenting, etc.) (11 articles, including 3 articles in patenting.)

The other 57 articles are summarized in the Sections 2 to 4.

2 RELATED STUDIES

Garg and Kumar (2010, [14]) analyzed 5317 articles and reviews published in 46 Indian science journals indexed by SCIE during 2006 indicated that these journals published mostly local papers. About 40 percent of the papers published in these journals were cited in international literature during January 2006-June 2009. The proportion of cited papers and the rate of citation varied for domestic, foreign and collaborative papers, as well as among disciplines and publishers. The study indicated that:

- Collaborative papers have the highest rate of citation per paper.
- The Indian *Journal of Medical Research* published by the Indian Council of Medical Research, New Delhi has the highest citation impact.
- Highest number of papers was cited in the discipline of medicine

Kademani and others (2007, [15]) noted that Indian scientists published a total of 182,111 papers (1990-2004) in SCI covered journals. They analyzed the broad features of Indian S&T by focusing on its publication growth characteristics, language, format and media of communication, research quality, institutional productivity, patterns of research collaboration, and broad and narrow subject areas of interests of Indian institutions and scientists. The authors have also made a broad comparison of India's research output with select countries, particularly with China.

Garg, Dutt and Kumar (2006, [16]) analyzed 11,067 articles of Indian scientists and indexed in SCI. The study indicated that academic institutions (universities and colleges) were the major contributors to the scientific publications. Aparna Basu (2013, 2012, 2010, 2006, 2001 and 2000, [17-22]) in a series of papers discussed:

- Differences in research publications of Indian scientists in India and the diaspora;
- Cognitive mobility or migration of authors between fields used in mapping a network of mathematics;
- The number of country journals indexed versus country's scientific productivity;
- Highly cited researchers; and
- International collaboration and its impact, in the context of science in India.

Harinarayana and Raju (2009, [23]) studied the impact of S.R.Ranganathan's (SRR's) seminal works, namely, *Five laws of library science, Prolegomena to library classification, and Colon classification* through citation analysis. The study is based on the data from the Google Scholar. Based on the data as on December 2008, Dr Ranganathan has received 894 citations, of which more than half (54.8%) is accounted for by the three books of Ranganathan.

2.1 Foreign Authors in Indian Journals

Garg and Kumar (2009, [24]) examined 2450 papers published by foreign authors in 284 Indian science journals from 1311 institutions spread over 102 countries. The study indicated that Asian countries are the largest contributors to these journals. Turkey, USA, Iran, China and Nigeria contributed 48% of the total foreign-authored publications. Most of the authors were from Turkey and Iran. Most of the papers were in the field of medicine, followed by chemistry and material science. The proportion of foreign authored contributions to Indian science journals witnessed a three-fold increase in 2006 as compared to July 1982 -- June 1984.

2.2 Indian Authors in Foreign Journals in LIS

Harinarayana, Mahadevaswamy and Vasantha (2008, [25]) studied articles by Indian authors published in foreign journals in LIS during 1970-2005. They analyzed 303 articles, from 18 foreign journals in LIS. The journal *Scientometrics* was the preferred foreign journal for Indian authors, with almost 44% of the articles published by them being reported in *Scientometrics*. While going through the Indian contributions in 18 international journals during the span of 36 years, it was found that only three authors have contributed more than 20 articles. This situation calls for more attention from Indian authors to increase their level of productivity in foreign periodicals. During 2000- 05, 131 articles (43.23%) were published showing that the trend of publishing in foreign journals is increasing

2.3 Works Related to Scientific Productivity

Harinarayana and Raju (2012, [26]) in their study analyzed the impact of research contributions of South Indian LIS teachers using citation analysis based on the data from Google Scholar relating to 1909 research papers published by the South Indian LIS teachers. About half of the data collected (48.40%) were articles published in journals. The DRTC and Karnataka University and University of Mysore published the most number of articles. Articles from SRELS Journal (28.45%) and *Information Studies* (9.63%) are visible in Google Scholar more than the other journals. 'Organization of Information' and 'Bibliometrics' are the most favored areas of research for South Indian LIS teachers.

Egghe and Ravichandra Rao (2002, [27]) developed a model to explain the distribution of papers, based on the fractional scores (with regard to the number of papers published) in mathematics, based on the articles covered in *Math Reviews* (1990.) Their paper "Duality Revisited: Construction of Fractional Frequency Distributions based on two dual Lotka's Laws," is the first attempt of this kind. They assumed two simple Lotka distributions with exponent 2 – one for the number of authors with n papers (total count) and the other for the number of papers with n authors. Based on the earlier convolution model of Egghe (1993, [28]), these authors reworked for discrete scores and produced a theoretical fractional frequency distribution (f(q),(q refers to fraction of a paper by an author.) with only one parameter. It is in very close agreement with observed data, produced earlier by Ravichandra Rao (1995, [29]). The f(q) was ultimately computed using $\phi(n)$ (distribution of papers) and $\psi(n)$ (distribution of authors). Further, Ravichandra Rao, Sahoo and Egghe (2003, [30]) and Sahoo (2006, [31]) obtained good results for different distributions for $\phi(n)$ and $\psi(n)$

2.4 Bibliometrics to Webometrics

Mahawar and Saini (2012, [32]) studied the issues concerning the use and awareness of 'Blogging' the act of posting blogs among LIS professionals. They discussed how far it is an effective means of communication for sharing information and knowledge. They also explored the nature of such inter-activities of LIS professionals. The authors have concluded that 'the blogs are worth investing as important tool for fostering professional communication and collaboration. The blog interconnected group of librarians.' Shukla and Poluru (2012, [33]) analyzed web presence of Indian State Universities (173) on the WWW and also found ways to get high web links that further help to improve presence on Web. They collected the data from Yahoo Site Explorer and Google Scholar. Further, they applied WISER (**W**eb **I**ndicators for **S**cience, T**E**chnology and Innovation **R**esearch) ranking method to know about the visibility and connectivity of universities on the Web. A WebCrawler Socscibot 4 was used to examine the pattern of link visibility and to create ADM (Alternative Document Model) Count Summary. Pajek, software for large network analysis was used as a graphical tool for creating inlinks topology. Their study shows that some state universities have more visibility compared with their counter parts. The authors also point out that the impact of maintaining institutional repositories, promotion of open access, academic researches, collaboration with other universities, online communities etc., are helpful in increasing the more visibility of the a university on the Web.

Jalal, Biswas and Mukhyopadhyay (2013, [34]) in their study on 'link analysis research' discussed the process of identifying hyperlinks to web pages in the Web environment. The paper dealt with history of link analysis, various approaches and measurement techniques of link analysis. Various link analysis methods and approaches are discussed. They have shown top level domain, (TLD), sub-level domain (SLD) and domain level link analysis. In another paper in 2010 [35], the authors described briefly the Indian higher educational system mentioning various types of universities having their websites. Web presence of Indian universities has been discussed in general and central universities in particular. Webometric data have been collected mainly through Yahoo! search engines using special query syntax. The authors have attempted to rank central universities in India using appropriate webometric indicators. Results revealed that based on WISER ranking University of Delhi gets top rank; Sikkim University occupied the last rank among central universities in India. The study also examined the link relationship through inlinks and outlinks among central universities using personal web crawler (- Socscibot 3.0.) Jalal, Biswas and Mukhyopadhyay (2010, [36]) focused their research in another article in 2010 on the Web presence and visibility of websites of Asian countries. The study highlighted the Web presence using webometric indicators, such as, Internet access, WebPages, number of Internet users, and link counts. They studied web presence using such popular search engines as AltaVista, Google, Yahoo and MSN. An attempt was also made to compute the Web Impact

Factor (WIF) for selected Asian countries. Jalal, Biswas and Mukhyopadhyaya (2009, [37]) discussed the trend from bibliometrics to webometrics and also discussed some application areas of Webometrics research, the methodology adopted for data collection, techniques and tools of Web analysis and the problems encountered in webometric research. Methods of computing Web Impact Factors and highlighted the research possibility in Webometric study. A webometric case study of 13 IITs and IIMs were presented. The analysis shows that the IIT, Bombay occupies the first place among the 13 IITs and the IIMs based on both absolute and logarithm values.

3 ANALYSIS OF MULTIPLE AUTHORSHIP

Sahoo (2006, [31]) in his study noted that the percentage of single authorship paper is decreasing – from 16% in 1989 to 12% in 2003, with one or two variations in the years, 1990, 1994 and 1999. In order to identify a probability distribution function, Sahoo attempted to fit several probability distributions (Poisson, Geometric, Lotka, and Negative Binomial) to the empirical distributions of both India data and world data. He argued further that:

(i) Poisson distribution can be a suitable model to explain the distribution of multiple authorship;

(ii) Negative binomial is the next best model to explain the distribution of multiple authorship; and

(iii) Lotka's model does not fit well – it is not even a good approximation.

Kundra (2002, [38]) in his thesis noted an increasing trend towards collaboration and large disparities in the rate of collaboration between 'pure' and 'applied' areas. He investigated collaboration influences in basic and applied fields of medical science in India. His findings clearly showed a higher degree of collaboration, i.e., an average of 21.95 papers in basic fields of medical science in contrast to an average of 7.63 papers per year in applied medicine. It is similar to the findings of other scholars who also reported a higher degree of international collaboration in basic sciences than in the applied fields.

Data on distributions of multiple authors in two journals namely, *JASIST* and *Scientometrics*, were collected and analyzed by Ravichandra Rao and Sahoo (2008, [39]). The number of authors per paper in both the journals is increasing indicating the trend towards collaboration with more than two authors. Anuradha and Urs (2007, [40]) analyzed international collaborative patterns as indicated in the Indian publications by tracking multi-author publications using *Science Citation Index* (SCI) database. Correspondence analysis is used for analysis and interpretation of the results. Roy (2004, [41]) analyzed 1637 research papers in Library and Information Science (LIS) published in 10 Indian LIS journals during the period 1991 to 2000. He showed that single authorship is much in vogue in LIS research work in India as compared to collaborative work in LIS. He found single authorship to be 66.7%, two authorships 26.45%, three authorship 5.68%, four authorship i0.97% and six authorship 0.06%. Gupta and Singh (2004, [42]) studied the research collaboration of India with Latin America, with the objectives: (i) To study the nature of Indian collaboration with Latin American countries in S & T, as reflected in co-authored research papers, (ii) To identify the specific subject areas of such collaboration, (iii) To study the impact of Indian collaborative research with Latin America in different fields, and (iv) To identify the major institutions involved in this collaborative research in India and Latin America respectively. Parameshwaran and Smitha (2001, [43]) measured the extent of collaborative authorship using Subramanyam's formula and the results helped the investigators to prove the hypothesis that the research papers by single authors are greater in number than collaborative work as covered by LISA.

There are a number of studies dealing with Collaboration. These are mentioned in Section 5 under different disciplines, as explained in Groups 1 to 8 in this paper.

4 GROWTH OF LITERATURE

There are a number of studies on growth of literature and its relation to obsolescence of literature; some of these are discussed below and some others under different disciplines.

Mahapatra and Jena (2006, [44]) described the growth of scientific research literature in Orissa, India, published during 1985-2004; the data set includes 875 research papers from 40 different periodicals. The authors have analyzed the data by their authorship pattern, year-wise growth, subject wise break up of papers, category of journals, place of origin, length of papers, and productivity of journals.

Sahoo (2006, [31]) in his thesis compared the growth of the journals with that of the articles, in the area of software studies. He observed that the correlation coefficient r between the number of journals and the articles is 0.9811. That is, 96% of the variation in y (articles) is due to the variation in x (journals) – higher the number of journals, higher the number of articles. However, in the case of world literature he observed that the correlation coefficient between number of journals and the number of articles published is only 0.8517. Ravichandra Rao and Divya (2010, [45]) studied the growth of literature in Malaria research. They also studied the relationship among journals, articles and authors. They observed that the number of journals, articles, and authors increased approximately exponentially. The number of articles in malaria research increased from 3,996 to 57,627 from 1955-1965 to 1996-2005. Also the number of journals has increased 503 to 3,072 from 1955-65 to 1996-2005. An attempt was also made to study the relationship among the three variables – journals, articles and authors. A multiple regression analysis was applied.

Sangam, Keshav and Agadi (2010, [46]) reported on the growth pattern of world marine engineering literature, based on the data from the Engineering Information CDROM COMPENDEX published by Elsevier for the period 1969-2005. They determined the growth rate of marine engineering literature by calculating relative growth rates and doubling time for publications. The criteria on which growth models are to be selected for application to marine engineering literature are briefly discussed. Sangam and Meera (2009, [47]) discussed the year wise (2000-2005) growth of Indian research papers in the thirteen subfields of chemical sciences. They investigated the pattern of authorship, type of collaborated research and the degree of collaboration linkages in the 13 subfields. Attempts were also made to evaluate growth v/s collaboration. They observed a high degree of collaboration in chemical sciences research in India.

Gupta and Karisiddappa (2000, [48]) used different approaches for studying the growth of scientific knowledge, as reflected in publications and authors. They applied selected growth models to the cumulative growth of publications and authors in theoretical population genetics from 1907 to 1980. They concluded that among the models studied, the power model is the one which best explains the cumulative growth of publication and author counts in theoretical population genetics. Gupta, and others (2002, [49]) found best fits with either power or logistic models, and called into question the utility of the Gompertz function for modeling S-shaped growth in the social sciences.

Egghe and Ravichandra Rao in their study in 2002 [51] observed that the cumulative distribution of the age of the most recent reference distribution is the dual variant of the first citation distribution. This model is different from the first citation distribution. In another study, Egghe and Rao (2001, [50]) have shown the general relation between the first citation distribution and the general citation age distribution. They have shown that if Lotka's exponent α = 2, both these distributions are the same. In the same study, they have argued that the distribution of nth citation is similar to that of the first citation distribution. Ravichandra Rao (2012, [52]) studied the relations among references, citations and authors, based on the data collected from two journals – *Annals of Mathematics* and *Econometrica*. The distribution of citations in the field of mathematics and econometrics was also identified as the lognormal distribution. He noted that the linear relation between references and citations is very weak.

Some Indian LIS journals are not indexed in WoS. However, articles published in Indian journals are cited by the SCI/SSCI source journals; these are available in WoS as cited references. Mahesh and Wadhwa (2012, [53]) used the 'cited reference search', to determine the citations received by Indian journals and compared it with the existing rankings of Indian LIS journals done by different authors who have used various methods. The authors have suggested to carry out further such studies on non-SCI-covered journals in other disciplines; it can ascertain the possible usefulness of adopting the WoS cited references search features for journal assessment.

Sagar and others (2009, [54]) studied a quantitative documentation of "Review Articles" published during 2000-2005 in the Science Citation Index (SCI). Records with "Review" in Document type field are extracted; a total of 2042 records by 5135 individual authors in over 640 individual journals are analyzed. Findings indicate that the average yearly growth rate is 11.04, and that 85.16 per cent of the total Review Articles are written in collaboration. Of these collaborative works, 2.9 percent of the collaborative papers are written with authors from 78 different countries. Collaboration of Indian reviewers with people from outside India is very significant.

Gupta, Kumar and Singh (2005, [55]) suggested a methodology for studying the quantitative profile of research and teaching institutes, with a view to get an idea about their major research contributions, performance and impact in different fields of science and technology. They concluded that mathematics, biology, and clinical medicine, although contributing relatively a smaller number of papers, secured the first three ranks in terms of average normalized impact factor per paper. They have also done fairly well in terms of percentage of collaborative papers, but fared badly in terms of contributing to high quality papers, with the exception of clinical medicine. Jeevan (2002, [56]) analyzed and evaluated research publications from 1994-1995 and 1996-1997 to assess various trends in publication patterns of researchers from the Indian Institute of Technology (IIT), Kharagpur, West Bengal. Some estimate of the quality aspect of these papers is assessed with the help of impact factor data for the journals.

Ravichandra Rao (2007, [57]) studied 'two hundred and fifty two references' from a bibliography on "optical flow estimation". He attempted to fit exponential, negative binomial and also lognormal distributions to the observed set of data.

- The exponential distribution fits the observed data for both the distributions of h and g very well; and
- The negative binomial distribution fits equally well for the empirical distributions of g. The negative binomial distribution fits the empirical distribution of h only at 0.01 levels.

Ravichandra Rao (2007, [57]), therefore, concluded that the exponential distribution is a suitable model to explain the distributions of *h* and *g*. However, theoretical explanations are yet to be explored in this regard.

5 OTHER RELATED WORKS

There are many other articles dealing with related topics; these articles are summarized under the following heads:

1) Library and Information Science and related topics (14 articles);
2) Mathematics, Physical Sciences (including Engineering and Technology) (28 articles);
3) Chemical Sciences (12 articles);
4) Biological Sciences (including Agricultural science and crop studies) (32 articles);
5) Health Sciences (13 articles); and
6) Humanities and Social Sciences (including management, economics, industrial research, patenting, etc.) (11 articles)

Group 1: Library and Information Science

Neelameghan and Sathish (2003, [58]) studied the knowledge diffusion in clusters of web-based communities. The links among the different clusters and with the original source was mapped. The authors have observed that the first application of the Lateral Relationship typology in a large thesaurus was in the Art and Architecture Thesaurus over a decade after the publication of the typology. Further, they point out that the diffusion of the idea in linguistic studies, web design, etc. occurred in a relatively shorter span of about 3 years, 2000-2003; it is due to the Internet/WWW. The discovery was that Relations Analysis (and Lateral Relations typology) is applicable and useful in several different domains - interdisciplinary subject areas and new subject areas. Sen (2002, [59]) traced the history of bibliometric research and related training activities at the INSDOC. The author has described briefly the objectives, facilities, services, research activities and publications of the NCB. The NCB could not grow the way it should have due to various factors. Initially, this was funded by NISSAT. It is unfortunate that the NCB is now almost a non-entity

Kumar and Dora (2012, [60]) observed that there was: (1) increase in the number of papers published by IIM (Ahmadabad) during 1999 to 2010, (2) an increase in collaborations among authors, (3) a decrease in single author publications, and most of the papers were centered around the multi-disciplinary subjects. Kumbhar (2012, [61]) analyzed the literature of classification published during 2000 to 2009. The author traced the pattern in scattering of literature on classification in library and information science (LIS) journals and concluded that the pattern conformed to the Bradford's law of scattering. He produced a rank list of journals publishing the literature on classification and identifies authorship patterns and the prominent contributors to the literature on classification.

Pradhan and Chandrakar's (2011, [62]) study presents a quantitative view of the growth of Indian scholarly literature in LIS versus the world as a whole, for the period 2000-2009. There were a total of 228 articles published in international LIS e-journals during 2000-2009 contributed by 300 authors among which 246 were Indian authors. During the span of 10 years, 10 Indian authors have contributed more than 5 articles each. Singh, Jain and Babbar (2011, [63]) studied research publications over a ten-year period from 1992-2002, to assess the trends in the publication (by library and information professionals) patterns in *DESIDOC Bulletin of Information Technology* The study revealed that 145 articles were published in the 60 issues of the journal. Out of the 145 publications, 97 (66.90%) articles are single authored papers. The study also revealed that 128 items (88.28%) were contributed from India and rest 17 items (11.72%) were from other countries.

Rajgoli (2011, [64]) observed that 12,536 references appended to 1012 papers published in four Indian LIS journals for the period 2002-2010. His study showed that there are 999 conference papers in all with an average of 0.99 conference paper per paper. Journal articles have emerged as the most important source of information among all the four journals followed by Web resources, books and conference proceedings.

Saxena, Gupta and Janhavi (2011, [65]) evaluated the application of h-index, g-index, and p-index on Indian engineering and technological institutes. A total of 40 institutes in India have been ranked by the three indices. The authors focused on the cluster analysis to segregate these institutes on the basis of ranks generated by these indices. The results show that g-index and h-index performed much on the similar lines. An attempt has thus been made to use other indices like p-index and ACPP method to find a viable segregation on the basis of attributes these indices deal with.

Patil (2010, [66]) examined articles published in *Herald of Library Science* for authorship pattern, degree of collaboration and geographical distribution of papers. The degree of collaboration is found to be 0.30. The geographical distribution shows that the contribution by Andhra Pradesh is the highest in India while Nigeria is at top among foreign countries. Nazim Mohammad and Ahmad (2007, [67]) analyzed scientific output on 'Information Literacy' to get an overview of research trends in the field and characterize its most important aspects and their evolution over the last quarter of the 20th century. Shafi and others (2007, [68]) have examined the articles published in on-line *D-Lib magazine* for authorship trend, contribution of teachers and professionals, country-wise contribution, degree of collaboration and productivity within different facets of digital /electronic libraries. The degree of collaboration is found to be 0.66.The study further showed more contribution from the teaching community compared to other professionals. Country-wise distribution showed that most of the contributions are from the USA and Germany while facet-wise distribution of articles indicated that most of the articles cover digital libraries and preservation followed by metadata /cataloguing.

Maheshwarappa, Tadasad, Ebnizar and Alur (2003, [69]) reviewed the literature in LIS on the use of Internet resources and services in different settings in two sections, namely, foreign and Indian literature. The authors have concluded that despite the growth in the number of users, the studies in LIS regarding the use of Internet resources and services in different settings are at its infancy.

Hadagali and Kumbar (2011, [70]) examined the use of electronic resources by faculty members and research scholars of universities of Karnataka State, India, in order to determine the level of use and different purposes of using electronic resources, and its impact on the academic community. A total of 604 questionnaires were distributed and 479 (79.63%) completed questionnaires were retuned, The authors have argued that the future of the library and information services in academic libraries depends upon major factors, like, availability of adequate manpower, IT infrastructure, and electronic resources.

Keshav, Hittalamani and Gowda (2008, [71]) discussed growth of literature in the field of sociology and the related authorship pattern; value of group co-efficient for collaborative research and geographical distribution of papers during 1999-21003. Their study shows that the highest number of papers (86) were published in 2001 and 2003. The number of single author papers is higher at 84% out of a total of 475. The value of group co-efficient (g_p) was only 0.16. The degree of collaboration among the co-authors was minimum (0.02) in articles written by five authors and maximum (0.12) in two-author papers. Keshav, Ganjihal and Gowda (2008, [72]) discussed bibliometric characteristics of scholarly research papers published in ACM Transactions on Information Systems (1989-2006 A total of 4,685 (average 260.3 per year) citations to the 295 research papers are reflected in SCI. It has been observed that the average Degree of Collaboration is 0.837. Further, it has been observed that:

- The vast majority of the papers originated from the North America.
- The number of two-authored papers is higher than the number of single-authored papers.
- Common topics of the papers in information systems include data processing, storage, and use/retrieval techniques, computer applications and database systems

Gururaj, Kumbar and Sumana (2009, [73]) analyzed the citation pattern in Current Science, a premier periodical in science published in India, for the years 2005 and 2006. The study is based on the 16,404 citations given in the articles published in the 48 issues. They studied the authorship pattern, types of publications, language-wise distribution, highly productive institutions, and periodicals preferred by cited scientists. They observed that two-authored papers constituted 26.4% with 4,332 citations. Current Science is ranked as the number one periodical with 508 citations.

Gururaj, Kumbar and Benahal (2009, [74]) attempted to identify the attributes of subject literature in Physics as reflected in theses submitted to Karnatak University, Dharwad during 1992-2006. They studied the 10, 057 citations given in the references in the 37 theses. They analyzed the data subject wise, form wise; they also studied authorship pattern, chronological distribution of journals and books, and half-life period of journals. The Journal of Chemical Physics ranked first among 548 journals. They observed that half-life period of journals is 33 years.

Amritraj (2012, [75]) attempted to identify the trends in using E-resources by various user groups. The author has studied the distribution of uses of e-resources with respect to place of publication, resource-wise, type of user, purpose-wise, subject-wise, year of publication, time lag in publication, language-wise, publication-wise etc. The study shows that academics prefer to use e-journals over other e-resources and that both print and e-resources complement each other.

In their article on 'Authorship pattern in library and information science journal literature', Paramjeet Kaur and Manpreet Kaur (2012. [76]) made a comparative analysis of authorship trends in USA, UK and India in LIS. Their study is based on nine LIS journals. They analyzed the data on gender, occupation, affiliation, geographic location and co-authorship. The nine journals selected for this study are published from USA, UK and India. A total of 269 articles by 471 authors were analysed. They observed that a large number of articles were contributed by male authors except in the case of USA. The LIS faculty contributed more articles 41% in comparison to practicing librarians, research scholars etc. Further, they observed that collaborative papers are predominant in all the journals studied. The LIS journals published from UK received more papers from other countries in comparison to journals published from USA and India

Application of Bradford's Law and Lotka's Law

Patra and Chand (2006, [77]) presented a bibliometric study of LIS research literature emanating from India based on the data abstracted in Library and Information Science Abstracts (LISA). Bradford's law of scattering is used to identify core journals of LIS wherein Indian authors publish their research output. To understand the productivity pattern of authors, Lotka's Law was applied. The identified core journals are mostly published from India. Indian authors' contribution in international journals is very low. Gupta and Khare (2013, [78]) examined the pattern of citations by the researchers of Dr. Harisingh Gour University, Sagar, applying Bradford's Law of Scattering. 255 periodicals were covered with 2953 citations, collected from 35 doctoral theses till the year 2010. They observed that the time span 1986-1995 was the most productive years of cited periodicals, mostly from USA and the most cited journal is *IASLIC Bulletin*. By applying the Bradford Law of Scattering, identified the core journals in the field of Library and information science. The authors concluded that the journal distribution pattern of the LIS doctoral theses does not fit the log-linear curve.

Group 2: Mathematics, Physical Sciences (including Engineering and Technology)

Mathematics

Bhaskaran (2012, [79]) examined growth of literature, relative growth rate and doubling time of publications, institution-wise and ranking of authors in research productivity of Graph theory during 2004-2011. The average number of papers published per year was 910.75. It is observed that RGR has decreased from 2005 (0.113) to 2011 (0.057). The doubling time (D_t) shows fluctuating trend from 2005 (6.132). Mamadpur and others (2011, [80]) analysed articles in *Baltic Astronomy* published during the years 2000 to 2008, with an objective to study distribution of contributions, authorship pattern of contributions, distribution of references, analysis of length of papers, etc. The degree of collaboration for the period 2000-2008 was 0.89. Authors have primarily relied on journals followed by books, conference proceedings and reports. Further, the authors noted that USA contributed maximum number of papers compared to other countries and India stood 21st in the ranked list. *Astrophysical Journal* topped the ranked list of journals cited by the authors followed by *Astronomy and Astrophysics*. It can be concluded that the top 20 journals cited by the authors cover almost 87.60 per cent of references and also that collaborative research is prevalent in astronomy research. Narang and Kumar (2010, [81]) analyzed 4798 references in 400 articles in five volumes - 34(2003) to 38(2007) and the first volume (1970) of the *Indian Journal of Pure and Applied Mathematics*. The objective was to examine the number of contributions and their distribution in different volumes, authorship pattern, foreign and Indian author contributions, citation analysis and number of pages used in each volume. Results indicate a decrease in the number of contributions in successive volumes. The most cited documents are articles from research journals.

Gupta and Dhawan (2007, [82]) analyzed the overall performance of four major performing sectors, namely universities & colleges, mission oriented R&D, institutes of national importance, and industry, in physics research in India during 1993-2001 in terms of publication growth and output and publication impact, using a number of quantitative indicators. They presented the data on comparative analysis of the performance of various sectors participating in physics research in India.

Nattar (2009, [83]) analyzed 829 articles published in the *Indian Journal of Physics* during the period 2004-2008 The author studied the distribution of contributions, authorship pattern, geographical distribution of contributions and the number of pages in each volume. Results indicated that highest numbers of papers qwere co-authoed. The contributions in this journal from India are slightly more than those from other countries. The growth and popularity of this journal is found to show an upward trend.

Garg, Sharma and Kumar (2008, [84]) analysis 369 items published in *Mausam* during 2003-2006 indicates that 72% items were research papers, 23% letters to the editor, 4% report on "Weather in India" and the rest 1% articles. Indian researchers belonging to the India Meteorological Department contributed most of the items. Papers on climatology, agricultural and environmental meteorology, synoptic meteorology, hydrometeorology, numerical weather forecasting and physical meteorology constituted about 56% of the total output. Time lag between receipt and acceptance of the manuscript was about 11 months, while the time lag between acceptance and publication of the manuscript was about 9 months.

Nuclear Science and Related Topics

Kademani and others (2009, [85]) attempted to highlight quantitatively the growth and development of world literature on Bhabha Scattering in terms of publication output as per International Nuclear Information System (INIS) (1970-2008), *Science Citation Index* (1982-2008), and *INSPEC* (1969-2008) databases. During 1969-2008 a total of 1305 papers were published by the scientists from different countries in the field Bhabha Scattering. Kademani, Vijai Kumar, Anil Kumar, Anil Sagar, Lalit Mohan, and Surwase have written several papers in the field of scientometrics with the objective to study and understand the various aspects of Indian publications. For example, in the following papers:

- World Literature on Thorium Research: A scientometric study based on Science Citation Index (Kademani and others, 2006, [86]);
- Scientometric Dimensions of Thorium Research in India (Kademani and others, 2006, [87]);
- Scientometric Dimensions of Nuclear Science and Technology Research in India: A study based on INIS (1970-2002) database (Kademani and others, 2006, [88]); and
- Scientometric Dimensions of Pulsed Laser Deposition Research: Global Perspective (2008,[89]).

The authors have:

- Provided detailed quantitative analysis of Indian contributions on thorium in terms of publications output as per INIS database during 1970-2004.
    1. A total of 2399 papers were published by Indian scientists on the subject of thorium.. There were only nine publications in 1970. Thereafter, a steady growth was observed except for the period 1983-1985;
    2. USA with 8049 (28.05 per cent) and India with 2399 (8.30 per cent) publications were the top two countries;
    3. Authorship and collaboration trend was towards multi-authored papers as 85.70% of the papers were collaborative. There were 79 international collaborative papers. Bilateral collaboration accounted for 90.14 per cent of total collaborative papers; and
    4. Bhabha Atomic Research Centre, Mumbai, topped the list with 1251 followed by Indira Gandhi Centre for Atomic Research, Kalpakkam with 168.
- Highlighted quantitatively the growth and development of world literature on thorium in terms of publication output as per *Science Citation Index* (1982-2004). During 1982-2004 a total of 3987 papers were published on "thorium".
    1. There were 94 countries involved in the research in this field. USA at the top with 1000 authorships (21.11%) followed by India with 498 authorships (10.51%).

2. Authorship and collaboration trend were towards multi-authored papers. Intensive collaboration was found during 1990-2004. There were 586 international collaborative papers. Bilateral collaboration accounted for 80.55 percent of total collaborative papers.

- Analyzed quantitatively the growth and development of Nuclear Science and Technology research in India in terms of publications output as reflected in International Nuclear Information System (INIS) (1970-2002) database.

  1. During 1970-2002 a total of 55313 papers were published by the Indian Nuclear scientists in various domains: Physics (23033), Chemistry (16368), Life and Environmental Sciences (7203), Engineering and Technology (6960), Other Aspects of Nuclear and Non Nuclear Energy (981) and Isotopes and Radiation Application (768).

- Studied the growth of world literature on pulsed laser deposition in terms of publications output as per *Science Citation Index* (1982-2006). During 1982-2006 a total of 8534 papers were published from 84 countries on pulsed laser deposition

Rajendran and Parihar (2007, [90]) discussed various bibliometric indicators of articles published by the Indian researchers in the field of laser science and technology during the period 1995-2005. SCOPUS - the indexing/abstracting online database was the main source for this study. Bibliometric techniques, such as Bradford's law, Lotka's law and the Subramanyam formula were used respectively to measure quantitative distribution of literature in sources/journals, author productivity, and the degree of collaboration among authors. The log-log plot drawn for distribution of literature in various sources/journals fits the typical Bradford S-shaped curve. The study identified 20 core sources and 23 core journals. The majority of authors contributed only one article (65.04%), which is larger than the 60% of original Lotka's data. The degree of collaboration among authors is 0.94.

Priya Girap and others (2011, [91]) studied the growth and development of world literature on Fuel Cell publications output as per INIS (1970-2008) database.

- During 1970-2008 a total of 3435 publications were published by the scientists in the field "Fuel Cell";
- There were 86 countries involved in research in this field. USA was the top producing country with 509 publications (17.56%) followed by Japan with 357

publications (12.3 1%). Authorship and collaboration trend was towards multi-authored publications. Intensive collaboration was found: during 1994-2008; and

- There were 321 international collaborative publications. Bilateral collaboration accounted for 89.72 percent of total collaborative publications.

Fiber Optics

Rajendran and others (2005, [92]) analyzed the global output of fiber optics research to examine the growth in fiber optics research during the period, 1999-2003. A total of 8,302 records were analyzed and the study presents data on the growth of literature year wise, country wise, authorship pattern, bibliographic forms, ranking of core periodicals and the nature of the research. It is concluded that approximately 1,500-1,700 articles are published annually on fiber optics and the majority are in English. About 45% of the articles are from conference proceedings and the contribution made by Indian authors was about 2% of the total. India ranks thirteenth in the worlds output of articles on fiber optics.

Aerospace Engineering

Guruprasad and others (2011, [93]) highlighted the role of the Net in spreading scholarly scientific communication. Their findings based on a questionnaire survey. They observed:

a. Aerospace scientists and engineers use Internet resources from their Desktop in their respective offices', followed by 'Access from their Homes'. Access from 'Cyber Café', 'The Organization's Library', 'other Departments' and 'another Library' occupy lesser priorities;
b. The average monthly usage of the Internet gets a mean value of 84.19 and have had exposure to the Net for at least 7 years;
c. The main purpose -- 'Sending and receiving e-mails', followed by 'Collecting general information' and 'Accessing e-Resources (e-Journals, e-Books and e-Databases)', and 'Download software for scientific research';
d. The main motivation factors to use the Net amongst this community are 'To update self-knowledge in the area of research';
e. The most frequently used search engines are 'Google', followed by 'Yahoo' and 'Alta Vista';

f. The most popular scientific web sites accessed and used are 'Google Scholar', followed by 'Google Book' and 'SCIRUS'; and
g. The biggest bottleneck faced by these scientists and engineers while accessing the Net are 'Very poor Internet connectivity (low speed)' followed by 'Getting irrelevant information' and 'Internet charges are high'.

Materials Science

Sahu, Goswamy and Choudhary (2011, [94]) analyzed R&D publication growth, its characteristics, research impact, quality, citation value, category of journals, core research areas, characteristics of productive authors with reference to the National Metallurgical Laboratory, an R&D organization under CSIR, India. The analysis shows that the majority of the authors of this laboratory published their research work in joint authorship (96.48%). The authors mostly published in reputed international journals;. 72.95% citing authors are from foreign countries and only 27.05% from India. Therefore, the R&D contributions made by scientists of CSIR-NML had a global impact in the fields of metallurgy and materials science. The h-index of the last decade was 25. Kademani and others (2011, [95]) analyzed publications on materials science in India for the period 1999-2008 based on the SCOPUS database. Their objective was to carry out a scientometric analysis of all materials science research publications by Indian scientists. The study analyzed the materials science publications in India for a period of ten years (1999-2008) based on the Scopus database. They observed that:

- A total of 14849 publications were published by the Indian scientists in materials science during 1999-2008 which received 94610 citations;
- The average number of publications per year was 1484.90. The average number of citations per publication was 6.37;
- The highest number of publications 1953 was published in 2007. The highest number of citations 12901 was received in 2003; and
- There were 11961 (80.55%) national collaborative publications and 2190 (14.75%) international collaborative publications by the scientists from India with 59 countries.

Indian Institute of Technology-Kharagpur topped the list with 1243 publications which received 7985 citations, followed by Indian Institute of Science-Bengaluru with 1052 publications and 8816 citations, and Bhabha Atomic Research Centre-Mumbai with 818 publications and 4252 citations.

Dhawan, Gupta, and Mohan (2003, [96]) analyzed materials science research in India for the period 1995-1999, based on a study of papers published by Indian scientists in collaboration with foreign researchers, as covered in *Material Science Citation Index* (MSCI). The results indicate that materials science in India is broad based and covers most of the important sub-areas, and is based on inherent strength. The top collaborating countries were the US, Germany, France, UK and Japan. Collaborative linkages with developing countries accounted for only about 10% of the total papers. Ten top Indian institutions contributed nearly 50% of the collaborated papers. The major areas of collaboration were theoretical studies, metals and alloys, electronic materials and super conducting materials. Walke, Dhawan and Gupta (2007, [97]) reported the status of Materials Science research in India during 1993-01. They presented the data on publication size and growth rate, and discussed media of communication, strength and weakness in the areas of research, quality of research output, nature of collaboration, and institutional productivity. The study finds that India's publications output in Materials Science has been growing steadily at about 7% per year.

Nanotechnology

Bhattacharya and Shilpa (2012, [98]) attempted to capture the contemporary position of nanotechnology development in China through bibliometric and innovation indicators. He argued that applying innovation indicators, such as, standards and products/processes developed along with bibliometric indicators provide a deeper insight of a country's development. His study shows China has been able to make an assertion in this area and has potentiality to forge ahead. It is emerging as a leading country in publication and standardization. Thirumagal (2012, [99]) studied publications on nanotechnology in India; the data were collected from the WoS database, for the period 2001-2011. The author has analyzed individual author's contribution, geographical distribution, and year-wise research in nanotechnology in India. Histcite and Bibexcel tools are used for data analysis. Karpagan, Gopalakrishnan and Ramesh Babu (2011, [100]) attempted to identify the publication trend on nanoscience and nanotechnology in the G-15 countries using SCOPUS database. They collected 7,55,656 bibliographic records in nanotechnology from SCOPUS database over the period of 18 years (i.e.) 1992-

2009. They have computed Relative Growth Rate, Doubling Time, Activity Index, and Growth Rate. Further this study examined the Indian Institutional performance by ranking.

Lalit Mohan and others (2010, [101]) studied the growth and development of Indian research in nanoscience and nanotechnology in terms of publication output as per *Science Citation Index* (1982-2008). The whole database contains 296,072 records on the subject and among them USA topped the list with 84,561 (28.56 per cent) followed by China with 43,393 (14.66 per cent) publications. During 1982-2008, a total of 8,326 (2.81 per cent) papers were published by Indian scientists in this field. The premier Indian institutes engaged in nanoscience and nanotechnology research are: Indian Institute of Science (IISc), Bangalore with 723 publications followed by IIT Kharagpur with 606 publications. Major portion of the publications (96.36 per cent) were prepared in collaboration with more than one author. India had collaboration with 67 other countries in the field.

Law of Scattering -- Physics Literature

Sudhier (2010, [102]) studied five-year (2004-2008) data of journals cited by the physicists at the IISc, Bangalore, to examine the applicability of Bradford's Law of Scattering, which include 690 periodicals containing 11,319 references collected from 79 doctoral theses during the period 2004-08. The author has prepared a ranked list of journals; *Physical Review-B* with 9.53 per cent citation, followed by *Physical Review-A* with 7.69 per cent, and *Astrophysical Journal* with 5.47 per cent citations were the most preferred journals. He noted that the journal distribution pattern of the IISc doctoral theses does not fit the Bradford's distribution pattern.

Computer Science

The research output of India in computer science during 1999-2008 was analyzed by Gupta, Kshitij and Verma (2011, [103]) ; they considered several parameters including total research output, its growth, rank and global publication share, citation impact, share of international collaborative papers and major collaborative partner countries and patterns of research communication in most productive journals. The publications output and impact of India was also compared with China, South Korea, Taiwan and Brazil. Gupta and others (2010, [104]) analyzed research output in computer science, in 11 sub-fields, in India during 1999-2008. The parameters studied include total research output, publications growth, citation impact, share of international collaborative publications, research communication in productive journals, characteristics of most productive institutions, authors, and high-cited papers. Suresh Kumar and Garg (2005, [105]) analyzed 2058 papers published by Chinese authors and 2678 papers published by Indian authors in computer science, 1971-2000; the study indicated that India's output is significantly higher than the Chinese output. The share of papers in journals covered by SCI for India was higher than those from China. However, no significant difference was noted in the impact of the research output of the two countries as seen by different impact indicators. Team research was more common in India as compared to China. Das and Karanjai (2002, [106]) studied 1,408 research papers published in international periodicals in computer science contributed by Indian scientists from 1991 to 2000. The scatter of literature is found to be a two-way process controlled by the number of institutions contributing literature and the number of periodicals publishing these contributions.

Group 3: Chemical Sciences

Thanuskodi (2011, [107]) presented a study dealing with bibliometric analysis of articles and references, contributed in *Indian Journal of Chemistry* from 2005-2009. The present study deals with bibliometric analysis of articles and references provided at the end of each article contributed in *Indian Journal of Chemistry* from 2005-2009. The authors concluded that most of the contributions are India. Maximum number of articles was contributed by two authors. This study also showed that majority of the contributors preferred core journals as the source of information. Nandi and Bandyopadhyay (2009, [108]) studied the research contributions in chemistry at the University of Burdwan. He analyzed 141 theses submitted from the Chemistry Department of the University during 1960-2000 and 979 articles produced based on them. The objective was to find the trend of research, article productivity, and choice of journals, authorship pattern and the position of the university in the state. In another article, Kumari (2009,[109]) studied the impact of literature in Synthetic Organic Chemistry (SOC) during 1998-2004. Adopting relative indicators - Absolute Citation Impact (ACI) and Relative Citation Impact (RCI), a cross national comparison was made at three levels of aggregations - global, Asian and Indian. The author concluded that G7 nations, being leaders for the volume of literature published and citations attracted are showing a decreasing trend over the years probably due to shifting and diversification of their research efforts to other emerging research fronts

Kademani and others (2007, [110]) analyzed the citations to 1733 publications published during 1970-1999 by the Chemistry Division at Bhabha Atomic Research Centre, Bumbai. The extent of citations received, in terms of the number of citations per paper, year-wise break up of citations, domain wise citations, self-citations and citations by others, diachronous self-citation rate, citing authors, citing institutions, highly cited papers, the categories of citing documents, citing journals and distribution of citations among them etc. were determined. During 1982-2003, the Division's publications received a total of 11041 citations. Citation time lag was zero for 144 (15.52%) papers and one year for 350 (37.72%) papers. Single authored publications (168) received 456 (4.13%) citations and 1565 multi-authored publications received 10585 (95.87%) citations.

An analysis of 6444 publications on Plastics, as indexed in *Biological Abstracts* on CD, during 1998-2002 was studied by Parvathamma and Gobbur (2007, [111]). Two or more authored papers constitute majority of the contributions and degree of collaboration amounts to 0.81. USA produces the largest number of documents related to Plastics and English is the most predominant language of the publications. Bibliometric analysis of 21,918 research publications of Indian polymer scientists, published during 1992 – 2006, taken from *Chemical Abstracts* database was studied by Parvathamma and Gobbur (2011, [112]). Results show that a majority of Indian polymer scientists publish in periodicals or registered them as patents. Among prolific authors, there is positive correlation between their publication productivity and (i) number of citations received and (ii) h-index, and negative correlation between publication productivity and web searches.

Kademani and others (2006, [113]) carried out a scientometric analysis of 724 papers published by the scientists of Analytical Chemistry Division at Bhabha Atomic Research Centre (BARC) during 1972-2003 in various domains of analytical chemistry. Scientometric evaluation of world's research output in Synthetic Organic Chemistry has been quantified for the periods 1989-1993 and 1998-2003 by Lalitha Kumari (2006, [114]). The global trends in publication output are mapped and a cross-country comparison of the relative activity in the subspecialty was examined. The Activity Index trend indicated that though quantitatively USA, Japan and European nations produce more publications, their Activity Index recorded a declining trend and leads to the conclusion that these nations are shifting their interest towards other emerging specialties. Asian countries, having recorded a linear increase in the Activity Index show that synthetic organic chemistry is still their priority.

Gunashekharan, Batcha and Shivaraman (2006, [115]) mapped the chemical sciences research in India with data collected from the CD-ROM version of *Chemistry Citation Index*, for the year 2002. Results indicated that approximately 4.5% of the global research and development output in chemical sciences was contributed in 2002 by Indian researchers and these researchers published 6,186 papers in 569 periodicals and 12 non-periodical sources. Over 45% of these papers appeared in periodicals with an impact factor less than 1.000 and about 2 percent of the papers were either published in periodicals with no impact factor or not indexed in JCR 2003.

Kademani and others (2005, [116]) made a analyze quantitative analysis of 475 papers published by the Bio-Organic Division of the BARC, Mumbai, during 1972-2002 in various domains of chemistry. Further, Kademani and others (2005, [117]) analyzed 1733 papers published by the teams comprising a total of 926 participating scientists at Chemistry Division of BARC during 1970-1999 in such domains as, Radiation & Photochemistry and Chemical Dynamics (649), Solid State Studies (558), Inorganic, Structural and Materials Chemistry (460) and Theoretical Chemistry (66) which were analyzed for year wise productivity, authorship pattern and collaboration facors.

Kannappanavar, Vijaya Kumar and Swamy (2004, [118]) discussed a bibliometric study to determine the productivity pattern of authors in chemistry in India and to determine the nature of the authorship patterns; the proportion of single versus multi-authored papers; and the degree of collaboration in the field. Further, they observed that team research is preferred rather than solo research. The degree of collaboration was calculated to be 0.76, with the absolute value varying from year to year in the range 0.72-0.83. The average number of authors per paper increased over time from 7.52 to 8.39.

Group 4: Biological Sciences (including Agricultural Science and Crop Studies)

Genetics

Kannappanavar and Roopashree (2011, [119]) discussed information use pattern of Indian geneticists. They nted that journals are heavily cited as compared to other forms of documents. The trend is towards team research. Aabout 48% of the journals cited are from the USA. The *Indian Journal of Genetics* is in the 14th place. Literature as old as 174 years have also been cited. Kumbar and Kumar (2011, [120]) identified the authorship trend and collaborative research in genetics and plant breeding, based on the data collected from the *Indian Journal of Genetics* and *Plant Breeding* published during 1998-2002. The study showed that 215 (44.24%) papers are two-authored. The degree of collaboration in research is 0.87 in genetics and plant breeding as a whole and ranged between 0.86 to 0.89 during 1998-2002.

Garg and others (2011, [121]) analyzed 32,574 papers published by USA, UK, China, India and Brazil in the field of "plant genetics and breeding" research during 2005-2009; their study indicates that USA produced the highest number of publications followed by China. The impact of research output is highest for UK. India contributed about 9 percent to the world publication output. The total Indian output originated from 1,806 institutions located in different parts of the country. About 41 percent of the total Indian output was concentrated among 23 institutions. Among the institutions, international institutes located in India had the highest impact. The proportion of single authored papers has decreased considerably and the share of internationally co-authored papers has remained almost steady during the period of study.

Garg and others (2010 [122]) analyzed 2,899 papers of Indian scientists during 1991-2008, which are indexed by SCIE. The study indicated that the growth of publications slow in the initial stages, but started increasing after 2000. The highest output was in the sub-field of molecular genetics. A significant proportion of papers were published in journals that originated from the advanced countries of the West and in journals with impact factor > 1. About 47% papers were cited more than 5 times.

Ram (2010, [123]) studied the use of Podophyllotoxin as Anti-Cancer Research. Out of the 948 articles, retrieved from WoS for the period of 1975-2007, 86.6% documents are indexed as journals and the remaining are other kinds of documents; Majority of the research on Podophyllum has been carried out in three countries - USA, China and India, The authorship patterns show that over 92% documents are by multiple authors.

Joshii, Kshitij and Garg (2010, [124]) examined the R&D efforts in the field of forest mycology (study of fungi) with a primary focus on the global trends of publication output and its citation impact for the papers published during 1987-2008. The results indicated that the number of publications has increased significantly especially during 2004 -2008. A total of 3313 publications are scattered in 6l9 journal titles originating from 50 countries and 839 institutions.

Mumtaz (2005, [125]) analyzed the literature on Nigella sativa (Habbat al-barakah or Black seed) with the objective to study the periodic growth of literature, author patterns, topical focus, and geographic origin of literature on the subject. The findings show the increase in the volume of literature from 1971 onwards starting from one citation per year growing to 46 papers per year during the late 1990s. One-third of the citations were received by very few. Four-fifths of the citations were the result of collaborative work. About two-fifths of the papers were published in 36 journals. India and Egypt are the leading contributors to this literature. Vijayakumar and Naqvi (2002, [126]) studied the authorship pattern of 'Azadirachta Indica' literature from 300 journals, revealing that joint research is quite significant; the degree of collaboration being 0.9402.

Biotechnology

Sevukan and Sharma (2008, [127]) presented an analysis of research performance of biotechnology faculties in central universities of India from 1997-2006, based on the data from two databases - PubMed, and NCBI and WoS. The results indicated that the growth of literature in biotechnology had steadily increased from 15 articles in 1997 to 43 articles in 2006 and two-authored publications predominated. Chand and Patra (2005, [129]) explored the chronological growth of Indian biotechnology. The study also shows the active authors, institutions and state wise distributions of research output in this field

Patra and Bhattacharya (2005, [128]) carried out a bibliometric analysis of oncology research in India. The data for the study has been downloaded from national centre for Biotechnology (NCBI), Pub Med. The study analyses literature growth trends. It also examines research activities in different countries worldwide. The study also identifies the active institutions in India, which published the cancer literature the most. Patra and Mishra (2006, [130]) analyzed the growth of the scientific literature in bioinformatics; the data were collected from NCBI, PubMed. Authors with single publication were predominant (73.58%) contrary to that predicted by Lotka's law.

Mukherjee (2011, [131]) studied the evaluation of Indian performance in the emerging fields of environmental sciences. The study indicates that the number of Indian papers in emerging research fronts in environmental science has been increasing during 2000–2009. However, the collaboration patterns according to institutional collaboration changed from "local papers" via "domestic papers" to "international papers".

Biradar (2006, [132]) studied the references in the articles published in *Indian Journal* of *Environmental Protection* published in 1994, 1999 and 2004. The objectives of the study were to determine the average number of references per article, the forms of materials used by the scientists, the nature of the authorship pattern and the degree of collaboration and the organization-wise contribution of articles. It was found that the team research was quite significant. The degree of collaboration varied from 0.78 to 0.95. The study also found that on an average 11.595 references are referred in each article. Universities contributed 31.6 per cent, followed by colleges (24 per cent). It is also observed that the proportion of single authored papers have decreased from 20.29 per cent in the year 1994 to 4.76 per cent in 2004.

Application of Bradford's Law and Lotka's Law

Sevukan and Sharma (2008, [127]) observed in biotechnology that the distribution of papers conforms to Lotka's law with $\alpha = 2.12$. However, the Bradford's law does not fit to the observed data. Bradford's principles were used by Patra and Mishra (2006, [130]) to identify core journals and Lotka's law applied to analyze author's productivity pattern. Twenty core journals were identified and the primary mode of dissemination of information was through journal articles. Authors with single publication were predominant (73.58%) contrary to that predicted by Lotka's law. Applicability of Lotka's law was examined by Chand and Patra (2005, [129]) for the authorship pattern. Productivity of authors is analyzed and a list of 35 authors publishing more than 10 papers is given. Bradford's law of scattering is used to identify the core journals which cover most of the research and development output of Indian biotechnology. Patra and Bhattacharya (2005, [128]) used Bradford law of scattering to identify the core journals for Indian cancer research literature. Lotka's law was used to study the authors' productivity pattern. Shukla, Saksena and Riswadkar (2001, [133]) applied Bradford's Law of scattering and Lotka's Law of productivity to bio-energy literature to determine whether or not the law holds good for ten abstracting services (eight international and two Indian). It was verified that literature related to bio-energy conforms to Bradford's law of scattering and that grouping of services (all services together) also yields a Bradford distribution. The new model developed in this study fits the data very satisfactorily, with the *r* value ranging from 0.952 to 0.998 (for papers from periodicals) and 0.989 to 0.998 (for papers from conference proceedings). The value of *p* (multiplication factor) for bio-energy literature ranged from 2.19 to 4.09 (except for IEA and ISA) for articles from periodicals and from 2.02 to 4.59 for papers from conference papers. Results of linear regression showed that Lotka's distribution holds good for bioenergy literature and the value of *n* ranged between 2.5 and 4.5. The K-S test confirmed these findings.

Agricultural Science

Choudhury and Sarkhel (2011, [134]) studied quantitatively agricultural research output in West Bengal for the period 1993-2007. The result shows that there has been a topsy-turvy growth in the research publication during the period. Top 50 journals with 30 or more papers have only 8 foreign journals. Kumar, Garg and Dutt (2009, [135]) analyzed 18,224 papers from 3439 institutions in 445 Indian science journals, retrieved from *Indian Science Abstracts* (ISA, 2006.) The study indicated that most of the articles are from academic institutions, followed by state agriculture universities and medical colleges; Punjab Agriculture University ranked first followed by Haryana Agriculture University. The highest number of papers was published in the disciplines of agriculture, forestry, animal husbandry and fisheries followed by medical and veterinary sciences. The Indian publication output in 2006 has increased considerably as compared to 1984. Garg, Kumar and Lal (2006, [136]) analyzed 16891 publications of Indian scientists during 1993-2002 and indexed by SCIE (WoS). It was noted that the publication output in the agricultural sciences is on the decline since 1998. "Dairy and animal sciences" followed by "veterinary sciences "constitute the largest component of the Indian agricultural research output. Agricultural universities and institutes under the aegis of ICAR are the major producers of research output.

Krishna and Kumar (2004, [137]) studied using citation analysis of 68 doctoral theses on Agriculture and Veterinary Sciences submitted to Rajasthan Agriculture University, Bikaner, during 1996 to 2000. The examined subjectwise authorship pattern and trend graph for books and journals. Ramesn and Nagaraju (2002, [138]) discussed various features of the quarterly *International Journal of Tropical Agriculture* for the period 1991-2000. They studied the year wise distribution of papers, authorship pattern, degree of collaboration, geographical location of contributors, types of affiliation, average length of articles and also examined the references. The study revealed dominance of Indian authors and multiple authorship belonging to the academic institutions.

Food Science and Technology

Vijay and Raghavan (2007, [139]) analyzed 779 articles published in five volumes 37(2000) to 41(2004) of *Journal Food Science and Technology*. A similar study was also carried out for the first volume of the same journal for the year 1964. The number of contributions and their distribution in different volumes, authorship pattern, foreign and Indian authored contributions, institution wise contribution, citations, types of publications cited, and geographical distribution of contributions national and international and physical growth of the journal were studied. In another paper, the authors (2005, [140]), have reported on the collaborative research and authorship trends in food science and technology in India. He examined and analyzed the authorship patterns in food science and technology periodicals, to (i) study the proportion of single-authored articles compared with multi-authored ones, (ii) determine the degree of collaboration in this field, and (iii) study the publication pattern of authors from different organizations. The results indicated that collaborative research was dominant in India and the degree of collaboration was 0.91. The average number of authors/paper also showed an upward trend from 4.89 in 1994 to 8.2 in 2003.

Crop studies

Sharma (2009, [141]) examined 2603 research articles published by the scientists of CPRI during 1991 to 2007; Results show that majority of the scientists preferred to publish research papers in joint authorship (82.67%) having 0.82 degree of collaboration. The study further shows no uniform pattern of literature growth but factors like fund availability, scientists' recruitment and their availability, and years that had special occasions like conferences, seminars etc. impact scientific productivity of the scientists during the period under review.

A scientometric analysis of major spices research literature published in Asian countries during 1968-2002 was undertaken using HORT-CD database by Senthilkumar and Amudhavalli (2005, [142]). Asian countries are the major producers, marketers, and consumers of spices in the world. The authors have identified the most prolific authors with their affiliations and key journals in major spices in the Asian region. In another study in 2007 [143], the authors have attempted to identify the high and low activity areas of Spices Research amongst the 36 Asian countries for the period 1968-2002, using HORT - CD database. The objectives of the study were to determine the priorities of the research interests and to study subject trends, gaps and similarity of research efforts amongst the Asian scholars working in this field. Using correspondence analysis, the relationship between countries and Spices Research is studied; also the dynamics of changes in research priorities, during the study period were also studied.

Dixit and Katare (2007, [144]) highlighted the research trend of cotton scientists by studying the patterns of articles published in the *Journal of the Indian Society of Cotton Improvement* for the period 1995-2004. Jena (2006, [145]) carried out a bibliometric analysis of the periodical *Indian Journal of Fiber and Textile Research* for the period 1996-2004, to study the trends such as the year wise distribution of articles, bibliographical distribution of citations, authorship pattern, citation pattern, average length of articles, number of tables and figures used, time lag, geographical distribution of authors and subject analysis. Concluded that the increasing trend in the number of contributions in the periodical from year to year shows the periodical is a respected primary publication by researchers in the area. Surendra Kumar and Kumar (2005, [146]) analyzed 743 research papers comprising 435 main articles and 308 short communications published in nine volumes 10 to 18, (1993 - 2001) in the *Journal of Oilseed Research*. The authors have analyzed the papers into year wise distribution, length of articles, use of tables, graphs and diagrams. Identifies authorship pattern and calculates collaboration coefficients. The paper analyses in detail citations given in these articles in various tables namely number of citations per article and types of documents used for citations. The paper also ranks periodicals, based on the law of scattering. In another study in 2004 [147], the authors have analyzed contributions of the National Research Centre for Soybean, Indore, India, for the period 1987-2001, with the objective to determine the average number of papers published per year, the types of documents publishing the papers along with names of the periodicals, subject and language distribution. The authorship pattern is also studied and provides a method for calculating the publication scores of individual authors and their respective ranks.

Ramesh, Ramanna and Hussain (2000, [148]) analyzed the papers published in the quarterly *International Rice Journal 'Oryza'* during 1986-1995. Attempted to analyze the yearly distribution of papers, authorship patterns, geographical location of contributors, subjects covered, average length or articles etc. Some suggestions for the future are made.

Senthilkumar and Vadivel (2004, [149]) analyzed the *Journal of Spices and Aromatic Crops* for the period 1992-2000. The objective was to study the various characteristics of literature on the subject. The authors have examined the year wise distribution of articles, authorship pattern, length of articles, subject wise breakup of articles and leading authors. Sivasubrananian (2000, [150]) reported results of a bibliometric study of articles published in the *Journal of Indian Coffee*, which is published by the Coffee Board since 1937 and has played a key role in the dissemination of coffee information all over the world. Analyzes the authorship pattern, the range and frequency of references cited and examines year-wise distribution of papers. It also shows subject wise breakup of the papers and average length of papers. Results indicate that the trend is towards single authorship and there exists a high degree of collaboration in-coffee research.

Group 5: Health Sciences

Bibliometric analysis of the *Indian Journal of Pharmaceutical Education and Research* reveals that journals are the predominant citation source followed by books. Kulkarni and others (2009, [151]) have shown that majority of the scientists preferred to publish research papers in multiple authorship and there is considerable time lag in publication of articles from the date of receipt of the papers.

Karpagan, Gopalakrishnan, Ramesh Babu and Natarajan (2012, [152])explored the growth of Stem Cell research in India during 2001-2010. Several parameters, such as, global publication share and rank, average citation per paper for 5 years block period, authorship pattern, collaboration index, Collaborative Coefficient, Degree of Collaboration, etc. have been computed.

Jain and Jacobs (2012, [153]) explored the progress in microbicide development by analyzing 317 papers from PubMed database. Majority of the papers (280), 88.33% appeared during the recent decade (2001-2010). Of the 133 journals, the four journals, namely *Sexually Transmitted Diseases, Antimicrobial Agents and Chemotherapy, Journal of Acquired Immune Deficiency Syndromes,* and *AIDS* contributed one-fourths (80 papers, 25.24%) of the total papers published by researchers from 22 countries with US on the top of the tally. The recent decade has witnessed considerable growth in research output in this field while a successful microbicide still remains elusive.

Gupta, Adarsha Bala and Kaur (2011, [154]) analyzed the research output of India in AIDS/HIV during 1999-2008. They studied several parameters such as the growth, rank and global publications share, citation impact, share of international collaborative papers, contribution of major collaborative partner countries, contribution of various subject-fields and using co-word analysis various diseases/ infections commonly associated with AIDS/HIV in India

Gupta and Adarsha Bala (2011, [155]) analyzed tuberculosis (TB) research output in India during 1998-2009; They considered different parameters such as, the growth, rank and global publications share, citation impact, share of international collaborative papers, contribution of major collaborative partner countries, contribution of various subject fields and by type of tuberculosis and patterns of research communication in most productive journals. SCOPUS Citation Database was used to collect the data for 10 years (1998-2009). India ranks third among the top 21 countries and its global publication share (7.73%) is higher than that of China (2.93%), South Africa (2.60%) and Brazil (2.47%). But its average annual publication growth rate and international collaborative publication share are lower than those of these countries. Dutt and Suresh Kumar (2010, [156]) analyzed 2,566 papers on Dengue research published during 1987 to 2008 and indexed by Science Citation Index. Their study indicated a gradual rise in the quantum of output. About 80% of the papers appeared in journals originating from USA, the UK, the Netherlands, France and Germany. Total output was from 74 countries of which 17 countries contributed 87% of the total output. The highest number of publications came from USA, followed by India. However, in the later block (1998-2008) the proportion of output of both USA as well as India declined as compared to the first block (1987-1997).

Singh, Ahmad and Nazim (2008, [157]) analyzed articles on plant Embeliaribes, with an objective to study an overview of research activity in this field and characterize its most important aspects. A total of 332 articles were collected from PubMed, Medicinal and *Aromatic Plants Abstract*, *Indian Science Abstracts* and *Biological Abstracts.* The analysis focused on growth of literature, authorship pattern, most prolific authors, core journals of the subject, most productive institutes and countries. Lotka's law and Bradford' law of scattering were applied to estimate the author productivity and core journals in the subject. Most articles involved collaboration between two or three authors Author productivity was not found to fit Lotka's law with a value of $\alpha = 2$. However, the distribution of articles in different journals was found fit Bradford's law of scattering with the distribution of journals as 1:n: n2.

Kurnar and Chand (2007, [158]) looked at the growth over time of Indian AIDS research output based on bibliographic data from PubMed and Web of Science. Authorship distribution was examined using Lotka's law. Bradford's law of scattering was used to identify core journals. The study identified active institutions and state-wide distributions of Indian AIDS research output. The yearly analysis of data shows that there is a rapid growth of literature from 1992 onwards. Still, in an international sense, relative productivity of India is low and requires more focused research and development. Saraswathi and Raghavendra (2005, [159]) carried out a bibliometric analysis in the area of cloning. Mahapatra and Panda (2004, [160]) described the growth trend in health science literature in Orissa published from 1993-2002. The study includes in its scope 118 research papers on "health literature" from 59 Indian and foreign journals. They analyzed the data by authorship pattern, year wise growth subject wise break up of papers, category of journals, country of origin, length of papers, and ranking of journals.

Biradar and Tippeswamy (2004, [161]) studied references in 62 M.D. Pediatric dissertations submitted to the J.J.M. Medical College, Davanagere. They computed the average number of references per dissertation, forms of documents, authorship pattern, and obsolescence of literature and percentage of cited periodicals available in the library. Results indicated that periodicals (79.12%) are the highly utilized source. Three authors have contributed 25% of the articles. 25.98% and 76.70% cited journals and journal articles respectively are available in the J.J.M. Medical College Library, Davanagere, and Karnataka. Nalini (2003, [162]) analyzed 31 articles on occupational health related problems studied in India and published in journals (most Indian but some in foreign journals) during the year 2000. Also, examines the institutions originating the articles: the major subject area covered was found to be that of health consequences of chemical and textile workers. Average length of articles, number of authors and the time span and number of citations are also analyzed.

Kundra and Tomov (2001, [163]) studied the collaboration patterns in Indian and Bulgarian epidemiology of neoplasms in 'MEDLINE' for 1966-1999. He analyzed selected papers of the 'Second Berlin Workshop on Scientometrics and Informetrics / Collaboration in Science and in Technology and First COLLNET Meeting, held in Berlin (Germany), 1-4 September 2000. Presents a scientometric analysis of the publication output of India and Bulgaria on the epidemiology of neoplasms as reflected in Medline on CD-ROM for 1966-1999. Indians published 347 papers in 24 domestic journals but 444 papers in 169 journals from 21 countries. Bulgarians published 88 papers in 6 Bulgarian journals but 63 papers in 39 journals from 13 countries. Some 17 journals from 8 countries contained papers by both Indian and Bulgarian authors. Oncology dominated with 46 different journals. Indians published papers in foreign journals of 30 thematic profiles; Bulgarians 12. The collaboration of Indians and Bulgarians resulted from joint bilateral projects and/or postgraduate studies abroad.

Neelameghan and Ravichandra Rao (2005, [164]) in their article on 'Bibliometric support to medical Historiography' discussed a general model for analyzing the patterns of incidence of certain communicable diseases in India in the 19th century. The authors have applied Bibliometric techniques in data analysis and interpreted the findings in relation to the health environment and preventive measures. The authors observed that the pattern of publications on cholera is a multi-modal distribution; also, that the growth of publications on communicable diseases conforms to a linear model, like the growth of highly cited papers.

Group 6: Humanities and Social Sciences (including management, economics, industrial research, patenting, etc.)

Rabindranath Tagore's songs known as Rabindra Sangit have become a symbol of cultural ethos of both India and Bangladesh. Ray and Sen (2012, [165]) studied the growth of literature on Rabindra Sangit. Ray and Sen (2012, [166]) in another study, analyzed the growth of poems of Gitanjali, their lengths, places and dates of writings, use of words, rank frequency of different words and to find out whether Gitanjali follows any bibliometric law. The rank-frequency distribution of words in Gitanjali does not follow Zipf's law but justifies the title of the kavyagrantha.

Sangam, Gupta and Kumar (2007, [167]) discussed the application of growth model with an objective to study the growth and dynamics of growth of Indian and Chinese publications in three sub-disciplines of social sciences namely., Economics,

Psychology and Sociology. Koganurmath, Angadi and Kademani (2002, [168]) analyzed 663 papers published by the social scientists of Tata Institute of Social Sciences (TISS) during 1990-2000 in diverse domains in the social sciences to study authorship pattern and collaboration. The results indicate that the collaboration coefficient of the 613 single-authored papers is 92.46 per cent, followed by 6.33 per cent (42 papers) for two-authored papers. Maximum collaboration coefficient was 0.13 during 1996-1997.

Eqbal and Raza (2005, [169]) studied quantitatively the Personnel Attitudes and Job Satisfaction. The aim of the study was to identify country, language, form, year wise distribution and authorship pattern, ranking of authors and journals. They collected data from *Psychological Abstracts* published from 1992-2001. The study showed that USA has contributed 59.53% of the papers and most of the papers are two-authored papers. The most productive journal was *Journal of Organizational Behavior.*

Mulla and Chandrasekhar (2011, [170]) studied 2,253 articles published on industry and trade during 2002-2006. The online database of the *Indian Science Abstracts* website (http://isa.niscair.res.in) was the main source for their study. The degree of collaboration in industrial and trade literature was 0.61. In the country wise contribution of documents, India contributed 69.86% of the total publication. In the state-wise contribution of documents Maharashtra stands first with 323 (14.34%). Among journals *Indian Journal of Fiber and Textile Research* is ranked first with 327 (27.88%) articles and among corporate bodies Procter & Gamble Company stands first with 172 (17.77%) documents. Sixty seven book reviews published in *Journal of Scientific and Industrial Research* during 2002-2007 were quantitatively analyzed by Sarala (2011, [171]). The analysis showed that 70% of the books reviewed were original works. Nearly 50% of the works were single authored. Documents reviewed comprised monographs (94%), yearbook, reviews and special issue of journal. About 60% of the books were published from New Delhi. 19 publishers were responsible for publishing 67 books. Price range of 44% Indian books was within Rs.251-500. Thirty one scientists belonging to 14 institutions were responsible for the review works.

Nandi and Bandyopadhyay (2008, [172]) studied the issues of *Indian Economic Review* 1998-2002. They examined authorship pattern, the degree of collaboration among authors and geographical distribution of the authors. They analyzed 1653 references in 68 research articles. The findings reveal that 43.25% references to books and 52.69% to journals. The authorship pattern study showed that the highest number of citations is by single authors. The degree of collaboration in "*Indian Economic Review*" is 0.33 and it gradually decreases during the study period. Geographical distribution of the authors showed that most of the contributors are from India with 48 authors (52.17%)

Debbarmann (2008, [173]) analyzed data on Indian patent applications; he obtained the data from the annual reports of the Controller General of Patents, Designs and Trademarks. His study shows that the patent filing activity (particularly in Biotechnology) has increased in India. Maharashtra, Delhi and Tamil Nadu are the leading states in patent filing in the country. Gupta (2005, [174]) examined the nature of international collaboration in patenting, with particular reference to the contributions made by scientists from India. The study shows a significant amount of contributions by inventors from India in collaboration with inventors from other countries in patenting. There is evidence of a gradual decline in individual inventor patents from India and contributions by teams of three inventors appear to be the maximum. Sujit and Martin (2004, [175]) examined the characteristics of Indian and Chinese patenting activities in the US patent system by delineating two categories of patents; "nationally assigned", and "invented not nationally assigned" patents Indian patents are mainly of utility type whereas China's activity falls in both utility and design, to the "nationally assigned" patents.

6 CONCLUDING REMARKS

Articles on scientometric research are published mostly in library science journals. The distribution of articles in different journals is as follows:

- *Annals of Library and Information Science* (37 articles).
- *SRELS Journal of Information Management* (32 articles)
- *COLLNET Journal of Scientometrics and Information Management* (18 articles).
- *DESIDOC Journal Library and Information Technology* (15 articles)
- Foreign Journals;
- *Journal of Scientometrics* (20 articles)
- *Malaysian journal of Library and Information Science* (6 articles)
- Other Indian and Foreign journals (14 articles)

- Other types of documents (Theses, Conference Proceedings and Reports)(25 articles)

Scientometric articles (since 2000 in India) mostly covered the following topics:

- Quantitative aspects of library and information studies;
- Journal productivity (by coverage, by citation, impact factor, h-index, sources of citations, immediacy of citations, age of sources cited, coverage in databases, etc.);
- Measures of productivity or author productivity, including studies related to multiple authorship (number of publications, impact factor, h-index);
- Growth of literature; and
- Quantitative analyses of science (National mapping of science -- science indicators at the macro level -- country-wise, language-wise, subject-wise, journal-wise etc.).

Scientometric research in India is centered around the quantitative analysis of the literature by subject wise and in a very few cases, it is country-wise. There is hardly any research on theoretical aspects of scientometrics. The survey indicates that:

- Proportion of single authorship is quite high in the field of library and information science, bio-informatics, social sciences (92 %!), and in economics;
- Proportion of multiple authorship is very high in chemistry, biological science, biotechnology, laser research (about 97.7 %!), thorium studies, etc.;
- Scientometric studies are also applied to prepare the scientists profiles;
- In library and information science, URLs are less cited, compared to that in other disciplines;
- There are hardly any studies on use and user studies, growth of collection, age distribution of documents, circulation statistics, co-citation, bibliographic coupling, co-word analysis, rank distribution of words, etc.; and
- There are a good number of articles related to Bradford's law and Lotka's law.

Science in general in India is growing; the Indian publications are now visible and it is increasing, this is what I could observe from the scientometric literature. No scientometric research is being carried out to evaluate and measure research outcome; there is also no evidence that the results of the scientometric research is being used in drafting science policy or in science administration.

7 ACKNOWLEDGEMENT

'This work is supported in part by the World Bank/Government of India research grant under the TEQIP programme (subcomponent 1.2.1) to the Centre for Knowledge Analytics and Ontological Engineering (KAnOE) at PES Institute of Technology, Bangalore, India. I thank Prof. A Neelameghan for his valuable suggestions in writing this paper'.

8 REFERENCES

1. Ravichandra Rao, I.K. and Suma, P. (1997) India's Coverage in COMPENDEX Plus in 1990 and 1994: An Analysis. *NISSAT report 1997* (Submitted by DRTC / ISI, Bangalore).
2. Dhawan, S.M. and Arunachalam, S. (1998) Physics Research in India: as reflected by INSPEC - Physics, 1990 & 1994. Report Submitted to NISSAT, Govt. of India.
3. Basu, Aparna and Nagpaul, P.S. (1998) National Mapping of Science. *NISTADS Report: # REP-248/98.*
4. Government of India, Department of Science and Technology, New Delhi. (2012) Bibliometric Study of India's Scientific Publication Outputs during 2001-10. Evidence Report for Changing Trends. Thomson Reuters.
5. Gupta, B.M. and Gupta, Prem. (2011) Analysis of India's S&T Research Capabilities and International Collaborative Strength, particularly in context of India-German Collaboration, 2004-09.
6. Arora, Jagadish and Trivedi, Kruti. (2012) Measuring Research Output and its Impact Using Bibliometric Indicators: Profiles of 50 Selected Universities. *INFLIBNET Centre*. Ahmedabad.
7. Erfanmanesh, Mohammadamin; Jahromi, Reza Basirian; Hosseini, Elahe and Gholamhosseinzadeh, Zohreb. (2013) Scientific Productivity, Impact and Collaboration of the top Asian Countries in Scopus During 1996-2010. *COLLNET Journal of Scientometrics and Information Management*, 7(1): 97-110.
8. Aslib Proceedings. (1948) 1: 102.
9. Ranganathan, S.R. (1969) Librametry and its Scope. *DRTC Annual Seminar*, 7. Paper DA.
10. Neelameghan, A. (1969) Librametry. *DRTC Annual Seminar,* 7. Paper LC.
11. Ravichandra Rao, I.K. and Neelameghan, A. (1992) From Librametry to Informetrics: An Overview and Ranganathan's Contributions. *Libri*, 42(3): 242-57.
12. Brookes, B.C. (1990) Biblio-, Sciento-, Infor-metrics??? What are we talking about? **In** L. Egghe and R. Rousseau (*Eds*) *Informetrics 89/90*. 31-43.
13. Ravichandra Rao, I.K. (1981) Document and User Distribution in Transaction Records of Canadian University Libraries. Ph. D. Thesis. *Faculty of Graduate Studies. School of Library and Information science*; the University of Western Ontario, London, Ontario, Canada.

14. Garg, K.C. and Kumar, S. (2010) An analysis of the citation pattern of Indian science journals indexed by SCIE. *Annals of Library and Information Studies*, 57(4): 365-372.
15. Kademani, B.S.; Sagar, A.; Kumar, V. and Gupta, B.M. (2007) Mapping of Indian publications in S&T: A scientometric analysis of publications in science citation index. *DESIDOC Bulletin of Information Technology*, 27(1): 17-34.
16. Garg, K.C.; Dutt, B. and Kumar, S. (2006) Scientometric profile of Indian science as seen through science citation index. *Annals of Library and Information Studies*, 53(3): 114-125.
17. Basu, Aparna. (2013) Some differences in research Publications of Indian Scientists in India and the Diaspora, 1986-2010. *Scientometrics (2013)*. DOI: 10.1000/s11192-012-0800.
18. Basu, Aparna and Wagner, Ronald (2012) 'Cognitive Mobility' or Migration of Authors between fields used in mapping a network of mathematics. *Scientometrics,* 91: 353-368.
19. Basu, Aparna (2010) Does a country's scientific productivity depend critically on the number of countries journals indexed? *Scientoemtrics*. 82: 507-516.
20. Basu, Aparna (2006) Using ISI's 'Highly Cited Researcher's to obtain a country level indicator of citation excellence. *Scientometrics*. 68(3): 361-375.
21. Basu, Aparna and Aggarwal, Ritu (2001) International Collaboration in Science in India and its Impact on International Performance. *Scientometrics*, 52(3): 379-394.
22. Basu, Aparna and Vinu Kumar, B.S. (2000) International Collaboration in Indian Scientific papers. *Scientometrics*, 48(3): 381-402.
23. Harinarayana, N.S. and Raju, Vasantha. (2009) Citation Analysis of SRR's works: A look through the Window of Google Scholar. *Information Studies*. 15(3): 165-178.
24. Garg, K.C. and Kumar, S. (2009) Foreign authored contributions to Indian science periodicals. *Annals of Library and Information Studies*, 56(2): 80-85.
25. Harinarayana, N.S.; Mahadevaswamy and Vasantha, R.N. (2008) Indian author productivity in international journals in library and information science: A study. *SRELS Journal of Information Management*, 45(4): 399-410.
26. Harinarayana, N.S. and Raju, V.N. (2012) Citation analysis of publications of LIS teachers in south India. *Information Studies*, 18(3): 143-161.
27. Egghe, L. and Ravichandra Rao, I.K. (2002) Duality Revisited: Construction Fractional Frequency Distributions based on two dual Lotka Laws. *Journal of the American Society for Information Science and Technology*. 53(10): 789-801.
28. Egghe, L. (1993) Consequence of Lotka's Law in the case of Fractional Counting of Authorship and of Author Count. *Math Computing Modeling*. 18(9): 63-77.
29. Ravichandra Rao, I.K. (1995) A stochastic Approach to Analysis of Distribution of Papers in Mathematics: Lotka's Law Revisited. *Proceedings of the Fifth Biennial Conference of the International Society for Scientometrics and Informetrics.* Royal College, River Forest, IL, 455-64.
30. Ravichandra Rao, I.K.; Sahoo, Bibhuti Bhusan and Egghe, L. (2003) A Distribution of papers based on Fractional Counting: An Empirical Study. *Proceedings of the 9th International Conference on Scientometrics and Informetrics.* Dalian University of Technology Press. Dalian, China. 241-250.

31. Sahoo, Bibhuthi Bhushan. (2006) Scientometric Study of Literature in Software Studies in India with a comparison to the World Literature. Ph.D. Thesis. *Department of Library and Information Science*, Pune University, Pune. India.
32. Mahawar, K.L. and Saini, O.P. (2012) Biblio-Blogsphere: A Platform for Communication among LIS Professionals. *COLLNET Journal of Scientometrics and Information management*. 6(2): 301-313.
33. Shukla, Svetal H and Polur, Lalitha. (2012) Webometric Analysis and Indicators of Selected Indian State Universities. *Information Studies*, 18(2): 70-104.
34. Jalal, Samir Kumar; Biswas, Subal Chandra and Mukhyopadhyay, Parthasarathy. (2013) Link Analysis Research of Indian Universities. *Information Studies*. 19(1): 5-28.
35. Jalal, Samir Kumar; Biswas, Subal Chandra and Mukhypadhyaya, Parthasarathy. (2010) Web-based Ranking and Link Analysis of Central Universities in India: A webometric Analysis. *Information Studies*. 16(1): 7-26.
36. Jalal, Samir Kumar; Biswas, S.C. and Mukhyopadhyaya, Parthasarathi. (2010) Web presence of selected Asian countries: A webometric study. *COLLNET Journal of Scientometrics and Information Management*, 4(2): 57-68.
37. Jalal, S.K.; Biswas, S.C. and Mukhyopadhyaya, P. (2009) Bibliometrics to webometrics. *Information Studies*, 15(1): 3-20.
38. Kundra, Ramesh. (2002) Quantitative Analysis of Medical Literature in India: A bibliometric study. Ph. D. Thesis. *Department of Library and Information Science*, Pune University, Pune, India.
39. Ravichandra Rao, I.K. and Sahoo, Bibhuthi Bhushan. (2008) Distribution of Multiple Authors: A case study of two Journals (*JASIST and Scientometrics*). *COLLNET Journal of Scientometrics* and *Information Management*. 2(1): 27-36.
40. Anuradha, K.T. and Urs, S.R. (2007) Bibliometric indicators of Indian research collaboration patterns: A correspondence analysis. *Scientometrics,* 71(2): 179-189. doi: http://dx.doi.org/10.1007/s11192-007-1657-4
41. Roy, P.C. (2004) Authorship pattern of Indian library science journals for the period of 1991-2000. *SRELS Journal of Information Management*, 41(4): 393-404.
42. Gupta, B.M. and Singh, M. (2004) India's collaboration with Latin America as reflected in co-authored papers. *DESIDOC Bulletin of Information Technology*, 24(3): 9-21.
43. Parameshwaran, M. and Smitha, K.G. (2001) Bibliometric analysis of LISA. *Annals of Library and Information Studies*, 48(4): 149-156.
44. Mahapatra, R.K. and Jena, P. (2006) Scientific research productivity on Orissa: A bibliometric analysis. *Annals of Library and Information Studies*, 53(1): 18-21.
45. Ravichandra Rao, I.K. and Divya Srivastava (2010) Growth of Journals, Articles and Authors in malaria research. *Journal of Informetrics.* 4(3): 249-256.
46. Sangam, S.L; Keshava and Agadi, A.B. (2010) Growth pattern of Marine Engineering Literature. *Information Studies*. 16(2): 113-120.

47. Sangam, S.L. and Meera. (2009) Research Collaboration Pattern in Indian Contributions to Chemical Sciences. *COLLNET Journal of Scientometrics and Information Management,* 3(1): 39-45.
48. Gupta, B.M. and Karisiddappa, C.R. (2000) Modeling the growth of literature in the area of theoretical population genetics. *Scientometrics*. 49(2): 321-55.
49. Gupta, B.M.; et al. (2002) Modeling the growth of world social science literature. *Scientometrics*, 53: 161-164.
50. Egghe, L and Ravichandra Rao, I.K. (2001) Theory of first citation distributions and applications. *Mathematical and Computer Modeling*, 34: 81-90
51. Egghe, L and Ravichandra Rao, I.K. (2002) Theory and Experimentation on the most recent reference Distribution. *Scientometrics,* 53(3): 371-87.
52. Ravichandra Rao, I.K. (2012) Relations Among the number of Citations, References and Authors: Revisited. *COLLNET Journal of Scientoemtrics and Information Management*. 6(1): 17-30.
53. Mahesh G and Wadhwa, N.K. (2012) Web of Science based Ranking of Indian Library and Information Science Journals. *COLLNET Journal of Scientometrics and Information Management*. 6(2): 279-299.
54. Sagar, A.; Kalyane, V.L.; Prakasan, E.R.; Garg, R.G. and Kumar, V. (2009) Scientometric highlights on science and technology related review articles affiliated to India. *Malaysian Journal of Library & Information Science*, 14(2).
55. Gupta, B.M.; Kumar, S. and Singh, Y. (2005) Research contributions and impact of research of Indian institute of technology, Roorkee, 1993 to 2001. *Annals of Library and Information Studies*, 52(1): 8-14.
56. Jeevan, V.K.J. (2002) Publishing research papers in journals: Trends in Indian institute of technology (IIT), Kharagpur. *SRELS Journal of Information Management*, 39(1): 73-92.
57. Ravichandra Rao, I.K. (2007) Distributions of Hirsch-index and g-index: An Empirical Study. *Proceedings of ISSI-2007*, CSIC, Madrid, Spain. June 25-27, Vol. II, 655-58.

Group 1: Library and Information Science and related topics

58. Neelameghan, A. and Sathish, K. (2003) Knowledge diffusion in clusters of web-based communities: A case study. IADIS/WBC International Conference on Web-bases Communities, Lisbon, Portugal.
59. Sen, B.K. (2002) INSDOC's contribution to bibliometrics. Annals of Library and Information Studies, 49(1): 1-6.
60. Kumar, H.A. and Dora, M. (2012) Research productivity in a management institute: An analysis of research performance of Indian institute of management Ahmadabad during 1999-2010. DESIDOC Journal of Library & Information Technology, 32(4): 365-372.
61. Kumbhar, R. (2012) Trends in classification literature: Analysis of literature published during 2000 to 2009. DESIDOC Journal of Library & Information Technology, 32(2): 179-185.

62. Pradhan, P. and Chandrakar, R. (2011) Indian LIS literature in international journals with specific reference to SSCI database: A bibliometric study. Library Philosophy and Practice (e-journal.) ISSN1522-0222. http://digitalcommons.unl/libphilprac/657.

63. Singh, Kunwar P; Jain, Arati and Babbar, Parveen. (2011) DESIDOC Bulletin of Information Technology: A Bibliometric Study. SRELS Journal of Information Management. 48(1): 57-68.

64. Rajgoli, I.U. (2011) Conference proceedings as a source of information in LIS research in India: A study based on citations. Annals of Library and Information Studies, 58(4): 346-354.

65. Saxena, A.; Gupta, B.M. and Jauhari, M. (2011) Research performance of top engineering and technological institutes of India: A comparison of indices. DESIDOC Journal of Library & Information Technology, 31(5): 377-381.

66. Patil, S.B. (2010) Herald of Library Science: A Bibliometric Study. SRELS Journal of Information Management. 47(3): 351-358.

67. Nazim, Mohammad and Ahmad. (2007) Main Research Trends In Information Literacy: A Bibliometric Study. SRELS Journal of Information Management, 44(1): 53-62.

68. Shafi, S.M.; Rather, Rafiq Ahmed; Jan Rosy and Shah, Gulam Jeelani. (2007) D-Lib Magazine: A Bibliometric Study. SRELS Journal of Information management, 44(3): 271-278.

69. Maheswarappa, B.S.; Tadasad, P.G.; Emmanuel Ebnazar, C. and Seema, A. Alur. (Sept 2003) Use of Internet Resources and Services: A Review of LIS literature. SRELS Journal of Information Management. 40(2): 157-167.

70. Hadagali, Gururaj, S. and Kumbar, B.D. (2011) Use of e-Resources in University Libraries of Karnataka State. Information Studies. 17(4): 211-224.

71. Keshava, V.P. Hittalamani; M.P. Gowda. (2008) Papers in select sociology journals (1999-2004): A bibliometric analysis. Information Studies, 14(1): 59-65.

72. Keshava, Girish A. Ganjihal, and M.P Gowda. (2008) ACM Transactions on Information Systems (1989-21006): A bibliometric study. Information Studies, 14(4): 223-234.

73. Gururaj S. Hadagali; B.D. Kumbar, and S. Sumana. (2009) Current Science: A bibliometric study. Information Studies, 15(1): 51-60.

74. Gururaj S. Hatagali; B.D. Kumbar and Amrut Benahal.(2009) Citation analysis of Ph.D. Theses submitted to Karnatak University, Dharwad, in the field of Physics./ Information Studies, 15(2): 115-127

75. Amrutraj Ravi Benahal. (2012) Use of e-resources by academia: An analysis of literature from 1995-2010. Information Studies, 18(2): 105-124.

76. Paramjeet Kaur Walia and Manpreet Kaur. (2012) Authorship pattern in library and information science journal literature. Information Studies, 18(3): 163-176.

77. Patra, S.K. and Chand, P. (2006) Library and information science research in India: A bibliometric study. Annals of Library and Information Studies, 53(4): 219-223.

78. Gupta, Jyothi and Khare, V.P. (2013) Application of Bradford's Law of Scattering to LIS Theses: Dr. Harisingh Gour University, Sagar, India. Information Studies, 19(3): 181-200.

Group 2: Mathematics, Physical Sciences (including engineering and technology)

79. Bhaskaran, C. (2012) Research Productivity of Graph Theory During 2004-2011: A Bibliometric Study. SRELS Journal of Information Management. 49(6): 683-691.
80. Mamdapur, Ghouse Modin N.; Govanakoppa, Rajalaxmi, A. and Rajgoli, Iqbalahmad, U. (2011) Baltic Astronomy (2000-2008) - A Bibliometric Study. Annals of Library and Information Studies, 58(1): 34-40.
81. Narang, Asha and Kumar, Anil. (2010) A Bibliometric Study of Indian Journal of Pure and Applied Mathematics. SRELS Journal of Information Management. 47(1): 31-39.
82. Gupta, B.M. and Dhawan, S.M. (2007) Role and Contribution of Various Performing Sectors in Indian Physics Output during 1993-01. COLLNET Journal of Information Management, 1(1): 33-51.
83. Nattar, S. (2009) Indian journal of physics: A scientometric analysis. International Journal of Library and Information Science, 1(4): 055-061.
84. Garg, K.C.; Sharma, P. and Kumar, S. (2008) Scientometric profile of the journal mausam. Annals of Library and Information Studies, 55(1): 76-80.
85. Kademani, B.S.; Surwase, Ganesh; Mohan, Lalit and Kumar, Vijai. (2009) Bhabha Scattering: A Scientometric View. DESIDOC Journal of Library & Information Technology, 29(4): 3-11.
86. Kademani, B.S.; Kumar, V.; Sagar, A. and Kumar, A. (2006) World literature on thorium research: A scientometric study based on science citation index. Scientometrics, 69(2): 347-364.
87. Kademani, B.S.; Kumar, V.; Sagar, A.; Kumar, A.; Mohan, L. and Surwase, G. (2006) Scientometric dimensions of thorium research in India. DESIDOC Bulletin of Information Technology, 26(3): 9-25.
88. Kademani, B.S.; Kumar, V.; Sagar, A. and Kumar, A. (2006) Scientometric dimensions of nuclear science and technology research in India: A study based on INIS (1970-2002) database. Malaysian Journal of Library & Information Science, 11(1): 23-48.
89. Surwase, G.; Kademani, B.S. and Kumar, V. (2008) Scientometric dimensions of pulsed laser deposition research: Global perspective. Annals of Library and Information Studies, 55(2): 101-110.
90. Rajendran, P. and Parihar, Y.S. (2007) A bibliometric study of laser literature in India, 1995-2005. Annals of Library and Information Studies, 54(2): 112-118.
91. Girap, Priya; Kumar, Anil; Mohan, Lalit and Surwase, Ganesh. (2011) Scientometric Dimensions of Fuel Cell Research as Reflected in INIS Database. SRELS Journal of Information Management. 48(3): 329-348.
92. Rajendran, P.; Babu, B.R. and Gopalakrishnan, S. (2005) Bibliometric analysis of fiber optics literature. Annals of Library and Information Studies, 52(3): 82-85.
93. Guruprasad, R.; Nikham, Khaiser; Marimuthu, P. and Mudkavi, Vidhyadhar Y. (2011) Impact of Internet on Scholarly Communications: A Survey of Aerospace Scientists and Engineers in Bangalore. Information Studies. 17(2): 65-88.

94. Sahu, A.K.; Goswami, N.G. and Choudhary, B.K. (2011) Research publications of National Metallurgical Laboratory during the year 2001-2010 - study on citation patterns. Annals of Library and Information Studies, 58(2): 151-160.
95. Kademani, B.S.; Sagar, A. and Bhanumurthy, K. (2011) Research and impact of materials science publications in India: 1999-2008. Malaysian Journal of Library & Information Science, 16(2): 63-82.
96. Dhawan, S.M.; Gupta, B.M. and Mohan, S. (2003) Materials science research and development in India: A scientometric analysis of international collaborative output. DESIDOC Bulletin of Information Technology, 23(2): 11-23.
97. Walke, Rajpal; Dhawan, S.M. and Gupta, B.M. (2007) Materials Science Research in India (1993-2001): A Scientometric Study. COLLNET Journal of Scientoemtrics and Information management, 1(2): 33-40.
98. Bhattacharya, Sujit and Shilpa. (2012) China Moving Ahead in the Global Nanotechnology Race: Evidence from Scientometric Study. COLLNET Journal of Scientometrics and Information Management, 6(1): 97-117.
99. Thirumagal, A. (2012) Bibliometric Study of Nanotechnology in India: An Analysis. SRELS Journal of Information management, 49(5): 577-587.
100. Karpagan, R; Gopalakrishnan, S. and Ramesh Babu, B. (2011) Publication Trend on Nanotechnology among G15 Countries. COLLNET Journal of Scientometrics and Information Management, 5(1): 61-80.
101. Lalit Mohan; Prakasan, E.R.; Kademani, B.S.; Surwase, G.; Kumar, A. and Kumar, V. (2010) Research trends in nanoscience and nanotechnology in India. DESIDOC Journal of Library & Information Technology, 30(2): 40-58.
102. Sudhier, K.G. (2010) Application of Bradford's Law of Scattering to the Physics Literature: A Study of Doctoral Theses Citations at the Indian Institute of Science. DESIDOC Journal of Library & Information Technology, 30(2): 3-14.
103. Gupta, B.M.; Kshitij, A. and Verma, C. (2011) Mapping of Indian computer science research output, 1999-2008. Scientometrics, 86(2): 261-283.
104. Gupta, B.M.; Kshitij, A. and Singh, Y. (2010) Indian computer science research output during 1999-2008: Qualitative analysis. DESIDOC Journal of Library & Information Technology, 30(6): 39-54.
105. Suresh Kumar and Garg, K.C. (2005) Scientometrics of Computer Science Research in India and China. Scientometrics, 64(2): 121-132.
106. Das, A.K. and Karanjai, A. (2002) Institutional distribution in computer science research in India: A study. Annals of Library and Information Studies, 49(1): 23-27.

Group 3: Chemical Sciences

107. Thanuskodi, S. (2011) Bibliometric analysis of the Indian journal of chemistry. Library Philosophy and Practice (e-journal). http://digitalcommons.unl/libphilprac/630.

108. Nandi, A. and Bandyopadhyay, A.K. (2009) Research contributions in chemistry at the university of Burdwan: An analytical study. Annals of Library and Information Studies, 56(3): 141-149.
109. Kumari, G.L. (2009) Synthetic organic chemistry research: Analysis by scientometric indicators. Scientometrics, 80(3): 559-570
110. Kademani, B.S.; Kumar, V.; Surwase, G.; Sagar, A.; Mohan, L.; Kumar, A. and Gaderao, C.R. (2007) Research and citation impact of publications by the chemistry division at Bhabha Atomic Research Centre. Scientometrics, 71(1): 25-57. doi: http://dx.doi.org/10.1007/s11192-007-1651-.
111. Parvathamma, N. and Gobbur, Devendra S. (2011) Scientific Productivity and Impact of Indian Polymer Scientists. COLLNET Journal of Scientometrics and information Management, 5(2): 205-215.
112. Parvathamma, N and Gobbur, Devendra, S. (2007) Mapping of Plastics Literature (1998-2002): A Bibliometric Study. SRELS Journal of Information Management, 44(4): 415-420.
113. Kademani, B.S.; Kumar, V.; Mohan, L.; Sagar, A.; Kumar, A.; Gaderao, C.R. and Surwase, G. (2006) Scientometric dimensions and publication productivity of the analytical chemistry division at Bhabha Atomic Research Centre. SRELS Journal of Information Management, 43(1): 5-20.
114. Kumari, L. (2006) Trends in synthetic organic chemistry research. cross-country comparison of activity index. Scientometrics, 67(3): 467-476. doi: http://dx.doi.org/10.1556/Scient.67.2006.3.8
115. Gunasekaran, S.; Batcha, M.S. and Shivaraman, P. (2006) Mapping chemical science research in India: A bibliometric study. Annals of Library and Information Studies, 53(2): 83-95.
116. Kademani, B.S.; Kumar, V.; Kumar, A.; Sagar, A.; Mohan, L.; Surwase, G. and Gaderao, C.R. (2005) Publication productivity of the bio-organic division at Bhabha atomic Research Centre: A scientometric study. Annals of Library and Information Studies, 52(4): 135-146.
117. Kademani, B.S.; Kumar, V.; Surwase, G.; Sagar, A.; Mohan, L.; Gaderao, C.R. and Prakasan, E.R. (2005) Scientometric dimensions of innovation communication productivity of the chemistry division at Bhabha Atomic Research Centre. Malaysian Journal of Library & Information Science, 10(1): 65-89
118. Kannappanavar, B.U.; Kumar, V. and Swamy, C. (2004) Publishing trends of Indian chemical scientists: A bibliometric study. Annals of Library and Information Studies, 51(1): 39-41.

Group 4: Biological Sciences (including agricultural Science and crop studies)

119. Kannappanavar, B.U. and Roopashree, T.N (2011) Journal of Genetics: A Bibliometric Study. SRELS Journal of Information Management, 48(6): 673-694.
120. Kumbar, M. and Kumar, N.G. (2011) Authorship trend and collaborative research in genetics and plant breeding. SRELS Journal of Information Management, 48(2): 113-122.

121. Garg, K.C.; Kumar, S.; Bhatia, V.K.; Ramasubramanian, V.; Kumar, A. and Kumari, J. (2011) Plant genetics and breeding research: Scientometric profile of selected countries with special reference to India. Annals of Library and Information Studies, 58(2): 184-197.
122. Garg, K.C.; Kumar, S.; Dutt, B. and Chakraborty, O. (2010) Scientometric profile of "genetics and heredity" research in India. Annals of Library and Information Studies, 57(3): 196-206.
123. Ram, S. (2010) Research practices in herbal medicinal plant: A case study of Podophyllotoxin. Annals of Library and Information Studies, 57(1): 65-71.
124. Joshi, Kirti; Kshitij, Avinash; Garg, K.C. (2010) Scientometric Profile of Global Forest Fungal Research. Annals of Library and Information Studies, 57(2): 130-139.
125. Mumtaz A. (2005) Nigella sativa: a bibliometric study of the literature on Habbat al-barakah. Malaysian Journal of Library & Information Science, 10(1): 1-18.
126. Vijayakumar, M and Naqvi, S.H. (2002) Authorship trend in 'azadirachta indicia' literature: A bibliometric study. SRELS Journal of Information Management, 39(4): 445-455.
127. Sevukan, R. and Sharma, J. (2008) Bibliometric analysis of research output of biotechnology faculties in some Indian central universities. DESIDOC Journal of Library & Information Technology, 28(6): 11-20.
128. Patra, S.K. and Bhattacharya, P. (2005) Bibliometric study of cancer research in India. DESIDOC Bulletin of Information Technology, 25(2): 11-18.
129. Chand, P. and Patra, S.K. (2005) Biotechnology research profile of India. Scientometrics, 63(3): 583-597
130. Patra, S.K. and Mishra, S. (2006) Bibliometric study of bioinformatics literature. Scientometrics, 67(3): 477-489. doi: http://dx.doi.org/ 10.1556/Scient.67.2006.3.9
131. Mukherjee, Bhasker. (2011) Evaluation of Indian Performance in the Emerging Fields of Environmental Sciences. COLLNET Journal of Scientometrics and Information Management, 5(1): 81-98.
132. Biradar, B.S. (2006) Indian journal of environmental protection: A study of citation pattern. Annals of Library and Information Studies, 53(3): 109-113.
133. Shukla, M.C.; Saksena, S. and Riswadkar, M.R. (2001) Application of Bradford's and Lotka's distribution to bioenergy literature: A study based on ten abstracting services. Annals of Library and Information Studies, 48(1): 3- 30.
134. Choudhury, Nitai Ray and Sarkhel, Juran Krishna. (2011) Mapping Agricultural Research in West Bengal, 1993-2007: A Bibliometric Study. COLLNET Journal of Scientometrics and Information Management, 5(1): 99-113.
135. Kumar, S.; Garg, K.C. and Dutt, B. (2009) Indian scientific output as seen through Indian Science Abstracts. Annals of Library and Information Studies, 56(3): 163-168.
136. Garg, K.C.; Kumar, S. and Lal, K. (2006) Scientometric profile of Indian agricultural research as seen through science citation index expanded. Scientometrics, 68(1): 151-166
137. Krishna, M.K. and Kumar, S. (2004) Authorship Trends in Agriculture Research: A Bibliometric Analysis. SRELS Journal of Information Management, 41(2): 229-

138. Ramesh, L.S.R.C.V. and Nagaraju, A.V.S.S. (2002) Publication pattern in 'international journal of tropical agriculture', 1991-2000: A bibliometric study. SRELS Journal of Information Management, 39(4): 457-465.

139. Vijay, K.R. and Raghavan, I. (2007) Journal of food science and technology: A bibliometric study. Annals of Library and Information Studies, 54(4): 207-212.

140. Vijay, K.R. (2005) Bibliometric study of research publication trends among Indian food scientists and technologists. Annals of Library and Information Studies, 52(3): 77-81.

141. Sharma, R.M. (2009) Research publication trend among scientists of central potato research institute: A bibliometric study. Annals of Library and Information Studies, 56(1): 29-34.

142. Senthilkumaran, P. and Amudhavalli, A. (2005) Research on spices in Asia: A bibliometric study. Journal of Library and Information Science (India), 30(1): 21-28.

143. Senthilkumaran, P. and Amudhavalli, A. (2007) Cross-national analysis on spices research in the Asian countries. COLLNET Journal of Scientometrics and Information Science, 1(2): 27-32.

144. Dixit, S. and Katare, V.V. (2007) A bibliometric analysis of the 'journal of the Indian society for cotton improvement' (1995-2004). Annals of Library and Information Studies, 54(2): 119-123.

145. Jena, K.L. (2006) A bibliometric analysis of the journal "Indian journal of fiber and textile research", 1996 - 2004. Annals of Library and Information Studies, 53(1): 22-30. Retrieved from http://search. proquest.com/docview/57640202?accountid=27563

146. Surendra Kumar and Kumar, S. (2005) A Bibliometric Study of the Journal of Oilseeds Research, Since 1993-2001. SRELS Journal of Information Management, 42(3): 305-334.

147. Surendra Kumar and Kumar, S. (2004) Productometric study of scientists of ICARs National Research Centre for Soybean (NRCS). Annals of Library and Information Studies, 51(1): 11-21.

148. Ramesh,L S.R.C.V.; Ramana, P.V. and Hussain, M.V. (2000) Publication pattern in oryza (oryza sativa L) from 1986-1995: A bibliometric study. SRELS Journal of Information Management, 37(3): 215-227.

149. Senthilkumaran, P and Vadivel, V. (2004) Journal of Spices and Aromatic Crops: A Bibliometric Appraisal. SRELS Journal of Information Management. 41(1): 121-131.

150. Sivasubramanian, V. (2000) Journal of Indian Coffee: A bibliometric survey. Annals of Library Science and Documentation, 47(2): 75-79.

Group 5: Health Sciences

151. Kulkarni, A.P.; Poshett, B. and Narwade, G.R. (2009) Indian journal of pharmaceutical education and research (1996-2006) -- A bibliometric analysis. Annals of Library and Information Studies, 56(4): 242-248.

152. Karagappan, R; Gopalakrishnan, S; Ramesh Babu, B and Natarajan, M. (2012) Scientometric Anaklysis of Stem Cell Research: A comparative study of India and other countries. COLLNET Journal of Scientometrics and Information Management, 6(2): 229-252.

153. Jain, N.C. and Jacobs, D. (2012) Microbicide development -- trends in original research published globally in PubMed-indexed journals. DESIDOC Journal of Library & Information Technology, 32(3): 261-264.
154. Gupta, B.M; Adarsh Bala and Kaur, Har. (2011) Mapping of AIDS / HIV Research in India: A scientometrics analysis of publications output during 1999-2008. COLLNET Journal of Scientometrics and Information Management, 5(2): 185-203.
155. Gupta B.M. and Adarsh Bala (2011) Mapping of Tuberculosis in India: A scientometric analysis of publications output during 1998-2009. COLLNET Journal of Scientometrics and Information management, 5(1): 33-51.
156. Dutt, Bharavi and Suresh Kumar (2010) Scientometric Profile of Global Dengue Research. COLLNET Journal of Scientometrics Information Management. 4(1): 81-93.
157. Singh, G.; Ahmad, M. and Nazim, M. (2008) A bibliometric study of embelia ribes. Library Review, 57(4): 289- 297.
158. Kurnar Patra, S. and Chand, P. (2007) HIV/AIDS research in India: A bibliometric study. Library & Information Science Research, 29(1): 124-134. doi: http://dx.doi.org/10.1016/j.lisr.2006.08.010
159. Saraswathi, P and Raghavendra, S. (2005) Cloning: A Bibliometric Analysis. SRELS Journal of Information Management, 42(1): 91-95.
160. Mahapatra, R.K. and Panda, K.C. (2004) Health research literature on Orissa: A bibliometric analysis. SRELS Journal of Information Management, 41(4): 383-392.
161. Biradar, B.S. and Tippeswamy, K. (2004) Information Use Pattern by Pediatrician: A Bibliometric Study. SRELS Journal of Information Management. 41(1): 107-120.
162. Nalini, J.K. (2003) Occupational health related publications in India: A bibliometric analysis of journals. SRELS Journal of Information Management, 40(1): 41-50.
163. Kundra, R. and Tomov, D. (2001) Collaboration patterns in Indian and Bulgarian epidemiology of neoplasms in 'Medline' for 1966-1999. Scientometrics, 52(3): 519-523.
164. Neelameghan, A and Ravichandra Rao, I.K. (2005) Bibliometric support to Medical Historiography: A case study of the incidence of communicable diseases in 19th century, 11(2): 79-92.

Group 6: Humanities and Social Sciences (including management, economics, industrial research, Patenting, etc.)

165. Ray, Partha Pratim and Sen, B.K. (2012) Rabindra Sangit (Songs of Rabindranath Tagore): A Bibliometric Study. SRELS Journal of Information Management, 49(4): 343-358.
166. Ray, Partha Pratim and Sen, B.K. (2012) Gitanjali (Song Offerings): A Bibliometric Study. SRELS Journal of Information Management. 49(6): 601-613.
167. Sangam, S.L.; Gupta, B.M. and Kumar, S. (2007) Modeling the growth of Indian and Chinese social science. Literature. SRELS Journal of Information Management, 44(4): 395-398.
168. Koganuramah, M.M.; Angadi, M. and Kademani, B.S. (2002) Bibliometric dimension of innovation communication productivity of Tata institute of social sciences. Malaysian Journal of Library and Information Science, 7(1): 69-76.

169. Eqbal, Monawwer and Raza, Masoom M. (2005) Literature on Personnel Attitudes and Job Satisfaction: A Bibliometric Study. SRELS Journal of Information Management, 42(1): 81-90.
170. Mulla, K.R. and Chandrashekara, M. (2011) Bibliometric analysis of literature on industry and trade. Information Studies, 17(2): 99-114.
171. Sarala, K.R. (2011) Book reviews published in Journal of scientific and industrial research during 2002-2007: A quantitative study. SRELS Journal of Information Management, 48(1): 101-107.
172. Nandi, A. and Bandyopadhyay, A.K. (2008) Indian economic review (1998-2002): A bibliometric study. SRELS Journal of Information Management, 45(1): 95-100.
173. Debbarman, S. (2008) A bibliometric study of Indian patent applications from 1995 to 2005. Annals of Library and Information Studies, 55(2): 153-163
174. Gupta, V.K. (2005) How Indian scientists collaborate in patenting. Annals of Library and Information Studies, 52(2): 47-50.
175. Bhattacharya, Sujit; Meyer, Martin. (2004) Commonalities and differences between scholarly and technical collaboration: an exploration of co-invention and co-authorship analyses. Scientometrics, 61(3): 443-456.

APPENDIX

Abbreviations

AIDS: Acquired Immune Deficiency Syndrome

ASLIB: Association for Information management

COLLNET: Global Interdisciplinary Research network for the Study of all aspects of Collaboration in science and Technology

COMPENDEX: An International database of S & T Literature – in the field of Engineering.

CPRI: Central Power Research Institute

CSIR: Council of Scientific and Industrial Research

DESIDOC: Defence Scientific Information and documentation Centre

DRTC: Documentation Research and Training Centre

HORT-CD: A Database of Literature in Horticulture in CD

ICAR: Indian Council of Agricultural Research

IIM: Indian institute of management

IISc: Indian Institute of Science

IIT: Indian institute of Technology

INFLIBNET: Information and Library network centre – an autonomous Inter-University Centre of the University Grants commission

INSPEC: An International database of S & T literature – filed of physics, computer, control, mechanical engineering, etc.

INSDOC: Indian National Scientific Documentation Centre

JCR: Journal Citation Report

K-S Test: Kolmogorov-Smirnov Test

LIS: Library and Information Science

LISA: Library and Information Science Abstracts

NCB: National Centre for Bibliometrics

NCBI: National Centre for Biotechnology Information

NISSAT: National Information system for Science and Technology

NISTADS: National Institute of Science Communication and Information Resources

PubMed: A database of literature in Medical science

SCI: Science Citation Index

SCIE: Science Citation Index Extended

SCIRUS: Comprehensive Science –specific search Engine

SLD: Sub-level Domain

SRELS: Sarada Ranganathan Endowment for Library Science

SSCI: Social Science Citation index

TLD: Top-level Domain

UNESCO: United Nations Educational Scientific and Cultural Organization

WIF: Web Impact factor

WISER: Web Indicators for Science, Technology and Innovation Research

WoS: Web of Science

WWW: World Wide Web

3

A Binary Tree as a Basic Model for Studying Hierarchies Using Q-Measures

Yuxian Liu[1]***; Raf Gun*** and ***Ronald Rousseau***

A binary tree is used as a model for a hierarchical structure. All nodes situated at the same height are assumed to form a group. The global and local Q-value, being measures for the extent to which a node plays a bridging function between groups, are determined. For the global Q-value this is can be done in two ways: a direct one and one via a recursion relation.

KEYWORDS: Global Q-measures, Local Q-measures, Rooted trees

1 INTRODUCTION

Although Prof. S.R. Ranganathan is best known for his Five Laws of Library Science, and for the introduction of the colon classification, most colleagues, and especially Indian colleagues know very well that S.R. Ranganathan began his professional career as a mathematician. All his life he had a keen interest in mathematics and statistics. The fact that he, in close collaboration with Prof. P. C. Mahalanobis, established the Documentation Research and Training Centre (DRTC) as a division of the Indian Statistical Institute (ISI) in Bangalore bears testimony of this dual interest. Moreover, already in 1948 Ranganathan proposed the term *Librametry* (Ranganathan, 1995) as a science, similar to biometrics and econometrics, to deal with large numbers in a library context. Clearly his view on librametry is close to the idea of statistics as applied in the context of librarianship, but explicitly including operations research. His view differed somewhat from the notion of bibliometrics as proposed by Pritchard (1969), which included citation studies and applications outside a pure library context. It should be noted that Otlet's notion of 'bibliométrie' (Otlet, 1934) is broader: it includes basic book measurements and statistics, but also the construction of indices, sociometric aspects and even – be it in vague terms – a mathematical theory comparable with thermodynamics in physics. For a recent discussion of scientometrics and its relation with other metrics, we refer the reader to (Zhang et al., 2013).

For the reasons mentioned above we hope that this article, which combines information science and mathematics, is suited to commemorate the celebration of the Golden Jubilee year of the Sarada Ranganathan Endowment for library Science. In this context we like to mention that nowadays we experience a world-wide phenomenon combining information and mathematics, namely social networks such as Facebook, LinkedIn, Academia, Worldfloat and QZone through which millions of persons exchange private as well as academic information on the Internet. Its formal analysis is an interdisciplinary academic field combining sociology, graph theory, social psychology, statistics and even physics. It is part of the emergent science of complex network theory.

In this contribution we will establish a formula (actually two forms of the same formula) characterizing a special relation in hierarchies. Details are presented further on.

2 NETWORKS

A network (mathematicians would say: a graph) consists of nodes or vertices connected by links or edges. If an edge is determined by an unordered pair of edges the network is said to be undirected. In this article we only consider this type of network. Depending on the network, it may occur that each node belongs to a larger subgroup. For instance, authors belong to a department, a university or a country; articles belong to a journal; journals belong to a publisher or a scientific discipline. Typically, in applications, some nodes are only important within their own group, whereas others are 'brokers' or 'bridges' between several groups in the network. Flom et al. (2004) introduced a new indicator, called *Q-measure*, reflecting the brokerage role of nodes between two groups in a connected, undirected, unweighted network. Rousseau (2005) introduced Q-measures to the field of library and information science, while later Guns, Liu and Mahbuba (2011) showed its applicability in informetric studies. The original definition has been extended to networks with more than two groups, as well as weighted and directed networks. In particular two variants: local and global Q-measures were introduced (Guns & Rousseau, 2009). Q-measures are another variant of betweenness centrality in which only shortest paths between nodes from different groups are taken into account.

3 Q-MEASURES: DEFINITIONS

Assume that there are S groups ($2 \leq S < +\infty$) in a network. The global Q-measure of node a is then defined as:

$$Q_G(a) = \frac{1}{C} \sum_{k,n} \left(\frac{1}{TP_{k,n}} \sum_{\substack{g \in G_k \\ h \in G_n}} \frac{p_{g,h}(a)}{p_{g,h}} \right) \quad (1)$$

where $C = \binom{S}{2} = \frac{S(S-1)}{2}$ is the number of ways to choose two different groups. $TP_{k,n}$ denotes the number of possible node combinations from groups G_k and G_n. Finally $p_{g,h}$ is the number of geodesics between nodes $g \in G_k$, $h \in G_n$ and $p_{g,h}(a)$ is the number of geodesics between nodes g and h (both different from a) that pass through a.

The local Q-measure for actor a belonging to group G_d with m_d nodes is defined as:

$$Q_L(a) = \frac{1}{S-1} \sum_{n \neq d} \left(\frac{1}{TP_{d,n}} \sum_{\substack{g \in G_d \\ h \in G_n}} \frac{p_{g,h}(a)}{p_{g,h}} \right) \quad (2)$$

4 A PERFECT HIERARCHY

In network studies random networks are often used as a kind of null-model (Maslov et al., 2004). In this contribution we study Q-measures for another type of basic model, namely the perfect hierarchy as represented by an undirected, unweighted tree with branching factor 2 (a rooted perfect binary tree) and height H. Each group consists of all nodes situated on the same height, i.e. each level in the tree is a group. Hence we have H+1 groups on levels 0,1,..., H. The root of the tree has height zero. This model can be used when studying the brokerage role of nodes in layers in networks that are more or less hierarchically ordered. It is easy to see that for reasons of symmetry each node in the same group (i.e. at the same height) has the same global and the same local Q-value.

As a start we note that a tree with height 0 has only one node, the root, which has – by definition – a local and a global Q-value equal to zero. A binary tree with height 1 has three nodes: the root and two nodes at level 1. Also these nodes have a local and a global Q-value equal to zero. The first non-trivial case is the tree with height H = 2. It is easy to see that the four nodes at level 2 have Q-values equal to zero. The root has global Q-value equal to 1/6 and, being a singleton group, local Q-value equal to zero; the two nodes at level 1 have global Q-value equal to 1/3 and local Q-value equal to 1/4.

5 GLOBAL Q-MEASURES OF NODES IN A PERFECT HIERARCHY

As the number of geodesics between two nodes in a tree is always one, equation (1) becomes:

$$Q_G(a) = \frac{2}{(H+1).H} \Sigma_{k,n} \left(\frac{1}{TP_{k,n}} \Sigma_{\substack{g \in G_k, \\ h \in G_n}} \; p_{g,h}(a) \right) \tag{3}$$

where $p_{g,h}(a)$ is 1(one) if node *a* is situated on the geodesic connecting nodes *g* and *h* and zero otherwise. When a tree has height H then, clearly, each node in group, i.e. level H has global Q-measure equal to zero. We consider now a node situated on level m with 0 < m < H. Then we first observe that if nodes g and h are on levels k and n such that k ≤ m and n < m then no geodesic connecting g and h passes through a. Now we divide $Q_G(a)$ into three sums:

$$Q_G(a) = \frac{2}{(H+1).H} * T$$

$$\text{where } T = \sum_{k>m} \left(\frac{1}{2^k.(2^m-1)} \sum_{\substack{g \in G_m \\ h \in G_k}} p_{g,h}(a) \right) + \sum_{\substack{k,n \\ k>m>n}} \left(\frac{1}{2^k.2^n} \sum_{\substack{g \in G_k \\ h \in G_n}} p_{g,h}(a) \right) + \sum_{\substack{k,n \\ k>n>m}} \left(\frac{1}{2^k.2^n} \sum_{\substack{g \in G_k \\ h \in G_n}} p_{g,h}(a) \right)$$

We refer to all descendants of *a* as *a*'s cone. This cone has two sub cones with the two children of *a* as roots. There are 2 level (m+1) nodes in *a*'s cone (namely the two children of node a) and generally 2^{k-m} nodes in this cone on level k (m < k ≤ H).

1) Case I: geodesics connecting level m and level k, k > m

If a node on level k is not situated in *a*'s cone then it can be connected directly (i.e. not passing through a) to all other nodes on level m and vice versa. The other ones pass through node a. Hence there are $2^{k-m}.(2^m-1)$ geodesics connecting level k and level m and passing through a.

Hence $\sum_{k>m}\left(\frac{1}{2^k.(2^m-1)}\sum_{\substack{g\in G_m\\ h\in G_k}} p_{g,h}(a)\right) = \sum_{k=m+1}^{H}\left(\frac{2^{k-m}.(2^m-1)}{2^k.(2^m-1)}\right) = \sum_{k=m+1}^{H}\frac{1}{2^m}$

$$= \frac{H-m}{2^m}$$

2) Case II: geodesics connecting level n and level k, k > m > n

Again we see that nodes on level k, situated outside *a*'s cone can be connected to level n without passing through *a* and vice versa. Hence there are $2^{k-m}.(2^n)$ geodesics connecting level k and level n and passing through a. Hence:

$$\sum_{k>m>n}\left(\frac{1}{2^k.2^n}\sum_{\substack{g\in G_n\\ h\in G_k}} p_{g,h}(a)\right) = \sum_{n=0}^{m-1}\sum_{k=m+1}^{H}\left(\frac{2^{k-m}.2^n}{2^k.2^n}\right) = m\left(\sum_{k=m+1}^{H}\frac{1}{2^m}\right) = \frac{m.(H-m)}{2^m}$$

3) Case III: geodesics connecting level n and level k, k > n > m

Geodesics connecting nodes on level k and situated outside *a*'s cone with nodes on level n pass through *a* if the end node is situated in *a*'s cone. This yields $(2^k - 2^{k-m}).2^{n-m}$ cases. Similarly, geodesics connecting nodes on level k situated inside *a*'s cone with nodes on level n outside *a*'s cone pass through *a*; there are $2^{k-m}.(2^n-2^{n-m})$ of this type. Finally we observe that a geodesic starting on level k in *a*'s cone reaches level n without passing through *a* if its end node (on level n) lies in the same sub cone as the begin node. Hence, if this does not happen, this geodesic, staying inside *a*'s cone passes through a. There are two times $2^{k-m-1}.2^{n-m-1}$ such geodesics. Adding these three contributions related to geodesics between levels k and n gives: $(2^k - 2^{k-m}).2^{n-m} + 2^{k-m}.(2^n-2^{n-m}) + 2^{k-m}.2^{n-m-1} = 2^{k+n}.(2^{-m} - 2^{-2m} + 2^{-m} - 2^{-2m} + 2^{-2m-1})$. Hence:

$$\sum_{k>n>m}\left(\frac{1}{2^k.2^n}\sum_{\substack{g\in G_n\\ h\in G_k}} p_{g,h}(a)\right) = \sum_{k=m+2}^{H}\sum_{n=m+1}^{k-1}\left(\frac{2^{k+n}.2^{-m+1}.(1-2^{-m}+2^{-m-2})}{2^k.2^n}\right)$$

As 2^{k+n} cancels we have a factor $2^{-m+1}(1-2^{-m} + 2^{-m-2})$ which does not depend on k or n. Hence we just have to count how many times this factor occurs. This is the sum of the first H-m-1 natural numbers or (H-m).(H-m-1)/2.

Bringing together the three cases yields, for *a* on level m in a tree of height H, such that

0 < m < H:

$$Q_G(a) = \frac{2}{(H+1).H}\left(\frac{H-m}{2^m} + \frac{m.(H-m)}{2^m} + \frac{(H-m).(H-m-1)}{2}.\frac{2.(1-2^{-m}+2^{-m-2})}{2^m}\right)$$

or:

$$Q_G(a) = \frac{(H-m).(1+m+(H-m-1).(1-2^{-m}+2^{-m-2}))}{(H+1).H.2^{m-1}} \tag{4}$$

Finally, there is still one case we have to consider, namely when *a* is the root of the tree. In this case half of the geodesics connecting any two (different) levels pass through *a*. This yields H-1 times ½ for geodesics between level H and another level, H-2 times ½ for geodesics between level H-1 and another level, leading to the sum of the first H-1 natural numbers, which is (H-1).H/2, times ½ in total. Hence, if *a* is the root:

$$Q_G(a) = \frac{2}{H.(H+1)}.\frac{(H-1).H}{2}.\frac{1}{2} = \frac{H-1}{2.(H+1)} \tag{5}$$

Using formulae (4) and (5) the following table (Table 1) gives the global Q values for all nodes in trees of height H = 0, ...,5

Table 1: Global Q-values for nodes on all levels in a binary tree with height at most 5, calculated using formulae (4) and (5).

H Level (m)	0	1	2	3	4	5
0	0	0	1/6	1/4	3/10	1/3
1		0	1/3	7/16	39/80	31/60
2			0	1/8	61/320	111/480
3				0	1/20	157/1920
4					0	1/48
5						0

We obtained also a recursion formula for the global Q-measure in a tree. It is shown in the appendix.

6 LOCAL Q-MEASURES OF NODES IN A PERFECT HIERARCHY

Nodes on level H and the root have local Q-measure equal to zero. Consider now node *a* on level m (0 < m < H). This node is never on a geodesic connecting another node on level m with a node on level n, n < m (a level nearer to the root).

Among the $2^{m+n}.(2^m -1)$ geodesics connecting level m and level m+1 there are $2.(2^m -1)$ passing through node *a*. Generally, among the $2^k.(2^m -1)$ geodesics connecting level m and level k (m+1 ≤ k ≤ H) there are $2^{k-m}.(2^m -1)$ ones passing through node *a*. Hence:

$$Q_L(a) = \frac{1}{H}.\left(\frac{2.(2^m-1)}{2^{m+1}.(2^m-1)} + \frac{2^2.(2^m-1)}{2^{m+2}.(2^m-1)} + \cdots + \frac{2^{H-m}.(2^m-1)}{2^H.(2^m-1)}\right) = \frac{1}{H}.\frac{H-m}{2^m} \quad (6)$$

7 SOME RELATIONS BETWEEN GLOBAL Q-VALUES ON DIFFERENT LEVELS

1) The global Q-value of the root increases for increasing H and has limit 0.5 We compare the root's Q_G value for height H and height H+1. Using formula (5) we have:

$$\frac{H-1}{2(H+1)} < \frac{(H+1)-1}{2((H+1)+1)}$$

$$\Leftrightarrow$$

$$(H-1).(H+2) < H.(H+1)$$

which is clearly satisfied. Also $\lim_{H\to\infty} \frac{H-1}{2\,(H+1)} = \frac{1}{2}$

2) The Q_G-value at level 1 is, for fixed H > 2, larger than the Q_G-value of the root (level 0). Using formulae (4) and (5) we have to prove that:

$$\frac{(H-1).(2+(H-2).\left(1-\frac{1}{2}+\frac{1}{2^3}\right))}{(H+1).H} > \frac{H-1}{2.(H+1)}$$

The left-hand side is larger than:

$$\frac{(H-1).(2+(H-2).\frac{1}{2})}{(H+1).H} = \frac{(H-1).(H+2)}{2\,(H+1).H} \quad (7)$$

Hence, it suffices to show that:

$$\frac{H+2}{H} > 1.$$

This is obviously correct. We note that also for H =2 the Q_G-value at level 1 is larger than the Q_G-value at level zero.

3) The Q_G-value at level 1 is, for fixed H > 2, larger than the Q_G-value at level H-1.

Using formula (4) for H =1 and H = H-1, and the lower bound for level 1 given by formula (7) we have to show that:

$$\frac{(H-1).(H+2)}{2\,(H+1).H} > \frac{1}{(H+1).2^{H-2}}$$

which is obviously correct.

8 NOTE

Recently Rousseau, Liu and Guns obtained a de-composition of a global Q-measure into a convex de-composition of a local Q-measure and a so-called external Q-measure. For details we refer to (Rousseau, Liu & Guns, 2013).

9 ACKNOWLEDGEMENT

Work for this submission was supported by NFSC grant no. 71173154.

REFERENCES

1. Flom, P.L.; Friedman, S.R.; Strauss, S. and Neaigus, A. (2004) A new measure of linkage between two sub-networks. *Connections*, 26(1): 62–70.
2. Guns, R.; Liu, YX and Mahbuba, D. (2011) Q-measures and betweenness centrality in a collaboration network: a case study of the field of informetrics. *Scientometrics*, 87(1): 133-147.
3. Guns, R. and Rousseau, R. (2009) Gauging the bridging function of nodes in a network: Q-measures for networks with a finite number of subgroups. **In**: Larsen, B. & Leta, J. (eds.), *Proceedings of ISSI 2009 – the 12th International Conference on Scientometrics and Informetrics*, 131–142.
4. Maslov, S.; Sneppen, M. and Zaliznyak, A. (2004) Detection of topological patterns in complex networks: correlation profile of the internet. *Physica A – Statistical Mechanics and its Applications*, 333: 529-540.
5. Otlet, P. (1934) *Traité de Documentation, le Livre sur le Livre* [Treatise on documentation; the book on the book]. Brussels: D. Van Keerberghen & Sons.
6. Pritchard, A. (1969) Statistical bibliography or bibliometrics? *Journal of Documentation*, 25(4): 348-349.

7. Ranganathan, S.R. (1995) Librametry and its scope (reprint). *JISSI. The International Journal of Scientometrics and Informetrics,* 1(1): 15-21.
8. Rousseau, R. (2005) Q-measures for binary divided networks: an investigation within the field of informetrics. *Proceedings of the 68th ASIST Conference,* 42: 675–696.
9. Rousseau, R.; Liu, YX and Guns, R. (2013) Mathematical properties of Q-measures. *Journal of Informetrics* (to appear).
10. Zhang, L.; Thijs, B. and Glänzel, W. (2013) What does scientometrics share with other "metrics" sciences? *Journal of the American Society for Information Science and Technology,* 64(7): 1515-1518.

Appendix

A recursion formula for the global Q-measure of a node.

The global Q-measure of a node a_H situated on level H-j (0 < j < H) can be calculated by the following recursion formula:

$$Q_G(a_H) = \frac{H-1}{H}\, Q_G(a_{H-1}) + \frac{2}{H.(H+1)} \cdot \frac{2^j}{2^H} \cdot \left[H + j - 1 - (j-1).\frac{2^{j-2}+2^{j-1}}{2^{H-1}}\right]$$

In this formula $Q_G(a_{H-1})$ denotes the global Q-measure of node *a* in a tree with H -1 levels. Recall that the global Q-measure of a node in the lowest existing level is always zero.

Finally, when a_H is the root of the tree we have the recursion:

$$Q_G(a_H) = \frac{H-1}{H}\, Q_G(a_{H-1}) + \frac{2}{H.(H+1)} \cdot \frac{H-1}{2}$$

Using the starting values for trees of height 0 and 1 we use the recursion formulae to calculate the global Q-values for all levels of all trees of height at most 5. The values are, of course, the same as those shown in Table 2.

Table 2. Global Q-values for nodes on all levels in a binary tree with height at most 5, calculated using the recursion formula.

H Level	0	1	2	3	4	5
0	0	0	1/6	$\frac{2}{4}\cdot\frac{1}{6}+\frac{2}{12}=\frac{1}{4}$	$\frac{3}{5}\cdot\frac{1}{4}+\frac{3}{20}=\frac{3}{10}$	$\frac{4}{6}\cdot\frac{3}{10}+\frac{4}{30}=\frac{1}{3}$
1		0	1/3	$\frac{2}{4}\cdot\frac{1}{3}+\frac{13}{48}=\frac{7}{16}$	$\frac{3}{5}\cdot\frac{7}{16}+\frac{18}{80}=\frac{39}{80}$	$\frac{4}{6}\cdot\frac{39}{80}+\frac{23}{120}=\frac{31}{60}$
2			0	$\frac{1}{8}$	$\frac{3}{5}\cdot\frac{1}{8}+\frac{37}{320}=\frac{61}{320}$	$\frac{4}{6}\cdot\frac{61}{320}+\frac{5}{48}=\frac{111}{480}$
3				0	$\frac{1}{20}$	$\frac{4}{6}\cdot\frac{1}{20}+\frac{31}{640}=\frac{157}{1920}$
4					0	$\frac{1}{48}$
5						0

A proof of the recursion formula can be obtained from the authors.

4

Scientometric Profile of Indian Science as Seen Through *Science Citation Index – Expanded* 2010-2011

K.C. Garg[1] and *S. Kumar*[2]

An analysis of 90958 papers published by Indian scientists and indexed by *Science Citation Index-Expanded (SCI-E)* during 2010-2011 indicates that academic institutions produced the highest number of papers contributing about 43% of the output. The highest number of papers was published in the discipline of chemical sciences. Highest impact as judged by the values of CPP and RCI was also made by chemical sciences. About 83% papers were published in journals originating froum outse India. US journals were the most preferred choice for publishing papers. About half of the papers were published in medium impact factor journals and 66% papers were cited one or more times. Indian Institute of Science (Bangalore) published the highest number of papers; and the Jawaharlal Nehru Centre for Advanced Scientific Research (Bangalore) made the highest impact.

KEYWORDS: Scientometric profile, Citation per Paper (CPP), Relative Citation Impact (RCI)

1 INTRODUCTION

Since Independence India has developed a large infrastructure for science and technology with the setting up of several universities and academic institutions, national laboratories, and autonomous research institutions. Presently there are more than 400 universities, 400 national laboratories, more than 1300 in-house R&D institutions of the industry recognized by the Department of Scientific and Industrial Research (DSIR) and several foundations and associations with S&T involvement. To boost the basic research in India, the Government of India has taken several new initiatives by opening several new IITs, National Institute of Science Education and Research (NISERs) and Indian Institute of Science Education and Research (IISERs). Thus, India's map is dotted with institutions that have capability to carry out 'research and development' in almost every discipline. In the past India's scientific output has declined, but is constantly on the rise now. Gupta and Garg [1] have pointed out some of the reasons for this decline.

Numerous bibliometric studies examining India's contribution to the scientific literature based on the journals indexed by *Science Citation Index –Expanded (SCI-E)* and *Scopus* databases have been published in the literature [2-6]. The present study is also an attempt in that direction. The basic aim of the study is to identify the contributions of different performing sectors, disciplines of the published output, communication behavior of Indian scientists, and identification of the most prolific institutions and their impact using different bibliometric indicators. *Science Citation Index-Expanded* (SCI-E) has been used as the data source for the study.

2 DATA AND METHODOLOGY

SCI-E, a product of Thomson Reuters (formerly Institute of Scientific Information, USA) was used for the present assessment of Indian science. Data was downloaded for the years 2010-2011 using 'India' in the country field ('cu') and year = 2010-2011. Downloaded data consist the name(s) of the authors with their affiliation, name of the journal with the publisher's information (which includes name of the publisher, city and country of publication), discipline of the journal as provided in the classification used by Thomson Reuters and the citations received by each article. Data was later enriched with impact factor of the journals and the agency to which contributing institutions belonged. Data was converted into Fox-Pro database and was analyzed to identify the contributions of different performing sectors, disciplines of the published output, communication behavior of Indian scientists, and identification of the most prolific institutions and their impact.

3 RESULTS AND DISCUSSION

SCI-E indexed 97,404 items published from India in 2010-2011. Of these, 84,759 (87%) were journal articles, 3139 (3.2%) letters, 3060 (3.1%) review articles and the rest 6424 (6.7%) were other items such as meeting abstracts, editorial material, correction, news items, biographical items, book reviews, reprints, software reviews and book chapters etc. Only 90958 items that were published as journal articles, reviews and letters have been subjected to detailed analysis as these are the main channels for communication. These articles originated from 10601 institutions located in different parts of the country and were scattered in 5700 foreign journals and 107 Indian titles. Detailed results of the analysis are provided in the following paragraphs.

4 DISTRIBUTION OF OUTPUT ACCORDING TO PERFORMING SECTORS

Bulk of funding to R&D in India comes from central government. Academic institutions (universities and colleges) are the hub for scientific research in India. Besides the academic institutions, the other government funded laboratories under the aegis of Council of Scientific and Industrial Research (CSIR), Department of Atomic Energy (DAE), Indian Council of Medical Research (ICMR), Indian Council of Agriculture Research (ICAR), State Agriculture Universities (SAUs), Department of Space (DOS), Department of Science and Technology (DST), Department of Biotechnology (DBT) and Defence Research and Development Organization (DRDO) are also actively engaged in research. Ministries under the central/state governments and private institutions approved by the Department of Scientific and Industrial Research (DSIR) also conduct scientific research. Table 1 presents the data on the distribution of output according to different performing sectors for 2000-01 and 2010-11. It indicates that the output during 2010-11 increased almost two and half times as compared to 2000-01. It indicates that academic institutions (universities and colleges) published the highest number (43.3%) of papers. These were followed by the output of Indian Institutes of Technology (IITs) including engineering colleges (19.5%), and medical colleges and hospitals (14.7%). These three performing sectors together published more than three-fourth (77.5%) of the output. Remaining output (22.5%) was scattered among the remaining performing sectors. Among these latter sectors the highest number of papers was published by CSIR.

Further analysis of data presented in Table 1 indicates that in absolute terms the output of all performing sectors except institutions under state governments have increased in 2010-11 as compared to 2000-01. However, proportional output of different performing sectors analyzed using TAI indicates a decrease in the output of different performing sectors in 2010-11 as compared to 2000-01. Here TAI= $\{(C_i / C_o)/(W_i / W_o)\}\times100$ where

C_i= Number of publications of the specific performing sector in the ith block;

C_o= Total number of publications of the specific performing sector during the period of study;

W_i= Number of publications of all performing sectors in the ith block; and

W_o= Total number of publications of all performing sectors during the period of study.

Based on the values of TAI it is observed that it has gone down for SAUs, DAE, DOS, DST, CSIR, ICAR, and ICMR. This is also reflected by decrease in percentage output of these sectors in 2010-11 as compared to the output in 2000-01. The highest decrease is in case of institutions under the state governments. The decrease is also significant in case of SAUs, DST and DOS. Fig. 1 graphically presents the change in TAI for different performing sectors.

Table 1: Distribution of Indian scientific output during 2010-2011

Sl. No.	Agency	Number of Publications (%)			TAI		
		2000-01	2010-11	Total	2000-01	2010-11	Change in TAI
1.	Academic Institutions	13743 (38.20)	39368 (43.28)	53111	91	103	12
2.	Engineering Colleges including IITs	5051 (14.04)	17729 (19.49)	22780	78	109	31
3.	Medical Colleges & Hospitals	3737 (10.39)	13404 (14.74)	17141	77	109	32
4.	Council of Scientific & Industrial Research	3687 (10.25)	8735 (9.60)	12422	105	98	-7
5.	Department of Atomic Energy	3032 (8.43)	4852 (5.33)	7884	136	86	-50
6.	State Agricultural Universities & Colleges	2014 (5.60)	3000 (3.30)	5014	142	84	-58
7.	Department of Science & Tech-nology	1606 (4.46)	3182 (3.50)	4788	118	93	-25
8.	Indian Council of Agriculture Research	1377 (3.83)	2893 (3.18)	4270	114	95	-19
9.	Private R&D institutions	769 (2.14)	2051 (2.25)	2820	96	102	6
10.	Department of Space	555 (1.54)	827 (0.91)	1382	142	84	-58
11.	Institutions under Central Government	548 (1.52)	1217 (1.34)	1765	110	96	-14
12.	Indian Council of Medical Research	532 (1.48)	1151 (1.27)	1683	112	95	-17
13.	DRDO	429 (1.19)	1410 (1.55)	1839	82	107	25

Sl. No.	Agency	Number of Publications (%)			TAI		
		2000-01	2010-11	Total	2000-01	2010-11	Change in TAI
14.	Institutions under State Governments	367 (1.02)	199 (0.22)	566	229	49	-180
15.	Foundations/Associations	295 (0.82)	667 (0.73)	962	108	97	-11
16.	Department of Bio-technology	202 (0.56)	640 (0.70)	842	85	106	21
17.	Others	316 (0.88)	1147 (1.26)	1463	76	109	33
	Total	35980 (100)	90958 (100)	126938			

DRDO: Defence Research and Development Organization

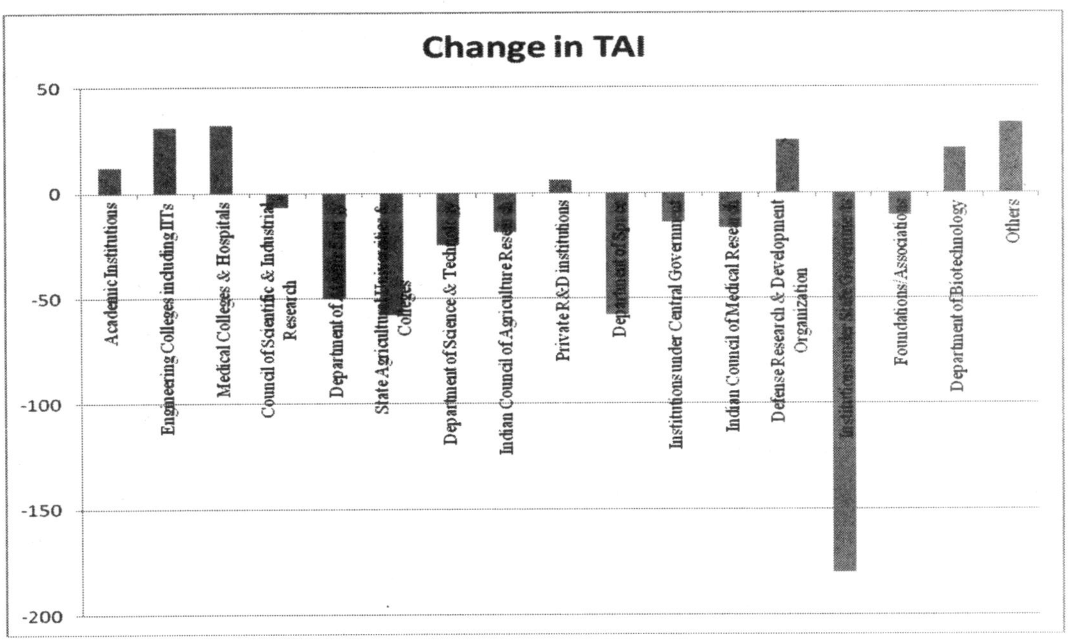

Fig. 1: Change in the values of TAI for 2001-01 and 2010-11

5 DISTRIBUTION OF OUTPUT ACCORDING TO DISCIPLINES

Table 2 presents the data on the distribution of output in different disciplines. More than one-fourth (26.7%) of the output was in the chemical sciences followed by physical and earth sciences. These two disciplines together constituted about half the Indian scientific output during 2010-2011. Mathe-matical sciences contributed only about 2% of the output. Using Citation per Paper (CPP) and Relative Citation Impact (RCI) authors examined the impact of the output in different disciplines and has been described below.

6 CITATION PER PAPER (CPP)

Citation per Paper (CPP) is a relative indicator computed as the average number of citations per paper. It has been widely used in bibliometric studies as it normalizes a large disparity in volumes of published output among disciplines, countries and institutions for a meaning full comparison of research performance. CPP = (Total number of citations for a discipline or country or an institution / total number of papers for India).

7 RELATIVE CITATION IMPACT (RCI)

Relative Citation Impact (RCI) was developed by Institute of Scientific Information (now Thomson Reuters, USA) and has been used by Joshi [7] *et al* to examine the impact of different countries and institutions in the field of forest fungal research. RCI measures both the influence and visibility of a nation's research in global context. Here RCI = (Disciplines or an institution's share of India's citations/Disciplines or institution's share of India's publications).

RCI = 1 indicates that the discipline's or institution's citation rate is equal to India's citation rate; RCI > 1 indicates that the discipline's or institution's citation rate is higher than India's citation rate and RCI < 1 indicates that discipline's or institution's citation rate is less than India's citation rate.

Data presented in Table 2 indicates that CPP for India was 3.13. It was highest (3.81) for the chemical sciences. The value of CPP for environmental sciences and physical & earth sciences was almost the same. CPP for life sciences and material sciences was also more than the Indian average. Surprisingly, the CPP for medical sciences was less than the Indian average. Similar trends were observed for the value of RCI for different disciplines.

Table 2: Distribution of output and impact according to different disciplines

Subject	Total papers*	Total citations*	CPP	RCI
Chemical sciences	24246(26.7)	92279(32.5)	3.81	1.22
Physical & Earth sciences	19975(22.0)	71999(25.3)	3.60	1.15
Medical sciences	18230(20.0)	51684(18.2)	2.84	0.91

Subject	Total papers*	Total citations*	CPP	RCI
Engineering sciences	15190(16.7)	45682(16.1)	3.01	0.96
Material sciences	12228(13.4)	39801(14.0)	3.25	1.04
Life sciences	12192(13.4)	42922(15.1)	3.52	1.13
Agricultural sciences	9809(10.8)	21226(7.5)	2.16	0.69
Environmental sciences	5707(6.3)	20625(7.3)	3.61	1.16
Mathematical sciences	3432(3.8)	6410(2.3)	1.87	0.60
Multi-disciplinary sciences	1856(2.0)	3826(1.4)	2.06	0.66
Total	**90958(100.0)**	**284403(100.0)**	**3.13**	**1.00**

* Sum of total papers and citations will be more than actual (90958) as several of the papers have been classified into more than one discipline.

8 COMMUNICATION BEHAVIOR OF INDIAN SCIENTISTS

This aspect was examined using two different characteristics of the journals used for communicating research results. These were publication in domestic journals vs. publications in international journals and the impact factor of the journals used for communicating research results.

9 DOMESTIC VS. INTERNATIONAL JOURNALS

Papers published by Indian scientists were scattered in 5700 titles published from abroad and 107 titles published from India. Analysis of data for the distribution of scientific output in domestic journals and in journals published from abroad is presented in Table 3. It indicates that 16.5% of the papers were published in domestic journals and the remaining 83.5% papers appeared in journals published from abroad which included both developed as well developing countries. The share of papers published in Indian journals has increased as compared to previous studies [8], because the number of journals indexed by SCI-E has increased considerably as compared to previous periods. Among the journals published abroad, about one-third of the papers appeared in journals originating from the US, followed by those that appeared from the UK, the Netherlands, Switzerland, Germany and France. This indicates that more than two-third (69%) of the papers published by Indian scientists appeared in journals published from these six countries. Remaining (24.7%) papers appeared in journals those originated from other developed and developing countries. From the pattern of publishing country of journals where Indian scientists published, it can be inferred that the Indian scientific output is well connected to the main stream science as more than two-third of the papers were published in journals originating from scientifically advanced countries of the West. Further analysis of data by publishing country of journals in different disciplines indicates that in all disciplines US journals were preferred for publishing papers except in environmental sciences, where the journals published from UK were preferred.

Table 3: Distribution of Indian S&T output according to Journal publishing countries

Sl. No.	Journal publishing countries	Number of Journals	Number of papers (%)
1	USA	2475	29988 (33.0)
2	UK	1208	18521 (20.4)
3	India	107	15025 (16.5)
4	Netherlands	541	11007 (12.1)
5	Switzerland	137	2990 (3.3)
6	Germany	219	2587 (2.9)
7	France	59	913 (1.0)
	Sub-total	**4746**	**81031 (89.2)**
	Other 67 countries	**1061**	**9927 (10.8)**
	Total	**5807**	**90958 (100)**

10 DISTRIBUTION OF PAPERS ACCORDING TO IMPACT FACTOR

Impact factor is an indicator of the prestige of the journal and depends upon the average rate of citations received by the articles published in it. Papers published in journals with higher IF by and large indicate more credit than papers published in journals with low IF. Papers published in high IF journals also indicate mainstream connectivity and readership. Based on the value of average impact factor (1.95), authors divided the impact factors into four categories. These are low 0-1 (low), >1≤ 3 (medium), > 3 ≤ 5 (high) and > 5 (very high). Distribution of output according to the range of impact factor is given in Table 4. It indicates that more than one-third (35.5%) papers were published in low impact factor journals. A significant number (46%) of papers were published in medium impact factor journals and the rest (18.5%) papers in high and very high impact factor journals. The share of papers in high and very high impact factor is very small as compared to other categories of impact factor. Based on this, one can infer that Indian scientific output is well connected to the mainstream science as about two-third of the published papers appeared in medium, high and very high impact factor journals.

Table 4: Distribution of output according to range of Impact factor of journals

Range of IF	# of Papers	% of Papers
0-1 (Low)	32338	35.5
>1 ≤ 3 (Medium)	41885	46.0
>3 ≤ 5 (High)	13031	14.4
>5 (Very high)	3704	4.1
Total	**90958**	**100.00**
Average 1.95		

11 CITATION ANALYSIS OF OUTPUT

Citation rates reflect the impact of published work on international community. Citation counts of authors or a group of authors is an indication of the influence of individuals or groups. The citation rate of a paper may be considered as a partial measure of its "impact" (rather than its quality or importance), where impact is defined as "its actual influence on surrounding research activity at a given time" [9].

The impact of research of any country or institution can be assessed by taking citation counts of the articles received over a period of time. In the present study citations were examined for the period of January 2010-May 2013. Table 5 presents the distribution of citations. It indicates that 90958 papers received 284403 citations in all. Thus the average rate of citation per paper for the Indian scientific output is 3.13. Of the total papers published by Indian scientists more than one-third (35.2%) of the papers did not get any citation and the rest were cited one or more times. Of the total cited papers about half (49%) were cited between 1-5 times and the remaining (16%) were cited more than five times. Of these 6% were cited more than 10 times. However, the proportion of papers that received more than 50 citations were very low. Based on the pattern of citations it can be concluded that the Indian scientific output is connected to the mainstream science as about two-third of the papers were cited one or more times. Appendix 1 lists the highly cited papers which received 200 or more citations. Data presented in Appendix 1 indicates that all the highly cited papers had international collaboration.

Table 5: Frequency of citations

Number of citations	# of Papers	% of Papers	Total citations
0	32016	35.2	0
1	16993	18.7	16993
2	10827	11.9	21654
3	7564	8.3	22692
4	5265	5.9	21060
5	3830	4.2	19150
6	2853	3.1	17118
7	2286	2.5	16002
8	1600	1.7	12800
9	1286	1.4	11574
10	1066	1.2	10660
11-20	3914	4.3	55096
21-50	1240	1.4	35576
> 50	218	0.2	24149
Total	**90958**	**100**	**2884403**
Citation per paper = 3.13			

12 PROLIFIC INSTITUTIONS AND THEIR IMPACT

Total output came from 10601 institutions located in different parts of the India. Of these 38 institutions contributed 0.5% or more of the output. These institutions produced about 40.5% of the total output and the remaining 59.5% output were produced by 10563 institutions. These prolific institutions belonged to different performing sectors. Highest number (18) of these institutions including Indian Institute of Science and Indian Statistical Institute belonged to academic sector, seven were the Indian Institutes of Technology (IITs), three were medical colleges and hospitals, four were CSIR institutes, three were DAE institutes, two were DST institutes and one was the ICAR institute. No institute could find place in the list of prolific institutions from ICMR and National Institutes of Technology. On comparing the rank of these institutions with earlier studies [10] it is observed that except Indian Institute of Science (Bangalore) and Bhabha Atomic Research Centre (Mumbai) there is a change in the ranking of all other institutions. One of the possible reasons for this may be inclusion of more Indian science journals in the list of journals indexed by SCI-E. During 2010-2011, SCI-E indexed 107 journals, while in 1997 it indexed a lesser number of journals.

Table 5 lists 38 prolific institutions along with their number of papers, the number of citations received by each institute and the values of CPP and RCI. Among all the institutes Jawaharlal Nehru Centre for Advanced scientific Research (JNCASR) had the highest value (6.87) of CPP followed by Indian Association for the Cultivation of Science (5.93) and Indian Institute of Chemical Technology (5.11). The value of CPP for JNCASR is more than twice the average value (3.13) for India. Other institutes for which the value of CPP is between 4 and 5 are University of Hyderabad, National Chemical Laboratory, Tata Institute of Fundamental Research and Punjab University. These institutes have higher values of CPP because they published more papers in the chemical science and physical sciences, which have higher values of CPP among all disciplines (Table 2). Among all the institutes 10 were having CPP less than the Indian average. These institutes also included All Indian Institute of Medical Sciences and Postgraduate Institute of Medical Education and Research. For Anna University and University of Allahabad the values of CPP were close to the Indian average. Among all the institutes Mangalore University and University of Mysore had the lowest values of CPP. RCI values also followed similar trends like the CPP. One of the possible reasons for low CPP and RCI for these institutes may be that they may be publishing in journals with low impact factor, which get fewer citations than those who have higher values of CPP and RCI.

Table 6: Impact of most prolific institutions*

#	Institution	Total papers	Papers (%)	Total citations	Citations (%)	CPP	RCI
1	IISC	2729	3.00	11702	4.11	4.29	1.37
2	BARC	2101	2.31	6749	2.37	3.21	1.03
3	IITKH	2030	2.23	7051	2.48	3.47	1.11
4	BHU	1907	2.10	7400	2.60	3.88	1.24
5	IITC	1681	1.85	5473	1.92	3.26	1.04
6	AIIMS	1663	1.83	4583	1.61	2.76	0.88
7	U DELHI	1574	1.73	5627	1.98	3.57	1.14
8	IITD	1479	1.63	4856	1.71	3.28	1.05
9	IITM	1414	1.55	4725	1.66	3.34	1.07
10	JAD U	1337	1.47	4755	1.67	3.56	1.14
11	IITK	1283	1.41	4427	1.56	3.45	1.11

#	Institution	Total papers	Papers (%)	Total citations	Citations (%)	CPP	RCI
12	IICT	1077	1.18	5499	1.93	5.11	1.64
13	PGIMER	1047	1.15	2324	0.82	2.22	0.71
14	IITR	1023	1.12	3730	1.31	3.65	1.17
15	ANNA U	973	1.07	2843	1.00	2.92	0.93
16	TIFR	950	1.04	4149	1.46	4.37	1.40
17	U CAL	950	1.04	3043	1.07	3.20	1.03
18	AMU	918	1.01	2919	1.03	3.18	1.02
19	PAN U	888	0.98	3841	1.35	4.33	1.38
20	ANNAM U	880	0.97	2718	0.96	3.09	0.99
21	IACS	863	0.95	5121	1.80	5.93	1.89
22	U HYD	772	0.85	3614	1.27	4.68	1.49
23	IITG	761	0.84	2727	0.96	3.58	1.14
24	NPL	683	0.75	2460	0.86	3.60	1.15
25	NCL	658	0.72	3055	1.07	4.64	1.49
26	U MAD	621	0.68	2161	0.76	3.48	1.12
27	IARI	612	0.67	1316	0.46	2.15	0.69
28	IGCAR	584	0.64	1230	0.43	2.11	0.67
29	MANG U	564	0.62	749	0.26	1.33	0.42
30	U PUNE	550	0.60	1925	0.68	3.50	1.13
31	U MYS	549	0.60	818	0.29	1.49	0.48
32	CDRI	532	0.58	2314	0.81	4.35	1.40
33	VIT U	531	0.58	1381	0.49	2.60	0.84
34	JNCASR	526	0.58	3613	1.27	6.87	2.19
35	U ALL	511	0.56	1549	0.54	3.03	0.96
36	U RAJ	464	0.51	1365	0.48	2.94	0.94
37	ISI	463	0.51	920	0.32	1.99	0.63
38	SGPGIMS	452	0.50	1578	0.55	3.49	1.10
Sub total		**35688**	**39.24**	**125348**	**44.07**	**3.51**	**1.12**
Other 10563 institutes		**55270**	**60.76**	**159055**	**55.93**	**2.88**	**0.92**
Total		**90958**	**100.00**	**284403**	**100.00**	**3.13**	**1.00**

*Appendix 2 lists full name and place of the institutes.

13 FINDINGS

- Scientific output during 2010-11 increased almost two and half times as compared to 2000-01. Academic institutions (universities and colleges) published the highest number (43.3%) of papers. Academic institutions, IITs and medical colleges/hospitals together published more than three-forth (77.5%) of the output. Proportional output of all performing sectors has decreased in 2010-11 as compared to 2000-01 except the academic institutions, IITs and medical colleges/hospitals;
- The highest output is in the discipline of chemical sciences followed by physical and earth sciences. The impact as seen by the values of CPP and RCI is also highest in these two disciplines;
- Indian scientists prefer to publish in journals published from abroad specially the US;
- Significant number of papers was published in medium impact factor journals and very few in high and very high impact factor journals;
- Two-third of the papers published by Indian scientists was cited one or more times in the literature; and
- Jawaharlal Nehru Centre for Advanced Scientific Research made the highest impact as seen by the values of CPP and RCI. However, Indian Institute of Science and Bhabha Atomic Research Centre published the highest number of papers.

REFERENCES

1. Gupta, B.M. and Garg, K.C. (2002) Is science in India on the decline? A rejoinder, *Current Science,* 83(12): 1431-32.
2. Arunachalam, S.; Srinivasan, R., and Raman, V. (1998) Science in India – A profile based on India's publications as covered by *Science Citation Index*-1989-1992, *Current Science*. 74: 433-441.
3. Garg, K.C. and Dutt, B. (1992) Bibliometrics of Indian science as reflected through Science Citation Index, *J. Sci. Indus. Res.* 51: 329-340.
4. Garg, K.C.; Dutt, B. and Kumar, S. (2006) Scientometric profile of Indian science as seen through Science Citation Index, *Annals of Library and Information Studies,* 53:114-125.

5. Gupta, B.M. and Dhawan, S.M. (2009) Status of India in science and technology as reflected in its publications output in the SCOPUS database – 1996-2006, *Scientometrics* 80: 473-490.

6. Kademani, B.S.; Sagar, A.; Kumar, V. and Gupta, B.M. (2007) Mapping of Indian publications in S&T: A scientometric analysis of publications in Science Citation Index. *DESIDOC Bulletin of Information Technology,* 27(1): 17-34.

7. Joshi, K.; Kshitij, A. and Garg, K.C. (2010) Scientometric profile of global forest fungal research. *Annals of Library and Information Science*, 57(1): 130-139.

8. Op cit 4.

9. King, J. (1987) A review of bibliometric and other science indicators and their role in research evaluation. *Journal of Information Science,* 13: 261-276.

10. Op cit 4.

Appendix 1: Highly cited Indian papers during 2010-11 (with 200 or more citations)

Sl. No.	Bibliographic Details	# of Citations
1.	Nakamura, K., Hagiwara, K., Hikasa, K. et al, Journal of Physics G-Nuclear and Particle Physics, 37 (7A) Jul 2010, 1 – 1422	3139
2.	Cohen, Myron S., Chen, Ying Q., McCauley, Marybeth et al , New England Journal of Medicine, 365 (6) Aug 11, 2011, 493 – 505	527
3.	Kumarasamy, Karthikeyan K, Toleman, Mark A., Walsh, Timothy R. et al, Lancet Infectious Diseases, 10 (9) Sep 2010, 597 – 602	485
4.	Granger, Christopher B., Alexander, John H., McMurray, John J. V. et al, New England Journal of Medicine, 365 (11) Sep 15, 2011, 981 - 992	391
5.	Boehme, Catharina C., Nabeta, Pamela, Hillemann, Doris et al, New England Journal of Medicine, 363 (11) Sep 9, 2010, 1005 - 1015	367
6.	Speliotes, Elizabeth K., Willer, Cristen J., Berndt, Sonja I. et al, Nature Genetics, 42 (11) Nov 2010, 937 - U53	365
7.	Kantarjian, Hagop, Shah, Neil P., Hochhaus, Andreas et al, New England Journal of Medicine, 362 (24) Jun 17, 2010, 2260 - 2270	317
8.	Connolly, Stuart J., Eikelboom, John, Joyner, Campbell et al, New England Journal of Medicine, 364 (9) Mar 3, 2011, 806 - 817	282
9.	Hudson, Thomas J., Anderson, Warwick, Aretz, Axel et al, Nature, 464 (7291) Apr 15, 2010, 993 – 998	249
10.	Butchart, Stuart H. M., Walpole, Matt, Collen, Ben et al, Science, 328 (5982) May28, 2010, 1164 – 1168	213

Appendix 2: Full names of prolific institutes

IISC	Indian Institute of Science, Bangalore
BARC	Bhabha Atomic Research Centre, Mumbai
IITKH	Indian Institute of Technology, Kharagpur
BHU	Banaras Hindu University, Varanasi
IITC	Indian Institute of Technology, Chennai
AIIMS	All India Institute of Medical Sciences, New Delhi
U DELHI	University of Delhi, Delhi
IITD	Indian Institute of Technology, Delhi
IITM	Indian Institute of Technology, Mumbai
JAD U	Jadavpur University, Jadavpur
IITKH	Indian Institute of Technology, Kanpur
IICT	Indian Institute of Chemical Technology, Hyderabad
PGIMER	Postgraduate Institute of Medical Education & Research, Chandigarh
IITR	Indian Institute of Technology, Roorkee
ANNA U	Anna University, Chennai
TIFR	Tata Institute of Fundamental Research, Mumbai
U CAL	University of Calcutta, Kolkata
AMU	Aligarh Muslim University, Aligarh
PAN U	Panjab University, Chandigarh
ANNAM U	Annamalai University, Annamalai
IACS	Indian Association for the Cultivation of Science, Kolkata
U HYD	University of Hyderabad, Hyderabad
IITG	Indian Institute of Technology, Guwahati
NPL	National Physical Laboratory, New Delhi
NCL	National Chemical Laboratory, Pune
U MAD	University of Madras, Chennai
IARI	Indian Agriculture Research Institute, New Delhi
IGCAR	Indira Gandhi Center for Atomic Research, Kalpakkam
MANG U	Mangalore University, Mangalore
U PUNE	University of Pune, Pune
U MYS	University of Mysore, Mysore
CDRI	Central Drug Research Institute, Lucknow
VIT U	Vellore Institute of technology University, Vellore
JNCASR	Jawaharlal Nehru Center for Advanced Scientific Research, Bangalore
U ALL	University of Allahabad, Allahabad
U RAJ	University of Rajasthan, Jaipur
ISI	Indian Statistical Institute
SGPGIMS	Sanjay Gandhi Postgraduate Institute of Medical Sciences, Lucknow

5

Scientometric Profile of Vector Borne Diseases: A Case Study of Global Japanese Encephalitis Research

K.C. Garg; Sandhya Dwivedi and ***S. Kumar***

An analysis of 2074 papers published on different aspects of Japanese Encephalitis (JE) during 1991 to 2010 and indexed by *Science Citation Index-Expanded* indicates that the output increased many folds since 1991 except for a significant dip in 2005. These papers were scattered in 501 journal titles, which originated from 29 different countries. Total output came from 62 countries of which 14 countries contributed 90% of the total output. The highest number of publications came from USA, followed by India. The publication activity increased significantly in China, South Korea, France, Austria, Singapore, Germany and decreased for Japan in the second block. Data indicates that about 87% of the total output is concentrated among 15 sub-disciplines and the remaining in other 53 sub-disciplines. Highest output (18%) is in the sub-discipline of virology. Among the prolific institutions, the publication output of institutions from the USA and Taiwan had higher impact. Citation per Paper (CPP) and Relative Citation Impact (RCI) were more than average for USA. All the Indian institutes listed under prolific institutions had made only a low impact.

KEYWORDS: Scientometric profile, Vector Borne disease, Citation Per Paper (CPP), Relative citation impact, Japanese Encephalitis Research

1 INTRODUCTION

Vector borne diseases are infections transmitted by the bite of infected arthropod species such as mosquitoes, ticks, triatomine bugs, sand flies, and black flies. Among these, different species of mosquitoes are responsible for the spread of malaria, dengue, chikungunya and Japanese encephalitis (JE). In the past, studies dealing with bibliometric assessment of different diseases like dementia [1], tuberculosis [2], diabetes [3], diarrhea [4], malaria [5], malaria vaccine [6], and dengue [7] have been published in the literature. However, there is no study that deals with the bibliometric assessment of the global output in JE. The present study is an attempt to fill that gap.

JE [8] is a zoonotic disease caused by an arbovirus, transmitted by Culex mosquitoes, which particularly breed in flooded rice fields. The disease is transmitted to man by the bite of infected mosquitoes. The clinical manifestations of the disease are rapid onset of high-grade fever, headache, neck stiffness, disorientation, coma, seizures, spastic paralysis and death. The fatality rate varies between 10% - 40% and those who survive do so with several neurological complications. In areas where the JE virus is common, encephalitis occurs mainly in young children, but can also affect adults.

JE is a leading cause of viral encephalitis and a significant cause of disability in Asia with 30,000 to 50,000 clinical cases reported annually. It occurs from the islands of the Western Pacific in the East to the Pakistan border in the West, and from Korea in the North to Papua New Guinea in the South. JE distribution is very significantly linked to irrigated rice production combined with pig rearing. Vaccine for JE is available since 1940 but, has not reached in many poor countries of Asia, because of the lack of awareness of the disease and its cost. This is an adequate intervention for travelers, but has limited public health value in areas where health services have limited resources. An inexpensive live-attenuated vaccine is used in China, but is not available elsewhere. Chemical vector control is not a solution, as the breeding sites (irrigated rice fields) are extensive. In some rice production systems faced with water shortages, however, certain water management measures (alternate wetting and drying) may be applied that reduce vector populations. Personal protection (using repellents and/or mosquito nets) will be effective under certain conditions. Eliminating the pig population is often a measure taken in the wake of outbreaks. Certainly, the introduction of pig rearing as a secondary source of income for rice-growing farmers in receptive areas must never be encouraged.

2 OBJECTIVES OF THE STUDY

The specific objectives of the study are as follows:

- To estimate the global output in JE and to examine the pattern of growth of publication output during 1990-2010;
- To study the geographical distribution of the research output and the change in their outputs during 1991-2000 and 2001-2010 using transformative activity index;

- To study the focus of research and activity profile of different countries in different sub-disciplines;
- To examine the pattern of citations of the research output and to identify highly cited papers; and
- To examine citation impact of different countries using different bibliometric indicators; and to identify the most prolific institutions and to compare their citation impact.

3 METHODOLOGY

Science Citation Index Expanded (SCI-E) was used as the source of data for the present study. The key word used for downloading the data was 'Japanese Encephalitis' in the topic field for the period 1990-2010. The search strategy yielded 2402 records that dealt with different aspects of JE research. Bibliographic details for each record included document type, title of the paper, author(s) and their affiliation, name of the journal with its place of publication and the number of citations received by each paper. From these downloaded records, 162 records were removed that were published as biography, meeting abstracts, corrections, editorial, news items, proceedings, reprints and book reviews. Of the remaining 2240 records, 166 records did not contain sufficient information like name of the institution and country and hence were not included in the analysis. Thus, the total number of papers included in the analysis was 2074.

Different approaches are available in scientometrics for count of authors and the most widely used is the first author approach (straight count), though it sometimes leads to bias as it under represents co-authors. However, authors of the present paper have used the same.

4 RESULTS AND ANALYSIS

4.1 4.1 Pattern of Research Output

During a period of 20 years (1991-2010), a total of 2074 papers were published on different aspects of JE. These papers were scattered in 501 journal titles, which originated from 29 different countries. Majority of these journals were published from USA (217), England (120), and The Netherlands (39). English was the most preferred language of communication as the number of articles published in English was 2046 (98.6%). Remaining 28 papers were published in French (16), German (4), Russian and Spanish (3 each), and Chinese and Korean one each. Table

1 lists top 18 journals with their country of publication and impact factor for 2010 where research results on JE were published. These 20 journals published 906 (43.7%) papers and the rest 1168 (56.3%) papers were scattered in 483 titles. *Lancet* had the highest impact factor among all the journals listed in Table 1.

Table 1: Most common journals used for publishing research results

#	Title of the Journal and country of publication	Number of Paper	JIF2010
1	Vaccine (England)	133	3.57
2	Journal of Virology (USA)	128	5.20
3	American Journal of Tropical Medicine and Hygiene (USA)	102	2.45
4	Virology (USA)	87	3.31
5	Journal of General Virology (England)	75	3.57
6	Journal of Medical Entomology (USA)	57	1.93
7	Journal of Virological Methods (Netherland)	38	2.14
8	Virus Research (Netherland)	38	2.91
9	Archives of Virology (Austria)	31	2.21
10	Emerging Infectious Disease (USA)	30	6.86
11	Japanese Journal of Infectious Disease (Japan)	30	1.37
12	Journal of Clinical Microbiology (USA)	26	4.22
13	Lancet (England)	23	33.63
14	Indian Journal of Medical Research (India)	23	1.83
15	Microbiology and Immunology (Japan)	22	1.23
16	Acta Virologica (Slovakia)	22	0.55
17	Antiviral Research (Netherland)	21	4.44
18	Trans. Royal Society of Tropical Medicine and Hygiene (England)	20	2.83
	Total	**906**	
	Other remaining journals	1168	
	Grand total	**2074**	

Fig. 1 shows the pattern of output during 1991-2010. The graph indicates that the output is increasing continuously with slight dips in the years 1992, 1996, 1999, 2009 and a significant dip in 2005. With an output of less than 50 in 1991, it increased manifold in later years and peaked in 2008 with 227 papers.

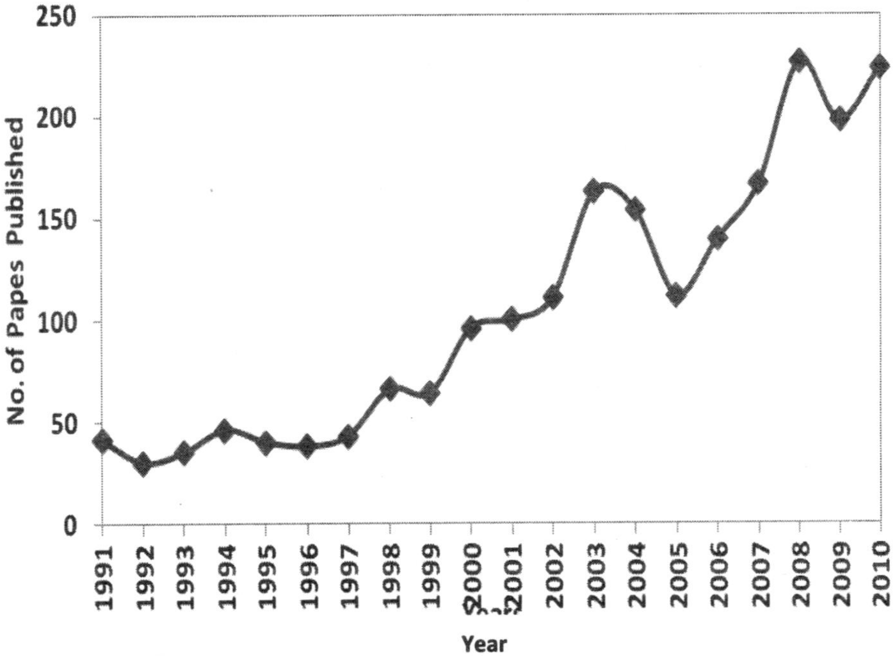

Fig.1: Growth pattern of world publication output

4.2 Geographical Distribution of Research Output

The total research output originated from 62 countries. Table 2 lists 14 prolific countries that produced 1% or more of the output. The share of these countries was about 90% of the total output. The geographical distribution of output for JE is similar to the output in the field of dengue [9] where the prolific countries contributed 87% of the total output. However, the ranking of prolific countries is different in JE as compared with that for dengue, but the top two producing countries are the same. Remaining 10% output was scattered among 48 countries. Among the most prolific countries US produced about one-fourth of publications, followed by India and Japan. These three countries together accounted for more than half (54%) of the total output. One of the probable reason for the US concentrating on JE research despite not being affected by the disease may be that many US soldiers stay in areas endemic to JE.

An examination of output for different countries in two blocks of 1991-2000 and 2001-2010 indicates that South Korea, France, Austria, Singapore, Brazil and Germany had very low output in the first block, but their output increased about eight times in the second block.

Table 2: Output in Japanese Encephalitis research in two different blocks

Country	1991-2000 No. of Papers (TAI)	2001-2010 No. of Papers (TAI)	Change in TAI	1991-2010 No. of Papers
USA	114 (95)	370 (102)	(+) 7	484
India	103 (114)	262 (95)	(-) 19	365
Japan	90 (134)	182 (89)	(-) 45	272
Taiwan	34 (85)	128 (105)	(+) 20	162
Australia	38 (104)	110 (100)	(-) 4	148
China	06 (31)	70 (122)	(+) 91	76
England	29 (155)	47 (83)	(-) 72	76
Thailand	21 (129)	45 (91)	(-) 38	66
South Korea	07 (50)	51 (116)	(+) 66	58
France	04 (29)	52 (122)	(+) 93	56
Austria	01 (12)	34 (129)	(+) 117	35
Singapore	05 (64)	27 (112)	(+) 48	32
Brazil	06 (102)	18 (100)	(-) 2	24
Germany	03 (58)	18 (114)	(+) 56	21
Other	51	148	--	199
Total	**512**	**1562**		**2074**

In order to study the change in the output in two blocks among prolific countries, we used Transformative Activity Index (TAI) suggested by Guan and Ma [10]. The methodology to calculate TAI is similar to what has been used by Garg and Kumar [11] and Garg *et al* [12] in their studies on computer science in India and China and global malaria vaccine research. The formula used for calculating TAI is as follows:

$$TAI=\{(C_i / C_o)/(W_i / W_o)\}\times 100 \text{ where}$$

C_i= Number of publications of the specific country in the ith block;

C_o= Total number of publications of the specific country during the period of study;

W_i= Number of publications of all countries in the ith block;

W_o= Total number of publication of all countries during the period of study.

Fig. 2 shows the change in the values of TAI for the prolific countries. From the figure, it is clear that the activity has increased significantly for China, South Korea, France, Austria, Singapore and Germany in the second block and it went down for Japan. The rise is substantial in case of Austria and France.

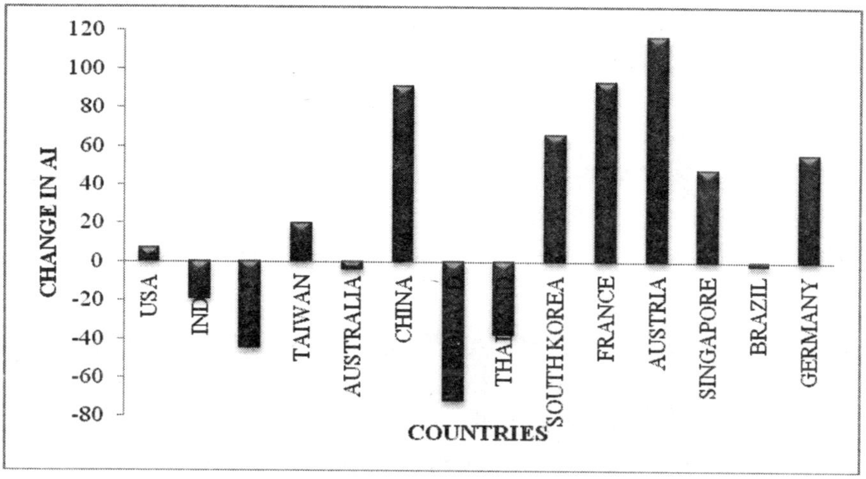

Fig. 2: Change in transformative activity Index

4.3 Focus of Research and Activity Profile of Prolific Countries

Based on the journal classification used by SCI-E, it is observed that global research efforts on JE are scattered in 68 sub-disciplines. Table 3 presents the distribution of output in different sub-disciplines. Analysis of data indicates that the main efforts are concentrated among 15 sub-disciplines, which accounted for about 87% of the total output and the remaining 13% output is scattered in other 53 sub-disciplines. Among these 15 sub-disciplines, about 18% of the output is concentrated in the sub-discipline of virology. The other sub-disciplines where the output is concentrated deals with different aspects of biochemistry, biotechnology, microbiology (S2 –S6) and medicine (S7 –S9).

Table 3: Scatter of publication output in major sub-disciplines

Subject Code	Subject	Papers (%)
S1	Virology	593(17.9)
S2–S6	Microbiology; biotechnology and applied microbiology; biochemistry and molecular biology; cell biology; genetics and hereditary	560(16.6)

Subject Code	Subject	Papers (%)
S7–S9	Tropical medicine; research & experimental medicine; general & internal medicine	477(14.2)
S10	Immunology	398(11.8)
S11	Infectious diseases	244(7.2)
S12	Public, environmental & occupational health	204(6.1)
S13	Neurosciences and neurology	175(5.2)
S14	Veterinary sciences	142(4.2)
S15	Entomology	141(4.2)
	Other 53 Subjects	436(12.9)
	***Total**	**3370**

* The total output is more than the actual output as several journals are classified in more than one sub-discipline.

Data was also analyzed to identify the focus of research for each prolific country using the activity index [13]. Reflecteing the values of activity index, Table 4 presents the data on the various sub-disciplines where different countries focused. It was found that different countries emphasized on different aspects of JE. The values of activity index presented in Table 3 indicate that except USA all countries emphasized on more than one sub-discipline.

Table 4: Sub-disciplines of focus by different countries

Country	Sub-disciplines of research activity
USA	S1(121)
India	S13(236), S7-S9(121)
Japan	S10(131), S15(128), S11(125)
Taiwan	S1(172), S2-S6(125)
Australia	S15(273), S14(212), S12(148)
China	S14(172), S13(162), S2-S6(135)
England	S13(125), S7-S9(121)
Thailand	S12(313), S11(148), S7-S9(152)
South Korea	S2-S6(138), S10(121)
France	S14(182), S11(169)
Austria	S10(222), S14(195), S7-S9(152)
Singapore	S13(202), S1(179), S10(125)
Brazil	S13(219), S2-S6(195), S7-S9(125)
Germany	S11(216), S13(182)

( ) Indicates activity index

4.4 Citation Pattern of the Research Output

Citation analysis measures the impact of each article by counting the number of times they were cited by other articles. High levels of citations to a scientific publication is interpreted as signs of scientific influence, impact, and visibility. An author's visibility can be measured through a determination of how often their publications have been cited in other authors' publications. Citation pattern of papers published is given in Table 5. Citations were examined from 1991-May 31, 2013 on which the data was downloaded. During this period 47004 citations were received by 2074 papers and the average rate of citation per paper is 22.7. Only a miniscule portion (4.4%) of papers did not get any citation and the rest 95.6 papers were cited one or more times. Of the total published papers 11% papers received 50 or more citations. Appendix 1 lists papers which received 150 or more citations. Most of the highly cited papers are from the USA.

Table 5: Distribution of Citation

No. of Citations	No. of Papers	Total Citations	No. of Citations	No. of Papers	Total Citations
0	92	0	11-20	407	6095
1	123	123	21-30	249	6281
2	92	184	31-40	134	4653
3	96	288	41-50	87	3931
4	76	304	51-75	116	7111
5	108	540	76-100	56	4877
6-10	380	2972	>100	58	9645
Total papers			**2074**		
Total citations			**47004**		
Citation/paper 4.5 4.7 ~ 23.00					

4.6 Prolific Countries and their Citation Impact

The scientific impact of prolific countries and prolific institutions was examined by using two relative indicators, namely Citation per Paper (CPP) and Relative Citation Impact (RCI).

Citation per Paper (CPP) is a relative indicator computed as the average number of citation per paper. It has been widely used in bibliometric studies as it normalizes a large disparity in volumes of published output among prolific countries and small nations for a meaningful comparison of research performance.

Citation per paper = (Total number of citations for a country or an institution / total number of papers for that country or institution)

Relative Citation Impact (RCI) was developed by the Institute of Scientific Information (now Thomson Reuters, USA) and has been used by Joshi [14] *et al* to examine the impact of different countries and institutions in the field of forest fungal research. RCI measures both the influence and visibility of nation's research in global context.

Relative Citation Impact (RCI) = (A Country's share of world citations /country's share of world publications).

RCI = 1 indicates that country's citation rate is equal to world's citation rate; RCI > 1 indicates that country's citation rate is higher than world's citation rate and RCI < 1 indicates that country's citation rate is less than world's citation rate.

Table 6 list 14 prolific countries with their total number of publications (TNP), total number of citations (TNC), share of world publications and citations as well as the values of CPP and RCI. The average value of CPP is 23 and is highest for England closely followed by USA. The value of CPP is significantly higher than average for Australia and Austria. CPP is considerably less than average for India, China, South Korea, Brazil, and Germany. It is lowest for China (8) and Brazil (10). The standing of different countries as judged by the values of RCI indicates that it is more than world average for England, USA, Australia, Austria, and Singapore. It is highest for England closely followed by USA. The value of RCI is less than world average for remaining countries listed in Table 5. The ranking of countries on these two parameters follow almost the similar trend.

Table 6: Prolific countries and their citation impact

Country	TNP	World's share (%)	TNC	World's share (%)	CPP*	RCI
USA	484	23.3	16705	35.6	35	1.5
India	365	17.6	4347	9.3	12	0.5
Japan	272	13.1	5420	11.5	20	0.9
Taiwan	162	7.8	3647	7.8	23	1.0
Australia	148	7.1	4385	9.3	30	1.3
China	76	3.7	606	1.3	8	0.4
England	76	3.7	2746	5.9	36	1.6
Thailand	66	3.2	1202	2.6	18	0.8

Country	TNP	World's share (%)	TNC	World's share (%)	CPP*	RCI
South Korea	58	2.8	760	1.6	13	0.6
France	56	2.7	1059	2.3	19	0.9
Austria	35	1.7	997	2.1	28	1.2
Singapore	32	1.5	773	1.7	24	1.1
Brazil	24	1.2	238	0.5	10	0.4
Germany	21	1.0	300	0.6	14	0.6
Others	199	9.6	3819	8.1	19	0.8
Total	**2074**		**47004**		**23**	

*CPP rounded off to the nearest whole number

4.7 Prolific Institutions and their Ranking

The total output came from 715 institutions located in different countries of the world. Table 7 lists 19 most prolific institutions that produced 20 or more papers on different aspects of JE. These institutions produced about 27% of the total output. Of these, highest number (7) institutions are in India, three each were from USA, Japan, and Taiwan, and one each from England, Australia and Thailand.

Table 7: Most prolific institutions and the impact of their output

Institute	TNP	World's share (%)	TNC	World's share (%)	CPP	RCI
University of Texas (USA)	52	2.51	1598	3.40	31	1.4
SGPIMS (India)	49	2.36	659	1.40	15	0.6
Centre of Disease Control and Prevention (USA)	40	1.94	1033	2.20	26	1.1
Kobe University (Japan)	37	1.78	775	1.65	21	0.9
National Institute of Virology (India)	37	1.78	335	0.71	9	0.4
Nagasaki University (Japan)	34	1.64	548	1.16	16	0.7
National Institute of Infectious Disease (Japan)	30	1.45	496	1.05	17	0.7
Indian Institute of Science (India)	30	1.45	488	1.04	16	0.7
National Brain Research Centre (India)	28	1.35	537	1.14	19	0.8
Academia Sinica (Taiwan)	25	1.21	1103	2.35	44	1.9
Washington University (USA)	23	1.11	1311	2.79	57	2.5
Liverpool University (England)	23	1.11	954	2.03	15	1.8

Institute	TNP	World's share (%)	TNC	World's share (%)	CPP	RCI
King George Medical College (India)	22	1.06	341	0.73	16	0.7
National Medical Defence Centre (Taiwan)	21	1.01	863	1.84	41	1.8
University Queensland (Australia)	21	1.01	712	1.51	34	1.5
China Medical University (Taiwan)	21	1.01	189	0.40	9	0.4
NIMHANS (India)	20	0.96	304	0.65	15	0.7
Mahidol University (Thailand)	20	0.96	159	0.34	8	0.4
Indian Council of Medical Research (India)	20	0.96	134	0.29	7	0.3
Others (696 institutes)	1521	73.34	34465	73.32	23	1.0
Total	2074	100	47004	100		

SGPIMS: Sanjay Gandhi Postgraduate Institute of Medical Sciences, Bangalore

NIMHANS: National Institute of Mental Health and Neuroscience, Bangalore

Among all the institutions listed in Table 7, University of Washington (USA) has the highest value of CPP as well as RCI. This is followed by Academia Sinica (Taiwan) and National Medical Defence Centre (Taiwan). Raw analysis of data indicates that these institutes publish in high impact factor journals, which in turn get more citations resulting in higher values of CPP and RCI. Other institutes that have higher values of CPP and RCI are also from the US, except University of Queensland (Australia). All other institutes listed in Table 6 have less than average values of CPP and RCI < 1. It indicates that these institutions might have published in low impact factor journals, which in turn get fewer citations.

5 CONCLUSIONS

- The output in JE has increased many folds since 1991 except a significant dip in 2005. Most of the papers have been published in journals originated from the advanced countries of the West.
- The total research output originated from 62 countries and 14 prolific countries that produced 1% or more of the output produced about 90% of the total output.
- The publication activity increased significantly for China, South Korea, France, Austria, Singapore and Germany and gone down for Japan in the second block.

- The main focus of research is spread among 15 sub-disciplines of which virology received the maximum attention. Different countries have focused on different sub-disciplines of research.
- As seen by the values of CPP and RCI, England followed by USA has made the highest impact and China and Brazil has the lowest impact. Among the prolific institutions University of Washington (USA) had the highest impact followed by Academia Sinica (Taiwan). All the Indian institutes listed under prolific institutions had made low impact.

REFERENCES

1. Gupta, B.M.; Kaur, H. and Kshitig, A. (2012) Dementia Research in India: A Scientometric Analysis of Research Output during 2002-11. *Annals of Library and Information Studies,* 59: 280-288.
2. Ramos, J.M.; Padilla, S.; Masia, M.; et. al. (2008) A bibliometric analysis of tuberculosis research indexed in Pub Med 1997-2006. *Inter. J. Tuberc. Lung Dis.,* 12:1461-68.
3. Krishnamoorthy, G.; Ramakrishnan, J. and Devi, S. (2009) Bibliometric analysis of literature on diabetes 1995-2004. *Annals of Library and Information Studies,* 56:150-155.
4. Khatun, A. and Ahmed, S.M.Z. (2011) A bibliometric analysis of diarrhoeal diseases in Bangladesh. *Annals of Library and Information Studies*, 58:109-117.
5. Garg, K.C.; Dutt, B. and Kumar, S. A preliminary scientometric investigation of malaria research, *Annals of Library and Information Studies*, 53: 43-53.
6. Garg, K.C.; Kumar, S.; Madhavi, Y. and Bahl, M. (2001) Bibliometrics of global malaria vaccine research. *Health Information and Library Journal*, 26: 22-31.
7. Dutt, B., Kumar, S., Garg, K.C., (2010) Scientometric profile of global dengue research. *Collnet Journal of Scientometrics and Information Management*, 4: 81-91.
8. www.nihfw.org/NDC/Documentation Services/National Health Programme/JAPANESE.
9. *Op cit* 7.
10. Guan, J. and Ma, N. (2004) A comparative study of research performance in computer science, *Scientometrics*, 61: 339-359.
11. Kumar, S. and Garg, K.C. (2005) Scientometrics of computer science research in India and China. *Scientometrics* 64:121-132.
12. Op cit 6.
13. Schubert, A. and Braun, T. (1986) Relative indicators and relational charts for comparative assessment of publication output and citation impact, *Scientometrics* 9: 281- 291.
14. Joshi, K.; Kshitij, A. and Garg, K.C. (2010) Scientometric profile of global forest fungal research. *Annals of Library and Information Science*, 57: 130-139.

Appendix 1: Highly cited papers

SN	Authors, Institute, Bibliographic Details	# Citations
1	Kato, H; Takeuchi O; Sato, S. et.al. Osaka University, Nature 441(2006)101-105	1094
2	Makangie, J. S; Gubler D.J; Petersen L.R., Curtin University, Nature Medicine 10 (2004) 98-109	356
3	Rigue-Perez, J.G; Clark, G.G; Gubler D.J. et.al. CDC, Lancet 352 (1998) 971-977	322
4	Mukhopadhyay, S; Khun Raj; Rossman, M.G, Purdue University, Nature Reviews Microbiology 3 (2005)13-22	254
5	Steele, K.E; Linn, M.J; Schoepp, R.J. et.al. Wild Life Conservation Society, Veterinary Pathology 37 (2000) 208-224	248
6	Farinati, F; Cradin, R; Demaria, N. et.al. Baptist Medical Centre, Journal of Hepatology 22 (1995) 449-456	246
7	Gubler D. J, US Department of Health and Human Service, Archives of Medical Research 33 (2002) 330-342	236
8	Westaway, E.G; Mackenzie J.M; Kenney, M.T. et.al. University Queensland, Journal of Virology 71 (1997) 6650-6661	218
9	Sejwar,J.J; Hadda M.B; Tierney, B.C. et.al. CDCP, JAMA- Journal of the American Medical Association 290 (2003) 511-515	193
10	Devis, B.S; Chang G.J.J; Cropp, B. et.al. US Department of Health and Human Service, Journal of Virology 75 (2001) 440-447	189
11	Oliphan, T; Eagle, M; Nybakken, T. et.al. ,Washington University, Nature Medicine 11 (2005) 522-530	186
12	Vaughn D.W; Hoke, C., Walter Reed Army Institute of Research, Epidemiological Reviews 14 (1992)197-221	183
13	Brinton M.A., Georgia State University, Annual Reviews of Microbiology 56 (2002) 371-402	183
14	Querec, T; Bennouna, S; Alkan, S.K. et.al. Emory University, Journal of Experimental Medicine 203 (2006) 413-424	167
15	Ratston R; Thudium, K; Berger, K. et.al. Chiron Corp, Journal of Virology 67 (1993) 6753-6761	166
16	Hann, J.N; Richie, S.A; Philips, D.A., Queensland Health, Medical Journal of Australia 165 (1996) 256-260	164
17	Fournier, D; Mutero, A., University of California, Comparative Biochemistry and Physiology C- Pharmacology Toxicology and Endocrinology 108 (1994) 19-31	153
18	Mason, P.W; Pincus, S; Fournier, M.J. et.al. Yale University, Virology 180 (1991) 294-305	151
19	Krishan, Manoj N; Ng. Alwin; Sukumaran, Bindu et.al. Yale University, Nature 455 (2008) 242-245	150

6

Research Performance of National Institutes of Technology (NITS) of India during 2001-2010: A Bibliometric Analysis

Adarsh Bala and ***Santosh Kumari***

This study analyses the research performance of National Institutes of Technology (NITs) of India during 2001-2010 on several parameters including NITs' overall contribution, its growth pattern, citation impact, the share of international collaboration, identification of significant participating countries in NITs' international collaboration, contribution and impact by different subject areas, identification of weak and strong subject areas, productivity and impact of prolific authors, pattern of communication of NITs' output in most productive journals and characteristics of high cited papers of NITs'. The Scopus Citation Database has been used to retrieve the data for 10 years (2001-10).

KEYWORDS: Bibliometrics, NIT, National Institute of Technology, India, Publication output

1 INTRODUCTION

National Institutes of Technology (NITs) are the premier institutes of engineering and technology in India. Initially NITs were known as Regional Engineering Colleges (RECs). In 2002, the Govt. of India's Ministry of Human Resource Development (MHRD), upgraded all the 17 existing RECs as National Institutes of Technology (NITs). In 2006, MHRD granted NIT status to three more colleges and in 2010 again the government announced setting up of ten new NITs. Presently there are thirty NITs scattered throughout the country with the idea of having one NIT in every major state of India with the view to achieving balanced regional development. Further in 2007, the government upgraded these twenty NITs to fully fledged technical universities. In this regard, the Indian Parliament passed legislation; the National Institutes of Technology Act in 2007 which designates each NIT an Institute of National Importance (INI).

NITs were setup with the objective of providing high quality education in engineering and technology to produce competent technical manpower for the country. These are rated just next to the Indian Institutes of Technology (IITs) in terms of quality of education, research and placements. NITs offers bachelors, masters and doctorate level courses in various branches of engineering and technology. Besides providing high quality technical education, NITs provide various facilities for their students, research scholars and faculty like hostel facilities (with Cable television, periodicals, News papers, Indoor Games and Internet facilities in all hostel rooms), high-speed LAN and internet connection infrastructure, Central Library with good collection of technical books, literature, fiction, scientific journals and other electronic material.

Engineering being one of the preferred choices among students after 10+2 and largest infrastructures of Indian engineering and technological institutions produce the highest number of engineering and technology graduates every year by offering state-of-the-art undergraduate, postgraduate, doctoral programmes and generating new knowledge by engaging in research. Very few studies are available on the evaluation of research output of these institutions; in these the scope is either limited to the rankings of engineering and technological institutes [1-3] or assessment of research output of individual institutes [4-6] or analysis of a particular subject area related to engineering and technology [7-10] on the basis of the publications output. In the absence of comprehensive studies on the evaluation of particular group of engineering and technological institutions of India on the basis of their research output, it was felt that there in a need to conduct a comprehensive study to analyze the research output of NITs of India.

2 OBJECTIVES OF THE STUDY

The main objectives of the present study of NITs are to: (i) Analyze their research output, its growth and publication share in the Indian context; (ii) Analyze their publications output under different subject areas; (iii) Identify the productive and weak subject areas of research; (iv) Study the patterns of international collaboration and identification of significant collaborating partners with NITs; (v) To identify and study the productive and quality profile of prolific NIT authors; (vi) Study the communication patterns of most productive journals; and (vii) Evaluate the characteristics of highly cited NIT papers.

3 METHODOLOGY

SCOPUS citation database [http://www.scopus.com/ search/] was used for the retrieval of publication data of NITs published during 2001-2010. To retrieve the data the following main string was formulated:

((((((AFFIL("**Bihar College of Engineering**") AND AFFIL(**patna**) AND AFFIL(**india**)) AND PUBYEAR AFT **2000** AND PUBYEAR BEF **2011**) OR ((AFFIL("**Government Engineering College**") AND AFFIL(**raipur**) AND AFFIL(**india**)) AND PUBYEAR AFT **2000** AND PUBYEAR BEF **2011**) OR ((AFFIL("**Tripura Engineering College**") AND AFFIL(**agartala**) AND AFFIL(**india**)) AND PUBYEAR AFT **2000** AND PUBYEAR BEF **2011**))) OR ((((AFFIL("**National Institute of Technology**") OR AFFIL("**NIT**") AND AFFIL(**india**)) AND PUBYEAR AFT **2000** AND PUBYEAR BEF **2011**) OR ((AFFIL("**Regional Engineering College**") OR AFFIL("**REC**") AND AFFIL(**india**)) AND PUBYEAR AFT **2000** AND PUBYEAR BEF **2011**))))) OR ((((AFFILORG(**national institute of technology**) AND AFFILCITY(**patna**)) AND PUBYEAR AFT **2000** AND PUBYEAR BEF **2011**) OR ((AFFILORG(**national institute of technology**) AND AFFILCITY(**agartala**)) AND PUBYEAR AFT **2000** AND PUBYEAR BEF **2011**) OR ((AFFILORG(**national institute of technology**) AND AFFILCITY(**raipur**)) AND PUBYEAR AFT **2000** AND PUBYEAR BEF **2011**))))

For citation data three years, two years and one year citation window was used for computing average citations per paper published during 2001-08, 2009 and 2010. For retrieving the data of individual NIT, separate strings of respective NIT was formulated with data range limited to 2001-2010. Similarly, for calculating the total international collaborative papers, a separate search strategy which combines India's collaboration with major countries was prepared and combined with NITs. For analyzing authors and journals output, separate search strategies for generating author and journal output was developed. The scope of this study is limited to the bibliometric analysis of publication output of 20 NITs. The Ten NITs started in 2010 (located at Arunachal Pradesh, Delhi, Goa, Manipur, Meghalaya, Mizoram, Nagaland, Puducherry, Sikkim and Uttrakhand) were excluded from this study.

4 ANALYSIS

4.1 NITs' Overall Research Output

The cumulative publication output of NITs' consists of 8841 papers with an average of 884 papers per year, giving an average annual growth rate of 38.45%, and registering an impact of 2.14 citations per paper (with total of 18878 citations) during 2001-2010. The research publications output of NITs' increased from 1374 papers to 7467 papers, achieving a growth of 443.23%, registering an increase in its citation impact from 1.90 citations per paper to 2.18 citations per paper during the block years from 2001-2005 to 2006-2010. Overall, the publication share of NITs' in national output varies from 0.58% to 3.40% during 2001-2010, showing an increase from 0.90% to 2.62% during 2001-2005 to 2006-2010. Out of the total published research output (8841 papers) of NITs', 66.41% are articles, 31.09% conference papers, 1.55% reviews, 0.24% notes, and 0.20% editorials, etc (Table 1).

Table 1: Cumulative NITs' research output, research quality and share in national output during 2001-2010

Sl. No.	Year	TP	TC	ACPP	Growth Rate	TP (India)	% Share*
1.	2001	142	304	2.14		24681	0.58
2.	2002	176	309	1.76	23.94	26599	0.66
3.	2003	215	394	1.83	22.16	30509	0.70
4.	2004	327	637	1.95	52.09	33067	0.99
5.	2005	514	971	1.89	57.19	37489	1.37
6.	2006	754	1799	2.39	46.69	44096	1.71
7.	2007	888	2840	3.20	17.77	49355	1.80
8.	2008	1434	4477	3.12	61.49	55452	2.59
9.	2009	1879	4586	2.44	31.03	61824	3.04
10	2010	2512	2561	1.02	33.69	73938	3.40
	Total	**8841**	**18878**	**2.14**			

TP- Total Papers, TC- Total Citations, ACPP- Average Citation per paper. *% publication share of NITs' in India's cumulative publication output in respective years.

5 RESEARCH PROFILE OF INDIVIDUAL NITS'

The individual output of NIT varied from 14 to 1134 papers, with an average productivity of 444 papers per organization during 2001-2010. Nine NITs have published higher number of papers than the group average. These are: NIT-Rourkela (1134 papers), NIT-Tiruchirappalli (1108 papers), NIT-Karnataka (753 papers), NIT-Durgapur (674 papers), NIT-Allahabad (662 papers), NIT-Warangal (619 papers), NIT-Kurukshetra (545 papers), NIT-Calicut (512 papers) and NIT-Hamirpur (467 papers). The average citation per paper of NITs was 2.31, which varied from 0.93 to 3.83 citations per paper during 2001-2010. Eight NITs' have scored higher impact than the group average of 2.31 citations per paper. The NIT-

Bhopal achieved the highest impact of 3.83 citations per paper, followed by NIT-Hamirpur (3.53), NIT-Silchar (3.40), NIT-Tiruchirappalli (2.59), NIT-Rourkela and NIT-Calicut (2.45 each), NIT-Karnataka (2.42) and NIT-Surat (2.34). The average h-index achieved by these NITs was 14.4 during 2001-10. Ten NITs' registered a higher h-index than the group average of 14.4. They are NIT-Rourkela with h-index of 24, followed by NIT-Bhopal (23), NIT-Tiruchirappalli (22), NIT-Hamirpur (21), NIT-Karnataka (20), NIT-Calicut (19), NIT-Allahabad and NIT-Warangal (18 each) and NIT-Durgapur and NIT-Kurukshetra (17 each) (Table 2).

Table 2: NITs' individual research output, growth and research quality during 2001-2010

Sl. No.	Name of NIT	TP	TC	ACPP	H-Index
1.	Rourkela	1134	2781	2.45	24
2.	Tiruchirappalli	1108	2865	2.59	22
3.	Karnataka	753	1819	2.42	20
4.	Durgapur	674	1458	2.16	17
5.	Allahabad	662	1457	2.20	18
6.	Warangal	619	1129	1.82	18
7.	Kurukshetra	545	1070	1.96	17
8.	Calicut	512	1256	2.45	19
9.	Hamirpur	467	1647	3.53	21
10.	Jalandhar	437	705	1.61	14
11.	Nagpur	390	702	1.80	12
12.	Surat	388	906	2.34	12
13.	Jaipur	342	448	1.31	11
14.	Bhopal	308	1180	3.83	23
15.	Silchar	179	609	3.40	14
16.	Jamshedpur	143	253	1.77	10
17.	Srinagar	111	114	1.03	6
18.	Raipur	75	120	1.60	5
19.	Agartala	26	31	1.19	2
20.	Patna	14	13	0.93	3
	Total *	**8887**	**20563**		

Total output of 20 NITs listed above (by adding all papers of each NIT) is more than the cumulative output of NITs as more than one NITs are involved in few papers.

6 RANK AND PUBLICATION SHARE OF EACH NIT

In the cumulative output of 20 NITs, the share of individual NIT varied from 0.16% to 12.83% during 2001-2010. Among these NITs, NIT-Rourkela scored the 1st

rank with its publication share of 12.83%, followed by NIT-Tiruchirappalli (2nd rank, 12.53% share) and NIT Karnataka (3rd rank, 8.52% share). NITs' that scored the positions between 4th to 9th by contributing more than 5% publication share during the same period are NIT-Durgapur, NIT-Allahabad, NIT-Warangal, NIT-Kurukshetra, NIT-Calicut and NIT-Hamirpur. 10th to 17th positions are scored by the NITs' located at Jalandhar, Nagpur, Surat, Jaipur, Bhopal, Silchar, Jamshedpur and Srinagar with their publication share ranging from 1.26% to 4.94% (Table 3).

Twelve NITs have shown rise in their publication share ranging from 0.16% to 4.40% during 2001-2005 to 2006-2010. Among these, NIT-Karnataka showed 4.4% rise and improved its rank from 8th to 3rd, followed by NIT-Allahabad (4.21% rise and rank improved from 10th to 4th), NIT-Surat (3.73% rise and rank improved from 17th to 9th), NIT-Nagpur 91.94% rise and rank improved from 13th to 11th), NIT-Calicut (1.68% rise and rank improved from 9th to 7th) and NIT-Durgapur (0.84% rise and rank improved from 6th to 5th). However, five NITs including NIT-Bhopal, NIT-Silchar, NIT-Raipur, NIT-Agartala and NIT-Patna remained at the same rank in spite of increase in their publication share during the same period. In contrast, NIT-Jaipur although showed 1.22% rise in its publication output, but showed declined in its rank from 12th to 13th from 2001-05 to 2006-10 (Table 3).

Eight NITs witnessed the decline in their publication share ranging from 0.01% to 5.03% during the block period from 2001-2005 to 2006-2010. Among them, NIT-Hamirpur witnessed the largest decline of 5.03% in publication share, followed by NIT-Warangal (4.98%), NIT-Kurukshetra (2.95%), NIT-Jamshedpur (2.65%), NIT-Rourkela (1.45%), NIT-Tiruchirappalli (0.93%), NIT-Srinagar (0.24%) and NIT-Jalandhar (0.01%). Decline in publication share of these NITs lead to the decline of publication ranking of these NITs, such as NIT-Hamirpur (from 4th to 12th), followed by NIT-Warangal (from 3rd to 6th), NIT-Kurukshetra (from 5th to 8th), NIT-Jamshedpur (from 11th to 17th) and NIT-Jalandhar (from 7th to 10th) from 2001-2005 to 2006-2010. In contrast, the rank of NIT- Rourkela, NIT-Triuchirappalli and NIT-Srinagar remains the same in spite of decrease in their publication share during same period (Table 3).

On analyzing the citation impact per paper of these NITs for their publication productivity from 2001-2005 to 2006-2010, it was observed that NIT-Bhopal and NIT-Surat registered the maximum increase of 3.82 and 2.19 citations per paper, respectively during this period. Seven NITs (NIT-Calicut, NIT-Silchar, NIT-Hamirpur,

NIT-Raipur, NIT-Agartala, NIT-Nagpur and NIT-Allahabad) have improved their citation impact per paper (from 1.05 to 1.49). Nine NITs have shown the marginal increase in their impact of average citation per paper. In contrast, two NITs (NIT-Warangal and NIT-Jaipur) have shown the decrease in their citation impact per paper (from 0.2-1.4) from 2001-05 to 2006-10. (Table 3)

Table 3: Publication output, share, rank and citation impact of individual NIT during 2001-2010

SN	Name of NIT	TP			% Publication Share*			Rank			ACPP		
				2001-10	2001-05	2006-10	2001-10	2001-05	2006-10	2001-10	2001-05	2001-05	2006-10
1.	Rourkela	193	941	1134	14.05	12.60	12.83	1	1	1	1.89	2.57	2.45
2.	Tiruchirappallli	183	925	1108	13.32	12.39	12.53	2	2	2	1.89	2.72	2.59
3.	Karnataka	66	687	753	4.80	9.20	8.52	8	3	3	1.56	2.50	2.42
4.	Durgapur	95	579	674	6.91	7.75	7.62	6	5	4	1.73	2.23	2.16
5.	Allahabad	54	608	662	3.93	8.14	7.49	10	4	5	0.83	2.32	2.20
6.	Warangal	154	465	619	11.21	6.23	7.00	3	6	6	2.88	1.48	1.82
7.	Kuruksheta	119	426	545	8.66	5.71	6.16	5	8	7	1.55	2.08	1.96
8.	Calicut	60	452	512	4.37	6.05	5.79	9	7	8	1.53	2.58	2.45
9.	Hamirpur	131	336	467	9.53	4.50	5.28	4	12	9	2.73	3.84	3.53
10.	Jalandhar	68	369	437	4.95	4.94	4.94	7	10	10	1.43	1.65	1.61
11.	Nagpur	38	352	390	2.77	4.71	4.41	13	11	11	0.58	1.93	1.80
12.	Surat	17	371	388	1.24	4.97	4.39	17	9	12	0.24	2.43	2.34
13.	Jaipur	39	303	342	2.84	4.06	3.87	12	13	13	1.49	1.29	1.31
14.	Bhopal	32	276	308	2.33	3.70	3.48	14	14	14	0.41	4.23	3.83
15.	Silchar	26	153	179	1.89	2.05	2.02	15	15	15	2.46	3.56	3.40
16.	Jamshedpur	53	90	143	3.86	1.21	1.62	11	17	16	1.51	1.92	1.77
17.	Srinagar	20	91	111	1.46	1.22	1.26	16	16	17	1.00	1.03	1.03
18.	Raipur	2	73	75	0.15	0.98	0.85	18	18	18	0.50	1.63	1.60
19.	Agartala	0	26	26	0.00	0.35	0.29	19	19	19	0.00	1.19	1.19
20.	Patna	0	14	14	0.00	0.19	0.16	20	20	20	0.00	0.93	0.93

* % publication share of each NIT in cumulative publication output of NITs

7 INTERNATIONAL COLLABORATION OF NITS

The NIT's cumulative international collaborative publication output consisted of 905 papers, accounting for 10.24% share in its publication output during 2001-10. The share of international collaborative publications of NITs have increased from 7.93% (109 papers) to 10.66% (796 papers) from 2001-2005 to 2006-2010. Similarly, the cumulative international collaborative papers of NITs received total of 1189 citations during 2001-10, registering an average citation impact per paper as 1.31, which declined from 2.17 to 1.20 from 2001-05 to 2006-10 (Table 4).

Table 4: NITs international collaborative research output and research impact during 2001-10

Sl. No.	Year	TP	ICP	TC	ACPP	% Share of ICP *
1.	2001	142	9	101	11.22	6.34
2.	2002	176	10	5	0.50	5.68
3.	2003	215	22	51	2.32	10.23
4.	2004	327	25	36	1.44	7.65
5.	2005	514	43	43	1.00	8.37
6.	2006	754	57	42	0.74	7.56
7.	2007	888	94	137	1.46	10.59
8.	2008	1434	137	189	1.38	9.55
9.	2009	1879	235	366	1.56	12.51
10	2010	2512	273	219	0.80	10.87
	Total	**8841**	**905**	**1189**	**1.31**	**10.24**
	2001-05	**1374**	**109**	**236**	**2.17**	**7.93**
	2006-10	**7467**	**796**	**953**	**1.20**	**10.66**

TP- Total Papers, ICP-International Collaborative Papers, TC- Total Citations, ACPP- Average Citation per paper. *% share of ICP in total output of NITs in respective year

8 INTERNATIONAL COLLABORATIVE RESEARCH PROFILE OF EACH NIT

On analyzing the international collaborative profile of individual NITs', it was noted that NIT-Tiruchirappallli has published the highest number (223) of international collaborative papers with 24.64% share in the cumulative international collaborative publication output of NITs' during 2001-10. NIT-Karnataka scored the second position (with 125 papers and 13.81% share), followed by NIT-Rourkela (with 95 papers and 10.50% share), NIT-Durgapur (with 85 papers and 9.39% share), NIT-Allahabad (with 57 papers and 6.30% share), NIT-Jaipur (with 49 papers and 5.41% share) and NIT-Calicut (with 47 papers and 5.19% share). The international collaborative publication output of other NITs' is less than 40 papers during 2001-10 (Table 5).

The international collaborative publication share of 20 NITs in their cumulative publication output varied from 3.43% to 21.43% during 2001-10. Eight NITs have shown an increase in their international collaborative publication share from 2001-2005 to 2006-2010: NIT-Jamshedpur (by 8.11%), NIT-Bhopal, (by 7.38%), NIT-Tiruchirappalli (by 6.44%), NIT-Kurukshetra (by 4.79%), NIT-Calicut (by 4.73%), NIT-Rourkela (by 1.36%), NIT-Allahabad (by 1.31%) and NIT-Warangal (by 1.04%). Six NITs' (NIT-Hamirpur, NIT-Surat, NIT-Silchar, NIT-Nagpur, NIT-Patna and NIT-

Agartala) have published international collaborative papers only during 2006-2010. Similarly, Six NITs' who have shown decrease in their international collaborative publication share during 2001-2005 to 2006-2010 are NIT-Karnataka, NIT-Durgapur, NIT-Jaipur, NIT-Jalandhar, NIT-Srinagar and NIT-Raipur (Table 5).

Table 5: Individual NITs international collaborative research output and share during 2001-2010

SN	Name of NIT	TP			ICP			% Share of ICP*			ICP % Share **
		2001-05	2006-10	2001-10	2001-05	2006-10	2001-10	2001-05	2006-10	2001-10	2001-10
1.	Tiruchirappalli	183	925	1108	27	196	223	14.75	21.19	20.13	24.64
2.	Karnataka	66	687	753	12	113	125	18.18	16.45	16.60	13.81
3.	Rourkela	193	941	1134	14	81	95	7.25	8.61	8.38	10.50
4.	Durgapur	95	579	674	12	73	85	12.63	12.61	12.61	9.39
5.	Allahabad	54	608	662	4	53	57	7.41	8.72	8.61	6.30
6.	Jaipur	39	303	342	8	41	49	20.51	13.53	14.33	5.41
7.	Calicutt	60	452	512	3	44	47	5.00	9.73	9.18	5.19
8.	Warangal	154	465	619	7	26	33	4.55	5.59	5.33	3.65
9.	Bhopal	32	276	308	1	29	30	3.13	10.51	9.74	3.31
10.	Kurukshetra	119	426	545	1	24	25	0.84	5.63	4.59	2.76
11.	Hamirpur	131	336	467	0	24	24	0.00	7.14	5.14	2.65
12.	Surat	17	371	388	0	20	20	0.00	5.39	5.15	2.21
13.	Silchar	26	153	179	0	18	18	0.00	11.76	10.06	1.99
14.	Jalandhar	68	369	437	3	12	15	4.41	3.25	3.43	1.66
15.	Nagpur	38	352	390	0	15	15	0.00	4.26	3.85	1.66
16.	Srinagar	20	91	111	3	8	11	15.00	8.79	9.91	1.22
17.	Jamshedpur	53	90	143	1	9	10	1.89	10.00	6.99	1.10
18.	Raipur	2	73	75	1	2	3	50.00	2.74	4.00	0.33
19.	Patna	0	14	14	0	3	3	0	21.43	21.43	0.33
20.	Agartala	0	26	26	0	1	1	0	3.85	3.85	0.11

TP- Total Papers, ICP-International Collaborative Papers, * ICP % share in respective NIT's cumulative output ** ICP % share of each NIT in cumulative ICP output of NITs (905 papers)

9 MAJOR COLLABORATING PARTNERS OF NITS

Among the top 15 collaborating countries that have significant collaboration with NITs' are USA with 22.76% international collaborative publication share, followed by Malaysia (13.48%), South Korea (11.05%), United Kingdom (8.73%), Germany (7.96%), Japan (7.40%), Australia, Singapore, Canada, France (varying its collaborative publication share from 3.20% to 5.41%), Taiwan, China, Brazil (varying its collaborative publication share from 2.21% to 2.98%) and other countries had less than 2% collaborative publication share during 2001-10 (Table 6). NITs witnessed both the rise and fall in their international collaborative publication share with these countries from 2001-05 to 2006-10. The collaborative linkages of NITs' have shown decrease with 12 countries with largest decrease (9.61%) with Singapore, followed by Japan (9.32%), Germany (7.64%), Taiwan (6%), USA (5.41%), U.K.(4.67%), South Korea (4.13%), Australia (2.19%), France (1.57%), China (1.16%), Canada(0.35%) and Thailand (0.2%). In contrast, the collaborative linkages of NITs' have shown increase with 3 countries with maximum increase (2.26%) with Denmark, followed by Brazil (1.47%) and Malaysia (0.73%) (Table 6).

Table 6: Number and share of major collaborative partners of NITs during 2001-10

Sl. No.	Country's Name	ICP			% Share of ICP*		
		2001 -05	2006- 10	2001 -10	2001 -05	2006 -10	2001 -10
1.	USA	30	176	206	27.52	22.11	22.76
2.	Malaysia	14	108	122	12.84	13.57	13.48
3.	S. Korea	16	84	100	14.68	10.55	11.05
4.	UK	14	65	79	12.84	8.17	8.73
5.	Germany	16	56	72	14.68	7.04	7.96
6.	Japan	17	50	67	15.60	6.28	7.40
7.	Australia	8	41	49	7.34	5.15	5.41
8.	Singapore	15	33	48	13.76	4.15	5.30
9.	Canada	6	41	47	5.50	5.15	5.19
10.	France	5	24	29	4.59	3.02	3.20
11.	Taiwan	9	18	27	8.26	2.26	2.98
12.	China	4	20	24	3.67	2.51	2.65
13.	Brazil	1	19	20	0.92	2.39	2.21
14.	Denmark	0	18	18	0.00	2.26	1.99
15.	Thailand	2	13	15	1.83	1.63	1.66
Total	**ICP of NITs'**	**109**	**796**	**905**	**100.00**	**100.00**	**100.00**

ICP-International Collaborative Papers, *The combined output of 15 foreign collaborating countries listed above in NITs' international collaborative output will be more than its total international collaborative papers as one or more foreign collaborating countries are involved in few collaborative papers.

10 SUBJECT PROFILE OF NITS

Among the broad subject wise contribution of NITs output, engineering sciences subjects together contributed the highest publication share of 81.93% during 2001-10, followed by physical sciences (with 40.47% share), life sciences (with 6.07% share) and health sciences (with 1.38% share) in the cumulative publication output of NITs during 2001-10. The publication share of NITs have increased in engineering sciences subjects by 1.87% (from 80.35% to 82.22%) and in health sciences subjects by 0.69% (from 0.80% to 1.49%), as against decrease in physical sciences subjects by 2.24% (from 42.36% to 40.12%) and in life sciences subjects by 0.48% (from 6.48% to 6.00%) from 2001-05 to 2006-10. The maximum average citation impact per paper (3.6) is scored by life sciences subjects, followed by physical sciences subjects (3.11 citations per paper), engineering sciences subjects (2.56 citations per paper) and health sciences subjects (2.12 citations per paper) during 2001-10.The average citations per paper witnessed an increase in life sciences subjects from 2.16 to 3.88, followed by physical sciences subjects from 1.92 to 3.34 and engineering sciences subjects from 1.90 to 2.68, as against the decrease in health sciences subjects from 2.45 to 2.09 from 2001-05 to 2006-10 (Table 7)

Table 7: Overall publication share and impact of NITs by broad disciplines during 2001-2010

Broad Subject Area	TP (% share)			TC (ACPP)		
	2001-2005	2006-2010	2001-2010	2001-2005	2006-2010	2001-2010
Engineering sciences	1104 (80.35)	6139 (82.22)	7243 (81.93)	2093 (1.90)	16442 (2.68)	18535 (2.56)
Physical sciences	582 (42.36)	2996 (40.12)	3578 (40.47)	1118 (1.92)	9999 (3.34)	11117 (3.11)
Life sciences	89 (6.48)	448 (6.00)	537 (6.07)	192 (2.16)	1740 (3.88)	1932 (3.60)
Health sciences	11 (0.80)	111 (1.49)	122 (1.38)	27 (2.45)	232 (2.09)	259 (2.12)

11 SUBJECT AREAS OF RESEARCH IN NITS

As per publication output data for 2001-2010 presented in Table 8-11. NITs research profile by 20 broad subject areas (as per general classification of SCOPUS database) emerges as follows:

High Productivity Subject Area - Engineering science, computer science, material science, physics and astronomy and chemistry are considered as the five high priority areas of NITs, each contributing publication share between 12.37% and 48.80% in the cumulative publication output of NITs during 2001-10. The highest publication share (48.80%) of NITs was in engineering science, followed by computer science (24.99%), material science (22.06%), physics and astronomy (15.04%) and chemistry (12.37%). The highest average citation impact per paper (4.27) for all its publications in high productivity subject areas was achieved in chemistry, followed by material science (3.35), physics and astronomy (3.03), engineering science (2.12) and computer science (1.13) during 2001-10 (Table 8)

Table 8: Research output, impact, and publication share of NITs in high productivity subject areas during 2001-2010

Subject	TP	TC	% Share	ACPP
Engineering college	4314	9133	48.80	2.12
Computer science	2209	2495	24.99	1.13
Material science	1950	6535	22.06	3.35
Physics and Astronomy	1330	4034	15.04	3.03
Chemistry	1094	4676	12.37	4.27

Medium Productivity Subject Area - Chemical engineering, energy, environmental science and mathematics are considered as four medium productivity subject areas of NITs, each contributing publication share between 7.50% and 9.74% in the cumulative publication output of NITs during 2001-10. Among these subject areas, the highest publication share of NITs was in chemical engineering (with 9.74% share), followed by energy (8.81% share), environmental science (7.95% share) and mathematics (7.50% share). The highest average citation per paper (4.71%) in these areas was observed in chemical engineering, followed by environmental science (3.68), energy (3.20) and mathematics (1.69) during 2001-2010. (Table 9)

Table 9: Research output, impact, and publication share of NITs in medium productivity subject areas during 2001-2010

Subject	TP	TC	% Share	ACPP
Chemical Engineering	861	4059	9.74	4.71
Energy	779	2493	8.81	3.20
Environmental Science	703	2590	7.95	3.68
Mathematics	663	1119	7.50	1.69

Low Productivity Subject areas - Earth and planetary science, biochemistry, genetics and molecular biology, agricultural and biological sciences, medicine and pharmacology, toxicology and pharmaceuticals are considered as low productivity subject areas, each contributing publication share between 1.30% and 3.30% in the cumulative publication output of NITs during 2001-2010. The highest average citation per paper (5.43) among these subject areas was observed in pharmacology, toxicology and pharmaceuticals, followed by biochemistry, genetics and molecular biology (3.69), agricultural and biological sciences (2.92), medicine (2.15), and earth and planetary sciences (1.53) during 2001-10 (Table 10).

Table 10: Research Output, Impact, and Publication share of NITs in low productivity subject areas during 2001-2010

Subject	TP	TC	% Share	ACPP
Earth & Planetary Science	292	448	3.30	1.53
Biochemistry, Genetics & Molecular Biology	279	1030	3.16	3.69
Agricultural & Biological Sciences	187	546	2.12	2.92
Medicine	119	256	1.35	2.15
Pharmacology, Toxicology & Pharmaceutics	115	624	1.30	5.43

Least Productivity Subject Areas - Immunology and microbiology, public health and neurosciences are considered as four least productivity subject areas contributing each < 1 percent in the cumulative publication output of NITs during 2001-10. The highest average citation per paper (4.10) among these areas was observed in immunology and microbiology, followed by neurosciences (3.64) and public health (3.62) during 2001-2010 (Table 11).

Table 11: Research output, impact, and publication share of NITs in least productivity subject areas during 2001-2010

Subject	TP	TC	% Share	ACPP
Immunology and Microbiology	30	123	0.34	4.10
Economics Econometrics and Finance	26	75	0.29	2.88
Public Health	26	94	0.29	3.62
Neuroscience	11	40	0.12	3.64

12 RESEARCH PROFILE OF MOST PROLIFIC AUTHORS OF NIT'S

The research performance of most prolific authors of NITs' during 2001-2010 in terms of their contributions, impact and h-index is presented in Table 12. Here 20 authors, who have published 35 and more papers, are considered as highly productive authors of NITs'. Among these 20 authors, 6 are affiliated to NIT-Tiruchirappalli, 3 each are affiliated to NIT-Hamirpur and NIT-Durgapur, 2 are affiliated to NIT-Warangal and 1 each is affiliated to NIT-Jalandhar, NIT-Kurukshetra, NIT-Karnataka, NIT-Surat, NIT-Calicut and NIT-Rourkela. These 20 authors together contributed 1034 papers with an average of 51.7 papers per author and accounts for 11.70% share in the cumulative publication output NITs' during 2001-10. Seven authors have published higher number of papers than the group average (51.7).These are R.Narayana Samy with 120 papers, followed by Ajay Kumar Sharma (76 papers), Shiv K. Chakarvarti (65 papers), T. Balasubramanian (64 papers), Arun M Isloor (58 papers), Baranthula Rajitha (55 papers) and Jagannath Sharma (53 papers).

Considering the quality/impact of papers, these 20 productive authors have received a total of 2986 citations for 1034 papers, with an average of 2.89 citations per papers during 2001-10. Nine authors have registered higher impact than the average citation impact of papers of all authors (2.89). These are: Amar Singh Singha with 8.58 citations per paper, followed by Z.V.P. Murthy (5.50), A.N. Haq (4.78), S.P. Ghosal (4.68), Sunil (4.60), P.Kumbhkar (4.29), J. Sharma (3.77), G.P. Unnikrishnan (3.47) and B. Rajitha (3.00). Similarly the average h-index achieved by these productive authors is 7.6 during 2001-10. Eleven authors who scored the higher h-index than the group average. They are A. S. Singha with h-index of 13, J. Sharma, Sunil and A. N. Haq (12 each), R. Narayana Samy (10), T. Balasubramanian, S.P. Ghoshal and G.P. Unnikrishanan (9 each) and B. Rajitha, Z.V.P. Murthy and P. Kumbhkar (8 each).

Table 12: Productivity and citation impact of NITs' top twenty authors during 2001-10

SN	Name	Affiliated NIT	TP	TC	ACPP	H-Index
1.	R Narayana Samy	NIT Tiruchirappalli	120	301	2.51	10
2.	Ajay Kumar Sharma	NIT Jalandhar	76	82	1.08	6

SN	Name	Affiliated NIT	TP	TC	ACPP	H-Index
3.	Shiv K Chakarvarti	NIT Kurukshetra	65	97	1.49	7
4.	Thailampillai K Balasubramanian	NIT Tiruchirappalli	64	137	2.14	9
5.	Arun M Isloor	NIT Surathkal	58	162	2.79	6
6.	Baranthula Rajitha	NIT Warangal	55	165	3.00	8
7.	Jagannath Sharma	NIT Hamirpur	53	200	3.77	12
8.	Sakti Prasad Ghosal	NIT Durgapur	47	220	4.68	9
9.	Sunil	NIT Hamirpur	47	216	4.60	12
10.	Amar Singh Singha	NIT Hamirpur	45	386	8.58	13
11.	Maheswarapu Sydulu	NIT Warangal	44	4	0.09	2
12.	Gopalkrishna Panicker Unnikrishanan	NIT Kozhikhode	43	149	3.47	9
13.	Seetha Raghavan	NIT Tiruchirappallli	42	9	0.21	2
14.	Z.V.P Murthy	NIT Surat	42	231	5.50	8
15.	Alok K Satapathy	NIT Rourkela	42	107	2.55	6
16.	A Noorul Haq	NIT Tiruchirappalli	41	196	4.78	12
17.	Mangalanathan Umapathy	NIT Tiruchirappallli	39	31	0.79	3
18.	Pathik Kumbhkar	NIT Durgapur	38	163	4.29	8
19.	Ajit Kumar Meikap	NIT Durgapur	38	87	2.29	6
20.	B. Venkataramani	NIT Tiruchirappalli	35	43	1.23	4

TP =Total Papers; TC = Total Citations; ACPP = Average Citations Per Paper

13 MEDIA OF COMMUNICATION OF NITS' IN MOST PRODUCTIVE JOURNALS

The research output of NITs' published in top 20 highly productive foreign and Indian journals during 2001-2010 is presented in Tables 13-14 .These productive journals together contributed 1059 papers, which accounts for 11.98% share in the cumulative publication output of NITs' during 2001-10, showing a decline in publication output from 16.08% share during 2001-05 to 11.22% share during 2006-10. Comparing the research output published in these highly productive foreign and India journals, it has been observed that foreign journals together contributed higher publication share of 7.26% than the Indian journals 4.72% in NITs' cumulative publication output during 2001-10.The publication share of foreign journals witnessed a marginal decrease from 7.28% to 7.26% in contrast to Indian journals witnessing a decline from 8.81% to 3.96% during 2001-05 to 2006-10.

Table 13: NITs' research productivity in Foreign Journals during 2001-2010

Sl. No.	Name of Foreign Journal	Total Papers		
		2001-05	2006-10	2001-10
1.	International. Journal of Advanced Manufacturing Technology	33	74	107
2.	Lecture Notes in Computer Science Including Subseries Lecture Notes in Artificial Intelligence and Lecture Notes in Bioinformatics	22	69	91
3.	Acta Crystallographic Section E Structure Reports Online	1	84	85
4.	Materials and Design	0	79	79
5.	Journal of Hazardous Materials	0	55	55
6.	Journal of Reinforced Plastics and Composites	8	43	51
7.	Journal of Materials Science	16	33	49
8.	Journal of Materials Processing Technology	12	32	44
9.	Electric Power Components and Systems	8	33	41
10.	Optik	0	40	40

Table 14: NITs' research productivity in Indian Journals during 2001-2010

Sl. No.	Name of Indian Journal	Total Papers		
		2001-5	2006-10	2001-10
1.	Communications in Computer and Information Science	0	54	54
2.	Indian Journal of Chemical Technology	15	36	51
3.	Journal of Structural Engineering Madras	12	37	49
4.	Transactions of the Indian Institute of Metals	11	31	42
5.	Indian Journal of Environmental Protection	27	14	41
6.	Indian Journal of Pure and Applied Physics	13	26	39
7.	Journal of Scientific and Industrial Research	9	27	36
8.	Bulletin of Materials Science	10	26	36
9.	Indian Journal of Physics	4	31	35
10.	IETE Journal of Research	20	14	34

14 HIGHLY CITED PAPERS

This section analyses the 100 high cited papers published by NITs' during 2001-2010. The papers receiving 36 and more citations are considered as high cited papers. The citations received by these papers vary from 36 to 349 per paper. Of these high cited papers, 84 appeared as articles, 14 as reviews and 1 each as short survey and letter. Considering the collaboration of these papers, 15 papers involve international collaboration (12 bilateral and 3 multilateral), 41 involve national collaboration and 44 papers have zero collaboration. Among these, 15 papers are from NIT-Rourkela followed by NIT-Tiruchirappalli (14 papers), NIT-Bhopal (11papers), NIT-Warangal (9 papers), NIT-Hamirpur (7 papers), NIT-Kurukshetra,(6 papers), NIT-Karnataka (6 papers), NIT-Silchar (6 papers), NIT-Durgapur (5 papers), NIT-Roorkee (4 papers), NIT-Calicut (4 papers), NIT-Allahabad (3 papers), NIT-Jalandhar (3 papers), NIT-Surat (2 papers), NIT-Nagpur (2 papers) and 1 paper each from other NITs'. Among the authors of these high cited papers, A.Mittal (NIT-Bhopal) published the maximum number of papers (6), followed by V.K. Gupta (NIT Roorkee) (5 papers), S. Chand (NIT Hamirpur), P.P. Sahay (NIT Silchar), D.P. Singh (NIT Kurukshetra) (3 papers each), S.P Ghosal (NIT Durgapur), H.M.Suryawanshi (NIT Nagpur), Z.V.P. Murthy (NIT Surat), B.S.Inbaraj (NIT Tiruchirappalli), S.Anandan (NIT Tiruchirappalli), A.N. Haq (NIT-Tiruchirappalli), M.Ahmaruzzaman (NIT Silchar), G. Radhakrishnamacharya, (NIT- Warangal) (with 2 papers each) and 1 paper each from other authors.. These 100 high cited papers were published in 82 journals including 7 papers in *Journal of Hazardous Materials*, 6 papers in *Journal of Colloid and Interface* Science, 5 papers in *IEEE Transactions on Power Delivery*, 4 papers each in *Advances in Colloid and Interface Science, Electric Power System Research, IEEE Transactions on Industrial Electronics*, 3 papers each in *Renewable Energy, Renewable and Sustainable Energy Reviews*, 2 papers each in *Tetrahedron Letters, Journal of Materials Science, International Journal of Machine tools and Manufacture, European Journal of Medicinal Chemistry, IEEE Transactions on Power System, Sensors and Actuators B: Chemical, International Journal of Advanced Manufacturing Technology, Bulletin of Materials Science, Semiconductor Science and Technology, Transition Metal Chemistry* and 1 paper each in others journals.

15 CONCLUDING REMARKS

The cumulative publication output of NITs' consist of 8841 papers with an average number of papers per year as 884, witnessing an average annual growth rate of 38.45%, registering an impact of 2.14 citations per paper (with total of 18878 citations) during 2001-10. Out of the total published research output (8841 papers) of NITs', 66.41% are published as articles, 31.09% as conference papers, 1.55% as reviews, 0.24% as notes, 0.20% as editorials, etc. The individual output of NITs varied from 14 to 1134 papers, with an average productivity of 444 papers per organization during 2001-2010. Nine NITs have published higher papers than the group average, eight NITs' have scored higher impact than the group average and ten NITs' registered the higher h-index than the group average.

The publication share of individual NIT varied from 0.16% to 12.83% during 2001-2010. NIT-Rourkela scored the 1st rank with its publication share of 12.83%. Twelve NITs have shown rise in their publication share, with NIT-Karnataka witnessing highest of 4.4 % rise and improved its rank from 8th to 3rd during 2001-05 to 2006-10. Similarly, NIT-Bhopal has registered the maximum increase of 3.82 citation impact per paper during 2001-05 to 2006-10.

The NIT's cumulative international collaborative publication output consisted of 905 papers, accounting for 10.24% share in its publication output during 2001-2010, registering an average citation impact per paper as 1.31, NIT-Tiruchirappallli has published the highest number (223) of international collaborative papers with 24.64% share in the cumulative international collaborative publication output of NITs' during 2001-10. USA is the major collaborating partner with NITs with 22.76% international collaborative publication share.

Among the broad subject wise contribution of NITs, engineering sciences subjects together contributed the highest publication share (81.93%) and life sciences subjects scored the maximum average citation impact per paper (3.6) during 2001-10. Engineering science, computer science, material science, physics and astronomy and chemistry are considered as the five high priority areas of NITs. In contrast, immunology and microbiology, public health and neurosciences are considered as least productivity subject areas of NITs.

The 20 most productive authors of NITs together contributed 1034 papers, accounting for 11.70% publications share in the cumulative publication output NITs' and registered an average impact of 2.89 citations per paper and an average h-index of 7.6 per author during 2001-2010.

The research output of NITs' published in top 20 highly productive foreign and Indian journals together contributed 1059 papers, which accounts for 11.98% share in the cumulative publication output of NITs' during 2001-10, showing a decline in publication output from 16.08% share during 2001-05 to 11.22% share during 2006-10. Among the 100 high cited papers 15 papers involve international collaboration (12 bilateral and 3 multilateral), 41 involve national collaboration and 44 papers have zero collaboration.

NITs were set up throughout the country with the idea of having one NIT in every major state of India to achieve balanced regional development and to provide high quality education in engineering and technology for producing competent technical manpower in the field of engineering, science and technology. These NITs were declared as Institute of National Importance in 2007 by the Indian government and are rated just next to the Indian Institutes of Technology (IITs) in terms of quality of education, research and placements. Although government had spent several crores on the development of these NITs, yet the research contribution and performance of only few NITs is at par with the other institutes of national importance like IITs. Thus, there is need to establish/strengthen R&D facilities in these institutes in collaboration with industries, need to create more national/international collaborative programmes, develop more research-oriented labs and centres and to increase the research facilities, infrastructure and resources to conduct research. Beside this, Govt. should fund the NITs based on performance so that the competition for excellence exists in them.

REFERENCES

1. Prathap, G. and Gupta, B.M. (2009) Ranking of Indian engineering and technological institutes for their research performance during 1999-2008. *Current Science*, 97(3): 304-306.
2. Gupta, B.M.; Bala, A. and Sharma, N. (2011) Ranking of Indian Institutions Contributing to Computer Science Research, 1999-2008. *Desidoc Journal of Library and Information Technology*, 31(6): 460-468.
3. Saxena, A.; Gupta, B.M. and Jauhari, M. (2011) Research Performance of Top Engineering and Technological Institutes of India: A Comparison of Indice. *Desidoc Journal of Library and Information Technology*. 31(5): 377-381.
4. Singh, Y.; Gupta, B.M. and Kumar, S. (2005) Research Contributions and Impact of Research of Indian Institute of Technology, Roorkee, 1993 to 2001. *Annals of Library and Information Studies,* 52(1): 8-14.
5. Jeyshankar, R.; Babu, B.R. and Rajendran, P. (2011) Research output of CSIR-Central Electro Chemical Research Institute (CECRI):A study. *Annals of Library and Information Studies*, 58(4): 301-306.

6. Vasishta, S. (2011) Assessment of Academic Research Output during 1996-2009: A Case Study of PEC University of Technology, Chandigarh. *Desidoc Journal of Library and Information Technology,* 31(2):136-142.
7. Dhawan, S.M. and Walke, R. (2007) Materials Science Research in India: A Scientometric Analysis. Desidoc *Journal of Library and Information Technology,* 27(1): 69-76.
8. Modak, J.M. and Madras, G. (2008) Scientometric analysis of chemical engineering publications. *Current Science,* 94(10): 1265-1272.
9. Nazim, M. and Ahmad, M. (2008) A bibliometric analysis on nanotechnology research. *Annals of Library and Information Studies.* 55(4): 292-299.
10. Gupta, B.M.; Kshitij, A. and Singh, Y. (2010) Indian Computer Science Research Output during 1999-2008: Qualitative Analysis. *DESIDOC Journal of Library and Information Technology.* 30(6): 39-54.

7

A Comparative Study of Mysore University and Karnatak University in S&T: Research Output, Citation Impact and Collaboration during 2001-10

B.D. Kumbar and ***B.M. Gupta***

The study provides a comparative assessment of the research contribution of the Mysore University and the Karnatak University in terms of publications output in science and technology, its growth and citation impact during 2001-10. It analyses the strong and weak subject areas of universities research and their citation impact. It describes the international collaborative share of research output of the universities at the overall level, indicating the contribution of the major collaborating partner countries. It also provides analyses of the national collaborating links of the two universities; with a view to study their collaborating linkages with academic institutions, institutes of national importance, research institutions and industry. It also studies the contribution and citation impact of the top 15 most productive authors and also the productivity of their most productive journals, where the two universities authors have published.

KEYWORDS: Mysore Univeristy, Karnatak University, Comparative study, Citation impact, Collaboration, S&T research output

1 INTRODUCTION

Karnatak University is the second university in established Karnatak after Mysore, which celebrated its diamond jubilee in 2009. It has been recognized for its excellence by NAAC, which has recently given it as "A" grade status. There are 48 postgraduate departments (of which 14 belong to science), 264 postgraduate faculty members and 4531 postgraduate students. It has also postgraduate centers at Karwar, Haveri and Gadag. For its scientific research it has received extra-mural funding from several agencies in the past, including University Grants Commission, Karnatak State, Department of Science and Technology, Indian Council of Agricultural Research, Nuclear Science Center, Department of Ocean Development, Department of Biotechnology, and Board of Research in Nuclear Science. The present paper analyses the contribution of Karnatak University in terms of publications in peer reviewed journals and citation impact in all fields of science and technology during 2001-10.

University of Mysore was established on 27th July, 1916 during the benevolent reign of the Maharaja of Mysore, His Highness Nalvadi Krishnaraja Wodeyar (1884-1940). University of Mysore is the first and one of the oldest Universities in the state of Karnatak. The genesis of the University of Mysore stems from a five year long in-depth reading and analysis on higher education across the globe. The mission of the University of Mysore, laid down in the 1916 regulations published in the Mysore Gazette Extraordinary, aims at 'promoting teaching and research in conventional and traditional domains of Arts, Humanities, Pure and Applied Sciences and Professional disciplines'. Sir. M Visvesvaraya (1860-1962) played a decisive role in the launch of the University.

Today, the University has 42 Postgraduate Departments at the Main Campus, Manasagangotri, 2 Postgraduate Centres, viz., Tubinakere in Mandya Dt., Hemagangotri in Hassan Dt. with 5 Postgraduate Departments each and one Satellite Centre at Chamarajanagar with 3 Postgraduate Departments. It is providing higher education to about 85 lakhs students, of which over 10,000 are Postgraduates. As many as 1400 students are from 50 countries pursuing higher studies in this University. Some of these countries are China, Iran, Jordan, Thailand, Indonesia, Egypt, Syria, Tanzania, Uzbekistan, Kajkhastan, Kirghizia, Mongolia, Uganda, Yemon, Kenya, Palestine, Srilanka, Bangladesh and Nepal.

Considering the progress of the University in all directions and its contributions to the society, the Ministry of Human Resource Development, Government of India has considered University of Mysore as `*Institution of Excellence*' and has awarded special grant of Rs.100 Crores for establishing Centre of Excellence in "*Biodiversity, Bioprospecting and Sustainable Development*" and also to strengthen infrastructural facilities in the University. University of Mysore is recipient of several research and other academic programs of UGC, CSIR, DST and DBT and other agencies of Govt. of India. It is pertinent to mention that very recently; University Grants Commission has awarded University of Mysore - *University with Potential for Excellence (UPE)* and has extended financial assistance of Rs.50 Crores for research activities and for holistic development of the University.

Various studies have been conducted in the past analyzing the growth, contribution and impact of individual organizations. Jeevan and Gupta [1-2] have analyzed the contribution and impact of Indian Institute of Technology, Kharagpur by suggesting a methodology for studying its quantitative profile. Singh, Gupta and Kumar [3] studied the research contribution and impact of Indian Institute of Technology, Roorkee during 1993-2001. Kumbar, Gupta and Dhawan [4] studied the growth and impact of research output of University of Mysore during 1996-2006. Tapaswi [5] studied the growth in the contribution and impact of a research organization (NIO, Goa).Gupta and Sangam [6] studied the contribution and impact of Karnatak University during 1999-2008 and compared its output with three other universities in Karnatak namely Mysore, Mangalore and Bangalore.

2 OBJECTIVES OF THE STUDY

The main objectives of this study are make a comparative study of the two universities of Karnatak, namely Mysore University and Karnatak University: (i) to analyze the publication output, growth and citation impact; (ii) to assess the share of national and international collaboration, its potential collaborating partners and countries; (iii) to study the distribution of its research output and impact under broad and narrow subject fields; (iv) to study the contribution and citation impact of its most productive authors and (v) to study the productivity of its most productive journals.

3 METHODOLOGY AND DATABASE USED

This study is based on the publication data retrieved from the Scopus international multidisciplinary bibliographical database [http://www.scopus.com/search/] for the 10 years (2001-10). The string used to retrieve the main data of the two universities was as follows:

(AF-ID ("Karnatak University India" 60029908)) and (LIMIT-TO
(PUBYEAR, 2011) or LIMIT-TO (PUBYEAR, 2010) or LIMIT-TO
(PUBYEAR, 2009) or LIMIT-TO (PUBYEAR, 2008) or LIMIT-TO
(PUBYEAR, 2007) or LIMIT-TO(PUBYEAR,2006) or LIMIT-TO
(PUBYEAR, 2005)or LIMIT-TO(PUBYEAR, 2004) or LIMIT-TO
(PUBYEAR, 2003) or LIMIT-TO (PUBYEAR, 2002))

The search using the above keywords becomes finally our main string. For searching on subjects, the following string was used:

(AF-ID ("Karnatak University India" 60029908)) and (LIMIT-TO (PUBYEAR, 2010) or LIMIT-TO (PUBYEAR, 2009) or LIMIT-TO (PUBYEAR, 2008) or LIMIT-TO (PUBYEAR, 2007) or LIMIT-TO (PUBYEAR, 2006) or LIMIT-TO (PUBYEAR,2005) or LIMIT-TO (PUBYEAR, 2004) or LIMIT-TO (PUBYEAR, 2003) or LIMIT-TO (PUBYEAR, 2002) or LIMIT-TO(PUBYEAR, 2001)) and (LIMIT-TO (SUBJAREA,"CHEM"))

For searching and calculating the total international collaborative papers, a separate search strategy, which combines India's collaboration with all major countries was prepared and this string was combined with the main string to generate the two universities total international collaborative output. For calculating national collaborating links, manual efforts were made to count these links with different type of institutions. For analyzing individual and journals output, the separate search strategies for generating author and journal outputs were developed, which later combined with the main string to generate the desired output. For citations data, three years, two year and one year citations window has been used for computing average citations per paper during 2002-9, 2010 and 2011.

4 ANALYSIS

4.1 Overall Publications Growth, Output and Citation Quality

The Karnatak University published 1615 papers during 2002-11, with an average number of papers per year as 161.5. In comparison, the Mysore University published 2911 with an average number of papers per year as 291.1. In terms of annual average growth rate of publications, the largest (15.09%) was achieved by Mysore University, followed by Karnatak University (9.44%) during 2002-11. In terms of growth of publications from 2002-06 to 2007-11, comparative larger growth (71.30%) was achieved by Mysore University than Karnatak University (37.17%) (Table 1). In terms of citation impact per paper (measured over a three year citation window), comparative higher impact (3.93) was registered by Karnatak University than Mysore University (2.39) during 2002-11. The citation impact per paper decreased from 4.19 to 3.72 in Karnatak University compared to decrease from 2.74 to 2.10 in case of Mysore University from 2002-06 to 2007-11. In terms of h-index, the higher (43) was achieved by Karnatak University, followed by University of Mysore (37) during 2002-11. In share of higher cited papers (25 or more since the publication till November 2012), relatively higher share (73.93%)

was registered by Karnatak University than University of Mysore (66.13%) during 2002-11. Similarly, the share of uncited (zero cited) papers (33.87%) was more in Mysore University compared to Karnatak University (26.07%) during 2002-11(Table 1-2).

Table 1: Overall publications output and citation impact of universities of Mysore and Karnatak, 2002-11

Period	University of Mysore		Karnatak University	
	TP	ACPP	TP	ACPP
2002	168	2.59	109	3.33
2003	137	2.52	128	3.45
2004	194	3.52	138	4.07
2005	228	2.02	131	4.28
2006	346	2.93	193	5.20
2007	366	3.05	178	5.31
2008	256	3.00	137	5.47
2009	333	2.96	184	4.96
2010	414	1.79	207	2.92
2011	469	0.89	210	0.94
2002-06	1073	2.74	699	4.19
2007-11	1838	2.19	916	3.72
2002-11	2911	2.39	1615	3.93

Table 2: Distribution of papers by citations of the of Two Universities of Mysore and Karnatak, 2002-11

Name	Number and Share of Papers in different Citation Range					Total
	100 & more	50-99	25-99	1-24	0	
University of Mysore	3 (0.10%)	14 (0.48%)	69 (2.37%)	1839 (63.17%)	986 (33.87%)	2911 (100.0%)
Karnatak University	5 (0.31%)	27 (1.67%)	95 (5.88%)	1067 (66.07%)	421 (26.07%)	1615 (100.0%)

4.2 National and International Collaboration

The number of cumulative international collaborative papers contributed by Mysore University and Karnatak University were 773 and 248 during 2002-11, constituting 26.55% and 15.36% share respectively of their total university output. The share of international collaborative papers of Mysore University has increased from 18.17% to 31.45%, in contrast to marginally decrease in Karnatak University from 15.74% to 15.07% from 2002-07 to 2007-11 (Table 3). The Mysore University and the Karnatak University collaborated with 47 and 75 countries respectively during 2002-11 (Table 3).

Table 3: Number and share of international collaborative papers of Mysore University and Karnatak University, 2001-10

Period	University of Mysore			Karnatak University		
	TP	ICP	%ICP	TP	ICP	%ICP
2002	168	15	8.93	109	11	10.09
2003	137	14	10.22	128	29	22.66
2004	194	29	14.95	138	14	10.14
2005	228	48	21.05	131	29	22.14
2006	346	89	25.72	193	27	13.99
2007	366	166	45.36	178	36	20.22
2008	256	58	22.66	137	28	20.44
2009	333	73	21.92	184	19	10.33
2010	414	138	33.33	207	24	11.59
2011	469	143	30.49	210	31	14.76
2002-06	1073	195	18.17	699	110	15.74
2007-11	1838	578	31.45	916	138	15.07
2002-11	2911	773	26.55	1615	248	15.36

Among the leading countries collaborating with Mysore University, United States tops the list with 36.87% share (285 papers), followed by Germany (134 papers, 17.34% share), United Kingdom (56 papers, 7.24% share), Japan (50 papers, 6.47% share), Iran (47 papers, 6.08% share), Poland (33 papers, 4.27% share), Denmark (21 papers, 2.72% share), etc. Among the collaborating countries, the share of United Kingdom has decreased from 10.89%, followed by Germany (9.74%), Japan (3.01%), South Korea (2.03%) and Singapore (0.83%), as against increase in case of United States (11.59%), Poland (4.34%), Iran (3.33%), Malaysia and Turkey (2.94% each), China (2.77%), Sweden (1.91%), South Africa (1.90%), France (1.04%), and Denmark (0.20%) from 2002-06 to 2007-11(Table 4).

Among the leading countries collaborating with Karnatak University, South Korea tops the list with 30.24% share (75 papers), followed by United States (57 papers, 22.98% share), United Kingdom (39 papers, 15.73% share), Finland (18 papers, 7.26% share), Australia (15 papers, 6.05% share), Taiwan (13 papers, 5.24% share), Switzerland (12 papers, 4.84% share), etc. Among the collaborating countries, the share of United States has decreased from 15.88%, followed by Switzerland (9.28%), Italy (4.73%), Malaysia (2.91%) and Greece (1.28%), as against increase in case of United Kingdom (20.09%), Finland (6.51%), Australia (5.97%), South Korea (3.70%), Israel, Netherlands, Portugal and Saudi Arabia (3.62% each),Taiwan (2.89%), China (2.53%), Estonia and Germany (1.99% each) from 2002-06 to 20007-11(Table 4).

Table 4: Number and share of collaborating countries in international collaborative papers of Karnatak and Mysore University, 2001-10

Collaborating Country	Karnatak University			Collaborating Country	Mysore University		
	2002-06	2007-11	2002-11		2002-06	2007-11	2002-11
South Korea	31 (28.18)	44 (31.88)	75 (30.24)	USA	55 (28.21)	230 (39.79)	285 (36.87)
USA	35 (31.82)	22 (15.94)	57 (22.98)	Germany	48 (24.62)	86 (14.88)	134 (17.34)
UK	5 (4.55)	34 (24.64)	39 (15.73)	U.K	30 (15.38)	26 (4.50)	56 (7.24)
Finland	4 (3.64)	14 (10.14)	18 (7.26)	Japan	17 (8.72)	33 (5.71)	50 (6.47)
Australia	3 (2.73)	12 (8.70)	15 (6.05)	Iran	7 (3.59)	40 (6.92)	47 (6.08)
Taiwan	4 (3.64)	9 (6.52)	13 (5.24)	Poland	2 (1.03)	31 (5.36)	33 (4.27)
Switzer-land	11 (10.0)	1 (0.72)	12 (4.84)	Denmark	5 (2.56)	16 (2.77)	21 (2.72)
Italy	6 (5.45)	1 ().72)	7 (2.82)	South Korea	8 (4.10)	12 (2.08)	20 (2.59)
China	2 (1.82)	6 (4.35)	8 (3.23)	Singapore	6 (3.08)	13 (2.25)	19 (2.46)
Estonia	1 (0.91)	4 (2.90)	5 (2.02)	China	1 (0.51)	19 (3.29)	20 (2.59)
Israel	-	5 (3.62)	5 (2.02)	Malaysia	-	17 (2.94)	17 (2.20)

Collaborating Country	Karnatak University			Collaborating Country	Mysore University		
	2002-06	2007-11	2002-11		2002-06	2007-11	2002-11
Malaysia	4 (3.64)	1 (0.72)	5 (2.02)	Turkey	-	17 (2.94)	17 (2.20)
Germany	1 (0.91)	4 (2.90)	5 (2.02)	Sweden	1 (0.51)	14 (2.42)	15 (1.94)
Netherlands	-	5 (3.62)	5 (2.02)	South Africa	-	11 (1.90)	11 (1.42)
Portugal	-	5 (3.62)	5 (2.02)	France	1 (0.51)	9 (1.56)	10 (1.29)
Greece	3 (2.73)	2 (1.45)	5 (2.02)				
Saudi Arabia	0 (0.00%)	5 (3.62)	5 (2.02)				
	110	**138**	**248**		**195**	**578**	**773**

4.3 National Collaboration Links

The share of national collaborating links in total university output in Mysore and Karnatak universities were 58.22% and 45.82% during 2002-11. Among total national collaborating links (1695 and 740) of both Mysore University and Karnatak University during 2002-11, the largest number of collaborating links (77.46% and 68.92%) are to academic institutions, followed by 10.32% and 16.35% to research institutions, 6.90% and 9.59% to institutes of national importance, 2.89% and 5.14% to industry, etc. Academic institutions include here universities, colleges, engineering colleges and medical colleges (Table 5).

Mysore University - Across 15 broad subjects, the national collaboration links varies from 0.28% in immunology and microbiology to 0.93% in physics. The national collaborating links trends of Mysore University is also generally reflected across 15 broad subjects, with few exceptions of agricultural and biological sciences, pharmacology, toxicology and pharmaceutics and computer science. The national collaborating links across 15 broad subjects, however, varied from 30.51% to 90.48% in academic institutions, research institutions (0.0% to 52.54%), institutes of national importance (from 0.0% to 18.18%) and industry (0.0% to 8.55%) (Table 6).

Table 5: Overall number and share of national collaborating links to various types of Institutions of Mysore University and Karnatak University, 2002-11

Type of Institution	Number of National Collaborating Links in Institutional Output		Share of National Collaborating Links in Institutional Output	
	Mysore University	Karnatak University	Mysore University	Karnatak University
Academic Institutions (AI)	1313	510	77.46	68.92
Institutes of National Importance (INI)	117	71	6.90	9.59
Research Institutions (RI)	175	121	10.32	16.35
Industry (INDU)	49	38	2.89	5.14
Others	42	7	2.48	0.95
Total National Collaborating Links	1695	740	(100.0)	(100.0)
Total Papers	2911	1615		
Share of National Collaborating Links in Institutional Output	58.23	45.82		

Table 6: Number and share of national collaborating links to various types of institutions across 15 broad subjects under Mysore University, 2002-11

Broad Subject	NCL	TP	% NCL	Share of National Collaborating Links				
				Acad. Inst.	RI	INI	INDU	OTH
Chem	508	908	0.56	83.46	3.54	4.72	7.87	0.39
Bioc	498	711	0.70	80.32	6.43	7.03	1.81	4.42
Phys	647	699	0.93	90.11	3.40	2.32	4.17	0.00
Mate	405	545	0.74	85.43	2.96	5.68	5.19	0.74
Agri	177	451	0.39	30.51	6.21	52.54	7.34	3.39
Phar	152	298	0.51	65.13	11.18	9.87	8.55	5.26
Comp	88	212	0.42	69.32	18.18	4.55	7.95	0.00
Envi	67	164	0.41	82.09	4.48	10.45	1.49	1.49
Engi	88	159	0.55	60.23	10.23	22.73	5.68	1.14
Medi	83	158	0.53	54.22	6.02	22.89	1.20	15.66
Ceng	53	148	0.36	75.47	5.66	7.55	7.55	3.77
Math	42	129	0.33	90.48	0.00	9.52	0.00	0.00
Immu	22	80	0.28	45.45	13.64	22.73	18.18	0.00
Eart	29	62	0.47	58.62	6.90	34.48	0.00	0.00
Ener	21	37	0.57	100.00	0.00	0.00	0.00	0.00

NCL=National Collaborating Links; TP=Total Papers Acad Inst=Academic Institutions; RI=Research Institutions; INI=Institute of National Importance, Indu=Industry

Karnatak University - Across 15 broad subjects, the overall national collaboration links varies from 8.82% in immunology and microbiology to 132.0% in computer science. The overall national collaborating links trends of Karnatak University are also generally reflected across its 15 broad subjects, with few exceptions. The national collaborating links across 15 broad subjects, however, varied from 33.33% to 92.45% in academic institutions, research institutions (0.0% to 35.69%), institutes of national importance (from 1.89% to 39.3%) and industry (0.0% to 833.33%) (Table 7).

Table 7: Number and share of national collaborating links to various types of institutions across 15 broad subjects under Karnatak University, 2002-11

Broad Subject	NCL	TP	% NCL	Share of National Collaborating Links				
				Acad. Inst.	RI	INI	INDU	OTH
Chem	255	708	36.02	48.24	35.69	7.84	8.24	
Bioc	132	255	51.76	71.21	9.85	15.2	2.27	1.52
Phys	216	244	88.52	82.41	6.48	10.2	0.93	
Mate	193	337	57.27	62.69	7.25	23.3	4.66	2.07
Agri	49	221	22.17	67.35	8.16	20.4	4.08	
Phar	50	182	27.47	82	10	2	6.00	
Comp	33	25	132.0	60.61		15.2		
Envi	39	54	72.22	46.15	12.8	20.5	15.38	5.13
Engi	54	84	64.29	70.37	9.26	13	7.41	
Medi	28	53	52.83	42.86	7.14	39.3	3.57	7.14
Ceng	66	206	32.04	43.94	7.58	36.4	12.12	
Math	53	68	77.94	92.45	5.66	1.89	0.00	
Immu	3	34	8.82	33.33		33.3	33.33	
Eart	9	20	45.00	77.78		22.2	0.00	
Ener	7	18	38.89	71.43		14.3	14.29	

NCL=National Collaborating Links; TP=Total Papers Acad Inst=Academic Institutions; RI=Research Institutions; INI=Institute of National Importance, Indu=Industry

4.4 Distribution of Papers by Broad Subject Fields

The largest priority was assigned to physical sciences (1658 papers, 56.96% share) in Mysore University, followed by life sciences (1277 papers, 43.87% share), engineering sciences (946 papers, 33.50% share) and health sciences (169 papers, 5.81% share) during 2001-10. The publication share of the university has increased in engineering sciences by 10.73% and health sciences by 3.44%), as against decrease in life sciences by 5.65% and physical sciences by 2.93% from 2002-06 to 2007-11 (Table 5). Similarly, the largest priority was assigned to physical sciences (1008 papers, 42.41% share) in Karnatak University output, followed by life sciences and engineering sciences (544 papers, 33.68% each) and health sciences (57 papers, 3.53% share) during 2001-10. The publications share of the university has increased in physical sciences by 10.41%, followed by engineering sciences (4.65%), life sciences by 2.13% and health sciences by 1.18% from 2001-05 to 2006-10 (Table 8-9).

Table 8: Distribution of Mysore University output by broad subject areas, 2002-11

Broad Subject	Number of Papers			Share of Papers		
	2002-06	2007-11	2002-11	2002-06	2007-11	2002-11
Physical Science	631	1027	1658	58.81	55.88	56.96
Life Science	509	768	1277	47.44	41.78	43.87
Engineering Science	276	670	946	25.72	36.45	32.50
Health Science	39	130	169	3.63	7.07	5.81
Total	**1073**	**1838**	**2911**	**100.00**	**100.00**	**100.00**

Table 9: Distribution of Karnatak University output by broad subject areas, 2002-11

Broad Subject	Number of Papers			Share of Papers		
	2002-06	2007-11	2002-11	2002-06	2007-11	2002-11
Physical Science	395	613	1008	56.51	66.92	62.41
Life Science	227	317	544	32.47	34.61	33.68
Engineering Science	217	327	544	31.04	35.70	33.68
Health Science	20	37	57	2.86	4.04	3.53
Total	**699**	**916**	**1615**	**100.00**	**100.00**	**100.00**

4.5 Distribution of Papers by Narrow Subject Fields

Physical Sciences - Within physical sciences (comprising of chemistry, physics, environment science, mathematics and earth and planetary sciences), the maximum emphasis in Mysore and Karnatak universities has been on chemistry (31.19% and 43.84%), followed by physics (24.01% and 15.11%), environment science (5.63% and 5.82%), mathematics (4.43% and 4.21%) and earth and planetary sciences (2.13% and 1.24%).

Table 10: Profile of Mysore and Karnatak Universities in Physical Sciences, 2002-11

	Mysore University				Karnatak University			
	No. of Papers	% of Papers	No. of Citations	ACPP	No. of Papers	% of Papers	No. of Citations	ACPP
	02-06	07-11	02-11	02-06	07-11	02-11	02-06	07-11
Chem	908	31.19	2527	2.78	708	43.84	2775	3.92
Phys	699	24.01	1716	2.45	244	15.11	739	3.03
Envi	164	5.63	228	1.39	94	5.82	178	1.89
Math	129	4.43	84	0.65	68	4.21	86	1.26
Eart	62	2.13	106	1.71	20	1.24	60	3.00
	2911				1615			

In terms of average citation per paper, the performance of physical science subjects are: chemistry (2.78 and 3.92), physics (2.45 and 3:03), environment science (1.39 and 1.89), mathematics (0.65 and 1.26) and earth and planetary sciences (1.71 and 3.00). Among the two universities, in terms of institutional share, Karnatak University has a edge in chemistry and environment science, in contrast to edge over physics, mathematics and earth and planetary sciences of Mysore University. The Karnatak University has however, performed better in terms of citation impact in all the five physical science subjects among these two universities (Table 10).

Life Sciences - Within life sciences (comprising of agricultural and biological sciences, biochemistry, genetics and molecular biology, pharmacology, toxicology and pharmaceutics and immunology and microbiology), the maximum emphasis in Mysore and Karnatak universities has been on biochemistry, genetics and molecular biology (24.42% and 15.79%), followed by agricultural and biological sciences (15.49% and 13.68%), pharmacology, toxicology and pharmaceutics (10.24% and 11.27%) and immunology and microbiology (2.75% and 2.10%). In terms of average citation per paper, the performance of life science is: biochemistry, genetics and molecular biology (3.04 and 2.89), agricultural and biological sciences (2.57 and 2.89), pharmacology, toxicology and pharmaceutics (4.49 and 6.49) and immunology and microbiology (2.30 and 2.74). Among the two universities, in terms of institutional share, Mysore University has a edge in biochemistry, genetics and molecular biology, agricultural and biological sciences and immunology and microbiology, in contrast to edge over pharmacology, toxicology and pharmaceutics of Karnatak University. The Karnatak University has however, performed better in terms of citation impact in three life science subjects, namely agricultural and biological sciences, pharmacology, toxicology and pharmaceutics and immunology and microbiology as against in only biochemistry, genetics and molecular biology by Mysore University (Table 11).

Table 11: Profile of Mysore and Karnatak Universities in Life Sciences, 2002-11

	Mysore University				Karnatak University			
	No. of Papers	% of Papers	No. of Citations	ACPP	No. of Papers	% of Papers	No. of Citations	ACPP
	02-06	07-11	02-11	02-06	07-11	02-11	02-06	07-11
Agri	451	15.49	1158	2.57	221	13.68	638	2.89
Bioc	711	24.42	2160	3.04	255	15.79	1149	4.51
Phar	298	10.24	1339	4.49	182	11.27	1182	6.49
Immu	80	2.75	184	2.30	34	2.10	93	2.74
	2911				**1615**			

Engineering Sciences - Within engineering sciences (comprising of engineering, material science, computer science, chemical engineering and energy), the maximum emphasis of Mysore university has been on material science (18.72%), followed by computer science (7.28%), engineering (5.39%), chemical engineering (5.08%) and energy (1.27%) during 2002-11. On the other hand, the maximum emphasis of Karnatak University has been on material science (20.87%), followed by chemical engineering (12.76%), engineering (5.20%), computer science (2.04%) and energy (1.27%) during 2002-11. In terms of average citation per paper, the citation impact of Mysore University and Karnatak University in engineering sciences is: material science (2.76 and 5.22), chemical engineering (2.95 and 6.79), engineering (2.24 and 2.69), computer science (1.56 and 2.45) and energy (0.84 and 5.44). Among the two universities, in terms of institutional share, Mysore University has a edge in engineering, computer science and energy, in contrast to edge over material science and chemical engineering of Karnatak University. The Karnatak University has however, performed better in terms of citation impact in all the five engineering science subjects (Table 12).

Table 12: Profile of Mysore and Karnatak Universities in Engineering Sciences, 2002-11

	Mysore University				Karnatak University			
	No. of Papers	% of Papers	No. of Citations	ACPP	No. of Papers	% of Papers	No. of Citations	ACPP
	02-06	07-11	02-11	02-06	07-11	02-11	02-06	07-11
Mate	545	18.72	1502	2.76	337	20.87	1760	5.22
Engi	157	5.39	351	2.24	84	5.20	226	2.69
Comp	212	7.28	330	1.56	33	2.04	81	2.45
Ceng	148	5.08	437	2.95	206	12.76	1399	6.79
Ener	37	1.27	31	0.84	18	1.11	98	5.44
	2911				**1615**			

Health Sciences: Within health sciences, we have included only medicine. In this subject, the institutional share of Mysore University and Karnatak University are 5.43% and 3.28% during 2002-11. In terms of average citation per paper, the citation impacts of these two universities are 2.72 and 3.13. Among the two universities, in terms of institutional share, Mysore University has a edge, but in terms of citation impact, Karnatak University has a edge in medicine (Table 13)

Table 13: Profile of Mysore and Karnatak Universities in Medicine, 2002-11

	Mysore University				Karnatak University			
	No. of Papers	% of Papers	No. of Citations	ACPP	No. of Papers	% of Papers	No. of Citations	ACPP
	02-06	07-11	02-11	02-06	07-11	02-11	02-06	07-11
Medi	158	5.43	430	2.72	53	3.28	166	3.13
	2911				**1615**			

4.6 Productivity and Citation Impact of Top 15 Most Productive Authors

Mysore University - The profile of the top 15 most productive authors of the Mysore University is given in Table 14, along with their productivity, affiliated department, citations received, average citations per paper and h-index. The 15 authors together have contributed 2017 papers (varying from 55 to 461), constituting 69.29% of the total university output and with the average productivity per author of 194.07 during 2002-11. Only two authors have scored higher productivity than the average productivity of all 15 authors. They are H.S. Yathirajan with 461 papers and B. Narayana with 317 papers. The average citation per paper received by these 15 authors was 2.54 (varying from 1.16 to 7.27). Only 5 authors have registered higher impact factor per paper than the average of all 15 authors. They are K. Byrappa with citation per paper of 7.27, followed by C. Ranganathaiah (3.54), K.S. Rangappa (3.35), D.C. Gowd (3.14) and B. Narayana (2.97). The average h-index registered by these 15 authors was 10.67 (varying from 5 to 17). Seven authors have registered higher h-index than the average h-index of all authors. They are: K.S.Rangappa with h-index of 17, followed by H.S.Yathirajan (16), K. Byrappa (13), C. Ranganathaiah (12), H.S. Shetty (12), B. Narayana (12) and P. Nagaraja (12).

Table 14: Productivity and citation profile of to 15 authors of Mysore University, 2002-11

Name	Department/ Center	TP	TC	ACPP	H-Index
H.S.Yathirajan	Chemistry	461	1173	2.54	16
B. Narayana	Chemistry	317	940	2.97	12
K.S.Rangappa	Chemistry	185	619	3.35	17
K. Basavaiah	Chemistry	166	270	1.63	10
J.S.Prasad	Physics	124	144	1.16	7
B.K. Sarojini	Chemistry	120	302	2.52	10
M.A. Sridhar	Physics	111	183	1.65	8
P. Nagaraja	Chemistry	85	175	2.06	12
C. Ranganathaiah	Physics	74	262	3.54	12
S. Naveen	Physics	68	83	1.22	5
D.S. Guru	Computer Science	67	126	1.88	9
H.S. Shetty	Applied Botany	65	165	2.54	13
D.C.Gowda	Chemistry	63	198	3.14	9
K. Byrappa	Materials Science	56	407	7.27	13
H.D. Revanasiddappa	Chemistry	55	70	1.27	7
Total		**2017**	**5117**	**2.54**	**10.67**
Total of the University		**2911**			
Share of Top 15 Authors in University Output		69.29			

TP=Total Papers; TC=Total Citations; ACPP=Average Citations per Paper

Karnatak University - The profile of the top 15 most productive authors of the Karnatak University is given in Table 15, along with their productivity, affiliated department, citations received, average citations per paper and h-index. The 15 authors together have contributed 1079 papers (varying from 36 to 233), constituting 66.81% of the total university output and with the average productivity per author of 71.93 during 2002-11. Only three authors have scored higher productivity than the average productivity of all 15 authors. They are T.M. Aminabhavi with 233 papers, S.T. Nandibewoor (184 papers) and H.N. Murthy with 75 papers. The average citation per paper received by these 15 authors was 5.56 (varying from 1.72 to 11.59). Only 6 authors have registered higher impact factor per paper than the average of all 15 authors. They are S.A. Patil with citation per paper of 11.59, followed by M.Sairam (9.02), T.M. Aminabhavi (8.51), J. Seetharamappa (6.80), N.N. Mallikarjuna (6.56) and M.Y. Kariduraganavar (6.17). The average h-index registered by these 15 authors was 14.07 (varying from 8 to 36). Six authors have registered higher h-index than the average h-index of all authors. They are: T.M. Aminabhavi with h-index of 36, followed by M. Sairam (18), J. Seetharamappa (17), S.A. Patil (16), H.N. Murthy (15) and S.T. Nandibewoor (15).

Table 15: Productivity and citation profile of to 15 authors of Karnatak University, 2002-11

Name	Department/ Center	TP	TC	ACPP	H-Index
T.M.Aminabhavi	Polymer Sc.	233	1982	8.51	36
S.T.Nandibewoor	Chemistry	184	563	3.06	15
H.N.Murthy	Botany	75	334	4.45	15
M.V.Kulkarni	Chemistry	64	150	2.34	9
J.Seetharamappa	Chemistry	59	401	6.80	17
K.B.Gudasi	Chemistry	54	205	3.80	12
S.A.Chitatadar	Chemistry	53	173	3.26	9
S.A.Patil	Polymer Sc.	51	591	11.59	16
K.M.Hosamani	Polymer Sc.	49	254	5.18	12
M.Y.Kariduraganavar	Polymer Sc.	48	296	6.17	14
B.G.Mulimani	Physics	45	154	3.42	10
M.Sairam	Polymer Sc.	45	406	9.02	18
N.N.Mallikarjuna	Polymer Sc.	45	295	6.56	10
V.K. Revankar	Chemistry	38	137	3.61	10
B.A.Shanbag	Zoology	36	62	1.72	8
Total		**1079**	**6003**	**5.56**	**14.07**
Total of the University		1615			
Share of Top 15 Authors in University Output		66.81			

TP=Total Papers; TC=Total Citations; ACPP=Average Citations per Paper

4.7 Media of Communication

Mysore University - The list of top 15 source journals is shown in Table 11. The share of the top 15 most productive journals in university output constitute 28.98% share of the total university output, which increased from 28.98% during 2002-06 to 30.47% during 2007-11 (Table 16).

Table 16: List of top 15 most productive Journals of the Mysore University, 2002-11

Sl. No.	Name of the Journal	Number of Papers		
		2001-10	2001-05	2006-10
1	Acta Crystallographica Section E. Structure Reports Online	106	329	435
2	Analytical Sciences X-Ray Structure Analysis Online	50	8	58
3	Archives of Phytopathology & Plant Protection	6	34	40
4	Journal of Applied Polymer Science	16	23	39
5	Molecular Crystals & Liquid Crystals	10	24	34
6	Journal of Chemical Crystallography	10	22	32
7	Asian Journal of Microbiology Biotechnology & Environmental Sciences	18	14	32
8	E-Journal of Chemistry	0	29	29
9	Indian Journal of Chemical Technology	22	6	28
10	Nature Environment & Pollution Technology	0	27	27
11	Indian Journal of Sericulture	6	20	26
12	Current Science	14	12	26
13	Indian Journal of Chemistry. Section B. Organic & Medicinal Chemistry	22	3	25
14	Synthetic Communication	14	6	20
15	Oxidation Communication	17	3	20
	Total	**311**	**560**	**871**
	Total of Country	**1073**	**1838**	**2911**
	Share of Top 15 Journals in Country Output	28.98	30.47	29.92

Karnatak University - The list of top 15 source journals is shown in Table 11. The share of the top 15 journals in university output constitute 28.23% share of the total university output, which declined from 34.91% during 2002-06 to 23.14% during 2007-11 (Table 17).

Table 17: List of top 15 most productive Journals of Karnatak University, 2002-11

Sl. No	Name of the Journal	Number of Papers		
		2001-10	2001-05	2006-10
1	Journal of Applied Polymer Science	62	30	92
2	Transition Metal Chemistry	25	19	44
3	Acta Crystallographica Section E. Structure Reports Online	18	23	41
4	Spectrochimica Acta. Part A. Molecular & Biomolecular Spectroscopy	9	27	36
5	European Journal of Medicinal Chemistry	3	23	26
6	Journal of Basic and Clinical Physiology and Pharmacology	18	7	25
7	Journal of Indian Chemical Society	15	8	23
8	Indian Journal of Chemistry. Section B. Organic & Medicinal Chemistry	17	6	23
9	Journal of Membrane Science	16	7	23
10	Polymer News	23	0	23
11	Current Science	10	11	21
12	Industrial and Engineering Chemistry Research	5	16	21
13	Journal of Coordination Chemistry	0	20	20
14	Indian Journal of Chemistry. Section A. Inorganic, Physical, Theoretical & Analytical Chemistry	10	9	19
15	Oxidation Communications	13	6	19
Total		**244**	**212**	**456**
Total of Country		**699**	**916**	**1615**
Share of Top 15 Journals in Country Output		34.91	23.14	28.23

5 SUMMARY AND CONCLUSION

The Mysore University and the Karnatak University have published 2911 and 1615 papers during 2002-11, witnessing an annual average productivity of 291.1 and 161.5 papers per year and an annual average growth rate of 15.09% and 9.44%, respectively. The citation impact per paper registered by these two universities (Mysore and Karnatak) were 2.39 and 3.93, decreasing from 2.74 to 2.10 and from 4.19 and 3.72 from 2002-06 to 2007-11. The h-index of the Mysore and Karnatak universities were 37 and 43 during 2002-11. The Mysore and Karnatak universities registered the high cited papers share (25 or more citations since the publication till November 2012) of 66.13% and 73.93% and the share of zero cited papers as 33.87% and 26.07%, respectively. The share of international collaborative papers in institutional output of these two universities were 26% and 15.36% during 2002-11, increasing from 18.47% to 31.45% in case of the Mysore University and decreasing from 15.75% to 15.07% in case of the Karnatak University from 2002-07 to 2007-11. The Mysore University and the Karnatak University participated in international collaborative research by collaborating with 47 and 75 countries respectively during 2002-11. In contrast to international collaborative share, the share of national collaborating links were 58.22% and 45.82% of the Mysore and Karnatak universities during 2002-11, the largest number of collaborating links (77.46% and 68.92%), however, were to academic institutions, followed by research institutions (10.32% and 16.35%), institutes of national importance (6.90% and 9.59%), industry (2.89% and 5.14%), etc.

In both the Mysore University and the Karnatak University, the largest priority was assigned to physical sciences (with 56.96% and 42.41% share), followed by life sciences (43.87% and 33.68% share), engineering sciences (33.50% and 33.68%) and health sciences (5.81% and 3.53%). Among the two universities in terms of institutional share in 15 broad subjects during 2002-11, the Mysore University has a edge in 10 broad subjects, namely physics, mathematics, earth and planetary sciences, biochemistry, genetics and molecular biology, agricultural and biological sciences, immunology and microbiology, engineering, computer science, energy and medicine, in contrast to Karnatak University in 5 subjects, namely chemistry, environment science, pharmacology, toxicology and pharmaceutics, material science and chemical engineering. Among the two universities in terms of citation impact in 15 broad subjects during 2002-11, Karnatak University has an edge in 14 broad subjects out of 15, such as physics, chemistry, mathematics, environment science, earth and planetary science, agricultural and biological sciences, pharmacology, toxicology and pharmaceutics, immunology and microbiology, engineering, computer science, energy, material science, chemical engineering and medicine, in contrast to the Mysore University only in one subject, namely biochemistry, genetics and molecular biology.

The top 15 most productive authors have together contributed 2017 papers (varying from 55 to 461) and 1079 papers (varying from 36 to 233) in the Mysore University and Karnatak University, constituting 69.29% and 66.81% publication share respectively of their total university output and with the average productivity per author of 194.07 and 71.93 during 2002-11.

From the above observations, it was observed that the Mysore University has contributed more paper in terms of overall research output, research output across subjects, international collaboration share, institutional share in 10 broad subjects and average author productivity per paper, but the Karnatak University has certainly faired better in terms of citation impact in overall output as well across 14 out of 15 broad subjects considered here for analysis. Although the Mysore University has contributed comparatively larger share of international collaborative papers than Karnatak University, but it has not helped in improving its citation quality. Both the universities have developed extensive national collaborating links, but mainly confined to academic institutions (includes universities, colleges, engineering colleges and medical colleges). However, the Karnatak University has comparatively larger share of its national collaborative links with institutes of national importance, research institutions and industry than the Mysore University. In case of both universities, the collaboration links to institutes of national importance, research institutions and industry are generally weak and more efforts should be made by them to increase these links for increasing their research output and citation quality.

REFERENCES

1. Jeevan, V.K.J. and Gupta, B.M. (2002) A scientometric profile of research output from Indian Institute of Technology, Kharagpur. *Scientometric,* 53(1): 165-68
2. Jeevan, V.K.J. and Gupta, B.M. (2001) R&D Performance of different departments of IIT, Kharagpur. *Journal of Library and Information Science*, 26(2): 129-43
3. Singh, Y.; Gupta, B.M. and Kumar, S. (2005) Research contributions and impact of research of Indian Institute of Technology, Roorkee, 1993-2001. *Annals of Library & Information Studies*, 52(1): 8-14
4. Kumbar, Mallinath; Gupta, B.M. and Dhawan, S.M. (2008) Growth and impact of research output of University of Mysore, 1996-2006: A case study. *Annals of Library & Information Studies*, 55(3): 185-95
5. Tapaswi, M.P. (2011) Growth in the productivity of an organization-Tracing the cause. **In**. S.L. Sangam et. al., Editors. *Scientometric Studies. Dharwad; Department of Library & Information Science*, Karnatak University. 56-62
6. Gupta, B.M. and Sangam, S.L. (2011) Contribution and impact of Karnatak University publications during 1999-2008: A study in comparison with three other universities in Karnatak. **In**. S.L. Sangam et. al. Editors. *Scientometric Studies. Dharwad; Department of Library & Information Science*, Karnatak University. 89-113

8

Contribution and Impact of Indian Agricultural Universities: A Performance: Analysis using Scientometric Techniques, 2007-11

B.M. Gupta; Anurag Saxena and ***P. Visakhi***

The study examined the contribution of twenty agricultural universities to the mainstream scientific literature during 2007-20011 along two distinct, but inter-related dimensions of quantity (number of papers, number of international collaborative papers) and quality of research output (assessed through the citations received) A number of measures are used for inter-field and inter-university comparisons. Inter-field comparisons are made at the level of 10 macro subject fields.

KEYWORDS: Indian Agricultural Universities, Impact of research, International Collaboration, Inter-field comparisons, Inter-university comparison

1 INTRODUCTION

Agriculture is the dominant sector of the Indian economy, growing at an average rate of 2.8 per cent. The sector provides the principal means of livelihood for over 58.4 per cent of India's population and contributes approximately one-fifth of total gross domestic product (GDP). Agriculture accounts for about 10 per cent of the total export earnings and provides raw material to a large number of industries. India is blessed with favorable climatic conditions for the production of a wide variety of crops. The country boasts of having the largest share of cultivated land, amounting to nearly 52 per cent of its total area. India is the second-largest producer of food in the world and holds the potential of being the biggest on global food and agriculture canvas [1].

Agricultural education forms the foundation for the development of requisite manpower for research, education, training, and transfer of technology to the field and extension activities throughout the country. Agriculture is a State subject and the prime responsibility for agricultural research, education, extension education and its development lies with the States. However, as the apex organization in the country, ICAR coordinates the research and extension education. The imparting of agriculture education and research in India at the central level is the sole responsibility of the ICAR. Under the ICAR, the Education Division which is headed by the Deputy Director General (Education) and five Assistant Directors General namely, ADG (HRD-I), ADG (HRD-II), ADG (Education Planning and Development), ADG (Accreditation), and

ADG (Home Science) - The Education Division of the ICAR since 1995 onwards conducts the All India Entrance Examination (AIEEA) for admission to 15 per cent of the seats reserved in SAUs, CUs (i.e., AMU, BHU, Biswa Bharti, Nagaland University, and CAU, Imphal) for UG degree (BSc, BTech., B.F. Sc, etc.) in agricultural sciences, namely, horticulture, agriculture engineering, dairy technology, forestry, food sciences, fishery sciences, home sciences, sericulture, agriculture marketing and cooperation. In addition to above activities, the Education Division of the ICAR also looks into the various important activities for the agriculture education in the country such as accreditation for quality assurance, global competitiveness in human resource development, distance education for reaching to the un-reached people [2].

The National Agricultural Education System (NAES) under the control of ICAR, New Delhi is the largest network of agricultural education and research in the whole world. It comprises of SAUs and their constituent colleges and the research institutes partially funded and controlled by

ICAR, which impart education, research and extension in all fields of agriculture science and technology and their allied fields. At present there are 210 constituent colleges of 44 SAUs and one central agricultural university (CAU), 5 deemed-to-be-universities (DUs), 17 national research centres (NRC), 50 central research institutes (CRI), 6 national bureaus (NBs), 25 project directorates (PDs) and 78 All India Coordinate Research Projects (AICRP) all functioning under the control of ICAR. In addition, about 50 agricultural colleges affiliated to 16 general universities and 7 Indian Institutes of Technology (IIT) are also imparting education and research in agriculture science and technology [2].

Our study makes an attempt to evaluate the role and contribution of 20 most productive agricultural universities of the country in the production of knowledge in the agricultural sciences and its allied disciplines. This evaluation is based on a number of bibliometric indicators, articles contributed to the mainstream literature as covered in the Scopus database during 2007-11, institutional specialization as reflected in institutional share and inter-institutional and international co-authorship links. Inter-institutional cooperation is visualized along two dimensions: (i) cooperation links of an institution with all other type institutions in different research field and (ii) cooperation links of an institution with other top 20 Indian agricultural universities covered in the study in different fields of study. The first dimension is concerned with the choice of research fields in terms of national collaboration, whereas the second dimension is concerned with the choice of partner institutions in India and abroad for research collaboration. A number of quantitative and qualitative indicators, based on publication counts and citations received and co-authorship links of research papers have been used to evaluate the most productive agricultural universities in India.

2 LITERATURE REVIEW

Sarkhel and Choudhury [3] analysed 2807 papers from Bidhan Chandra Krishi Viswavidalaya derived from CAB Abstracts from 1993-2007. It analyses department-wise and subject-wise quantum of publications, authorship pattern and journals used for publications are identified. Hussain and Mushtaq [4] analysed 19260 papers of 18 central universities with a view to analyze year-wise and subjects wise distribution of publications, the modes of communication, the most prolific authors, language used and identification of the preferences of source titles for communication. Sevukan, Nagarajan,and Sharma [5] analysed 348 records in plant sciences by faculty members of central universities derived from SCI, with a focus on document type, authorship pattern, collaboration at different levels, author and journal productivities, etc. Using Pubmed and SCI databases, Sevukan and Sharma [6] analyses 334 records from 1997-2006 of biotechnology faculties of 10 central universities with a view to ascertain the growth of literature, source of publications, identification of prolific authors, institutions and journals, etc. Anitha [7] studied the growth of literature, sources of publications, identification of prolific authors, institutions, core journals, etc,. in the field of biology by faculties in central universities of India for the period 2000–10. Nagpal [8] examined the contribution of Indian universities to the mainstream scientific literature during 1987–1989 along two distinct, but inter-related dimensions of quantity (number of papers) and quality of research output (assessed through the impact factors of journals). A number of relative indicators are constructed for inter-field and inter-institution comparisons Inter-field comparisons are made at the level of eight macro-fields Inter-institution comparisons cover thirty three institutions which had published at least 150 articles in three years.

3 OBJECTIVES

The study seek to examine the patterns of research and scientific cooperation of twenty most productive agricultural universities in India during the five year period (2007-11), based on publications covered in refereed journals as covered in Scopus international multidisciplinary bibliographic database, using few bibliometric indicators. The study is concerned with following issues: (i) What is the contribution of these agricultural universities to mainstream literature in agriculture and allied research fields?; (ii) What are the linkages of agricultural universities among themselves and with institutions abroad?; What are the similarities and differences among the agricultural universities in the emphasis given to different scientific fields in their RandD?; and What are the similarities and differences among the agricultural universities in the choice of scientific fields for inter-institutional and international cooperation?

4 METHODOLOGY

This study used Scopus International Database [http://www.scopus.com/search/] to extract relevant data on twenty agricultural universities for the last 5 years (2007-11). Separate search strategies were developed of each university for analyzing its total output, citation impact, international collaboration and subject-wise output. These search strategies were combined to get desired combined output of all 20 agricultural universities. For citations data, three years, two years, one year citation windows have been used for computing average citations per paper in all papers during 2007-09, 2010 and 2011. For example, for papers published in 2007 to 2009, citation window is three years. For papers published in 2010, citation window is two years from 2010-2012, and for papers published in 2011 citation window is one year 2011-12. For identifying international collaborative papers, a separate search strategy was prepared. For national collaboration linkages, manual count of linkages with different types of institutions of the address field was undertaken. For classification of data under various subjects, Scopus classification as provided in the database has been used. The study was restricted to 10 main scientific fields. There is some overlapping of papers under these subject areas. As a result, if we count the number of papers published under these subjects, it comes out more than the cumulative publication output of individual university.

5 ANALYSIS

The 20 Indian top agricultural universities together have published 9272 papers, constituting 2.75% of the Indian research output during 2007-11. The research output of these 20 agricultural universities increased from 1701 in 2007 to 2112 papers in 2011, witnessing an annual average growth rate of 5.71%.

Table 1: Total output and International Collaboration, 2007-11

Year	TP	ICP	%ICP
2007	1701	230	13.52
2008	1720	179	10.41
2009	1738	162	9.32
2010	2001	238	11.89
2011	2112	240	11.36
Total	**9272**	**1049**	**11.31**

5.1 Productivity, Citation Impact and Collaboration

5.1.1 Productivity

On adding individual productivity, impact and international papers of 20 top agricultural universities during 2007-11, their total output consists of 10539 papers, varying from 138 to 1588, and witnessing an average productivity per organization of 526.95. Five universities have produced more papers than the average productivity of all universities. These are Indian Agricultural Research Institute, Delhi (IARI-DELHI) with 1588 papers, followed by Indian Veterinary Research Institute, Bareillly (IVRI-BAREILLY) (1413 papers), Punjab Agricultural University, Ludhiana (PUNJAU-LUDH) (1083 papers), GB Pant University of Agriculture and Technology, Nainital (GBPUAT-NAIN) (871 papers) and CCS Haryana Agricultural University, HIsar (CCHAU-HISAR) (787 papers) (Table 2).

Table 2: Publication profile of top 20 agricultural universities, 2007-11

Name	Abbreviation	2007-11					
		TP	TC	ACPP	HI	ICP	% ICP
Indian Agricultural Research Institute, Delhi	IARI-DELHI	1588	4698	2.96	28	219	13.79
Indian Veterinary Research Institute, Bareilly	IVRI-BAREILLY	1413	2701	1.91	19	108	7.64

Name	Abbreviation	2007-11					
		TP	TC	ACPP	HI	ICP	% ICP
Punjab Agricultural University, Ludhiiana	PUNJAU-LUDH	1083	1939	1.79	20	152	14.04
GB Pant University of Agricul-ture & Techno-logy, Nainital	GBPUAT-NAIN	871	1122	1.29	15	72	8.27
CCS Haryana Agricultural University, Hisar	CCSHAU-HISAR	787	862	1.10	14	83	10.55
Tamilnadu Agricultural University, Coimbatore	TAMILAU-COIM	771	1414	1.83	18	137	17.77
National Dairy Research Institute, Karnal	NDRI-KARN	657	1358	2.07	17	66	10.05
Tamilnadu Veterinary & Animal Science University, Chennai	TAMVASU-CHENN	591	639	1.08	15	33	5.58
University of Agricul-tural Sciences, Bangalore	UAS-BANG	422	847	2.01	14	116	27.49
Maharana Pratap University of Agricul-ture & Techno-logy, Udaipur	MPUAT-UDAIP	398	417	1.05	9	31	7.79
West Bengal University of Animal & Fishery Science, Kolkata	WBUAFS-KOLK	252	550	2.18	13	14	5.56
Kerala Agricultural University, Hisa	KERAU-TRISS	227	342	1.51	10	23	10.13
Rajasthan Agricultural University, Bikaner	RAJAU-BIKA	220	171	0.78	6	6	2.73
Dr YSP University of Horticult-ure & Forestry, Solan	DYSPUHF-SOLA	220	196	0.89	7	15	6.82
Orissa University of Agricul-ture & Techno-logy, Bhuba-neswar	ORISUAT-BHUB	214	182	0.85	7	11	5.14
Acharya NG Ranga Agri-cultural University, Hyderabad	ANGRAU-HYDE	191	298	1.56	10	20	10.47
Bidhan Chandra Krishi Viswa-vidyalaya, Mohanpur	BKCV-MOHAN	187	347	1.86	9	13	6.95
Sher-e-Kashmir University of Agricul-tural Science & Techno-logy, Jammu	SKUAST-JAMM	163	126	0.77	6	15	9.20
CSK Himachal Pradesh Krishi Viswavidyalaya, Palampur	CSKHPKV-PALAM	146	169	1.16	8	13	8.90
Assam Agricultural University, Jorhatt	ASSAU-JORH	138	174	1.26	8	15	10.87
	Total (526.95)	**10539**	**18552**	**1.76**	**12.65**	**1162**	**11.03**

TP=Total Papers; TC=Total Citations; ACPP=Average Citation Per Paper; HI=h--index; ICP=International Collaborative Papers

The total papers (10539) of these 20 agricultural universities have received 18552 citations on a three year citation window, registering an average citation per paper of 1.76 (varying from 0.77 to 2.96). Eight organizations have registered higher citation impact per paper than the average impact of all universities. These are Indian Agricultural Research Institute, Delhi (IARI-DELHI) with a citation impact per paper of 2.76, followed by West Bengal University of Animal and Fishery Science, Kolkata (WBUAFS-KOLK)(2.18), National Dairy Research Institute, Karnal (NDRI-KARN)(2.07), University of Agricultural Sciences, Bangalore (UAS-BANG)(2.01), Indian Veterinary Research Institute, Bareilly (IVRI-BAREILLY)(1.91), Bidhan Chandra Krishi Viswavidyalaya, Mohanpur (BKCV-MOHAN)(1.86), Tamilnadu Agricultural University, Coimbatore (TAMILAU-COIM)(1.83) and Punjab Agricultural University, Ludhiiana (PUNJAU-LUDH)(1.79). The average h-index registered by these 20 agricultural universities was 12.65, varying from 6 to 28. Ten organizations have registered higher h-index values than the average h-index of all universities. They are IARI-DELHI with h-index value of 28, followed by PUNJAU-LUDH (20), IVRI-BAREILLY (19), TAMILAU-COIM (18), NDRI-KARN (17), GBPUAT-NAIN and TAMVASU-CHENN (15 each), UAS-BANG and CCSHAU-HISAR (14 each) and WBUAFS-KOLK (13).

5.1.2 International Collaboration

The 20 universities together have published 1049 international collaborative papers, constituting 11.31% share in the total output of these universities, decreasing from 13.52% in 2007 to 11.36% in 2011. The 20 agricultural universities together collaborated with 83 countries of the world during 2007-11. Around 24 countries have published 10 and more collaborative papers. Of these 25 countries, the largest number and share (32.32%) of papers was published with United States, followed by UK (10.39% share), Germany (9.25% share), Australia (7.91% share), China (6.96% share), Canada (6.67% share), Iran, South Korea, Philippines and Japan (with publication share varying from 4.77% to 5.43%), Ethiopia, France, Taiwan, Switzerland and Netherlands (with publication share varying from 2.00% to 2.38%) and Spain, Kenya, Sri Lanka, Pakistan, Bangladesh, Sweden, Singapore and Malaysia (with publication share varying from 0.95% to 1.72%) (Table 3).

Among the most productive foreign organizations collaborating with Indian agricultural universities during 2007-11, the largest number of papers (51) comes from International Rice Research Institute, Philippines, followed by Kansas State University, Manhattan, USA and University of Florida, USA (18 papers each),

University of Adelaide, Australia (17 papers), University of Western Australia (16 papers), Wageningen University Research Center, Netherlands, Technische Universitat Munchen, Germany and Gyeongsang Nationl University, South Korea (15 papers each), Centro Internacional de Mejoramiento de Maiz y Trigo and University of Saskatchewan, Canada (14 papers each), McGill University, Canada (13 papers), USDA Agricultural Research Service, Washington DC, USA, University of Manitoba, Canada, City University of Hong Kong, China and University of Kentucky, USA (11 papers each) (Table 4)

Table 3: Share of various countries in the total International Collaborative papers of agricultural universities, 2007-11

Collaborating Country	No. of Papers	% Share of Papers	Collaborating Country	No. of Papers	% Share of Papers
USA	339	32.32	Taiwan	24	2.29
UK	109	10.39	Switzerland	22	2.10
Germany	97	9.25	Netherlands	21	2.00
Australia	83	7.91	Spain	18	1.72
China	73	6.96	Kenya	15	1.43
Canada	70	6.67	Sri Lanka	14	1.33
Iran	57	5.43	Pakistan	12	1.14
South Korea	52	4.96	Bangladesh	11	1.05
Philippines	52	4.96	Sweden	11	1.05
Japan	50	4.77	Singapore	11	1.05
Ethiopia	25	2.38	Malaysia	10	0.95
France	24	2.29	Thailand	10	0.95
Mexico	24	2.29	**Total**	**1049**	**100.00**

Table 4: Most productive foreign organizations collaborating with Indian agricultural universities, 2007-11

Sl. No.	Name of Foreign Organization	No. of Papers
1	International Rice Research Institute, Philippines	51
2	Kansas State University, Manhattan, USA	18
3	University of Florida, USA	18
4	University of Adelaide, Australia	17
5	University of Western Australia	16
6	Wageningen University Research Center, Netherlands	15
7	Technische Universitat Munchen, Germany	15

Sl. No.	Name of Foreign Organization	No. of Papers
8	Gyeongsang Nationl University, South Korea	15
9	Centro Internacional de Mejoramiento de Maiz y Trigo	14
10	University of Saskatchewan, Canada	14
11	McGill University, Canada	13
12	USDA Agricultural Research Service, Washington DC, USA	11
13	University of Manitoba, Canada	11
14	City University of Hong Kong, China	11
15	University of Kentucky, USA	11

5.1.3 National Collaboration

The national collaboration links of 20 agricultural universities consists of 4630, accounting for 43.93% share of their total research output during 2007-11. The share of national collaboration links varies from 26.41% to 81.31% and with average number of national collaboration links per university as 231.5. Twelve universities have registered more than average national links (43.93%) of all agricultural universities. They are ORISUAT-BHUB with national collaboration links of 81.31%, followed by ANGRAU-HYDE (76.96%), ASSAU-JORH (71.74%), SKUAST-JAMM (68.10%), RAJAU-BIKA (65.45%), WBUAFS-KOLK (63.89%), BKCV-MOHAN (55.08%), IVRI-BAREILLY (54.07%), UAS-BANG (50.95%), NDRI-KARN (48.86%), IARI-DELHI (46.66%) and MPUAT-UDAIP (45.98%). Of the total national collaboration links, the largest share of collaboration links (50.26%) were to academic institutions (varying from 27.27% to 75.86%), followed by research institutions (45.36%)(varying from 26.23% to 62.30%), institutes of national importance (3.80%) (varying from 0.0% to 15.85%), industry (1.32%) (0.0% to 6.80%) and others (0.99%) (0.0% to 6.86%) (Table 5).

Table 5: National collaboration linkages of 20 agricultural universities, 2007-11

	TP	TNCL	% TNCL	National Collaboration Links by Type of Institutions					Inter University Coll. Links
				Academic Institution	Research Institution	Institution of National Importance	Industry	Others	
IARI-DELHI	1588	741	46.66	38.73	55.20	5.80	0.00	0.27	106
IVRI-BAREILLY	1413	764	54.07	55.10	42.67	0.52	0.65	1.05	174

	TP	TNCL	% TNCL	National Collaboration Links by Type of Institutions					Inter University Coll. Links
				Academic Institution	Research Institution	Institution of National Importance	Industry	Others	
PUNJAU-LUDH	1083	286	26.41	47.90	45.10	6.29	0.70	0.00	56
GBPUAT-NAIN	871	319	36.62	75.86	42.95	8.15	1.25	0.00	78
CCSHAU-HISAR	787	215	27.32	57.67	39.53	1.86	0.93	0.00	70
TAMILAU-COIM	771	232	30.09	42.24	55.17	0.00	1.72	0.86	26
NDRI-KARN	657	321	48.86	44.55	50.16	0.93	1.56	2.80	53
TAMVASU-CHENN	591	186	31.47	61.83	26.34	4.30	5.38	2.15	29
UAS-BANG	422	215	50.95	43.72	41.86	5.58	5.58	3.26	18
MPUAT-UDAIP	398	183	45.98	56.83	26.23	15.85	1.09	0.00	18
WBUAFS-KOLK	252	161	63.89	35.40	52.80	6.83	0.62	4.35	41
KERAU-TRISS	227	102	44.93	53.92	37.25	1.96	0.00	6.86	21
RAJAU-BIKA	220	144	65.45	55.56	43.06	0.69	0.69	0.00	33
DYSPUHF-SOLA	220	66	30.00	27.27	71.21	0.00	0.00	1.52	8
ORISUAT-BHUB	214	174	81.31	50.00	43.10	2.30	2.30	2.30	27
ANGRAU-HYDE	191	147	76.96	55.78	40.14	2.72	0.00	1.36	19
BKCV-MOHAN	187	103	55.08	47.57	35.92	6.80	6.80	2.91	17
SKUAST-JAMM	163	111	68.10	59.46	40.54	0.00	0.00	0.00	48
CSKHPKV-PALAM	146	61	41.78	34.43	62.30	0.00	3.28	0.00	20
ASSAU-JORH	138	99	71.74	47.47	52.53	0.00	0.00	0.00	19
	10539	**4630**	**43.93**	**50.26**	**45.36**	**3.80**	**1.32**	**0.99**	**44.05**

The average number of inter-university links per university was 44.05, which varies from 17 to 174. Eight universities had more than the average interuniversity links of all 20 agricultural universities. They are IVRI-BAREILLY with collaboration links of 174, followed by IARI-DELHI (106), GBPUAT-NAIN (78), CCSHAU-HISAR (70), PUNJAU-LUDH (56), NDRI-KARN (53), SKUAST-JAMM (48) and WBUAFS-KOLK (41) (Table 5). The largest number (33) of inter-university collaboration links are between IVRI-BAREILY and GBUAT-NAIN, followed by IVRI-BAREILY and NDRI-KARN (30 links), IVRI-BAREILY and TAMVASU-CHEN (25 links), IVRI-BAREILY and WBUAFS-KOLK (24 links), IARI-DELHI and GBPUAT-NAIN (23 links), PUNJAU-LUDH and CCSHAU-HISAR (21 links), IARI-DELHI and CCSHAU-HISAR (19 links), NDRI-KARNAL and SKUAST-JAMU (15 links), IVRI-BAREILY and SKUAST-JAMU (13 links), RAJAU-BIKA and MPUAT-UDAI (12 links), IVRI-BAREILLY and ORISUA-BHUB (12 links), IVRI-BAREILY and CCSHAU-HISAR (12 links), IARI-DELHI and MPUAT-UDAI (10 links), etc.

5.2 Subject-Wise Distribution of Papers

5.2.1 Agricultural and Biological Sciences

The 20 agricultural universities together contributed 5945 papers in agricultural and biological sciences, constituting 60.88% share of total publication output of universities and 16.22% of the output of India in agricultural and biological sciences during 2007-11.

On individually analyzing the profile of 20 agricultural universities in agricultural and biological sciences during 2007-11, nine universities output were found to be having more than the average productivity (297.25) of all universities. They are IARI-DELHI with 1160 papers, followed by PUNJAU-LUDH (827 papers), IVRI-BAREILY (682 papers), TAMILAU-COIM (611 papers), CCSHAU-HISAR (607 papers), GBPUAT-NAIN (462 papers), NDRI-KARN (441 papers), TAMVASU-CHENN (432 papers) and UAS-BANG (305 papers).

Eight universities have registered higher citation impact per paper than the average impact (1.52) of all universities. These IARI-DELHI with a citation impact per paper of 2.29, followed by NDRI-KARN (1.97), WBUAFS-KOLK (1.76), PUNJAU-LUDH (1.68), TAMILAU-COIM and UAS-BANG (1.62 each), CSKHPKV-PALAM (1.54) and ASSAU-JORH (1.54). Nine universities have registered higher h-index values than the average h-index (10.7) of all universities. They are IARI-DELHI with h-index value of 22, followed by PUNJAU-LUDH (19), TAMILAU-COIM (17), TAMVASU-CHENN (15), UAS-BANG and CCSHAU-HISAR (14 each), NDRI-KARN, IVRI-BAREILY and GBPUAT-NAIN (13 each).

Seven universities have achieved international collaborative publication share higher than the average international collaborative publication share (10.36%) of all organizations. They are UAS-BANG with international collaborative publication share of 25.90%, followed by PUNJAU-LUDH (16.44%), TAMILAU-COIM (15.71%) ASSAU-JORH (13.13), IARI-DELHI (13.10), KERAU-TRISS (11.24%) and CCSHAU-HISAR (10.71%). Nine universities have more than the average national collaborative links (54.68%) of all universities. They are ORISUAT-BHUB with national collaboration links of 135.34%, followed by UAS-BANG (88.52%), ANGRAU-HYDE (85.31%), SKUAST-JAMM (79.44%), CSKHPKV-PALAM (70.48%), ASSAU-JORH (67.68%), RAJAU-BIKA (67.24%), IVRI-BAREILY (64.66%) and KERAU-TRISS (55.03%). The average number of inter-university links per university was 32.3, which varied from 6 to 94. Six universities had more than the average interuniversity links of all 20 agricultural universities. They are IVRI-BAREILLY with collaboration links of 94, followed by IARI-DELHI (84), GBPUAT-NAIN (59), NDRI-KARN (55), PUNJAU-LUDH (41) and SKUAST-JAMM (34)(Table 5). The largest number (27) of inter-university collaboration links in agricultural and biological sciences are between IVRI-BAREILY and NDRI-KARN, followed by IARI-DELHI and GBPUAT-NAIN (22 links), IVRI-BAREILY and GBPUAT-NAIN (19 links), IARI-DELHI and CCSHAU-HISAR (18 links), PUNJAU-LUDH and CCSHAU-HISAR (16 links), IVRI-BAREILY and WBUAFS-KOLK (13 links) and RAJAU-BIKA and MPUAT-UDAI (12 links), etc.

Thirteen universities have more institutional share more than the average institutional share (68.76%) of all universities. They are DYSPUHF-SOLA with average institutional share of 87.27%, TAMILAU-COIM (79.25%), RAJAU-BIKA (79.09%), CCSHAU-HISAR (77.13%), PUNJAU-LUDH (76.36%), ANGRAU-HYDE (74.87%), BKCV-MOHAN (74.87%), KERAU-TRISS (74.45%), TAMVASU-CHENN (73.10%), IARI-DELHI (73.05%), UAS-BANG (72.27%), CSKHPKV-PALAM (71.92%) and ASSAU-JORH (71.74%).

Table 6: Profile of agricultural universities in agricultural and Biological Sciences, 2007-11

Name (Abbreviated)	2007-11											
	TP	TC	ACPP	TIO	INSH	HI	ICP	%ICP	NCLIN	%NCLIN	IUCL	ICP
IARI-DELHI	1160	2658	2.29	1588	73.05	22	152	13.10	491	42.33	84	152
PUNJAU-LUDH	827	1389	1.68	1083	76.36	19	136	16.44	176	21.28	41	136
IVRI-BAREILY	682	890	1.30	1413	48.27	13	39	5.72	441	64.66	94	39
TAMILAU-COIM	611	990	1.62	771	79.25	17	96	15.71	167	27.33	18	96
CCSHAU-HISAR	607	690	1.14	787	77.13	14	65	10.71	180	29.65	31	65
GBPUAT-NAIN	462	480	1.04	871	53.04	13	33	7.14	224	48.48	59	33

Name (Abbreviated)	2007-11											
	TP	TC	ACPP	TIO	INSH	HI	ICP	%ICP	NCLIN	%NCLIN	IUCL	ICP
NDRI-KARN	441	870	1.97	657	67.12	13	39	8.84	219	49.66	55	39
TAMVASU-CHENN	432	615	1.42	591	73.10	15	7	1.62	122	28.24	18	7
UAS-BANG	305	495	1.62	422	72.27	14	79	25.90	270	88.52	18	79
MPUAT-UDAIP	210	152	0.72	398	52.76	5	13	6.19	84	40.00	23	13
DYSPUHF-SOLA	192	141	0.73	220	87.27	6	14	7.29	42	21.88	6	14
RAJAU-BIKA	174	92	0.53	220	79.09	5	5	2.87	117	67.24	27	5
KERAU-TRISS	169	231	1.37	227	74.45	9	19	11.24	93	55.03	18	19
ANGRAU-HYDE	143	186	1.30	191	74.87	8	11	7.69	122	85.31	17	11
BKCV-MOHAN	140	212	1.51	187	74.87	9	13	9.29	61	43.57	14	13
WBUAFS-KOLK	123	217	1.76	252	48.81	8	7	5.69	59	47.97	30	7
ORISUAT-BHUB	116	81	0.70	214	54.21	4	7	6.03	157	135.34	27	7
SKUAST-JAMM	107	92	0.86	163	65.64	5	10	9.35	85	79.44	34	10
CSKHPKV-PALAM	105	162	1.54	146	71.92	8	10	9.52	74	70.48	18	10
ASSAU-JORH	99	152	1.54	138	71.74	7	13	13.13	67	67.68	14	13
Total	**5945**	**8137**	**1.52**	**10539**	**68.76**	**10.7**	**616**	**10.36**	**3251**	**54.68**	**32.3**	**616**

TP=Total Papers; TC=Total Citations; ACPP=Average Citation Per Paper; TIO=Total Papers of the Institute; INSH=Institute Share in Total Papers; HI-Index; ICP=International Collaborative Papers; NCIL=National Collaborative Links; IUCL=Inter-University Collaborative Links

5.2.2 Veterinary Science

The 20 agricultural universities together contributed 2087 papers in veterinary science, constituting 22.51% share of total publication output of universities and 33.24% of the output of India in veterinary science during 2007-11.

On individually analyzing the profile of 20 agricultural universities in veterinary science during 2007-11, four universities were found to have more than the average productivity (120.35) of all universities. They are IVRI-BAREILY with 887 papers, followed by TAMVASU-CHENN (432 papers), NDRI-KARN (294 papers) and GBPUAT-NAIN (179 papers).

Only one university has registered higher citation impact per paper than the average impact (4.33) of all universities. This is IVRI-BAREILY with citation impact per paper of 10.19; (iii) Six organizations have registered higher h-index values than the average (4.15) h-index of all universities. They are TAMVASU-CHENN with h-index value of 15, followed by IVRI-BAREILY (14), WBUAFS-KOLK and NDRI-KARN (7 each), PUNJAU-LUDH (6) and SKUAST-JAMM (5);

Table 7: Profile of agricultural universities in Veterinary Science, 2007-11

Name (Abbreviated)	2007-11										
	TP	TC	ACPP	TIO	INSH	HI	ICP	%ICP	NCLIN	%NCLIN	IUCL
IVRI-BAREILY	887	9036	10.19	1083	81.90	14	40	4.51	330	37.20	50
TAMVASU-CHENN	432	615	1.42	591	73.10	15	7	1.62	122	28.24	18
NDRI-KARN	294	217	0.74	657	44.75	7	17	5.78	162	55.10	40
GBPUAT-NAIN	179	68	0.38	771	23.22	4	4	2.23	137	76.54	32
WBUAFS-KOLK	114	172	1.51	191	59.69	7	3	2.63	50	43.86	20
CCSHAU-HISAR	109	74	0.68	787	13.85	3	7	6.42	70	64.22	12
SKUAST-JAMM	81	53	0.65	163	49.69	5	5	6.17	61	75.31	25
ORISUAT-BHUB	56	32	0.57	187	29.95	4	0	0.00	32	57.14	11
KERAU-TRISS	55	10	0.18	220	25.00	2	0	0.00	32	58.18	4
PUNJAU-LUDH	43	72	1.67	1413	3.04	6	4	9.30	26	60.47	4
RAJAU-BIKA	41	22	0.54	227	18.06	3	1	2.44	35	85.37	11
CSKHPKV-PALAM	34	24	0.71	146	23.29	3	2	5.88	23	67.65	2
MPUAT-UDAIP	28	9	0.32	398	7.04	2	0	0.00	7	25.00	4
ASSAU-JORH	20	3	0.15	138	14.49	1	1	5.00	18	90.00	2
UAS-BANG	11	2	0.18	422	2.61	1	1	9.09	9	81.82	1
BKCV-MOHAN	7	2	0.29	214	3.27	1	0	0.00	9	128.57	4
ANGRAU-HYDE	6	1	0.17	220	2.73	1	0	0.00	11	183.33	0
IARI-DELHI	5	8	1.60	1588	0.31	2	1	20.00	10	200.00	0
TAMILAU-COIM	3	3	1.00	871	0.34	1	0	0.00	1	33.33	0
DYSPUHF-SOLA	2	1	0.50	252	0.79	1	0	0.00	1	50.00	0
Total	**2407**	**10424**	**4.33**	**10539**	**25.05**	**4.15**	**93**	**3.86**	**1146**	**75.07**	**12**

Nine universities have achieved international collaborative publication share higher than the average international collaborative publication share (3.86%) of all universities. They are IARI-DELHI with international collaborative publication share of 20.00%, followed by PUNJAU-LUDH (9.30%), UAS-BANG (9.09%), CCSHAU-HISAR (6.42), SKUAST-JAMM (6.17), CSKHPKV-PALAM (5.88%), NDRI-KARN (5.78%), ASSAU-JORH (5.00%), and IVRI-BAREILY (4.51). Eight universities have more than average national collaboration links (75.07%) of all universities. They are IARI-DELHI with national collaboration links of 200.0%, followed by ANGRAU-HYDE (183.33%), BKCV-MOHAN (128.57%), ASSAU-JORH (90.00%), RAJAU-BIKA (85.37%), UAS-BANG (81.82%), GBPUAT-NAIN (76.54%) and SKUAST-JAMM (75.31%). The average number of inter-university links per university was 12, which varied from 0 to 50. Six universities had more than the average interuniversity links of all 20 agricultural universities. They are IVRI-BAREILLY with collaboration links of 50, followed by NDRI-KARN (40 links), GBPUAT-NAIN (32 links), SKUAST-JAMM (25 links), WBUAFS-KOLK (20 links) and TAMVASU-CHENN (18 links). The largest number (27) of inter-university collaboration links are between IVRI-BAREILY and GBPUAT-NAIN (26 links), followed by IVRI-BAREILY and NDRI-KARN (23 links), IVRI-BAREILY and TAMVASU-CHENN (15 links), IVRI-BAREILY and WBUAFS-KOLK (13 links), IVRI-BAREILLY and SKUAST-JAMM (10 links), NDRI-KARN and SKUAST-JAMM (8 links) and IVRI-BAREILLY and ORISUAT-BHUB (8 links).

Six agricultural universities had more institutional share than the average institutional share (25.05%) of all universities. They are IVRI-BAREILY with average institutional share of 81.90%), followed by TAMVASU-CHENN (73.10%), WBUAFS-KOLK (59.69%), SKUAST-JAMM (49.69%), NDRI-KARN (44.75%) and ORISUAT-BHUB (29.95%) (Table 7)

5.2.3 Biochemistry, Genetics and Molecular Biology

The 20 agricultural universities together contributed 1366 papers in biochemistry, genetics and molecular biology, constituting 14.73% share of total publication output of agricultural universities and 3.19% share of the output of India in biochemistry, genetics and molecular biology during 2007-11.

On individually analyzing the profile of 20 agricultural universities in biochemistry, genetics and molecular biology during 2007-11, eight universities were found to have more than the average productivity (71.3) of all universities. They are IARI-DELHI with 415 papers, followed by IVRI-BAREILY (201 papers), PUNJAU-

LUDH (152 papers), NDRI-KARN (128 papers), GBPUAT-NAIN (120 papers), TAMILAU-COIM (117 papers), UAS-BANG (100 papers) and CCSHAU-HISAR (76 papers).

Five universities have registered higher citation impact per paper than the average impact (3.37) of all universities. They are WBUAFS-KOLK with citation impact per paper of 4.17, followed by IARI-DELHI (3.85), CSKHPKV-PALAM (3.73), NDRI-KARN (3.63) and TAMVASU-CHENN (3.39). Seven universities have registered higher h-index values than the average h-index (7) of all universities. They are IARI-DELHI with h-index value of 20, followed by IVRI-BAREILY (13), PUNJAU-LUDH (12), NDRI-KARN (11), TAMVASU-CHENN and UAS-BANG (10 each) and TAMILAU-COIM (9).

Six universities have achieved international collaborative publication share higher than the average international collaborative publication share (22.30%) of all university. They are UAS-BANG with international collaborative publication share of 41.00%, followed by ASSAU-JORH (37.50%), TAMILAU-COIM (27.35%), CSKHPKV-PALAM (26.82%), ANGRAU-HYDE (22.58%) and PUNJAU-LUDH (22.37%). Six universities have secured higher national collaboration links than the average national links (64.80%) of all universities. They are WBUAFS-KOLK with national collaborating links of 103.48%, followed by ORISUAT-BHUB (95.12%), ANGRAU-HYDE (93.55%), ASSAU-JORH (87.50%), RAJAU-BIKA (78.26%) and TAMVASU-CHENN (73.44%). The average number of inter-university links per university was 4.65, which varied from 1 to 27. Eight universities had more than the average interuniversity links of all 20 agricultural universities. They are IARI-DELHI with collaborating links of 27, followed by GBPUAT-NAIN (16 links), CCSHAU-HISAR (14 links), IVRI-BAREILY (13 links), NDRI-KARN (7 links), TAMVASU-CHENN (5 LINKS), WBUAFS-KOLK (5 LINKS), etc. The largest number (10) of inter-university collaboration links in biochemistry, genetics and molecular biology are between IARI-DELHI and GBPUAT-NAIN, followed by IARI-DELHI and CCSHAU-HISAR (8 LINKS), TAMVASU-CHENN and IVRI-BAREILY (4 links), etc

Ten agricultural universities had more institutional share than the average share (13.57%) of all universities. They are IARI-DELHI with average institutional share of 26.13%, followed by PUNJAU-LUDH (23.70%), NDRI-KARN (19.48%), ORISUAT-BHUB (19.16%), CSKHPKV-PALAM (17.81%), ANGRAU-HYDE (16.23%), TAMILAU-COIM (15.18%), IVRI-BAREILY (14.22%), PUNJAU-LUDH (14.04%) and GBPUAT-NAIN (13.78%) (Table 8).

Table 8: Profile of agricultural universities in Biochemistry, Genetics and Molecular Biology, 2007-11

Name (Abbreviated)	2007-11										
	TP	TC	ACPP	TIO	INSH	HI	ICP	%ICP	NCLIN	%NCLIN	IUCL
IARI-DELHI	415	1599	3.85	1588	26.13	20	87	20.96	246	59.28	27
IVRI-BAREILY	201`	590	2.93	1413	14.22	13	33	16.42	118	58.71	13

Name (Abbreviated)	2007-11										
	TP	TC	ACPP	TIO	INSH	HI	ICP	%ICP	NCLIN	%NCLIN	IUCL
PUNJAU-LUDH	152	380	2.50	1083	14.04	12	34	22.37	47	30.92	3
NDRI-KARN	128	465	3.63	657	19.48	11	16	12.50	74	57.81	7
GBPUAT-NAIN	120	220	1.83	871	13.78	7	13	10.83	62	51.67	16
TAMILAU-COIM	117	392	3.35	771	15.18	9	32	27.35	44	37.61	2
UAS-BANG	100	296	2.96	422	23.70	10	41	41.00	61	61.00	1
CCSHAU-HISAR	76	120	1.58	787	9.66	6	9	11.84	41	53.95	14
TAMVASU-CHENN	64	217	3.39	591	10.83	10	12	18.75	47	73.44	5
ORISUAT-BHUB	41	37	0.90	214	19.16	3	3	7.32	39	95.12	4
ANGRAU-HYDE	31	87	2.81	191	16.23	5	7	22.58	29	93.55	2
WBUAFS-KOLK	29	121	4.17	252	11.51	6	5	17.24	30	103.45	5
CSKHPKV-PALAM	26	97	3.73	146	17.81	5	7	26.92	14	53.85	2
MPUAT-UDAIP	25	45	1.80	398	6.28	4	3	12.00	17	68.00	4
DYSPUHF-SOLA	25	32	1.28	220	11.36	4	3	12.00	4	16.00	1
RAJAU-BIKA	23	49	2.13	220	10.45	4	4	17.39	18	78.26	3
ASSAU-JORH	16	22	1.38	138	11.59	3	6	37.50	14	87.50	5
KERAU-TRISS	13	12	0.92	227	5.73	3	1	7.69	8	61.54	1
BKCV-MOHAN	13	16	1.23	187	6.95	3	1	7.69	6	46.15	2
SKUAST-JAMM	12	13	1.08	163	7.36	2	1	8.33	5	41.67	3
Total	**1426**	**4810**	**3.37**	**10539**	**13.57**	**7**	**318**	**22.30**	**924**	**64.80**	**4.65**

TP=Total Papers; TC=Total Citations; ACPP=Average Citation Per Paper; TIO=Total Papers of the Institute; INSH=Institute Share in Total Papers; HI-Index; ICP=International Collaborative Papers; NCIL=National Collaborative Links; IUCL=Inter-University Collaborative Links

5.2.4 Environment Science

The 20 agricultural universities together contributed 760 papers in environment science, constituting 8.20% share of total publication output of agricultural universities and 3.58% of the output of India in environment science during 2007-11.

On individually analyzing the profile of 20 agricultural universities in environment science during 2007-11, seven universities were found to have more than the average productivity (43.05) of all universities. They are IARI-DELHI with 178 papers, followed by PUNJAU-LUDH (131 papers), GBPUAT-NAIN (89 papers), TAMILAU-COIM (84 papers), CCSHAU-HISAR (56 papers), MPUAT-UDAIP (46 papers) and IVRI-BAREILY (45 papers);

Five universities have registered higher citation impact per paper than the average impact (2.37) of all universities. They are KERAU-TRISS with citation impact per paper of 4.45, followed by IARI-DELHI (3.99), IVRI-BAREILY (3.89), BKCV-MOHAN (3.74) and NDRI-KARN (2.83). Seven organizations have registered higher h-index values than the average h-index (5) of all universities. They are IARI-DELHI with h-index value of 13, followed by IVRI-BAREILY (10), TAMILAU-COIM and PUNJAU-LUDH (9 each), CCSHAU-HISAR, UAS-BANG and GBPUAT-NAIN (6 each).

Table 9: Profile of agricultural universities in Environment Science, 2007-11

Name (Abbreviated)	2007-11										
	TP	TC	ACPP	TIO	INSH	HI	ICP	%ICP	NCLIN	%NCLIN	IUCL
IARI-DELHI	178	710	3.99	1588	11.21	13	25	14.04	80	44.94	10
PUNJAU-LUDH	131	240	1.83	1083	12.10	9	10	7.63	49	37.40	11
GBPUAT-NAIN	89	128	1.44	871	10.22	6	7	7.87	33	37.08	4
TAMILAU-COIM	84	195	2.32	771	10.89	9	21	25.00	22	26.19	3
CCSHAU-HISAR	56	99	1.77	787	7.12	6	9	16.07	26	46.43	7
MPUAT-UDAIP	46	48	1.04	398	11.56	5	2	4.35	15	32.61	0
IVRI-BAREILY	45	175	3.89	1413	3.18	10	8	17.78	23	51.11	6
UAS-BANG	41	69	1.68	422	9.72	6	18	43.90	34	82.93	2
BKCV-MOHAN	35	131	3.74	187	18.72	5	0	0.00	25	71.43	1
ANGRAU-HYDE	24	42	1.75	191	12.57	4	3	12.50	13	54.17	2
NDRI-KARN	18	51	2.83	657	2.74	4	4	22.22	8	44.44	5
ORISUAT-BHUB	18	26	1.44	214	8.41	3	0	0.00	17	94.44	4
ASSAU-JORH	17	15	0.88	138	12.32	3	1	5.88	14	82.35	6
TAMVASU-CHENN	14	17	1.21	591	2.37	2	1	7.14	8	57.14	0
RAJAU-BIKA	13	8	0.62	220	5.91	2	0	0.00	6	46.15	1
DYSPUHF-SOLA	13	5	0.38	220	5.91	2	0	0.00	8	61.54	4
SKUAST-JAMM	13	8	0.62	163	7.98	2	0	0.00	8	61.54	6
KERAU-TRISS	11	49	4.45	227	4.85	5	4	36.36	5	45.45	0
WBUAFS-KOLK	10	19	1.90	252	3.97	3	0	0.00	12	120.00	2
CSKHPKV-PALAM	5	7	1.40	146	3.42	1	1	20.00	3	60.00	1
Total	**861**	**2042**	**2.37**		**8.26**	**5**	**114**	**13.24**	**409**	**47.50**	**3.75**

TP=Total Papers; TC=Total Citations; ACPP=Average Citation Per Paper; TIO=Total Papers of the Institute; INSH=Institute Share in Total Papers; HI-Index; ICP=International Collaborative Papers; NCIL=National Collaborative Links; IUCL=Inter-University Collaborative Links

Seven universities have achieved international collaborative publication share higher than the average international collaborative publication (13.24%) share of all universities. They are UAS-BANG with international collaborative publication share of 43.9%, followed by KERAU-TRISS (36.66%), TAMILAU-COIM (25.00%), NDRI-KARN (22.22%), CSKHPKV-PALAM (20.00%), IVRI-BAREILY (17.78%) and CCSHAU-HISAR (16.07%). Nine universities have received higher national share of national collaborative linkages than the average national collaborative linkages (47.50%) of all universities. They are WBUAFS-KOLK with national collaborative linkage share of 120.0%, followed by ORISUAT-BHUB (94.44%), UAS-BANG (82.93%), ASSAU-JORH (82.35%), BKCV-MOHAN (71.43%), SKUAST-JAMM and DYSPUHF-SOLA (61.54% each), CSKHPKV-PALAM (60.99%), TAMVASU-CHENN (57.14%), ANGRAU-HYDE (54.17%) and IVRI-BAREILY (51.11%). The average number of inter-university links per university was 3.75, which varied from 0 to 11. Ten universities had more than the average interuniversity links of all 20 agricultural universities. They are PUNJAU-LUDH with collaborative links of 11, followed by IARI-DELHI (10 linkages), CCSHAU-HISAR (7 linkages), IVRI-BAREILY (6 linkages), ASSAU-JORH (6 linkages), SKUAST-JAMM (6 linkages), etc. The largest number (4) of inter-university collaboration links in environment science are between IARI-DELHI and ASSAU-JORH, followed by IVRI-BAREILY and ORISUAT-BHUB (3 linkages), PUNJAU-LUDH and CCSHAU-HISAR (3 linkages), NDRI-KARN and SKUAST-JAMM (3 linkages), etc.

Ten agricultural universities had more institutional share than the average share (8.26%) of all universities. They are BKCV-MOHAN with average institutional share of 18.72%, followed ANGRAU-HYDE (12.57%), ASSAU-JORH (12.32%), PUNJAU-LUDH (12.10%), MPUAT-UDAIP (11.56%), IARI-DELHI (11.21%), TAMILAU-COIM (10.89%), GBPUAT-NAIN (10.22%), UAS-BANG (9.72%) and ORISUAT-BHUB (8.41%) (Table 9).

5.2.5 Immunology and Microbiology

The 18 agricultural universities together contributed 778 papers in immunology and microbiology, constituting 8.39% share of total publication output of agricultural universities and 6.68% of the output of India in immunology and microbiology during 2007-11.

On individually analyzing the profile of 20 agricultural universities in immunology and microbiology during 2007-11, seven universities were found to have more than the average productivity (45.78) of all universities. They are IVRI-

BAREILY with 239 papers, followed by IARI-DELHI (142), NDRI-KARN (75), TAMILAU-COIM (67), TAMVASU-CHENN (59), GBPUAT-NAIN (54) and CCSHAU-HISAR (52).

Seven universities have registered higher citation impact per paper of 4.31, followed by GBPUAT-NAIN (3.81), IARI-DELHI (3.66), IVRI-BAREILY (3.51), NDRI-KARN (3.48), ASSAU-JORH (3.40) and TAMVASU-CHENN (3.34). Nine universities have registered higher h-index values than the average h-index (5.89) of all universities. They are IVRI-BAREILY with h-index value of 15, followed by IARI-DELHI (14), GBPUAT-NAIN (11), NDRI-KARN and TAMVASU-CHENN (9 each), CCSHAU-HISAR (8), PUNJAU-LUDH and TAMILAU-COIM (7 each) and UAS-BANG (6).

Six universities have achieved international collaborative publication share higher than the average international collaborative publication share (16.99%) of all universities. They are TAMILAU-COIM with international collaborative publication share of 40.30%, followed by ASSAU-JORH and CSKHPKV-PALAM (40.0% each), UAS-BANG (20.0%), CCSHAU-HISAR (19.23%) and WBUAFS-KOLK (18.75%). Eight universities have more share than the average share (64.32%) of all national collaboration linkages of the universities. They are ASSAU-JORH and MPUAT-UDAIP with 100% share of national collaboration linkages, followed by ORISUAT-BHUB (93.75%), IARI-DELHI (80.28%), CCSHAU-HISAR (76.92%), BKCV-MOHAN (75.00%), ANGRAU-HYDE (71.43%) and IVRI-BAREILY (70.71%). The average number of inter-university links per university was 3.70, which varied from 0 to 22. Seven universities had more than the average interuniversity links of all 20 agricultural universities. They are IVRI-BAREILLY with collaborative links of 22, followed by CCSHAU-HISAR (11 linkages), IARI-DELHI (10 linkages), WBUAFS-KOLK (5 linkages), GBPUAT-NAIN (5 linkages), TAMVASU-CHENN (4 linkages), etc. The largest number (7) of inter-university collaboration links in immunology and microbiology are between IVRI-BAREILLY and CCSHAU-HISAR, followed by IVRI-BAREILLY and WBUAFS-KOLK (5 links), IVRI-BAREILLY and GBPUAT-NAIN (4 linkages), IVRI-BAREILLY and TAMVASU-CHENN (4 links), IARI-DELHI and ANGRAU-HYDE (3 links), IARI-DELHI and CCSHAU-HISAR 3 links), etc.

Eight agricultural universities had more institutional share than the average institutional share (6.31%) of all universities. They are IVRI-BAREILY with average institutional share of 16.91%, followed by NDRI-KARN (11.42%), TAMVASU-CHENN (9.98%), IARI-DELHI (8.94%), TAMILAU-COIM (8.69%), ORISUAT-BHUB (7.48%), CCSHAU-HISAR (6.61%) and WBUAFS-KOLK (6.35%) (Table 10).

Table 10: Profile of agricultural universities in Immunology and Microbiology, 2007-11

Name (Abbreviated)	2007-11										
	TP	TC	ACPP	TIO	INSH	HI	ICP	% ICP	NCLIN	%NCLIN	IUCL
IVRI-BAREILY	239	840	3.51	1413	16.91	15	39	16.32	169	70.71	22
IARI-DELHI	142	520	3.66	1588	8.94	14	23	16.20	114	80.28	10
NDRI-KARN	75	261	3.48	657	11.42	10	9	12.00	33	44.00	2
TAMILAU-COIM	67	175	2.61	771	8.69	7	27	40.30	30	44.78	0
TAMVASU-CHENN	59	197	3.34	591	9.98	9	9	15.25	32	54.24	4
GBPUAT-NAIN	54	206	3.81	871	6.20	11	7	12.96	38	70.37	5
CCSHAU-HISAR	52	142	2.73	787	6.61	8	10	19.23	40	76.92	11
PUNJAU-LUDH	37	115	3.11	1083	3.42	7	2	5.41	10	27.03	1
UAS-BANG	25	58	2.32	422	5.92	6	5	20.00	16	64.00	4
WBUAFS-KOLK	16	69	4.31	252	6.35	4	3	18.75	10	62.50	5
ORISUAT-BHUB	16	5	0.31	214	7.48	2	1	6.25	15	93.75	1
DYSPUHF-SOLA	11	7	0.64	220	5.00	2	0	0.00	1	9.09	0
KERAU-TRISS	7	15	2.14	227	3.08	3	1	14.29	3	42.86	0
ANGRAU-HYDE	7	2	0.29	191	3.66	1	0	0.00	5	71.43	3
CSKHPKV-PALAM	5	8	1.60	146	3.42	2	2	40.00	3	60.00	3
ASSAU-JORH	5	17	3.40	138	3.62	3	2	40.00	5	100.00	0
BKCV-MOHAN	4	4	1.00	187	2.14	1	0	0.00	3	75.00	1
MPUAT-UDAIP	3	2	0.67	398	0.75	1	0	0.00	3	100.00	2
	824	**2643**	**3.21**	**10156**	**6.31**	**5.89**	**140**	**16.99**	**530**	**64.32**	**3.70**

TP=Total Papers; TC=Total Citations; ACPP=Average Citation Per Paper; TIO=Total Papers of the Institute; INSH=Institute Share in Total Papers; HI-Index; ICP=International Collaborative Papers; NCIL=National Collaborative Links; IUCL=Inter-University Collaborative Links

5.2.6 Pharmacology, Toxicology and Pharmaceutics

The 19 agricultural universities together contributed 342 papers in pharmacology, toxicology and pharmaceutics, constituting 3.69% share of total publication output of agricultural universities and 1.09% of the output of India in pharmacology, toxicology and pharmaceutics during 2007-11.

On individually analyzing the profile of 19 agricultural universities in pharmacology, toxicology and pharmaceutics, six universities were found to have more than the average productivity (19.32) of all universities. They are IVRI-BAREILY with 80 papers, followed by IARI-DELHI (55 papers), PUNJAU-LUDH (41 papers), GBPUAT-NAIN and CCSHAU-HISAR (31 papers each) and WBUAFS-KOLK (20 papers);

Six universities have registered highest citation impact per paper (2.40) than the average impact of all universities. They are ANGRAU-HYDE with citation impact per paper of 6.80, followed by TAMVASU-CHENN (4.45), IARI-DELHI (3.82), IVRI-BAREILY (3.13), TAMILAU-COIM (2.77) and GBPUAT-NAIN (2.65). Five universities have registered higher h-index values than the average h-index (3.26) of all universities. They are IVRI-BAREILY with h-index value of 10, followed by IARI-DELHI (9), GBPUAT-NAIN (6), ORISUAT-BHUB (4) and PUNJAU-LUDH (4).

Table 11: Profile of agricultural universities in Pharmacology, Toxicology & Pharmaceutics, 2007-11

Name (Abbreviated)	2007-11										
	TP	TC	ACPP	TIO	INSH	HI	ICP	% ICP	NCLIN	%NCLIN	IUCL
IVRI-BAREILY	80	250	3.13	1413	5.66	10	10	12.50	39	200.0	7
IARI-DELHI	55	210	3.82	1588	3.46	9	4	7.27	29	135.7	2
PUNJAU-LUDH	41	61	1.49	1083	3.79	4	2	4.88	12	127.3	4
GBPUAT-NAIN	31	82	2.65	871	3.56	6	3	9.68	23	120.0	3
CCSHAU-HISAR	31	20	0.65	787	3.94	3	1	3.23	11	100.0	5
WBUAFS-KOLK	20	19	0.95	252	7.94	2	0	0.00	16	100.0	1
ORISUAT-BHUB	19	34	1.79	214	8.88	4	0	0.00	19	80.0	2
NDRI-KARN	15	27	1.80	657	2.28	3	2	13.33	12	80.0	5
UAS-BANG	14	24	1.71	422	3.32	3	1	7.14	19	74.2	0
TAMILAU-COIM	13	36	2.77	771	1.69	3	3	23.08	8	62.5	0
BKCV-MOHAN	12	18	1.50	187	6.42	3	0	0.00	7	61.5	0
TAMVASU-CHENN	11	49	4.45	591	1.86	3	0	0.00	14	58.3	1
SKUAST-JAMM	8	3	0.38	163	4.91	1	0	0.00	5	52.7	4
ANGRAU-HYDE	5	34	6.80	191	2.62	3	2	40.00	6	50.0	0
MPUAT-UDAIP	4	3	0.75	398	1.01	1	0	0.00	2	48.8	1
RAJAU-BIKA	3	7	2.33	220	1.36	2	0	0.00	3	35.5	0
KERAU-TRISS	2	3	1.50	227	0.88	1	0	0.00	0	29.3	0
DYSPUHF-SOLA	2	0	0.00	220	0.91	0	0	0.00	0	0.0	0
CSKHPKV-PALAM	1	1	1.00	146	0.68	1	0	0.00	2	0.0	1
Total	**367**	**881**	**2.40**	**10401**	**3.43**	**3.26**	**28**	**7.63**		**74.51**	**1.80**

TP=Total Papers; TC=Total Citations; ACPP=Average Citation Per Paper; TIO=Total Papers of the Institute; INSH=Institute Share in Total Papers; HI-Index; ICP=International Collaborative Papers; NCIL=National Collaborative Links; IUCL=Inter-University Collaborative Links

Five universities have achieved international collaborative publication share higher than the average international collaborative publication share (7.63%) of all universities. They are ANGRAU-HYDE with international collaborative publication share of 40.00%, followed by TAMILAU-COIM (23.08%), NDRI-KARN (13.33%), IVRI-BAREILY (12.50%) and GBPUAT-NAIN (9.68%). Eight universities have achieved national collaborative linkages share more than the average share of national collaborative linkages (74.51%) of all universities. They are CSKHPKV-PALAM with national collaborative linkages share of 200.00%, followed by UAS-BANG (135.7%), TAMVASU-CHENN (127.3%), ANGRAU-HYDE (120.0%), ORISUAT-BHUB (100.0%), RAJAU-BIKA (100.0%), WBUAFS-KOLK (80.0%), NDRI-KARN (80.0%) and GBPUAT-NAIN (74.2%). The average number of inter-university links per university was 1.80, which varied from 0 to 7. Eight universities had more than the average interuniversity links of all 20 agricultural universities. They are IVRI-BAREILLY with collaborative links of 7, followed by CCSHAU-HISAR (5 linkages), NDRI-KARN (5 linkages), PUNJAU-LUDH (4 linkages), SKUAST-JAMM (4 linkages), GBPUAT-NAIN (3 linkages), etc. The largest number (3) of inter-university collaboration links in pharmacology, toxicology and pharmaceutics is between CCSHAU-HISAR and PUNJAU-LUDH and SKUAST-JAMM, followed by IVRI-BAREILLY and WBUAFS-KOLK (5 links), IVRI-BAREILLY and GBPUAT-NAIN (4 linkages), IVRI-BAREILLY and ORISUAT-BHUB (2 links) and IVRI-BAREILLY and NDRI-KARN (2 links), etc.

Nine agricultural universities had more institutional share than the average share (3.43%) of all universities. They are ORISUAT-BHUB with average institutional share of 8.88%, followed by WBUAFS-KOLK (7.94%), BKCV-MOHAN (6.42%), IVRI-BAREILY (5.66%), SKUAST-JAMM (4.91%), CCSHAU-HISAR (3.94%), PUNJAU-LUDH (3.79%), GBPUAT-NAIN (3.56%) and IARI-DELH (3.46%) (Table 11).

5.2.7 Medicine

The 20 agricultural universities together contributed 443 papers in medicine, constituting 4.78% share of total publication output of agricultural universities and 0.64% of the output of India in medicine during 2007-11.

On individually analyzing the profile of 20 agricultural universities in medicine during 2007-11, six universities were found to have more than the average productivity (24.2) of all universities. They are IVRI-BAREILY with 137 papers, followed by IARI-DELHI (63 papers), NDRI-KARN (53 papers), TAMVASU-CHENN (40 papers), PUNJAU-LUDH 939 papers) and WBUAFS-KOLK (25 papers).

Four universities have registered higher citation impact per paper than the average impact (3.84) of all universities. They are CSKHPKV-PALAM with citation impact per paper of 8.00, followed by KERAU-TRISS (6.60), IARI-DELH (6.33) and NDRI-KARN (4.70). Eight universities have registered higher h-index values than the average h-index (4.8) of all universities. They are IVRI-BAREILY with h-index value of 14, followed by IARI-DELHI (13), NDRI-KARN (10), TAMVASU-CHENN and PUNJAU-LUDH (9 each), UAS-BANG, WBUAFS-KOLK and GBPUAT-NAIN (5 each).

Nine universities have achieved international collaborative publication share higher than the average international collaborative publication share (20.04%) of all universities. They are UAS-BANG with international collaborative publication share of 41.18%, followed by ANGRAU-HYDE (40.00%), CSKHPKV-PALAM and SKUAST-JAMM (33.33% each), CCSHAU-HISAR (27.78%), TAMVASU-CHENN (27.50%), NDRI-KARN (22.64%), IARI-DELHI (20.63%) and PUNJAU-LUDH (20.51%). Eight universities have achieved share of national collaborative links more than the average share (65.50%) of national collaborative links. They are RAJAU-BIKA with national collaborative links of 200.0%, ANGRAU-HYDE (120.0%), NDRI-KARN (94.34%), WBUAFS-KOLK (88.0%), IARI-DELHI (76.19%), ORISUAT-BHUB (72.73%), GBPUAT-NAIN (70.83%), SKUAST-JAMM (66.67%).The average number of inter-university links per university was 1.80, which varied from 0 to 15. Five universities had more than the average interuniversity links of all 20 agricultural universities. They are IVRI-BAREILLY with collaborative links of 15, followed by NDRI-KARN (6 linkages), SKUAST-JAMM (4 linkages), GBPUAT-NAIN (3 linkages), CCSHAU-HISAR (3 linkages), etc. The largest number (3) of inter-university collaboration links in medicine are between IVRI-BAREILLY and NDRI-KARN, followed by IVRI-BAREILLY and GBPUAT-NAIN (3 linkages), IVRI-BAREILLY and CCSHAU-HISAR (3 linkages), NDRI-KARN and SKUAST-JAMM (3 linkages), etc.

Five agricultural universities had more institutional share than the average institutional share (4.59%) of all universities. They are WBUAFS-KOLK with average institutional share of 9.92%, followed by IVRI-BAREILY (9.70%), NDRI-KARN (8.07%), TAMVASU-CHENN (6.77%) and ORISUAT-BHUB (5.14%) (Table 12).

Table 12: Profile of agricultural universities in Medicine, 2007-11

Name (Abbreviated)	2007-11										
	TP	TC	ACPP	TIO	INSH	HI	ICP	% ICP	NCLIN	%NCLIN	IUCL
IVRI-BAREILY	137	510	3.72	1413	9.70	14	27	19.71	85	62.04	15
IARI-DELHI	63	399	6.33	1588	3.97	13	13	20.63	48	76.19	1

Name (Abbreviated)	2007-11										
	TP	TC	ACPP	TIO	INSH	HI	ICP	% ICP	NCLIN	%NCLIN	IUCL
NDRI-KARN	53	249	4.70	657	8.07	10	12	22.64	50	94.34	6
TAMVASU-CHENN	40	152	3.80	591	6.77	9	11	27.50	25	62.50	1
PUNJAU-LUDH	39	142	3.64	1083	3.60	9	8	20.51	20	51.28	0
WBUAFS-KOLK	25	73	2.92	252	9.92	5	2	8.00	22	88.00	1
GBPUAT-NAIN	24	68	2.83	871	2.76	5	2	8.33	17	70.83	3
CCSHAU-HISAR	18	49	2.72	787	2.29	4	5	27.78	10	55.56	3
UAS-BANG	17	52	3.06	422	4.03	5	7	41.18	11	64.71	0
TAMILAU-COIM	15	27	1.80	771	1.95	3	2	13.33	4	26.67	0
ORISUAT-BHUB	11	17	1.55	214	5.14	2	0	0.00	8	72.73	1
MPUAT-UDAIP	10	8	0.80	398	2.51	2	2	20.00	1	10.00	0
SKUAST-JAMM	6	8	1.33	163	3.68	2	2	33.33	4	66.67	4
CSKHPKV-PALAM	6	48	8.00	146	4.11	2	2	33.33	0	0.00	0
KERAU-TRISS	5	33	6.60	227	2.20	4	0	0.00	2	40.00	0
ANGRAU-HYDE	5	19	3.80	191	2.62	3	2	40.00	6	120.00	1
BKCV-MOHAN	4	1	0.25	187	2.14	1	0	0.00	2	50.00	0
DYSPUHF-SOLA	3	1	0.33	220	1.36	1	0	0.00	0	0.00	0
ASSAU-JORH	2	1	0.50	138	1.45	1	0	0.00	0	0.00	0
RAJAU-BIKA	1	3	3.00	220	0.45	1	0	0.00	2	200.00	0
Total	**484**	**1860**	**3.84**	**10539**	**4.59**	**4.8**	**97**	**20.04**	**317**	**65.50**	**1.80**

TP=Total Papers; TC=Total Citations; ACPP=Average Citation Per Paper; TIO=Total Papers of the Institute; INSH=Institute Share in Total Papers; HI-Index; ICP=International Collaborative Papers; NCIL=National Collaborative Links; IUCL=Inter-University Collaborative Links

5.2.8 Chemistry

The 20 agricultural universities together contributed 278 papers in chemistry, constituting 3.00% share of total publication output of agricultural universities and 0.53% of the output of India in chemistry during 2007-11.

On individually analyzing the profile of 18 agricultural universities in chemistry during 2007-11, six universities were found to have more than the average productivity (17.39) of all universities. They are PUNJAU-LUDH with 61 papers, followed by GBPUAT-NAIN (55), IARI-DELH (38 papers), CCSHAU-HISAR (34 papers), MPUAT-UDAIP (24 papers) and IVRI-BAREILY (21 papers).

Nine universities have registered higher citation impact per paper than the average impact (2.36) of all universities. They are TAMVASU-CHENN with citation impact per paper of 8.67, followed by IVRI-BAREILY (7.62), ANGRAU-HYDE (5.43), IARI-DELHI (4.29), ORISUAT-BHUB (4.20), BKCV-MOHAN (3.17), UAS-BANG (2.55), TAMILAU-COIM (2.53) and WBUAFS-KOLK (2.43). Seven universities have registered higher h-index values than the average h-index (3.22) of all universities. They are IARI-DELHI and PUNJAU-LUDH with h-index value of 7 each, IVRI-BAREILY and GBPUAT-NAIN (6 each), ANGRAU-HYDE, UAS-BANG and TAMILAU-COIM (4 each).

Table 13: Profile of agricultural universities in Chemistry, 2007-11

Name (Abbreviated)	2007-11										
	TP	TC	ACPP	TIO	INSH	HI	ICP	% ICP	NCLIN	%NCLIN	IUCL
PUNJAU-LUDH	61	88	1.44	1083	5.63	7	7	11.48	16	26.23	3
GBPUAT-NAIN	55	75	1.36	871	6.31	6	5	9.09	33	60.00	2
IARI-DELHI	38	163	4.29	1588	2.39	7	7	18.42	21	55.26	0
CCSHAU-HISAR	34	19	0.56	787	4.32	3	2	5.88	14	41.18	2
MPUAT-UDAIP	24	7	0.29	398	6.03	2	0	0.00	3	12.50	0
IVRI-BAREILY	21	160	7.62	1413	1.49	6	2	9.52	14	66.67	4
TAMILAU-COIM	15	38	2.53	771	1.95	4	7	46.67	13	86.67	1
NDRI-KARN	12	22	1.83	657	1.83	3	2	16.67	6	50.00	4
UAS-BANG	11	28	2.55	422	2.61	4	2	18.18	17	154.55	1
SKUAST-JAMM	9	13	1.44	163	5.52	2	0	0.00	7	77.78	7
WBUAFS-KOLK	7	17	2.43	252	2.78	3	0	0.00	4	57.14	0
ANGRAU-HYDE	7	38	5.43	191	3.66	4	1	14.29	7	100.00	1
BKCV-MOHAN	6	19	3.17	187	3.21	2	0	0.00	1	16.67	0
ORISUAT-BHUB	5	21	4.20	214	2.34	2	0	0.00	3	60.00	1
TAMVASU-CHENN	3	26	8.67	591	0.51	1	0	0.00	2	66.67	0
RAJAU-BIKA	3	5	1.67	220	1.36	2	0	0.00	3	100.00	0
CSKHPKV-PALAM	2	0	0.00	146	1.37	0	0	0.00	2	100.00	0
Total	**313**	**739**	**2.36**	**9954**	**3.14**	**3.22**	**35**	**11.18**	**166**	**53.04**	**1.30**

TP=Total Papers; TC=Total Citations; ACPP=Average Citation Per Paper; TIO=Total Papers of the Institute; INSH=Institute Share in Total Papers; HI-Index; ICP=International Collaborative Papers; NCIL=National Collaborative Links; IUCL=Inter-University Collaborative Links

Six universities have achieved international collaborative publication share higher than the average international collaborative publication share (11.18%) of all universities. They are TAMILAU-COIM with international collaborative publication share of 46.67%, followed by IARI-DELHI (18.42%), UAS-BANG (18.18%), NDRI-KARN (16.67%), ANGRAU-HYDE (14.29%) and PUNJAU-LUDH (11.48%). Twelve universities have scored the share of national collaborating links more than the average national collaborating links (53.04%) of all universities. They are UAS-BANG with national collaborating links share of 154.55%, followed by ANGRAU-HYDE, RAJAU-BIKA and CSKHPKV-PALAM (100.0% each), TAMILAU-COIM (86.67%), SKUAST-JAMM (77.78%), IVRI-BAREILY and TAMVASU-CHENN (66.67% each), GBPUAT-NAIN and ORISUAT-BHUB (60.0% each), WBUAFS-KOLK (57.14%) and IARI-DELH (55.26%). The average number of inter-university links per university was 1.30, which varied from 0 to 7. Six universities had more than the average interuniversity links of all 20 agricultural universities. They are SKUAST-JAMM with collaborative links of 7, followed by NDRI-KARN (4 linkages), IVRI-BAREILY (4 linkages), PUNJAU-LUDH (3 linkages), etc. The largest number (3 each) of inter-university collaboration links in chemistry is between PUNJAU-LUDH and SKUAST-JAMM and between NDRI-KARN and SKUAST-JAMM, etc.

Seven agricultural universities had more institutional share than the average institutional share (3.14%) of all universities. They are GBPUAT-NAIN with average institutional share of 6.31%, followed by MPUAT-UDAIP (6.03%), PUNJAU-LUDH (5.63%), SKUAST-JAMM (5.52%), CCSHAU-HISAR (4.32%), ANGRAU-HYDE (3.66%) and BKCV-MOHAN (3.21%) (Table 13)

5.2.9 Engineering

The 20 agricultural universities together contributed 360 papers in engineering, constituting 3.88% share of total publication output of agricultural universities and 0.62% of the output of India in engineering during 2007-11.

On individually analyzing the profile of 20 agricultural universities in engineering during 2007-11, six universities were found to have more than the average productivity (24.30) of all universities. They are GBPUAT-NAIN with 129 papers, followed by MPUAT-UDAIP (101 papers), PUNJAU-LUDH (47 papers), TAMILAU-COIM (46 papers), IARI-DELH (37 papers) and CCSHAU-HISAR (37 papers.

Eight universities have registered higher citation impact per paper than the average impact (1.34) of all universities. They are WBUAFS-KOLK with citation impact per paper of 14.33, followed by TAMVASU-CHENN (9.33), NDRI-KARN (5.33), ANGRAU-HYDE (3.44), IARI-DELHI (3.08), DYSPUHF-SOLA (2.33), BKCV-MOHAN (2.14) and IVRI-BAREILY (1.58). Nine universities have registered higher h-index values than the average h-index (2.60) of all universities. They are IARI-DELHI. MPUAT-UDAIP and GBPUAT-NAIN with h-index value of 6 each, followed by NDRI-KARN and TAMILAU-COIM (4 each), WBUAFS-KOLK, ANGRAU-HYDE, BKCV-MOHAN and PUNJAU-LUDH (3 each).

Eleven universities have achieved international collaborative publication share higher than the average international collaborative publication share (10.49%) of all universities. They are TAMVASU-CHENN with international collaborative publication share of 100.00%, followed by KERAU-TRISS (50.00%), ANGRAU-HYDE and UAS-BANG (33.33% each), BKCV-MOHAN (28.57%), WBUAFS-KOLK (16.67%), TAMILAU-COIM (15.22%), ORISUAT-BHUB (13.33%), ASSAU-JORH (12.50%), NDRI-KARN (11.11%) and MPUAT-UDAIP (10.89%). Thirteen universities have scored the share of national collaborating links more than the average national collaborating links (45.47%) of all universities. They are IVRI-BAREILY with national collaborating links share of 116.67%, followed by BKCV-MOHAN, WBUAFS-KOLK, CSKHPKV-PALAM, TAMVASU-CHENN and KERAU-TRISS (100.0% each), UAS-BANG (83.22%), DYSPUHF-SOLA (66.67%), IARI-DELH (64.86%), ANGRAU-HYDE (55.56%), ORISUAT-BHUB (53.33%), MPUAT-UDAIP (50.50%) and SKUAST-JAMM (50.0%).The average number of inter-university links per university was 0.85, which varied from 0 to 3. Ten universities had more than the average interuniversity links of all 20 agricultural universities. They are GBPUAT-NAIN and TAMILAU-COIM with collaborative links of 3 each, followed by MPUAT-UDAIP, IVRI-BAREILY and KERAU-TRISS (2 each), etc. The largest number (2 each) of inter-university collaboration links in chemistry is between IVRI-BAREILY and GBPUAT-NAIN and between TAMILAU-COIM and KERAU-TRISS.

Seven agricultural universities had more institutional share than the average institutional share (4.61%) of all universities. They are MPUAT-UDAIP with average institutional share of 25.38%, followed GBPUAT-NAIN (14.81%), ORISUAT-BHUB (7.01%), TAMILAU-COIM (5.97%), ASSAU-JORH (5.80%), ANGRAU-HYDE (4.71%) and CCSHAU-HISAR (4.70%) (Table 14)

Table 14: Profile of agricultural universities in engineering, 2007-11

Name (Abbreviated)	2007-11										
	TP	TC	ACPP	TIO	INSH	HI	ICP	% ICP	NCLIN	%NCLIN	IUCL
GBPUAT-NAIN	129	114	0.88	871	14.81	6	10	7.75	41	31.78	3
MPUAT-UDAIP	101	113	1.12	398	25.38	6	11	10.89	51	50.50	2
PUNJAU-LUDH	47	25	0.53	1083	4.34	3	2	4.26	14	29.79	0
TAMILAU-COIM	46	30	0.65	771	5.97	4	7	15.22	13	28.26	3
IARI-DELHI	37	114	3.08	1588	2.33	6	3	8.11	24	64.86	1

Name (Abbreviated)	2007-11										
	TP	TC	ACPP	TIO	INSH	HI	ICP	% ICP	NCLIN	%NCLIN	IUCL
CCSHAU-HISAR	37	6	0.16	787	4.70	2	1	2.70	15	40.54	1
ORISUAT-BHUB	15	2	0.13	214	7.01	1	2	13.33	8	53.33	0
IVRI-BAREILY	12	19	1.58	1413	0.85	2	1	8.33	14	116.67	2
NDRI-KARN	9	48	5.33	657	1.37	4	1	11.11	2	22.22	0
ANGRAU-HYDE	9	31	3.44	191	4.71	3	3	33.33	5	55.56	1
ASSAU-JORH	8	7	0.88	138	5.80	1	1	12.50	3	37.50	0
BKCV-MOHAN	7	15	2.14	187	3.74	3	2	28.57	7	100.00	1
UAS-BANG	6	5	0.83	422	1.42	2	2	33.33	5	83.33	1
WBUAFS-KOLK	6	86	14.33	252	2.38	3	1	16.67	6	100.00	0
SKUAST-JAMM	4	1	0.25	163	2.45	1	0	0.00	2	50.00	0
CSKHPKV-PALAM	4	0	0.00	146	2.74	0	0	0.00	4	100.00	0
TAMVASU-CHENN	3	28	9.33	591	0.51	2	3	100.00	3	100.00	0
DYSPUHF-SOLA	3	7	2.33	220	1.36	2	0	0.00	2	66.67	0
KERAU-TRISS	2	2	1.00	227	0.88	1	1	50.00	2	100.00	2
RAJAU-BIKA	1	0	0.00	220	0.45	0	0	0.00	0	0.00	0
Total	**486**	**653**	**1.34**	**10539**	**4.61**	**2.6**	**51**	**10.49**	**221**	**45.47**	**0.85**

TP=Total Papers; TC=Total Citations; ACPP=Average Citation Per Paper; TIO=Total Papers of the Institute; INSH=Institute Share in Total Papers; HI-Index; ICP=International Collaborative Papers; NCIL=National Collaborative Links; IUCL=Inter-University Collaborative Links

5.2.10 Energy

The 20 agricultural universities together contributed 85 papers in energy, constituting 0.92% share of total publication output of agricultural universities and 0.80% of the output of India in energy during 2007-11.

On individually analyzing the profile of 15 agricultural universities in energy during 2007-11, five universities were found to have more than the average productivity (6.8) of all universities. They are MPUAT-UDAIP with 31 papers, followed by PUNJAU-LUDH (21 papers), GBPUAT-NAIN (16 papers), IARI-DELHI (9 papers) and TAMILAU-COIM (7 papers).

Four universities have registered higher citation impact per paper than the average impact (5.41) of all universities. They are IARI-DELHI with citation impact per paper of 16.78, followed by CCSHAU-HISAR (15.75), ANGRAU-HYDE (9.50) and PUNJAU-LUDH (7.10). Four universities have registered higher h-index values than the average h-index (2) of all universities. They are PUNJAU-LUDH with h-index value of 9, followed by MPUAT-UDAIP (6), IARI-DELHI (4) and GBPUAT-NAIN (3).

Four universities have achieved international collaborative publication share higher than the average international collaborative publication share (11.76%) of all universities. They are ORISUAT-BHUB with international collaborative publication share of 50.00%, followed by CCSHAU-HISAR (25.00%), MPUAT-UDAIP (16.13%) and TAMILAU-COIM (14.29%). Eight universities have scored the share of national collaborating links more than the average national collaborating links (56.86%) of all universities. They are UAS-BANG, ORISUAT-BHUB and ANGRAU-HYDE with national collaborating links share of 150.0% each, followed by DYSPUHF-SOLA, BKCV-MOHAN and ASSAU-JORH (100.0% each), IARI-DELH (77.78%) and PUNJAU-LUDH (71.43%).

Four agricultural universities had more institutional share than the average institutional share (1.22%) of all universities. They are MPUAT-UDAIP with average institutional share of 7.79%, followed PUNJAU-LUDH (1.94%), GBPUAT-NAIN (1.84%) and ANGRAU-HYDE (1.05%) (Table 15).

Table 15: Profile of agricultural universities in Energy, 2007-11

Name (Abbreviated)	2007-11										
	TP	TC	ACPP	TIO	INSH	HI	ICP	%ICP	NCLIN	%NCLIN	IUCL
MPUAT-UDAIP	31	132	4.26	398	7.79	6	5	16.13	13	100.00	0
PUNJAU-LUDH	21	149	7.10	1083	1.94	9	2	9.52	15	56.86	0
GBPUAT-NAIN	16	20	1.25	871	1.84	3	2	12.50	8	100.00	0
IARI-DELHI	9	151	16.78	1588	0.57	4	0	0.00	7	56.86	0
TAMILAU-COIM	7	3	0.43	771	0.91	1	1	14.29	0	100.00	0
CCSHAU-HISAR	4	63	15.75	787	0.51	1	1	25.00	2	56.86	
UAS-BANG	2	2	1.00	422	0.47	1	0	0.00	3	100.00	0
KERAU-TRISS	2	0	0.00	227	0.88	0	0	0.00	0	56.86	0
DYSPUHF-SOLA	2	5	2.50	220	0.91	1	0	0.00	2	100.00	0
ORISUAT-BHUB	2	1	0.50	214	0.93	1	1	50.00	3	56.86	0
ANGRAU-HYDE	2	19	9.50	191	1.05	1	0	0.00	3	100.00	0
NDRI-KARN	1	3	3.00	657	0.15	1	0	0.00	0	56.86	0
TAMVASU-CHENN	1	0	0.00	591	0.17	0	0	0.00	0	100.00	0
BKCV-MOHAN	1	4	4.00	187	0.53	1	0	0.00	1	56.86	0
ASSAU-JORH	1	0	0.00	138	0.72	0	0	0.00	1	100.00	0
Total	**102**	**552**	**5.41**	**8345**	**1.22**	**2.0**	**12**	**11.76**	**58**	**56.86**	

TP=Total Papers; TC=Total Citations; ACPP=Average Citation Per Paper; TIO=Total Papers of the Institute; INSH=Institute Share in Total Papers; HI-Index; ICP=International Collaborative Papers; NCIL=National Collaborative Links; IUCL=Inter-University Collaborative Links

6 SUMMARY

The twenty Indian agricultural universities together have published 9272 papers, constituting 2.75% of the Indian research output during 2007-11. Their research output increased from 1701 in 2007 to 2112 papers in 2011, witnessing an annual average growth rate of 5.71%. The productivity of individual agricultural university during 2007-11 varied from 138 to 1588, and witnessing an average productivity per organization of 526.95. The agricultural universities have registered an average citation per paper of 1.76, which varied from 0.77 to 2.96. These 20 agricultural universities have published 1049 international collaborative papers with 83 countries, constituting 11.31% share in the total output of these universities, decreasing from 13.52% in 2007 to 11.36% in 2011.Of the collaborating countries, the largest share (32.32%) of papers was published with United States, followed by UK (10.39% share), Germany (9.25% share), Australia (7.91% share), China (6.96% share), Canada (6.67% share), Iran, South Korea, collaboration links of 20 agricultural universities accounts for 43.93% share (4630 papers) of their total research output during 2007-11. The share of national collaboration links varies from 26.41% to 81.31% and with average number of national collaboration links per university as 231.5. Of the total national collaboration links, the largest share of collaboration links (50.26%) were to academic institutions (varying from 27.27% to 75.86%), followed by research institutions (45.36%)(varying from 26.23% to 62.30%), institutes of national importance (3.80%)(varying from 0.0% to 15.85%), industry (1.32%) (0.0% to 6.80%) and others (0.99%) (0.0% to 6.86%).

The average number of inter-university links per university was 44.05, which varies from 17 to 174. The largest number of interuniversity links (174) is made by IVRI-BAREILLY, followed by IARI-DELHI (106), GBPUAT-NAIN (78), CCSHAU-HISAR (70), PUNJAU-LUDH (56), NDRI-KARN (53), and SKUAST-JAMM (48), WBUAFS-KOLK (41) .etc. The largest number (33) of inter-university collaboration links are between IVRI-BAREILY and GBUAT-NAIN, followed by IVRI-BAREILY and NDRI-KARN (30 links), IVRI-BAREILY and TAMVASU-CHEN (25 links), IVRI-BAREILY and WBUAFS-KOLK (24 links), IARI-DELHI and GBPUAT-NAIN (23 links), PUNJAU-LUDH and CCSHAU-HISAR (21 links), IARI-DELHI and CCSHAU-HISAR (19 links), NDRI-KARNAL and SKUAST-JAMU (15 links), IVRI-BAREILY and SKUAST-JAMU (13 links), etc

The 20 agricultural universities together contributed 5945 papers (with 60.88% share in universities output and 16.22% in Indian subject output) in agricultural and biological sciences, 2087 papers (with 22.51% share in universities output and 33.24% in Indian subject output) in veterinary science, 1366 papers (with 14.73% share in universities output and 3.19% in Indian subject output) in biochemistry, genetics and molecular biology, 778 papers (with 8.39% share of in university output and 6.68% share in Indian subject output) in immunology and microbiology, 760 papers (with 8.20% share in universities output and 3.58% in Indian subject output) in environment science, 342 papers (with 3.69% share of in university output and 1.09% share in Indian subject output) in pharmacology, toxicology and pharmaceutics, 443 papers (with 4.78% share of in university output and 0.64% share in Indian subject output) in medicine, 360 papers (with 3.88% share of in university output and 0.62% share in Indian subject output) in engineering , 278 papers (with 3.0% share of in university output and 0.53% share in Indian subject output) in chemistry and 85 papers (with 0.92% share of in university output and 0.80% share in Indian subject output) in energy during 2007-11.

In terms of average institutional share of 20 agricultural universities in different subjects , the largest share (68.76%) was in agricultural and biological sciences, followed by veterinary sciences (25.05%), biochemistry, genetics and molecular biology (13.57%), environment science (8.26%), immunology and microbiology (6.31%), engineering (4.61%), medicine (4.59%), pharmacology, toxicology and pharmaceutics (3.43%), chemistry (3.14%) and energy (1.221%) during 2007-11.

The average productivity per university (297.25) was highest in agricultural and biological sciences, veterinary sciences (120.35), biochemistry, genetics and molecular biology (71.3), immunology and microbiology (45.78), environment science (43.05), engineering (24.30), medicine (24.20), pharmacology, toxicology and pharmaceutics (19.32), chemistry (17.39) and energy (6.8) during 2007-11.

The largest average citation impact per paper (5.41) by 20 agricultural universities was made in energy, followed by veterinary science (4.33), immunology and microbiology (4.31), medicine (3.84), biochemistry, genetics and molecular biology (3.37), environment science (2.37), pharmacology, toxicology and pharmaceutics (2.40), chemistry (2.36), agricultural and biological sciences (1.52) and engineering (1.34) during 2007-11.

The highest average h-index value (10.7) of 20 agricultural universities was achieved by agricultural and biological sciences, followed by biochemistry, genetics and molecular biology (7), immunology and microbiology (5.89), environment science (5), medicine (4.8), veterinary science (4.15), pharmacology, toxicology and pharmaceutics (3.26), chemistry (3.22), engineering (2.60) and energy (2.0) during 2007-11.

The average share of international collaborative papers of 20 agricultural universities was highest (22.30%) in biochemistry, genetics and molecular biology, followed by medicine (20.04%), immunology and microbiology (16.99%), environment science (13.24%), energy (11.76%), chemistry (11.18%), engineering (10.49%), agricultural and biological sciences (10.36%), pharmacology, toxicology and pharmaceutics (7.63%) and veterinary science (3.86%) during 2007-11.

The average share of national collaborating links of 20 agricultural universities was highest (75.07%) in veterinary science, followed by pharmacology, toxicology and pharmaceutics (74.51%), medicine (65.50%), biochemistry, genetics and molecular biology (64.80%), immunology and microbiology (64.32%), energy (56.86%), agricultural and biological sciences (54.68%), chemistry (53.04%), environment science (47.50%) and engineering (45.47%) during 2007-11.

Among the various subjects, the average number of interuniversity collaboration links was highest (32.3) in agricultural and biological sciences, followed by veterinary sciences (12), biochemistry, genetics and molecular biology (4.65), environment science (3.75), immunology and microbiology (3.70), pharmacology, toxicology and pharmaceutics (1.80), medicine (1.80), chemistry (1.30), engineering (0.85) and energy (0).

REFERENCES

1. Agriculture sector in India. November 2012. http://www.ibef. org/industry/agriculture-india.aspx (Accessed on December 24, 2012).
2. K.P. Singh. (2012) Growth and Development of Agricultural Education, Research, and Libraries in India. *DESIDOC Journal of Library and Information Technology*, 32(1): 5-14.
3. Sarkhel, J.K. and Choudhury, Nitani Ray. Contribution of Bidhan Chandra Krishi Viswavidalaya to agricultural research: A bibliometric study. *Annals of Library and Information Studies December 2010,* 57(4): 348-55.
4. Hussain, Shabahat and Mushtaq, Muzamil. (2011) Scientometric study of Indian central universities: A picture from Scopus. *Journal of Indian Library Association,* 47(3-4): 5-12.

5. Sevukan, R.; Nagarajan, M. and Sharma, Jaideep. Research output of faculties of plant sciences in central universities of India: A bibliometric study. Annals of Library and Information Studies September 2007, 54(3), 129-39.
6. Sevukan, R and Sharma, Jaideep. Bibliometric analyses of research output of biotechnology faculties in some Indian central universities. *DESIDOC Journal of Library and Information Technology November 2008*, 28(6): 11-20.
7. Anitha, N. Research trends of biology in selected central universities. http://www.authorstream.com/Presentation/anitharajan-1196687-research-trends-of-biology-in-slected-central-universities-autosaved/
8. Nagpal, P.S. (2005) Contribution of Indian universities to the mainstream scientific literature: A bibliometric assessment. *Scientometrics January*, 32(1): 11-36.

9

Acknowledgements in Research Papers in Electronics and related Fields: 2008-2012

Susanta Koley and ***B.K. Sen***

Studies the acknowledgements incorporated in research papers on electronics and related fields appearing during 2008-2012 in *IETE Technical Review*, and *IETE Journal of Research*, official publications of The Institution of Electronics and Telecommunication Engineers (IETE). Results show that nearly 35% articles contains acknowledgements; on average acknowledgement per articles is 2.2; mostly acknowledgements relates to financial support. Only 21% of acknowledgements address to the PIC [Peer Interactive Communication], and two persons are acknowledged two times. The number of articles with acknowledgements is higher in *IETE Technical Review* compared to IETE *Journal of Research*. The number of PIC acknowledgements in electronics research is very low compared to other journals. Forty-two percent articles acknowledge one addressee and 1% articles acknowledges up to ten addressees at a time.

KEYWORDS: Acknowledgement, *IETE Journal of Review*, *IETE Journal of Research*, Bibliometrics, Electronics Research.

1 INTRODUCTION

Acknowledgements form one of the parts of a printed work. It is also found in doctoral thesis, journal articles, project reports and so on. According to Kyland and Tse (2004) "Acknowledging the assistance and contributions of others is now a well-established feature of the scholarly communication process". It is a practice to give due respect to individual(s) or organization(s) for assistance to complete a research article, book, thesis, dissertation, project or experiments, by way of funding, comment, encouragement or any other support to the worker (s) or reseacher(s). The practice of acknowledgement does have certain social functions and cognitive significance (Tiew and Sen, 2002: 43). Cheng (2012) opines that it is an 'interpersonal relationship' along with the 'writers' socio-cultural values and identity in academia'. Giles and Councill (2004) defined acknowledgments as "a wide range of relationships among people, agencies, institutions, and research." Its location varies and is found in separate pages after the dedication page in books and theses; and after conclusion and before references in journal articles.

The present study is a bibliometric analysis of acknowledgements found in electronics research papers. The scale and significance of acknowledgements vary from field to field, and from journal to journal. Cronin, Mckenzie and Stiffler (2004) have shown such variations in library and information science (LIS) journals and commented that 'a small number of individuals are highly acknowledged and a majority are mentioned infrequently'. Similarly, Tiew and Sen (2002) have also recorded that PIC acknowledgements are more or less the same with those found in LIS. Other works on the same lines were carried out by Mackintosh (1972) in the field of sociology. Davis and Cronin (1993) showed that acknowledgements related to intellectual indebtedness. Kyland (2004) studied varieties of acknowledgements taking 240 doctoral and MA dissertations written by non-native speakers of English in a variety of disciplines at five Hong Kong universities. Cheng's study was based on Masters' theses only. Rigby's (2011) was related to systematic grants and funding bodies.

2 SCOPE

The source journals of this study are *IETE Journal of Research* (f.1955) and *IETE Technical Review* (f.1984) which are published by the Institution of Electronics and Telecommunication Engineers, New Delhi. Since their inception they have been publishing, original research and review papers describing the state-of–the art technologies.

This study covers 546 source articles, of which 298 articles pertain to *IETE Journal of Research* (V. 54-58), and 248 articles to *IETE Technical Review* (V.25-29) published during 2008-2012. Of these articles, 191 articles contain acknowledgments.

3 OBJECTIVES

The objectives of this study are to find out the

1. number of articles with acknowledgements;
2. number of acknowledgement in articles;
3. types of acknowledgements;
4. average number of acknowledgement per article;
5. PIC acknowledgements; and
6. number of addressees acknowledged at a time.

4 METHODOLOGY

Data obtained were examined, classified and analyzed keeping the objectives in view. Finally results were tabulated and discussed.

5 RESULTS AND DISCUSSION

5.1 Articles with Acknowledgements

Table 1: No. of articles with acknowledgements

Journal / Year	*IETE Technical Review*			*IETE Journal of Research*		
	No. of Articles	Number of Articles with Acknowledgements	%	No. of Articles	Number of Articles with Acknowledgements	%
2008	53	08	15.09	57	14	24.57
2009	47	13	27.66	47	13	27.66
2010	51	29	56.87	50	15	30.00
2011	53	19	35.85	72	29	40.28
2012	44	21	47.73	72	30	41.67
Total	**248**	**90**	**36.29**	**298**	**101**	**33.90**

Table 1 shows the number of articles with acknowledgements in the research articles of *IETE Technical Review* and *IETE Journal of Research*. Out of 248 articles of *IETE Technical Review*, 90(36.29%) articles contain acknowledgements. Maximum number of articles, i.e. 51(56.87%) contained acknowledgements in 2010 and minimum number 8 (15.09%) in 2008. In case of *IETE Journal of Research*, the scenario is as follows. Out of 298 articles, 101 contained acknowledgements. Maximum number of articles, i.e. 30(41.67%) contained acknowledgements in 2012, and minimum number 14(24.56%) in 2008. In other words, trend of use of acknowledgement in *IETE Technical Review* has increased from 15.09 % in 2008 to 56.87% in 2010 and thereafter it has ups and downs. In the case of *IETE Journal of Research* an upward trend is observed during the period (Fig.1).

5.2 Number of Acknowledgements

The acknowledgements per article is given in Table 2.

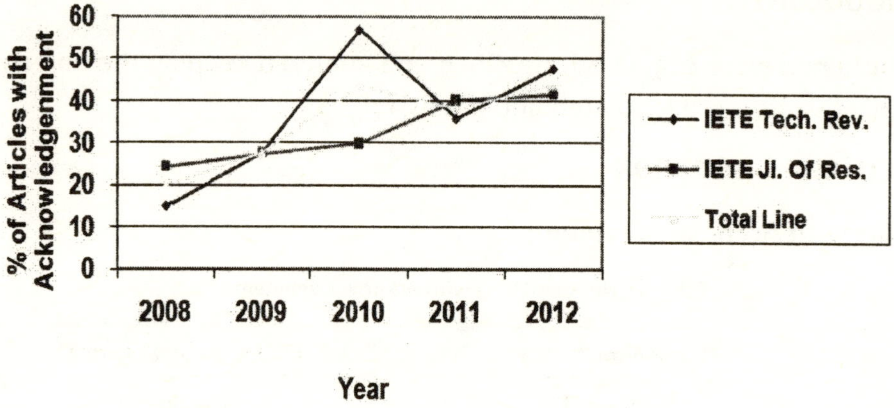

Fig. 1: Trends of use of acknowledgement

Table 2: Acknowledgements per article

Journals / Years	*IETE Technical Review*			*IETE Journal of Research*		
	No. of Articles with Acknowledge-ments	No. of Acknowledge-ments	Average	No. of Articles with Acknowledge-ments	No. of Acknowledge-ments	Average
2008	08	13	1.63	14	42	3.00
2009	13	33	2.54	13	25	1.93
2010	29	66	2.28	15	32	2.14
2011	19	37	1.95	29	69	2.38
2012	21	49	2.34	30	64	2.14
Total	90	198	2.20	101	232	2.30

Table 2 shows the frequency of acknowledgements appearing in both the source journals. In *IETE Technical Review* the highest average number of acknowledgements per article is in 2009 (2.54) and lowest number in 2008 (1.63). For *IETE Journal of Research*; the highest number is in 2008 (3.00 per article) and the lowest number in 2009 (1.93). On average, each article recorded 2.20 and 2.30 acknowledgements in both the journals respectively. Comparatively, the average number of acknowledgements is more or less the same in the two journals.

5.3 Types of Acknowledgement

For this study, acknowledgements have been categorized according to various supports or assistance, such as access support (AS), peer interactive communication (PIC), moral support (MS), technical support (TS), editorial support (ES), clerical support (CS), financial support (FS), unclassified (UC) (Cronin, McKenzie and Rubio, 1993; Tiew and Sen, 2002; Wikipdia,). Table 3 and 4 shows acknowledgements according to categories.

Table 3: Acknowledgements according to Categories: *IETE Technical Review*

Year	AS	MS	TS	FS	ES	CS	PIC	UC	Total
2008	01	02	04	06	-	-	-	-	13
2009	04	04	02	21	-	-	02	-	33
2010	02	06	03	46	03	-	-	06	66
2011	02	02	-	32	-	-	-	01	37
2012	-	03	-	37	01	-	08	-	49
Total	**09**	**17**	**09**	**142**	**04**	-	**10**	**07**	**198**
%	**4**	**9**	**4**	**72**	**2**	-	**5**	**4**	**100**
Rank	**IV**	**II**	**IV**	**I**	**VII**	-	**III**	**IV**	

Table 4: Acknowledgments according to Categories: *IETE Journal of Research*

Year	AS	MS	TS	FS	ES	CS	PIC	UC	Total
2008	04	05	04	07	01	06	12	03	42
2009	02	02	06	06	04	-	05	-	25
2010	03	09	04	08	03	-	-	05	32
2011	17	04	15	20	-	-	11	02	69
2012	03	09	14	35	01	-	02	-	64
Total	**29**	**29**	**43**	**76**	**09**	**06**	**30**	**10**	**232**
%	**12**	**12**	**19**	**33**	**4**	**3**	**13**	**4**	**100**
Rank	**IV**	**IV**	**II**	**I**	**VI**	**VIII**	**III**	**VI**	

Tables 3 and 4 present acknowledgements according to categories. The highest number of acknowledgements in *IETE Technical Review* is in the FS category (72%); followed by MS category (9%); PIC category (5%); AS, TS (4% each), ES category (2%). In *IETE Journal of Research*, the largest number is in FS category (33%), then others according to rank are TS (19%), PIC (13 %), AS and MS (12% each), ES (4%), CS (3%). In both the cases, only 4% of acknowledgements could not be classified due to non-availability of proper information i.e. Unclassified category.

Table 5: Total Acknowledgements by Categories

Year	AS	MS	TS	FS	ES	CS	PIC	UC	Total
2008	05	07	08	13	01	06	12	03	55
2009	06	06	08	27	04	-	07	-	58
2010	05	15	07	54	06	-	-	11	98
2011	19	06	15	52	-	-	11	03	106
2012	03	12	14	72	02	-	10	-	113
Total	**38**	**46**	**52**	**218**	**13**	**06**	**40**	**17**	**430**
%	**9**	**11**	**12**	**51**	**3**	**1**	**9**	**4**	**100**
Rank	**IV**	**III**	**II**	**I**	**VII**	**VIII**	**IV**	**VI**	

Table 5 shows total acknowledgements by categories. It is seen from the Table that FS category accounts for the highest number (51%), followed by TS (12%), MS (11%), PIC and AS (9%), ES (3%) and CS (1%). It should be noted that financial support is the highest (51%) in total acknowledgements which is seen in Tables 3 and 4 also since no research activity is possible without money.

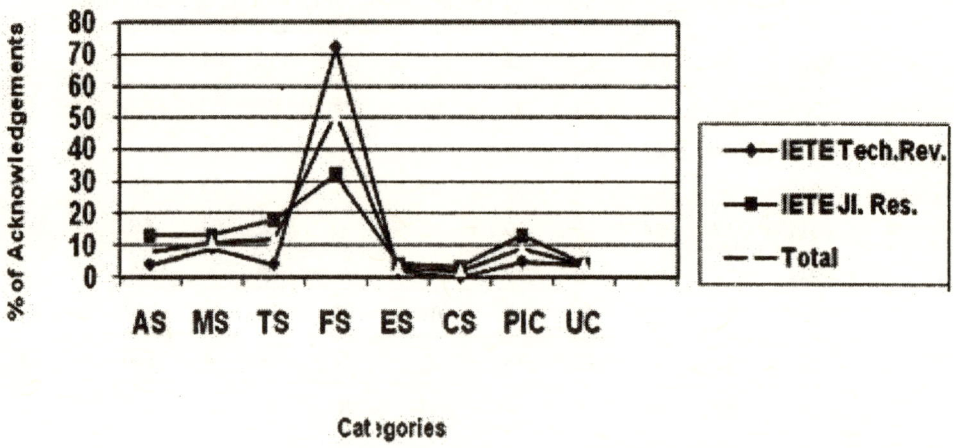

Fig. 2: Graphic presentation of acknowledgements

5.4 PIC Acknowledgement

"PIC" stands for Peer Interactive Communication i.e. communication with human resource or subject experts of the related field of researchers. As generally conceptual support is taken from such human resource or experts, this is also called as "conceptual support". Acknowledgement of conceptual support helps for identifying intellectual debt and this is considered to be important as valuable as citations (Giles and Councill, 2004; Wikipedia, n.d.).

Table 6: Acknowledgements of PIC

Year	IETE Tech. Review			IETE Journal of Research			Total		
	Articles with Acknow-ledgement	Number of Acknowledge-ment of PIC	%	Articles with Acknow-ledgement	Number of Acknow-ledgement of PIC	%	Articles with Acknow-ledgement	No. of PIC Acknow-ledgement	%
2008	08	00	-	14	12	86	22	12	55
2009	13	02	15	13	05	38	26	07	27
2010	29	00	-	15	-	-	44	-	-
2011	19	00	-	29	11	38	48	11	23
2012	21	08	38	30	02	7	51	10	20
Total	**90**	**10**	**11**	**101**	**30**	**35**	**191**	**40**	**21**

Table 6 shows acknowledgement of PIC in *IETE Technical Review*, and *IETE Journal of Research*. From the first source journal, it is seen that the highest number of PIC acknowledgement has been recorded in 2012 (38%) while the lowest number (15%) in 2009 and the average is only 11%. No PIC acknowledgement is seen in 2008, 2010 and 2011. Besides, in case of second source journal, the highest number of PIC acknowledgments (86%) in 2008 that is very high, whereas lowest number (7%) in 2012 and its average is 35%. Over all, PIC acknowledgement has decreased from 55% in 2008 to 20% in 2012, and average is 21%. From the above discussion, it may be noted that the average of individual journal (11% and 35%) and even of total (24%) are very low as compared to other journals as mentioned by Tiew and Sen (2002). However, the number of PIC Acknowledgement in electronics research is rather low. Graphically, a comparison can be drawn between the data furnished by Tiew and Sen with the data of the present study.

Table 7: Comparison of PIC Acknowledgement

Name of Journals	Code Name	Average in %
Journal of Documentation	JD	56.5
Journal of American Society of Info. Science	JASIS	54.9
Information Processing & Management	IPM	49.5
College and Research Libraries	CRL	46.2

Name of Journals	Code Name	Average in %
Library Quarterly	LQ	42.6
Psychology Review	PR	78.1
American Sociology Review	ASR	92.6
American Historical Review	AHR	83.7
Journal of Natural Rubber Research	JNRR	44.0
IETE Technical Review (selected for present study)	ITR	11.0
IETE Journal of Research (selected for present study)	IJR	35.0

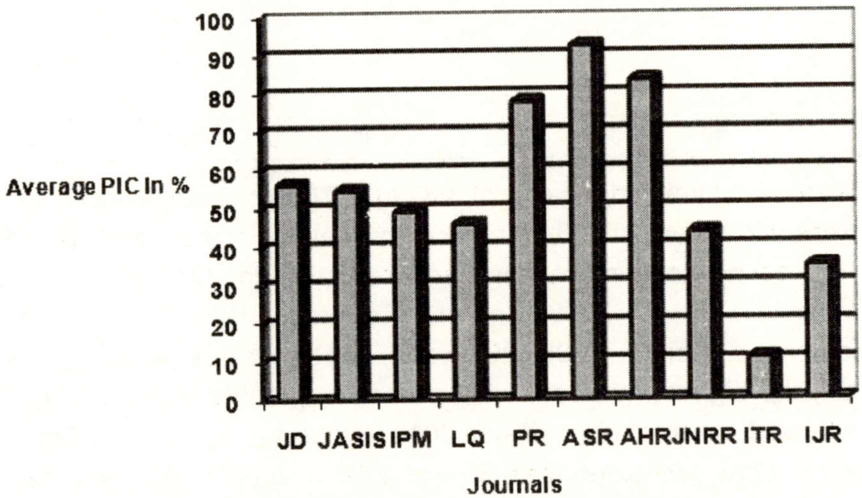

Fig. 3: Comparison of PIC Acknowledgement

5.5 Frequency of Persons acknowledged in PIC Acknowledgement

Only two persons have been acknowledged two times. They are P.K. Mukhopadhyay, Head, Electronics Division, BARC and P.S. Dhekne, Associate Director (E), E and I Group, BARC.

5.6 Acknowledgement to Addressee(s)

Addressee is that person to whom due respect or gratitude or thanks or gratefulness or indebtedness is expressed in the acknowledgement for the support in creating or completing any work successfully. Addressee may be person, institution, agency, co-author/ co-workers, peers, friends or family members or well-wishers, subject mentors, etc. Cheng (2012: 9-10) has given several semantic definitions of acknowledgements. One simple definition is as follows: expression of 'thanking' or 'gratefulness' to the "addressee (s)' for some 'reasons'. The single quoted facets themselves indicates subject-matter of acknowledgement i.e. information of these three facets is generally furnished is an acknowledgement.

Table 8: Pattern of Acknowledgement

Acknowledgement to Addressees	No of Articles with Acknowledgements	Percentage
One	82	42
Two	53	27
Three	30	16
Four	10	6
Five	05	3
Six	05	3
Nine	04	2
Ten	02	1
Total	**191**	**100**

Table 8 shows pattern of acknowledges in electronics research papers i.e. according to number of addressee(s) appearing in an acknowledgement at a time. This reports that 42% articles contains acknowledgement to one addressee, followed by 27% articles with acknow-ledgement to two addressees, 16% with acknowledgement to three addressees, 6% with acknowledgement to four addressees. Only 2% articles contain acknowledgement to nine addressees, and 1% with acknowledgement to ten addressees at a time.

6 CONCLUSIONS

Expression of gratitude, gratefulness or thanking is an old practice in Indian societies. Its impacts are recognized by the community of students, authors, researchers also. From this study, the following facts have been noted:

1. Only 35% articles in electronics research contain acknowledgement, which is very low compared to other areas;
2. The average acknowledgement per article is 2.2;
3. Most of the acknowledgements appear is related to the financial category accounting for 51% of total acknowledgement, as research cannot run without funds;

4. Of the source articles, articles with acknow-ledgement in IETE Technical Review is 36.29%, whereas 33.89% in IETE Journal of Research. Averages are 2.2 and 2.3 respectively;
5. Only 21% of total acknowledgement is found to be PIC Acknowledgement that is very less than others, and of which, only two persons have been acknowledged two times; and
6. Highest ten addressees has been acknowledged articles at a time in 1% of the articles. It indicates many addressees can be acknowledged in one acknowledgement at a time.

REFERENCES

1. Cheng, Stephanie W. (2012) A Contrastive study of master thesis acknowledgements by Taiwanese and North American students. *Online Journal of Modern Linguistics*, 2(1): 8-17. doi: 10.4236/ojml.2012.21002
2. Cronin, B.; McKenzie, G., and Rubio, L. (1993) The norms of acknowledgement in four humanities and social sciences disciplines. *Journal of Documentation*, 49(1): 29-43.
3. Cronin, Blaise; Mckenzie, Gail and Stiffler, Michael. (1992) Patterns of Acknowledgement. *Journal of Documentation*, 48(2): 107-122. Davis, C. H. & Blaisie Cronin (1993).
4. Acknowledgements and intellectual indebtedness: A bibliometric conjecture. *Journal of the American Society for Information Science*, 44(10): 590-592.
5. Giles, C. Lee and Councill, Isaac G. (2004) Who gets acknowledged: Measuring scientific contributions through automatic acknowledgement indexing. **In** *`PANS Proceedings of the National Academy of Sciences of the United States of America*, 101(51): 17599-17604. Retrieved from http://intl. pnas.org on 10.12.2012.
6. Kyland, K. (2004) Gradates' gratitude: the generic structure of dissertation Acknowledgements. *English for Specific Purposes*, 23:303–324.doi: 10.1016/S0889-4906(03)00051-6
7. Kyland, K. and Tse, P. (2004) I would like thank my supervisor: Acknowledgements in graduate dissertations. *International Journal of Applied Linguistics*, 14(2): 259-275. doi:10.111/j.1473-4192. 2004.00062.x
8. Mackintosh, K.H. (1972) Acknowledgement patterns in sociology. Ph.D. dissertation, University of Oregon.
9. Rigby, J. (2011) Systematic grant and funding body acknowledgement data for publications: An Examination of new controversies for bibliometrics. *Manchester Business School Working Paper*, Number 611. Retrieved from http://www.mbs. ac.uk/research/workingpapers.aspx on 15.12.2012
10. Tiew, W.S. and Sen, B.K. (2002) Acknowledgement patterns in research articles: A Bibliometric study based on Journal of Natural Rubber Research 1986-1997. *Malaysian Journal of Library and Infiormation Science*, 7(1): 43-56.
11. Wikipedia: Free encyclopedia. (n.d.) Acknowledgement (Creative arts). Retreived from www. en.wikipedia.org/wikj/ Acknowledgement_(creative_arts) on.05.03.2012.

10

Research Collaboration in the Field of Social Sciences

S.L. Sangam and ***Shivaranjini, S. Mogali***

In this paper, an attempt has been made to investigate the pattern of authorship, type of collaborated research and the degree of collaboration in the field of Social Sciences. The data was collected from social science citation index of ISI Thomson Reuters, for the period of twelve years i.e. 2000-2011. Author publications have been divided into three block periods 2000-2003, 2004-2007, and 2008-2011. The Collaborative Index (CI) and Degree of Collaboration (DC) and Collaboration Coefficient (CC) have been calculated. These are increasing from one block to another indicating a progressive trend in collaborative research.

KEYWORDS: Collaboration, Collaborative index, Degree of collaboration, Collaboration coefficient

1 INTRODUCTION

In recent times collaboration is an integral part of research. It is a mutual involvement of participants in a coordinated effort to overcome certain problems together. The collaborative interactions are characterized by shared goals, symmetry of structure and a high degree of negotiation, interactivity and interdependence. The sharing of goals may be interdisciplinary, interdepart- mental or interinstitutional. The interdisciplinary collaboration has increased the productivity of research and encouraged the development of innovative new strategies in investigations. Social Science domain is a vast discipline and there is a scope for interdisciplinary growth through collaborative work done by Social Scientist who may belong to different disciplines.

It has been found from the earlier studies that collaboration in research varies from discipline to discipline and for the same discipline from time to time and from one country to another. Some of the notable studies in the field are Subramanyam (1993), Maheshwarappa (1987), Gupta (2000), Sangam (2009), Kretschmer (2004) etc. In the present study an attempt has been made to know the Authorship pattern and Collaborative measures in the Social Sciences.

2 METHODOLOGY AND DATABASE

The present study has been done by referring to Social Science Citation Index of ISI Web of Knowledge published by Thomson Reuters. According to the index the Social Science has a large number of subfields and the quantum of literature output is too much to handle. Therefore only 31 subfields of Social Sciences have been selected for analytical study. Further these 31 subfields have been grouped into five main fields: Psychology, Economics, Sociology, Political Science and History. The data on authorship pattern and collaborative measures have been considered for the period 2000 to 2011 only. The collaborative Index, Degree of Collaboration and Collaboration Coefficient were determined based on year-wise output of publications.

3 ANALYSIS AND INTERPRETATION

3.1 Single *vs* Multi-authored Papers

Table 1 shows the distribution of total number of single and multi-author publications in three block periods 2000-2003, 2004-2007, and 2008-2011. In psychology there is an increasing trend both in single author publications and collaborative author publications; however, a slight increase is seen in collaborative author publication in 2008-2011. In economics there is an increasing trend in single author publications and collaborative author publications but in 2000-2003 and 2004-2007, Single Author (SA) is more than Collaborative Publications (CP) while in 2008-2011 CP is more than SA. It indicates that collaboration is increasing. In sociology also in the first two block periods SA predominates over CP, while in the third it shows CP predominating over SA. It indicates increasing trend of collaboration. In Political Science there is a constant increase both is SA and CP in all the three block periods. However, only a slight increase in CP is observed in block 2008-2011. In case of history there is a constant increase in SA while the CP shows a sudden increase up to 65.57% in the third block period showing trend towards collaboration. The overall inference is that the collaborative publication shows an increasing trend.

Table 1: Distribution of single author publication and collaborative author publications in three block periods during2000-2003, 2004-2007 and 2008-2011

Block Period	Psycology				Economics				Sociology			
	SA		CP		SA		CP		SA		CP	
	T	%	T	%	T	%	T	%	T	%	T	%
2000-2003	132	23.66	345	21.93	192	24.09	280	16.88	555	35.04	254	25.45

Block Period	Psycology				Economics				Sociology			
	SA		CP		SA		CP		SA		CP	
	T	%	T	%	T	%	T	%	T	%	T	%
2004-2007	165	29.57	466	29.62	255	31.99	405	24.41	485	30.62	231	23.15
2008-2011	261	46.77	762	48.44	350	43.91	974	58.71	544	34.34	513	51.4
Total	**558**	**100**	**1573**	**100**	**797**	**100**	**1659**	**100**	**1584**	**100**	**998**	**100**

Contd...

Block Period	History				Political Science			
	SA		SA		SA		CP	
	T	%	T	%	T	%	T	%
2000-2003	40	25.32	11	18.03	64	23.1	16	18.6
2004-2007	48	30.38	10	16.39	61	22.02	20	23.26
2008-2011	70	44.3	40	65.57	152	54.87	50	58.14
Total	**158**	**100**	**61**	**100**	**277**	**100**	**86**	**100**

SA=Single Author, CP= Collaborative Publication T= Total %=Percentage

4 DISTRIBUTION OF PUBLICATIONS BY NUMBER OF AUTHORS

Table 2 shows the distribution of publications by the number of authors in five main subdiscipines. In psychology the number of authors 4 and above are 641 which is the highest; it is 375 for three authors which is least, whereas single and two authors are almost equal in number. This is an indication that team of researchers are more in psychology. When we consider the number of authors block-wise, there is an increasing trend in single, two, three and four and above authorship. In Economics two author papers are 893 followed by single author 797 and then three author collaboration 502 and lastly four and more authorship 264. Here also there is an increasing trend in all the four categories of authorship.

Table 2: Distribution of publications classifieds by number of authors in Block Period during 2000-2003, 2004-2007 and 2008-2011

Block Period	Psycology				Economics				Sociology			
	S	D	T	Four & Above	S	D	T	Four & Above	S	D	T	Four & Above
2000-2003	132	144	74	127	192	171	86	23	555	135	66	53
2004-2007	165	161	114	191	255	235	119	51	485	111	60	60
2008-2011	261	252	187	323	350	487	297	190	544	224	146	143
Total	**558**	**557**	**375**	**641**	**797**	**893**	**502**	**264**	**1584**	**470**	**272**	**256**

Contd...

Block Period	Political Science				History			
	S	D	T	Four & Above	S	D	T	Four & Above
2000-2003	64	9	4	3	40	5	4	2
2004-2007	61	13	5	2	48	4	3	3
2008-2011	152	27	13	10	70	18	7	15
Total	277	49	22	15	158	27	14	20

S= Single author; D=Double author; T=Three author; F= Four author

In sociology single author publications are more in number 1584; it decreased to 470 for two authors and 272 for three authors and only 256 in four and above author collaborations. The single author number in first block is more and decreased in second block and again increased in third; this trend hold even if for two and three authors also. In Political science the maximum contribution is by single authors and it has decreased as the number of authors increased. Single and four and more authors show decreasing trend in the second block whereas two and three author collaborations show consistent increase. Again, in History also the major share is of single authorship, then two authors, four and more authors and lastly three author collaborations. The block-wise distribution shows an increasing trend in single and four and more author collaborations, while two and three authors category shows a little decrease in the second block period. The overall picture shows that the major contributions are from single authors.

4.1 The Relative Growth of Single-authored vs Multi-authored Contributions

Table 3 shows the relative growth of single and multi-author publications analyzed in terms of relative frequency of publications. The relative frequency has been calculated by taking the number of publications (single / multi-author) and by dividing the same by total number of publications (single / multi-author).

Table 3: Relative Frequency of Publications by number of authors in block period during 2000-2003, 2004-2007 and 2008-2011

Block Period	Psychology				Economics				Sociology			
	S	D	T	F & above	S	D	T	F & Above	S	D	T	F & above
2000-2003	0.2366	0.2585	0.1973	0.1981	0.2409	0.1915	0.1713	0.0871	0.3504	0.2872	0.2426	0.207
2004-2007	0.2957	0.289	0.304	0.298	0.3199	0.2632	0.2371	0.1932	0.3062	0.2362	0.2206	0.2344
2008-2011	0.4677	0.4524	0.4987	0.5039	0.4391	0.5454	0.5916	0.7197	0.3434	0.4766	0.5368	0.5586

Condt...

Block Period	Psychology				Economics			
	S	D	T	F & above	S	D	T	F & above
2000-2003	0.231	0.184	0.182	0.2	0.253	0.185	0.286	0.1
2004-2007	0.22	0.265	0.227	0.133	0.304	0.148	0.214	0.15
2008-2011	0.549	0.551	0.591	0.667	0.443	0.667	0.5	0.75

S= Single author; D=Double author; T=Three author; F= Four author

In Psychology the relative frequency is showing an increasing trend and more so in case of four and more authorship collaborations. In Economics a similar trend is observed. In Sociology there is a decrease compared to the 1st block in Single, Two and Three authors frequency. Again it has increased in the third block. In four and more authorship category there is an increase block by block. In Political Science the single and four and more authorship contributions are less frequent in the second block where as double and three authors category the frequency has increased gradually. In History the frequency of single and four and more authorship has increased considerably from one block to another block period whereas two and three authorship collaborations has decreased in the second block compared to that in the first block period. In psychology there is an increase from one block to another block in all categories of authorship. In economics also a similar trend is observed. In Sociology the second block shows a decrease in the category of single, double and three authors collaboration, whereas in four and more authorship collaboration there is an increase compared to the first block period. In Political Science except single and four and more authorship collaboration in the 2004-07 block an increasing trend is observed in two and three author collabrations. In history except in the second block that too in double and three authored publications there is an increase in all other categories of authorship. The overall figures shows that the frequency of publications is more in the period 2008-2011 in all the five subjects which clearly indicates the positive trend of collaborative publications.

4.2 Collaboration Measures

The measures Degree of Collaboration (DC), first suggested by Subramanyam (1993) which takes the proportion of co-authored publications in the total number ofpublications, the Collaboration Index (CI), first suggested by Lawani, which takes the mean number of authors per publication has been studied. Table 4 shows the mean number of authors per publication in Psychology, 2.41 in the block 2000-2003 that increased to 2.56 in 2008-2011. The degree of collaboration remains the same in all the three block periods. In Economics also the mean of collaborative index 1.87 in the first block and increased to 2.25 in the last block period, whereas the DC is almost same with little increase. In Sociology, Political Science and History the Collaborative mean is the same which is lower in the first block but gradually increased in the second and third blocks. The same phenomenon is also observed in DC also. The results obtained by the computation shows that the CI and DC are increasing along the time period indicating the team work pattern of the professionals in the field of Social Science.

Table 4: Collaboration publications in different block periods during 2000-2003, 2004-2007 and 2008-2011

Block Period	Psychology		Economics		Sociology		Political Science		Histroy	
	CI	DC	CI	DC	CI	DC	CI	DC	CI	DC
2000-2003	2.41	0.89	1.87	0.78	1.53	0.55	1.33	0.4	1.37	0.43
2004-2007	2.52	0.9	1.95	0.8	1.57	0.57	1.36	0.45	1.33	0.38
2008-2011	2.56	0.9	2.25	0.88	1.89	0.73	1.41	0.47	1.7	0.63

CI= Collaboration Index; DC= Degree of Collaboration

4.3 Basic Statistics of Authorship data in Different Subject Fields in 3 Block Periods

Table 5 presents the basics statistics of authorship data in different subject fields in three block periods 2000-2003, 2004-2007 and 2008-2011.

Table 5: Basic Statistics of authorship data in different subject fields in three block periods 2000-2003, 2004-2007 and 2008-2011

Block Period	Statistics						Statistics			
	Psycology		Economics		Sociology		Political Science		Histroy	
	Mean	Variance	Mean	Variance	Mean	Variance	Mean	Variance	Mean	Variance
2000-2003	2.4109	2.3987	1.8729	1.8654	1.5266	1.5237	1.325	1.3031	1.3725	1.3356
2004-2007	2.5246	2.5145	1.9485	1.9427	1.574	1.5706	1.358	1.3353	1.3276	1.2972
2008-2011	2.5591	2.5527	2.247	2.2432	1.894	1.8906	1.4109	1.401	1.7	1.6737

It is observed that the mean value has increased from one block period to another in psychology, economics sociology and political science whereas there is slight decrease in the second block period with respect to history. In psychology the mean value 2.41 has increased to 2.55; in Economics the mean value 1.87 increased to 2.24, in Sociology the mean value 1.5 increased to 1.89, and in Political

Science the mean value 1.32 increased to 1.41. This indicates the increasing trend of collaborative research publication. Whereas in History the mean value in first block period is 1.37 and decreased to 1.32 in second block and again increased to 1.70 in the third block. As far as variance is concerned the same pattern is noted but the degree of variance varies from subject to subject. The highest contribution is from psychology, followed by economics, sociology, history and last political science.

4.4 Application of Selected Probability Distribution to the Distribution of Authorship in Publication

Five subdiscipines of social science viz Psychology, Economics, Sociology, Political Science and History during the block periods 2000-2003, 2004-2007, 2008-2011 have been chosen to explore the goodness of fit by applying Lotka's Geometric, and Truncated Poisson statistical distributions. Table 6 shows in Psychology the Lotka's inverse power law decreased from 0.19(2000-2003) to 0.03(2008-2011). The geometric distribution shows 0.293 to 0.2837 in the second block and again decreased to 0.2809 in the last block. And the Truncated Poisson distribution shows 2.41 in the first block and raised to 2.52 in the second block and again increased to 2.55 in the last block.

Table 6: Parameter value obtained from application of selected probability distribute one to the distribution of authorship in publications in different subject in block periods from 2000-2003, 2004-2007, 2008-2011

Block Period	Parameter Value								
	Psychology			Economics			Sociology		
	Lotka α	Geom P	Poison λ	Lotka α	Geom P	Poison λ	Lotka α	Geom P	Poison λ
2000-2003	0.19	0.2932	2.4109	1.373	0.3481	1.8729	1.747	0.3957	1.33
2004-2007	0.22	0.2837	2.5246	1.085	0.3392	1.9485	1.589	0.3885	1.57
2008-2011	0.03	0.2809	2.5591	0.41	0.308	2.247	1.015	0.3455	1.89

Contd...

Block Period	Parameter Value					
	Political Science			History		
	Lotka α	Geom P	Poison λ	Lotka α	Geom P	Poison λ
2000-2003	2.265	0.43	2.325	2.87	0.4215	1.3725
2004-2007	2.423	0.42	2.358	2.059	0.4296	1.3276
2008-2011	2.013	0.41	1.4108	1.36	0.3704	1.7

In Economics the Lotka's inverse power law decreased from 1.373(2000-2003) to 0.41(2008-2011). The geometric distribution shows 0.3481 to 0.308 in the last block. And the Truncated Poisson distribution shows increasing trend i.e 1.8729 in the first block and raised to 2.247 in the last block.

In Sociology the Lotka's inverse power law shows 1.747(2000-2003) to 1.015(2008-2011). The geometric distribution shows 0.3957 to 0.3455 in the last block. And the Truncated Poisson distribution shows increasing trend i.e 1.33 in the first block and raised to1.89 in the last block.

In Political Science the Lotka's inverse power law shows 2.265 (2000-2003) and little increase in the second block (2.423) and again decreased to 2.013(2008-2011). The geometric distribution shows 0.43 to 0.41 in the last block. And the Truncated Poisson distribution shows 2.325 in the first block and raised to2.358 in the second block and again decreases to 1.4108 in the last block.

In History the Lotka's inverse power law shows 2.87(2000-2003) and little decrease in the second block (2.059) and again decreased to 1.36(2008-2011). The geometric distribution shows 0.4215 in the first block and raises to 0.4296 and then decreases to 0.3704 in the last block. And the Truncated Poisson distribution shows 1.37 in the first block and decreases to1.32 in the second block and again increases to 1.7 in the last block.

In Psychology, Economics, Sociology, Political Science there is an increasing trend in Truncated Poisson value. Similarly the geometric distribution shows decreasing trend from one block to another block in all the five subjects. As far as lotka's inverse power law varies from subject to subject and from one block to another.

4.5 Chi-Square value and degree of Freedom obtained from fitted distribution to the distribution of authorship in publications in different block periods from 2000-2003, 2004-2007, 2008-2011 (Table 7)

The chi-square value and degree of freedom obtained from fitted distribution of authorship in publications in different block periods from 2000-2003, 2004-2007, 2008-2011.

In order to understand the distribution pattern of authorship and their goodness of fit in publication pattern Lotka's Geometric and Truncated Poisson distributions have been applied. In Table 7 the psychology in the first block period Lotka's chi-square value is 22.63 decreased to 20.35 during second block and again raised to 36.33 in the third block. Geom Chi-Square value shows an increase from 345.04 to 935.11 and in case of Poisson the chi-square increased from 91.81 to 255 .3.Similarily in Economics during the first block the Lotka's chi-square value 85.10 decreases to 68.63 and again raised to 109.18 in the last block. Where as Geom Chi-square value and Poisson value there is an increasing trend from one block to another. In case of sociology during the first block the Lotka's chi-square value is 8.247 and raised to 23.05 and again falls down to 11.18 during the last block period. The Geom Chi-square raises from first block to second block and fall down in the third block. Where as there is a constant decrease from one block to another block in the Poisson chi-square value. In case of Political Science the Lotka's chi-square value, Geom, Poisson values during 2004to 2007 block show comparatively less than the first block and third block . In History the Lotka's, Geom, and Poisson chi-square values have increased from one block to another block.

Table 7: Chi-Square value and degree of Freedom obtained from fitted distribution to the distribution of authorship in publications in different block periods from 2000-2003, 2004-2007, 2008-2011

Block Periods	Statistical Model for distribution																	
	Psychology						Economics						Sociology					
	Lotka		Geom		Poison		Lotka		Geom		Poison		Lotka		Geom		Poison	
	1	2	1	2	1	2	1	2	1	2	1	2	1	2	1	2	1	2
2000-2003	22.635	4	345.04	4	91.81	4	85.103	4	251.39	4	44.581	4	8.247	4	565	4	348.45	4
2004-2007	20.352	4	537.19	4	144.4	4	68.636	4	317.65	4	46.581	4	23.05	4	595	4	326.21	4
2008-2011	36.34	4	935.11	4	255.3	4	109.18	4	745.54	4	69.998	4	11.18	4	523	4	254.35	4

Contd...

Block Periods	**Statistical Model for distribution**											
	Political Science						**History**					
	Lotka		**Geom**		**Poison**		**Lotka**		**Geom**		**Poison**	
	1	**2**	**1**	**2**	**1**	**2**	**1**	**2**	**1**	**2**	**1**	**2**
2000-2003	2.185	4	101.9	4	52.769	4	9.2156	4	61.843	4	32.599	4
2004-2007	0.36	4	87.31	4	41.71	4	9.3677	4	83.021	4	46.019	4
2008-2011	4.174	4	217.2	4	112.58	4	11.5183	4	89.416	4	56.392	4

1= Chi-Sqaure Value; 2= Df

5 CONCLUSION

The latest research trends show that they are more data intensive than earlier research due to the proliferation of digital technologies and the demand for solutions in today's era of fast paced innovation. Similarily the movement towards collaborative innovation is affecting scientific research, bringing scientists from different disciplines together in their pursuit of solutions to today's challenges. In particular, teams that work collaboratively can obtain greater resources, recognition and reward when facing competition for finite resources. The collaboration is not limited to individual scientists; it is extended even up to institutions, communities, and nations and so on. The concept of team work is in vogue because of various funding agencies. The investigation of such nature may be found useful in understanding the research and communication patterns of various disciplines, and hence would be helpful in planning more effective research and communication systems.

REFERENCES

1. Subramanyam, K. (1993) Bibliometric Studies as research collaboration: a review. *Journal of Information* Science, 6: 35
2. Maheshwarappa, B.S (1987) Research Collaboration in different disciplines of applied science in India: a bibliometric Study, *IASLIC Bullitin*, 105-114
3. Gupta,B.M (2000) Application of statistical models to the collaborative publications. Data in Theoretical population Genetics .*Malaysian Journal of Library and Information Science*, 5(1): 37-51.
4. Sangam, S.L. and Meera (2009) Research Collaboration Pattern in Indian Contribution to Chemical Sciences. *COLLNET Journal of Scientometrics and Information Management*, 3(1): 39-45.
5. Kretschmer, H (2009) Authorproductivity and Geodistance in Bibliographic co-authorship networks, and visibility on the web. *Scientometrics,* 60(3): 409-420.

11

Scientometric Study of Carbon Nanotube Research in India

Bidyarthi Dutta and ***Durga Sankar Rath***

This paper reports on a scientometric study of 834 articles on Carbon nanotube research in India spanning over the years 1999 to 2012 downloaded from *Web of Science*. The study analyses literature growth trends, which shows an initiation of potential growth of research in this subject since 2008. It also examines collaborations with different countries. The authorship pattern, document types involved and active Indian institutions co-coordinating research in this subject have also been studied. Bradford law of scattering was applied to identify the core journals and Lotka's law to study the authors' productivity pattern.

KEYWORDS: Scientometrics, Informetrics, Bibliometrics, Carbon nanotube, Nanotechnology, Nanoscience, Bradford's law, Lotka's law, Research trend, India

1 INTRODUCTION

Emerging technologies shape existing societies since time immemorial. It is well known that invention of fire and wheel radically altered the then societal functions. Similarly information and communication technology (ICT) totally changed the global scenario since the eighties of the last century followed by biotechnology and nanotechnology. NBIC is an acronym for Nanotechnology, Biotechnology, Information technology and Cognitive science, is currently the most popular term for emerging and converging technologies, and was introduced into public discourse through the publication of *Converging Technologies for Improving Human Performance*, a report sponsored in part by the U.S. National Science Foundation [1]. Nanotechnology is the engineering of functional systems at the molecular scale. It is not a particular technology applicable to a specific area of industry, but a broad spectrum of technological innovations functioning at nanoscale (1 nanometer = 10^{-9} meter). Nanotechnology is not just a subject domain from this viewpoint, but may be reckoned as a broad discipline embracing a large number of specific subjects. The conceptual root of nanotechnology can be traced to 1959

Richard Feynman's talk *There's Plenty of Room at the Bottom*, in which he described the possibility of synthesis via direct manipulation of atoms. The term "nano-technology" was coined by Norio Taniguchi in 1974. Inspired by Feynman's idea, K. Eric Drexler used the term "nanotechnology" in his 1986 book *Engines of Creation: The Coming Era of Nanotechnology*, which proposed the idea of a nanoscale "assembler" that would be able to build a copy of itself and of other items of arbitrary complexity with atomic control [2].

Carbon nanotubes (CNTs) are allotropes of carbon with a cylindrical nanostructure. It is a special type of material that is widely used in fabricating products at nano scale. It is an important material of nanotechnology. Nanotubes have been constructed with length-to-diameter ratio of up to 132,000,000:1, significantly larger than for any other material. These cylindrical carbon molecules have unusual properties, which are valuable for nanotechnology, electronics, optics and other fields of materials science and technology. The material Carbon nanotube thus embraces so many specific subject domains. In particular, owing to their extraordinary thermal conductivity and mechanical and electrical properties, carbon nanotubes find applications as additives to various structural materials [3]. National Aeronautics and Space Administration [4] (NASA) defined Carbon nanotube as a new form of carbon, configurationally equivalent to two dimensional graphene sheet rolled into a tube. It is grown now by several techniques in the laboratory and is just a few nanometers in diameter and several microns long, which can be metallic or semiconducting and offers amazing possibilities to create future nanoelectronic devices, circuits and computers.

Research on Carbon nanotube thus explores potentially resourceful facets of nanotechnology and in India, significant growth in the research literature on this domain has been observed during the last few years as reflected from *Web of Science* database. This paper reports out a scientometric study of Carbon nanotube literature contributed by Indian authors. Significant scientometric studies have been carried out in the field of nanotechnology. The mapping of innovative research in India in this field was studied by Bhattacharyya [5]. Some other important contributions include Kostoff [6], Meyer [7] and Leydesdorff [8]. This paper does not cover the entire area of nanotechnology but focuses on Carbon nanotube research in India only, a thrust facet of active research in this area. The scientometric study of global trend of Carbon nanotube research was done by Marx and Barth [9] in 2010.

2 OBJECTIVES

The principal objectives of the study are to find:

- Pattern of growth of literature since 1999 to 2012;
- Authorship pattern of the articles and to find out core authors;
- Core journals of this subject domain;
- Applicability of Bradford's law and Lotka's law;
- Collaborating countries;
- Document types in which Carbon nanotube literature is published;
- Core Indian institutions carrying out research in this subject; and
- Specific thrust areas as the domain of Carbon nanotube.

3 SCOPE AND METHODOLOGY

Scientometric study is a statistical method of counting to evaluate and quantify the growth of a subject. The research trend during the said time span would be clearly understood from this study and a predictive projection may be made for an anticipatable future. There are several areas in science, social science and arts for which scientometric studies have been carried out. Scientometric studies of the subject areas like cancer [10], HIV/AIDS [11], biotechnology [12],bibliometrics [13], library and information science [14], bioinformatics [15] etc. were carried out by Patra et al. and scientometric studies in physics by Kumara [16] et al. Other scientometric studies in different subject domains include Jain [17] (Laser research), Kademani [18] (Thorium research), Stanhill [19] (climatology), Garg [20] (Laser patent literature), Upadhye [21] (physics Noble lectures), Lee [22] (molecular and cell biology), Schummer [23] (chemistry), Braun [24] and Gupta [25] (Fullerene research). Bibliometric analysis of patents for Carbon nanotube research has been done by Gupta [26]. The general definition and scope of scientometrics for all major science subjects in the context of web resources (cybermetrics) was discussed by Sen [27].

The data for this study was downloaded from the *Web of Science* database. For downloading the data, the search term applied was "Carbon nanotube" AND Author address= "India". This may be considered as central keyword of the topic discussed. As indicated by Lancaster [28], main heading includes synonyms, near-synonyms and homonyms. Therefore, the maximum retrieval may be expected by using this expresion. A total of 834 records spanning over the years 1999 to 2012 were downloaded from *Web of Science* on 2nd May, 2013. Each record contains English language abstract with detailed bibliographic information, e.g. author, name of journal, author address, affiliation, keywords, cited items etc. The downloaded data was analysed for source items to find out the research trend. The temporal variation pattern of different variables involved was studied by using the software *Findgraph*. Observed data are in approximate conformity with Bradford's [29] and Lotka's [30] distributions.

4 DATA ANALYSIS

4.1 Growth of Literature

Fig. 1 shows temporal variation of publications on Carbon nanotube research since 1999 to 2012. Out of the 834 publications during this time span, nearly three-fourth, i.e. 76% appeared after 2008 and the remaining one-fourth, (i.e. only 24%) appeared before 2008 as evident from Fig. 2. Most number of literature was published during the last two years, 2011 and 2012 that accounts for almost half (48%) of the total publications. The number of documents published along with corresponding percentages are presented in Table 1. It is evident that, in India Carbon nanotube research has gained momentum very recently and presently it is growing in full swing.

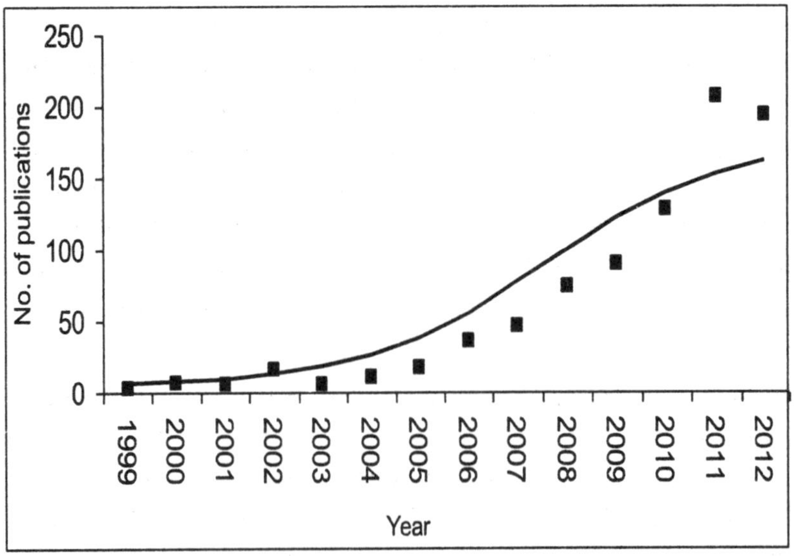

Fig. 1: Temporal variation of publications

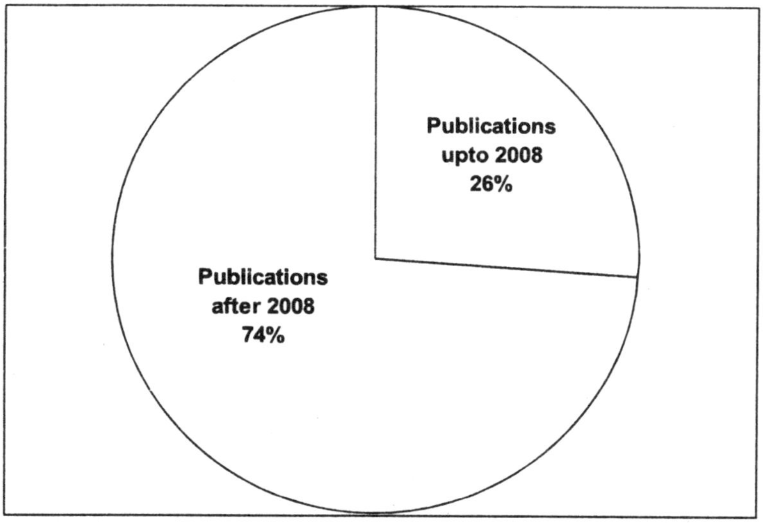

Fig. 2: Percentage distribution of publications before and after 2008

Table 2: Distribution of authorship pattern over all literature

Year	No. of publications	% of total publications
1999	3	0.4%
2000	6	0.7%
2001	5	0.6%
2002	16	1.9%
2003	5	0.6%
2004	10	1.2%
2005	17	2.0%
2006	36	4.3%
2007	46	5.5%
2008	74	8.9%
2009	89	10.7%
2010	127	15.2%
2011	206	24.7%
2012	194	23.3%
Total	**834**	**100%**

The growth pattern of published literature is in good consonance with the logistic equation presented in Equation 1.

$$y = 5 + 170/(1 + \exp(5.25 - 0.55*x)) \quad (1)$$

Where y represents number of publications literature over the years and x represents corresponding time span starting from 1999. This function involves exponential function in the denominator. The mean graph of Figure (1) represents the Equation (1).

4.2 Authorship Pattern

Table 2 presents authorship pattern for all publications. The authorship pattern is graphically presented in Fig. 3. It is observed that two-authored and three – authored publications (51%) are higher than the other modes of authorship. Single-authored publications are significantly low, only 2% and more than seven authored publication is also low, i.e. only 4%. Hence it is clear that team research is dominant here with tiny team size, i.e. number of members are mostly 2, 3, 4 and 5 that accounts 81% of total strength. Large teams are hardly involved here.

Table 2: Distribution of authorship pattern over all literature

Number of authors	Authorship	Frequency or number of publications
1	Single-authored	16 (1.9%)
2	2-authored	231 (27.7%)
3	3-authored	196 (23.5%)
4	4-authored	161 (19.3%)
5	5-authored	92 (11%)
6	6-authored	71 (8.5%)
7	7-authored	30 (3.6%)
8	8-authored	15 (1.8%)
9	9-authored	11 (1.3%)
10	10-authored	5 (0.6%)
11	11-authored	3 (0.4%)
12	12-authored	2 (0.2%)
13	13-authored	1 (0.1%)

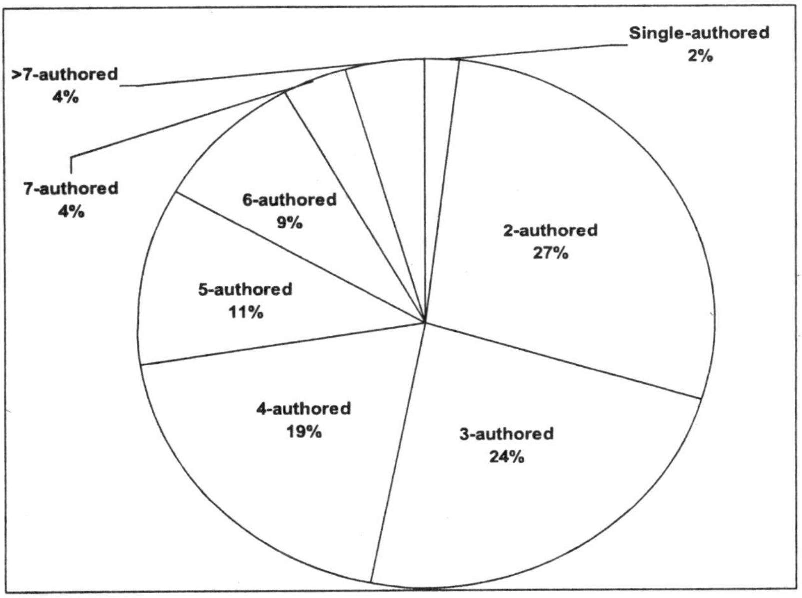

Fig. 3: Distribution of authorship pattern

4.3 Author productivity and Lotka's law

Lotka's law states that the number of authors making contributions is about $1/n^2$ of those making one; and the proportion of all contributors, that make a single contribution, is about 60 percent. This means that out of all the authors in a given field, 60 percent will have just one publication, and 15 percent will have two publications ($1/2^2$ times of 60). Seven percent authors will have three publications ($1/3^2$ times of 60), and so on. According to Lotka's law of scientific productivity, only six percent of the authors in a field will produce more than 10 articles. Lotka's law, when applied to large bodies of literature over a fairly long period of time, can be accurate in general, but not statistically exact. The general form of Lotka's law can be expressed as $y=c/x^n$ where y=percentage of authors, x=number of articles published by an author, c=constant and –n=slope of the log-log plot. In this study, 1148 authors contributed 834 articles; on an average 1.4 authors per article. Among 1148 authors, 569 authors (49.6%) contributed only one article; 306 authors (26.7%) contributed two articles and 111 (9.7%) authors contributed three articles. Hence the author productivity in Indian Carbon nanotube research approximately conforms to Lotka's law. Actually the number of two-authored articles is comparatively higher than single-authored articles in this case. In general, single-authored articles amount to nearly 60% and two-authored article 15%. But here single-authored articles amount to nearly 50%, i.e. 10% less than usual value, which was added to two-authored articles to make it nearly 25%, i.e. 10% more than the usual value of 15%. Fig. 4 shows the graph in which the number. of authors is plotted against the number of publications. The log-log plot of cumulative number of authors and their cumulative number of contributions gives an approximate straight line which is not in exact conformation with Lotka's law, but approximately so.

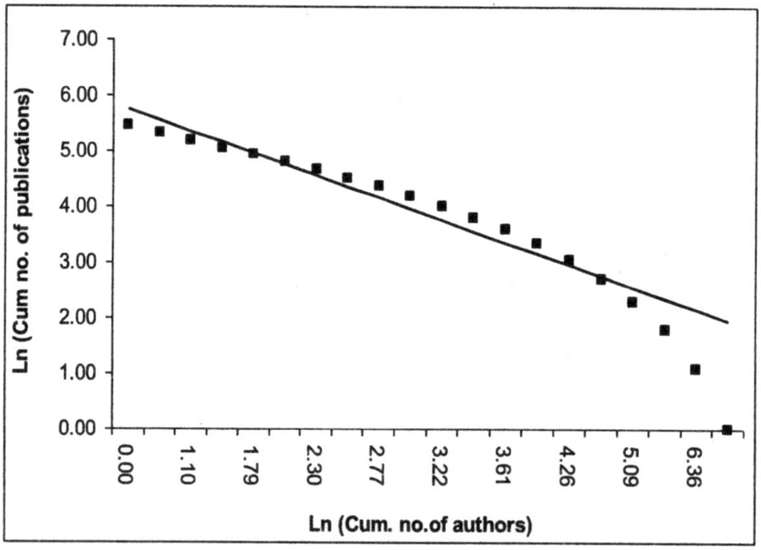

Fig. 4: ln (cum. no. of authors) *vs.* ln (cum. no. of pub.) plot

Table 3: Top twenty contributing authors with more than ten contributions each

Authors' name (surname first)	Number of articles contributed	Percentage of articles contributed
Ramaprabhu S	31	3.71
Rao C N R	25	2.99
Sood A K	21	2.51
Sharma S C	19	2.27
Govindaraj A	18	2.15
Kawazoe Y	18	2.15
Gopalakrishnan S	15	1.79
Ghosh S	14	1.68

Authors' name (surname first)	Number of articles contributed	Percentage of articles contributed
Menon R	14	1.68
Sarkar S	14	1.68
Goyal R N	13	1.56
Harsha S P	13	1.56
Iyakutti K	13	1.56
Srivastava A K	13	1.56
Das C K	12	1.44
Singh B P	12	1.44
Misra D S	11	1.32
Pillai V K	11	1.32
Srivastava A	11	1.32
Subramanian V	11	1.32

The list of top twenty authors who contributed more than twenty articles is given in Table 3 above. It is observed that S. Ramaprabhu is the most productive author with 31 publications followed by C. N. R. Rao and A. K. Sood in second and third positions respectively.

4.4 Collaboration Pattern

Of the 834 contributions in total, 271 papers were contributed due to collaborative research work of India with other countries. The topmost collaborating country is USA (25.8% contribution) followed by Japan (14.8%) in the second position, South Korea (13.3%) in the third position, France (5.5%) in the fourth position and Taiwan (5.2%) in the fifth position. The next five countries in decreasing order of contributions are Germany, Saudi Arabia, Singapore, England and Canada respectively. The list of collaborating countries is presented in Table 4 and the relative percentage contribution is presented in Fig. 5.

Table 4: List of collaborating countries

Collaborating countries	No. and % of contributions
USA	70 (25.8%)
Japan	40 (14.8%)
South Korea	36 (13.3%)
France	15 (5.5%)
Taiwan	14 (5.2%)
Germany	12 (4.4%)
Saudi Arabia	11 (4.1%)
Singapore	11 (4.1%)

Collaborating countries	No. and % of contributions
England	9 (3.3%)
Canada	7 (2.6%)
Italy	6 (2.2%)
Poland	6 (2.2%)
Portugal	5 (1.8%)
Belgium	4 (1.5%)
Ireland	4 (1.5%)
Peoples R China	4 (1.5%)
Spain	4 (1.5%)
Iran	3 (1.1%)
Australia	2 (0.7%)
Finland	2 (0.7%)
North Ireland	2 (0.7%)
Sweden	2 (0.7%)
Switzerland	2 (0.7%)

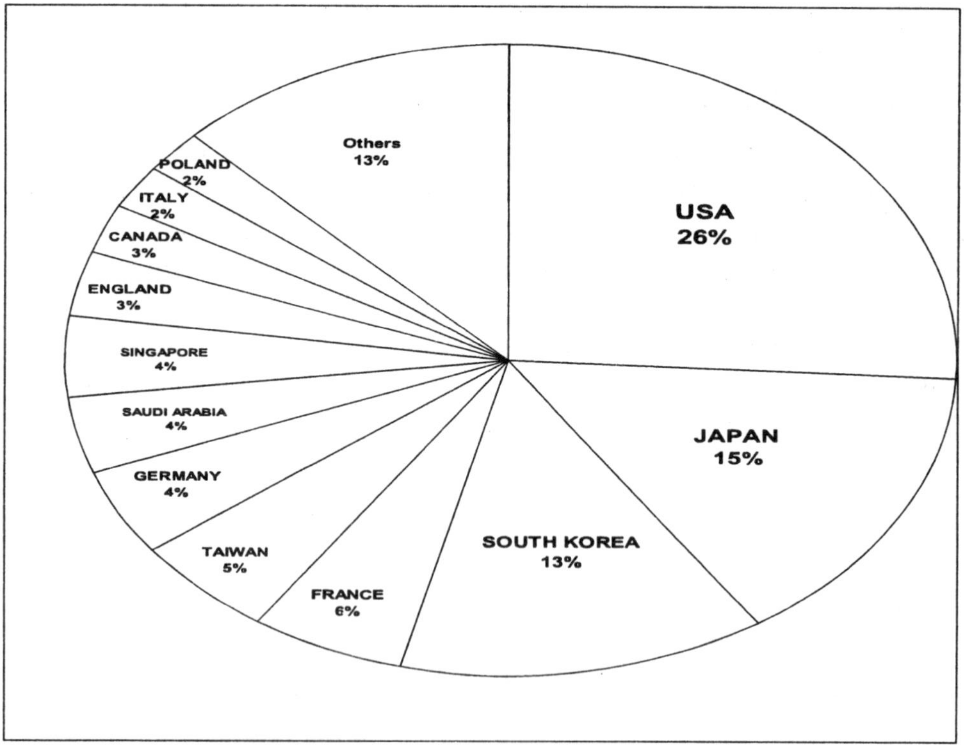

Fig. 5: Percentage distribution of contributors over collaborating countries

4.5 Document Type

Out of 834 publications, journal articles amount to 776 accounting for 93%; and conference and seminar papers amount to 58 accounting for 7%. It is thus evident that journal articles are most prefered form of research publication in this subject area. The strength of seminar and conference papers as probable research outcome is far behind the journal articles. Other forms of research outcomes are totally absent in this subject area.

4.6 Core Journals and Bradford's Law

In all, 270 journals, published 834 articles. The scattering of articles over journals may be studied using Bradford's law of bibliographic scattering. The Bradford's distribution is generally used for identify the 'core' journals. Core journals are central to a subject because they produce a subject's maximum probable content. Fig. 6 shows Bradford plot, where cumulative number of articles is plotted against the journal's rank.

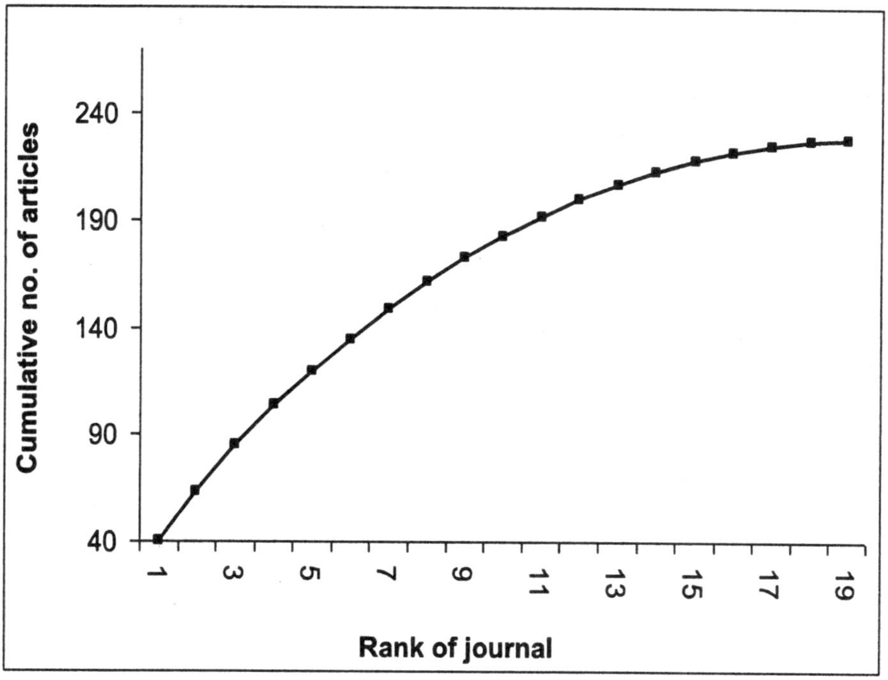

Fig. 6: Journal-rank *vs*. cumulative no. of articles plot

In all, 834 articles were published in 270 journals. The division of all articles in three equal zones retaining 277 articles in each zone shows the corresponding Bradford's ratio of number of journals as follows:

$$16 : 53 : 201$$

This ratio can be rewritten as:

$$16*(1 : 3.3 : 12.6)$$

This ratio may be approximated with the following values, $16*(1 : 3 : (3)^2)$, which is in consonance with the Bradford's pattern, i.e. $k*(1 : n : n^2)$, where k is the Bradford's multiplier. In this study, k = 16 and n = 3. The number of core, allied and alien journals in Carbon nanotube is thus 16, 53 and 201 respectively. The list of core journals is given in Table 5, which reveals that of the 16 core journals, only one (the last one in Table 5) journal is Indian, the 12th journal (rank 7) is published from UK, and remaining all fourteen journals are published from USA. Maximumnumber of journals (five) are published by Elsevier while the three publishers American Chemical Society, American Institute of Physics and American Scientific Pub. bring out two journals each. Also, all these 16 journals are closed-access. Indian scientists in this subject publish their articles mostly in international journals. Indian journals are rare in this subject. Of these journals, the *Journal of Materials Chemistry* has the highest 2011 Impact Factor, i.e. 5.968, followed by *Carbon* (IF = 5.378) and *Journal of Physical Chemistry C* (IF = 4.805). The lowest Impact Factor is for *Bulletin of Material Science* (0.88), the only Indian journal here.

Table 5: List of core journals in the subject domain carbon nanotube

Sl. No.	Rank	Journals	Publisher and place	Impact Factor (2011)	5-year Impact Factor	Immediacy Index	No. & % of articles published therein
1	1	Journal of Nanoscience and Nano-technology	American Scientific Pub. (USA)	1.563	1.574	0.208	40 (4.8%)
2	2	Nano-technology	Institute of Physics (USA)	3.979	4.017	0.665	23 (2.8%)
3	3	Applied Physics Letters	American Institute of Physics (USA)	3.844	3.787	0.661	22 (2.6%)

Sl. No.	Rank	Journals	Publisher and place	Impact Factor (2011)	5-year Impact Factor	Immediacy Index	No. & % of articles published therein
4	4	Carbon	Elsevier (USA)	5.378	6.008	1.081	19 (2.3%)
5	4	Journal of Applied Physics	American Institute of Physics (USA)	2.168	2.169	0.369	19 (2.3%)
6	5	Electrochimica Acta	Elsevier (USA)	3.832	4.039	0.45	16 (1.9%)
7	5	Journal of Applied Polymer Science	John Wiley (USA)	1.289	1.413	0.218	16 (1.9%)
8	5	Sensors and Actuators B Chemical	Elsevier (USA)	3.898	3.751	0.355	16 (1.9%)
9	6	Chemical Physics Letters	Elsevier (USA)	2.337	2.215	0.45	15 (1.8%)
10	6	Physical Review B	American Physical society (USA)	3.691	3.405	0.889	15 (1.8%)
11	7	International Journal of Hydrogen Energy	Elsevier (USA)	4.054	4.402	0.591	14 (1.7%)
12	7	Journal of Materials Chemistry	Royal Society of Chemistry (UK)	5.968	5.992	1.088	14 (1.7%)
13	7	Journal of Physical Chemistry C	American Chemical Society Pub. (USA)	4.805	5.049	0.72	14 (1.7%)
14	8	Journal of Computational and Theoretical Nanoscience	American Scientific Pub. (USA)	0.912	0.871	0.099	13 (1.6%)

Sl. No.	Rank	Journals	Publisher and place	Impact Factor (2011)	5-year Impact Factor	Immediacy Index	No. & % of articles published therein
15	9	Journal of Physical Chemistry B	American Chemical Society Pub. (USA)	3.696	4.061	0.715	11 (1.3%)
16	10	Bulletin of Materials Science	Indian Academy of Science (India)	0.88	1.333	0.024	10 (1.2%)

In accordance with 5-year impact factor, the topmost journal is *Carbon* (6.008), followed by *Journal of Materials Chemistry* (5.992) and *Journal of Physical Chemistry C* (5.049). Also, the ranking by immediacy index gives the top three journals as *Journal of Materials Chemistry* (1.088), *Carbon* (1.081) and *Physical Review B* (0.889). Out of the 16, only 4 journals have impact factor below 2, i.e. *Journal of Nanoscience and Nanotechnology*, *Journal of Applied Polymer Science*, *Journal of Computational and Theoretical Nanoscience* and lastly *Bulletin of Materials Science*. The remaining twelve journals have impact factor above 2. Thus Indian scientists doing research in this field greatly prefer publication in high impact journals.

4.7 Subject Domains Covered

The bibliographic records as obtained from *Web of Science* which has subject categories of its own. The subject categories described by different descriptors indicate both specific domains and broad disciplines as well. Any particular record may contain several descriptors as actual subject coverage mostly claims a fairly large number of descriptors for accurate coverage of the content. The list of descriptors indicating both broad and specific domains is presented in Table 6. Here some of the broad descriptors are: biology, biophysics and environmental sciences. Some broad areas consist of few specific facets, e.g. biochemistry, biotechnology, computer science, science and technology and medical science. Some other broad areas consist of fairly large number of specific facets, e.g. physics, chemistry, engineering science and material science. The contribution of articles from these four areas is very large compared to others. Also, the contribution from nanoscience and nanotechnology under the broad category of science and technology is very high. The five subject areas - physics, chemistry, engineering science, material science and nanoscience and nanotechnology may be considered as core subject domains for Carbon nanotube. The top ten subject descriptors indicating core subject zone covering the subject Carbon nanotube is presented in Table 6A. These ten subject descriptors cover 80% of all articles. Majority of these ten descriptors belong to the broad subject physics followed by material science and chemistry.

The term or descriptor Carbon nanotube may be categorized as a keyword, but as there are quite a large number of articles belonging to this descriptor, it is not logically incorrect to reckon Carbon nanotube as a specific subject domain. Now as observed this domain covers so many disciplines of science and engineering that it may be recognized as an inter-disciplinary topic. As this subject is formed from several facets belonging to some other broad subjects, the mode of formation of the same may be categorized under distillation at per Ranganathan's scheme of subject formation mechanism that was further modified by Gopinath and Seetharama [31]. There are similarities between the mode of formation of subjects like microbiology, management sciences or forestry with Carbon nanotube. In this mode, some common facets distilled out from several subjects to form clusters that eventually shaped in to another new subject.

Table 6: List of broad subjects and specific domains at per *Web of Science* categories

Descriptors indicating broad subject areas	Descriptors indicating specific subject areas	No. of articles contributed	% of articles contributed
Biochemistry	Biochemical research methods	10	0.58%
	Biochemistry & molecular biology	17	0.98%
Biology		4	0.23%
Biophysics		16	0.92%
Biotechnology	Biotechnology & applied microbiology	9	0.52%
Chemistry	Chemistry-analytical	54	3.12%
	Chemistry-inorganic nuclear	4	0.23%
	Chemistry-multidisciplinary	119	6.87%
	Chemistry-physical	164	9.47%
	Electrochemistry	2	0.12%
Computer science	Computer science with interdisciplinary applications	6	0.35%
	Crystallography	81	4.68%
	Energy fuels	21	1.21%

Descriptors indicating broad subject areas	Descriptors indicating specific subject areas	No. of articles contributed	% of articles contributed
Engineering science	Engineering-chemical	13	0.75%
	Engineering-civil	2	0.12%
	Engineering-electrical and electronic	31	1.79%
	Engineering-environmental	3	0.17%
	Engineering-manufacturing	5	0.29%
	Engineering-mechanical	11	0.64%
	Engineering-multidisciplinary	5	0.29%
	Metallurgy & metallurgical engineering	12	0.69%
Environmental sciences		5	0.29%
	Instruments and instrumentation	26	1.50%
Material science	Materials science-biomaterials	12	0.69%
	Materials science-ceramics	4	0.23%
	Materials science-characterization testing	3	0.17%
	Materials science-coatings films	21	1.21%
	Materials science-composites	20	1.16%
	Materials science-multidisciplinary studies	296	17.10%
	Materials science-textiles	4	0.23%
	Polymer science	7	0.40%
Science & technology	Multidisciplinary sciences	17	0.98%
	Nanoscience and nanotechnology	197	11.38%
	Telecommunications	5	0.29%
Medical science	Pharmacology & pharmacy	2	0.12%
	Experimental medicine research	8	0.46%
Physics	Physics-applied	205	11.84%
	Physics-atomic molecular & chemical	48	2.77%
	Physics-condensed matter	146	8.43%
	Physics-fluids plasmas	6	0.35%
	Physics-mathematical	3	0.17%
	Physics-multidisciplinary	22	1.27%
	Physics-spectroscopy	71	4.10%
	Physics-optics	3	0.17%
	Physics-thermodynamics	3	0.17%
	Physics-mechanics	8	0.46%

Table 6A: List of core facets

Descriptors indicating core subject areas	No. and % of article contributions

Multidisciplinary materials science	296 (17.1%)
Applied physics	205 (11.8%)
Nanoscience and nanotechnology	197 (11.4%)
Physical chemistry	164 (9.5%)
Condensed matter physics	146 (8.4%)
Multidisciplinary chemistry	119 (6.9%)
Crystallography	81 (4.7%)
Spectroscopy	71 (4.1%)
Analytical chemistry	54 (3.1%)
Atomic, molecular and chemical physics	48 (2.8%)
All	1381(79.8%)

Fig. 7: Relative distribution of different broad subjects over Carbon nanotube

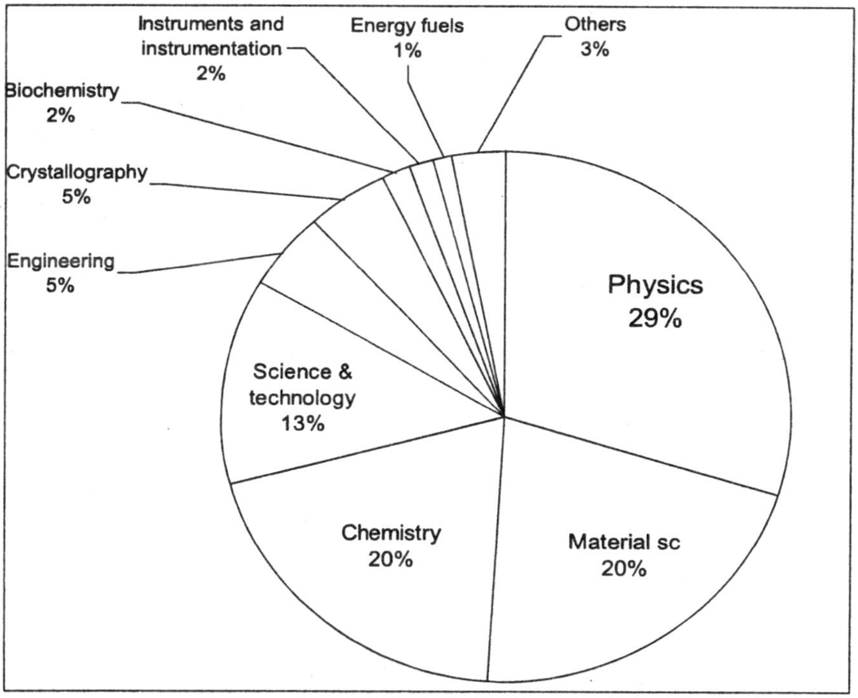

4.8 Institutional Distribution

In this study, 834 articles have been analysed contributed by 1148 authors. The authors' affiliations show 1148 authors are affiliated to 332 institutions, i.e. 1.4 authors per institution on an average. The affiliating institutions are categorized in thirteen types of sectors as listed in Table 7. Highest percentage of authors are from the university sector (24.8%) followed by IITs (20.7%) and foreign institutions (17%). Then comes CSIR (9%) followed by IISc (8.5%). The authors affiliated to foreign institutions work in collaboration with Indian institutions. It is a notable feature that foreign collaborative research in this subject is substantial. The list of top twelve affiliating institutions is given in Table 8 that accounts for nearly 46% of authors' affiliation. Of these, only one institution is a foreign one, while the remaining eleven institutions are Indian. IITs, IISc and JNCASR are top three institutions accounting for 32% affiliations. Only three universities have appeared in the list of top twelve, viz. Banaras Hindu University, University of Delhi and Madurai Kamraj University. The other important top-ranked institutions are NPL, NCL, other CSIR labs, BARC and IACS. It is an important finding that although collectively the university sector is the topmost, individually IITs and IISc are the foremost ones. The relative distribution of different sectors is presented in Fig. 8.

Table 7: Different categories of affiliating institutions

Categories of institutions	Abbreviation used in Fig. 8	No. and % of authors affiliated
Indian Universities	Univ	288 (24.8%)
Indian Institute of Technology	IIT	240 (20.7%)
Foreign Institutions	FI	197 (17.0%)
Council of Scientific and Industrial Research	CSIR	104 (9.0%)
Indian Institute of Science	IISc	99 (8.5%)
Dept. of Atomic Energy	DAE	49 (4.2%)
Dept. of Science and Technology	DST	47 (4.1%)
Jawaharlal Nehru Centre for Advanced Scientific Research	JNCASR	39 (3.4%)
Non-Govt. Institutions	Non-Govt	30 (2.6%)
Indian Colleges	College	26 (2.2%)
National Institute of Technology	NIT	21 (1.8%)
Defence Research and Development Organization	DRDO	17 (1.5%)
Indian Space Research Organization	ISRO	2 (0.2%)

Table 8: Top twelve affiliating institutions

Top twelve affiliating institutions	No. and % of authors affiliated
Indian Institute of Technology (IIT)	238 (20.7%)
Indian Institute of Science (IISc)	99 (8.5%)
Jawaharlal Nehru Centre for Advanced Scientific Research (JNCASR)	39 (3.4%)

Top twelve affiliating institutions	No. and % of authors affiliated
Banaras Hindu University (BHU)	28 (2.1%)
Bhabha Atomic Research Centre (BARC)	28 (2.1%)
National Physical Laboratory (NPL)	27 (2%)
National Chemical Laboratory (NCL)	24 (1.8%)
CSIR (other than NPL And NCL)	22 (1.7%)
University of Delhi (DU)	20 (1.5%)
Indian Association for the Cultivation of Sciences (IACS)	19 (1.4%)
Madurai Kamaraj University (MKU)	19 (1.4%)
Tohoku University (TU)	19 (1.4%)

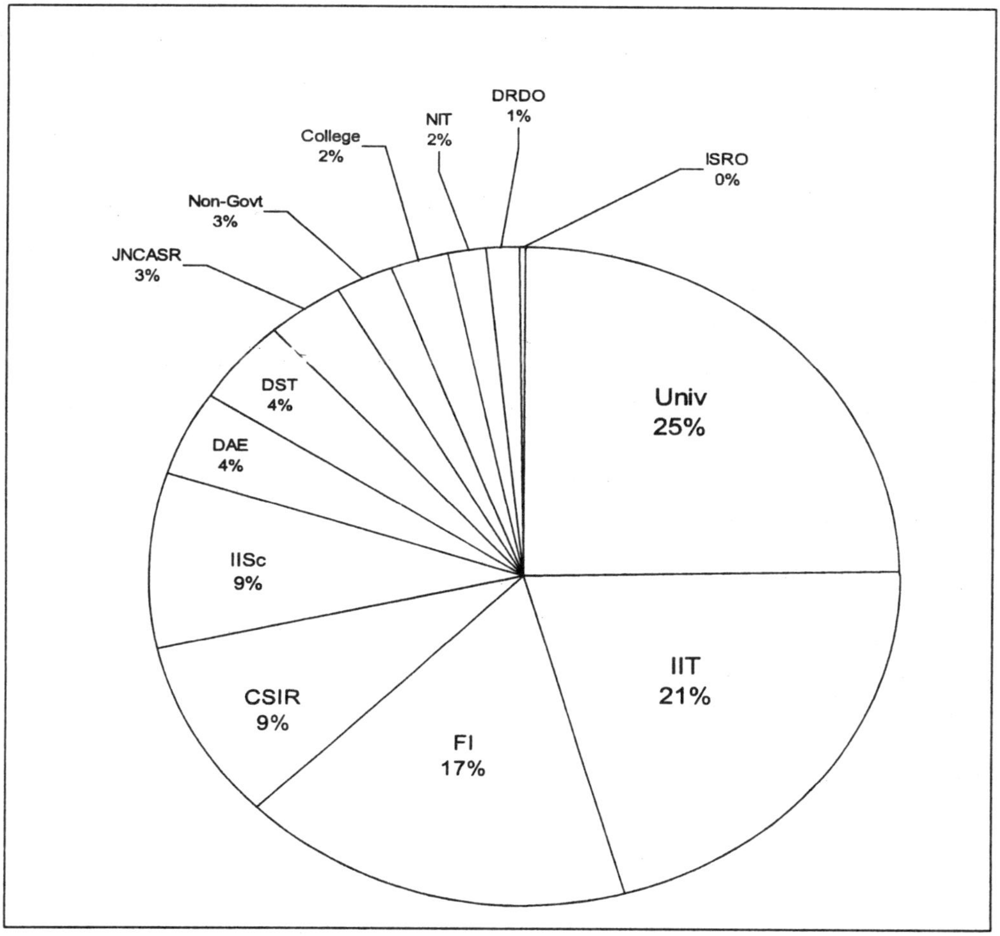

Fig. 8: Relative distribution of affiliation among different sectors

5 CONCLUSION

This study deals with the scientometric analysis of Indian Carbon nanotube research as reported in *Web of Science*. The study shows that Carbon nanotube research in India is increasing. The research was started in 1999 and notable increase occurred since 2008, with the maximum hike in 2011. The Carbon nanotube research in India is mainly a collaborative effort with USA as top-ranked collaborating country. The study of authorship pattern shows dominance of two-authored and three-authored articles. As this research field is an experimental one, solo research is almost nil. Team research is prominent with tiny team size while large teams are hardly involved. The author productivity pattern does not stricly conform to Lotka's law, but only approximately. The core journals of this subject area have been identified by applying Bradford's law of scattering. Almost all core journals are published from USA and has a fairly high impact factor. The subject domain analysis shows that it is an interdisciplinary area with many overlapping subjects. Subjects like physics, chemistry, material science and nanoscience & nanotechnology are in closely associated with the subject of Carbon nanotube. The analysis of institutional pattern shows that the top three sectors, namely. university, IIT and foreign institutional affiliation account for nearly two-third (66%) of total number of authors. Also, individually IITs, IISc and JNCASR are top three affiliating institutions. Other universities involved in Carbon nanotube research include BHU, DU and MKU, and potential laboratories are NPL, NCL , BARC and IACS. Thus Carbon nanotube research in India though started in the recent past gained thrust and importance within a few years. It is a budding topic of active interdisciplinary research with high prospects.

6 ACKNOWLEDGEMENT

The academic assistance from Dr. Anup Kumar Das, Documentation Officer, School of Social Sciences, Jawaharlal Nehru University, New Delhi is gratefully acknowledged.

REFERENCES

1. http://en.wikipedia.org/wiki/Emerging_technologies (Retrieved on 4/6/2013 at 3.47 PM)
2. http://en.wikipedia.org/wiki/Nanotechnology (Retrieved on 4/6/2013 at 4.04 PM)
3. http://en.wikipedia.org/wiki/Carbon_nanotube (Retrieved on 4/6/2013 at 4.10 PM)
4. http://www.ipt.arc.nasa.gov/carbonnano.html (Retrieved on 4/6/2013 at 4.17 PM)

5. Bhattacharya, S. and Shilpa. (2011) Mapping nanotechnology research and innovation in India. *DESIDOC Journal of Library and Information Technology*, 31(5): 349-58.

6. Kostoff, R.N. et al. (2006b) The structure and infrastructure of the global nanotechnology literature. *Journal of Nanoparticle Research*, 8: 301-21.

7. Meyer, M. (2007) What do we know about innovation in nanotechnology? Some propositions about an emerging field between hype and path-dependency. *Scientometrics*, 70(3): 779-810.

8. Leydesdroff, L. (2007) Betweenness centrality as an indicator of the interdisciplinarity of scientific journals. *Journal of American. Society of Information Science and Technology*, 58(9): 1302-319.

9. Marx, W. and Barth, A. (2010) Carbon nanotubes- a scientometric study, *Carbon Nanotubes*, Jose Mauricio Marulanda (Ed.), ISBN: 978-953-307-054-4, InTech, Available from: http://www.intechopen.com/books/ carbon-nanotubes/carbon-nanotubes-a-scientometric-study

10. Patra, S. K. and Bhattacharya, P. (2005) Bibliometric study of cancer research in India, *DESIDOC Journal of Library & Information Technology*, 25(2): 11-18.

11. Patra, S. K. and Chand, P. (2007) HIV/AIDS research in India: A bibliometric study, *Library & Information Science Research*, 29(1): 124-34.

12. Patra, S. K. and Chand, P. (2005) Biotechnology research profile in India, *Scientometrics*, 63(3): 583-97.

13. Patra, S. K.; Bhattacharya, P. and Verma, N. (2006) Bibliometric study of literature on bibliometrics, *DESIDOC Journal of Library & Information Technology*, 26(1): 27-32.

14. Patra, S. K. and Chand, P. (2006) Library and information science research in India: A bibliometric study, *Annals of library and information studies*, 53(4): 219-23.

15. Patra, S. K. and Mishra, S. (2006) Bibliometric study of bioinformatics literature, *Scientometrics*, 67(3): 477-89.

16. Kumara, A. et al. Bibliometric and Scientometric Studies in Physics and Engineering: Recent Ten Years Analysis, 2009. **In** *Putting Knowledge to Work: Best Practices in Librarianship, Mumbai (India), 1-2 May 2009. [Conference Paper]*

17. Jain, A. and Garg, K.C. (1992) LASER research in India: scientometric study and model projections, *Scientometrics*, 23(3): 395-415.

18. Kademani, B.S. et. al. (2006) World literature on thorium research: A scientometric study based on Science Citation Index, *Scientometrics*, 69(2): 347-64.

19. Stanhill, G. (2001) The growth of climate change science: a scientometric study, *Climatic Change*, 48(2-3): 515-24.

20. Garg, K.C. and Padhi, P. (1998) Scientometric study of LASER patent literature, *Scientometrics*, 43(3): 443-54.

21. Upadhye, R.P. et. al. (2004) Scientometric analysis of synchronous references in the Physics Nobel lectures, 1981-1985: A pilot study, *Scientometrics*, 61(1): 55-68.

22. Lee, C.K. (2003) A scientometric study of the research performance of the Institute of Molecular and Cell Biology in Singapore, *Scientometrics*, 56(1): 95-110.

23. Schummer, J. (1997) Scientometric studies on chemistry I: the exponential growth of chemical substances, 1800-1995, *Scientometrics*, 39(1): 107-23.

24. Braun, T; Schubert, A.P. and Kostoff, R.N. (2000) Growth and trends of Fullerene research as reflected in Its journal literature, *Chemical Review*, 100: 23-37.

25. Gupta, V.K. (1999) Technological trends in the area of Fullerenes using bibliometric analysis of patents, *Scientometrics*, 44(1): 17-31.

26. Gupta, V.K. and Pangannaya, N.B. (2000) Carbon nanoitubes: bibliometric analysis of patents, *World Patent Information,* 22(3): 185-9.

27. Sen, B.K. Cybermetrics-Meaning, Definition, Scope and Constituents WIS-2004, International Workshop on *Webometrics, Informetrics and Scientometrics*, (eds.). Hildrun Kretschmer, Yogendra Singh, and Ramesh Kundra,. (2-5 March, 2004).Organised by Society for Information Science, New Delhi, and Indian Institute of Technology, Roorkee, India, pp. 310-315

28. Lancaster, F.W. (1986) Vocabulary control for information retrieval, Ed. 2. Information Resources, Arlington, V.A.

29. Bradford, S.C. (1934) Sources of information on specific subjects. *Engineering: An Illustrated Weekly,* 137(3550): 85-6.

30. Lotka, A.J. (1926) The frequency distribution of scientific productivity. *Journal of the Washington Academy of Science,* 16: 317-23.

31. Ranganathan S.R. (1967) *Prolegomena to Library Classification*. London: Asia Publishing House.

12

Current Trends in Webometrics Research

N.S. Harinarayana and ***Vasantha Raju, N.***

Webometrics is the quantitative analysis of Web phenomena. The growth of Web technologies has opened new avenues for Web researchers for measurement and analyses of the phenomenon. Webometrics is traditionally used for quantifying Web data related to footprints of researchers or institutions on the Web measured in terms of their research publications and other parameters. The paper looks at the recent developments in webometrics research in light of emergence of social Web and big data, and their applications in new research fronts and future perspective of webometrics research. The paper also discusses about the recent developments in research techniques in webometrics such as query splitting and virtual memetics in the social network sites. It is observed that the growth of Web technologies has possibly posed new challenges for traditional citation databases which have been extensively used so far for measuring research impact of universities, institutions or individual researchers. The new trend has shown that impact measures are in the verge of acceptance as new method for measurement of academic and research contributions. One notable example for this is altmetrics. In the nutshell the paper gives an overview of the emerging trends and impact measuring techniques used in webometrics research.

KEYWORDS: Webometrics, Research impact, Web.2.0, Social web, Big data

1 INTRODUCTION

Webometrics is the quantitative study of Web related phenomena (Thelwall, Vaughan and Björneborn, 2005). The growth of Web as a major source of information attracted a large number of researchers in applying traditional bibliometrics and scientometrics techniques to the new form of communication medium that is World Wide Web (WWW). The term 'webometrics' was first coined by Almind and Ingwersen (1997) in their seminal paper entitled *"Informetric analysis of the World Wide Web: A methodological approach to 'webomtetrics'"* published in the *Journal of Documentation*.

Björneborn and Ingwersen (2004), defines webometrics as "the study of the quantitative aspects of the construction and use of information resources, structures and technologies on the Web drawing on bibliometric and informetric approaches". According to Mike Thelwall, webometrics is "the study of Web-based content with primarily quantitative methods for social science research goals using techniques that are not specific to one field of study" (Thelwall, 2009), which emphasizes a small subset of a relatively larger number of applied methods for use in the social sciences. The purpose of this alternative definition helped to publicize appropriate methods outside of the information science discipline rather than to replace the original definition within information science.

The introduction of Web Impact Factor (WIF) by Ingewersen (1998) which was similar to that of Web of Science's (WOS) Journal Impact Factor (JIF) for assessing the website helped webometrics to establish itself as a method to assess Web phenomena. The WIF measure may be defined as the number of Web pages in a Web site receiving links from other Web sites, divided by the number of Web pages published in the site that are accessible to the crawler. As the Web became a major source of information, key areas were identified to apply webometrics techniques to the Web. The phenomenal growth of Internet technologies mainly the social Web and the emergence of big data have opened up new opportunities for using webometrics for studying Web phenomena. This paper attempts to document the current developments and trends in webometrics research. The coverage is not intended to be comprehensive, but provides a birds-eye-view of the current methods in webometrics.

2 FROM BIBLIOMETRICS TO WEBOMETRICS

Library and Information Science (LIS) domain has a long history of measuring the research output of an organization or individual using quantitative techniques derived from mathematics and other subfields. Sociology of science, librametrics, bibliometrics, scientometrics and informetrics are some of the terms, to name a few, used often for measuring the research contributions. The term Bibliometric was first used in 1969 by Pritchard and he defined it as "the application of mathematical and statistical methods to books and other media of communication" (Pritchard, 1969). By 1970 the term Bibliometrics gained considerable attention and mentioned in LIS literature including *Library and Information Science Abstracts* (LISA) and other LIS literature (Hood and Wilson, 2001). The introduction of *Science Citation Index* (SCI) in the early 60s by the Institute of Scientific Information (ISI) now Thomson Reuters, has played a significant role in making Bibliometrics an area of research for measuring research productivity and network of researchers or institutions.

The term Scientometrics was first coined by Vassily V. Nalimov and Z. M. Mulchenko in 1969. The term 'scientometrics' is the Russian equivalent of 'naukometriya'. Scientometrics though overlaps with the term 'bibliometrics' has a wider ambit compared to bibliometrics. Scientometrics has been defined as "the study of the quantitative aspects of science as a discipline or economic activity. It is part of the sociology of science and has application to science policy-making. It involves quantitative studies of scientific activities, including, among others, publication, and so overlaps with bibliometrics to some extent" (Tague-Sutcliffe, 1992, p. 1).

As the field of bibliometrics and scientometrics expanded, a new term 'informetrics' was introduced to include the wide ambit of information science research in the early 1990s. A per the definition of the term by Tague-Sutcliffe (1992, p. 1), informetrics is "the study of the quantitative aspects of information in any form, not just records or bibliographies, and in any social group, not just scientists. Thus it looks at the quantitative aspects of informal or spoken communication, as well as recorded, and of information needs and uses of the disadvantaged, not just the intellectual elite. It can incorporate, utilise, and extend the many studies of the measurement of information that lie outside the boundaries of both bibliometrics and scientometrics. ...Two phenomena that have not, in the past, been seen as a part of bibliometrics or scientometrics, but fit comfortably within the scope of informetrics are: definition and measurement of information, and types and characteristics of retrieval performance measures. "Since the 1990s the term 'informetrics' has been often used in the world of quantitative analysis of scholarly communications. As the Web gain its momentum and became major source of information and scholarly communication shifting its boundaries from print to online, researchers in scienotmetrics and informetrics have tried to quantify Web pages or sites, because of this shifts, new term 'webometrics' was coined in 1997 by Almind and Ingwersen (1997). Today 'webomterics' has become a major area of research in LIS domain and has also spread its tentacles across other subject fields (*See* Fig. 1 for citations received for Webometrics from other subject domains) which is discussed in the later part of this paper.

3 WEBOMETRICS RESEARCH TECHNIQUES AND ITS APPLICATIONS

As mentioned above Webometrics is the quantitative analysis of Web phenomena. It includes link analysis, Web citation analysis, search engine evaluation and Web data analysis. Each of these is briefly discussed below.

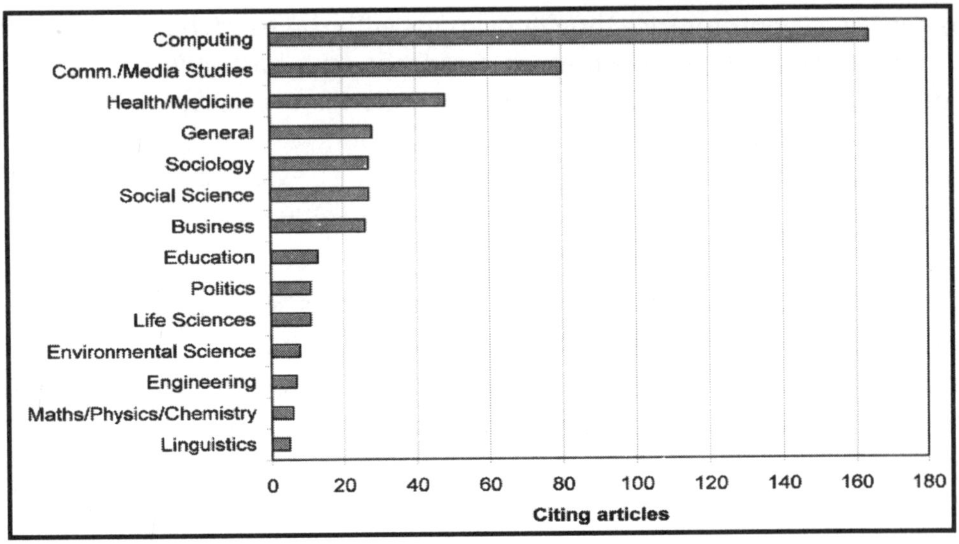

Fig 1: Disciplines of non-library and information science articles citing webometrics[1]

3.1 Link Analysis

Link analysis is the quantitative study of hyperlinks between Web pages. Early webometrics studies conducted this type of research extensively. Link analysis has been used sfor identifying the patterns in academic or scholarly Web spaces. Link analysis has direct analogies in traditional bibliometric studies. In traditional bibliometric related studies, the researcher often used to do studies by measuring or quantifying the research contributions of an organization or researchers; in a similar way link analysis can be done for identifying the popularity of the websites, and also to measure which links of Web sites or pages are more popular and why? The Web crawling tools such as SocSciBot (http://www.socscibot.wlv.ac.uk) introduced by the Statistical Cybermetrics Research Group at the University of Wolverhampton, UK and other freely available link analysis Web crawlers have made the process of crawling Web data simpler. Some of the major studies in this field of research have been reviewed by Kousha (2005) in his paper entitled "*Webometrics and scholarly communications: An overview*".

3.2 Web Citation Analysis

Another key area of Webometrics research is Web citation analysis. Web citation analysis is nothing counting online citations to published items such as journal articles. Earlier, bibliographic citations found in traditional citation indexing

---

1 Adapted from "Webometrics: Emerged or doomed," M. Thelwall, 2010, Information Research, 15 (4).

databases such as SCI, SSCI, and Hand ACI were considered as major source for identifying the impact of research publications. The Web provided new methods to overcome the limitations of the bibliographic citation databases by helping in finding Web citations for articles published online largely for open access journals. Research on Web citations have found that there was correlation between the citations found in bibliographic citations and citations found on the Web for particular research papers (Vaughan and Shaw, 2003). The introduction of Google Scholar has helped webometricians to use this citation database to identify the impact of the research publications easily. The introduction of tools such as Google Scholar and Altemetrics the research in this area has seen considerable growth in recent times. Two of the research publications mentioned below on this subject throw more light on how this kind of studies can be conducted using Webometrics. One is done by Kousha and Thelwall (2007) on Google Scholar and Google Web/URL Citations and Kousha and Thelwall (2008) study on Google scholar.

3.3 Search Engine Evaluation

Another key area of research in Webometrics is evaluating search engines. The major webometric studies have concentrated on the coverage of the Web and the accuracy of the reported results. It was known that none of the search engines have indexed whole of the information available on the Web. Still 70% of the information available on the Web has not been indexed by any of the search engines (Metayer, 2010).

The accuracy of the data obtained through commercial engines was also a very contentious issue in Webometrics; and many studies have raised questions about the validity and reliability of data obtained through search engines (Bar-Ilan, 2004; Kousha, 2005). Many of the search engines such as Alta Vista (which was initially used by many webometricians for link analysis), Yahoo and Bing now have stopped providing advanced link search commands feature (Thelwall, 2012).

3.4 Describing the Web

Some descriptive types of webometrics studies have also been done to understand the Web characteristics. The studies which fall under this category, include measuring the average Web page size, kind of meta tags used, average use of technologies, overall Web structures and other parameters. Apart from this Web dynamics research have also been conducted. Such work is concerned with measuring, characterizing and modeling changes in the Web. One notable example is that of Koehler (2002, 2004) studies on changing pattern of Web pages or sites.

Later webometrics was used extensively for studying social aspect research in emerging Web 2.0 environment, which is discussed below.

4 CURRENT TRENDS IN WEBOMETRICS

The advancements in Web technologies, mainly with the emergence of Web 2.0 tools or social Web like Blogs, social network sites such as MySpace, Facebook, Free video hosting sites YouTube, Twitter, a microblogging tool opened up new opportunities for webometrics to understand and analyze these new Web technologies. The ability to crawl and analyses huge data sets automatically has proved webometrics as a potential method for studying these new media tools.

4.1 Measuring Web 2.0 or Social Web

Various studies on blogs and social networking sites have been conducted using webometrics as a research method. A blog - a personal online diary in which entries or posts organized in reverse chronological sequence - contains huge corpus of data which can be used for identifying a public opinion on a particular subject matter or interesting trends. . Blogs have become important online space for sharing personal opinions or sentiments. Blog feature such as archiving retrospective data, easy search options, information on any given topic and other similar features have made this form a fertile ground for social science research. Blogs have become a large scale freely accessible source of public opinions about major topics which have not been there previously except in standard national survey data (Thelwall, 2013). Blogs can be used for examining public opinion about a person or public figure, or also identifying the trends on a particular topic. Similarly, Twitter - a microblogging tool – is also used for identifying trends or sentiment behavior. However Twitter has some difference with blogs in the content and its organization of information. Twitter posts are much shorter compared to blog postings and also ephemeral in nature (Thelwall, 2013).

Blogs and twitters have been used in webometrics research to identifying the starting point for discussion of an issue (Thelwall, 2007), identifying long term trends (Wilkinson and Thelwall, 2012), identifying key issues (Thelwall and Stuart, 2007) and comparative time series analysis (Thelwall, 2007).

Webomerics research has also been used in social Web for analyzing comments and sentiments on a particular topic of interest to Web users (Thelwall, Buckley and Paltoglou, 2011). These types of methods are new to social science research (e.g., sentiment analysis). Apart from these areas of research webometrics has also been used for analyzing social networks. A social network is a social structure made up of individuals (or organizations) called "nodes", which are tied (connected) by one

›r more specific types of interdependency, such as friendship, kinship, common nterest, financial exchange, dislike, sexual relationships, or relationships of beliefs, :nowledge or prestige (Wikipedia, 2013). The study on "Co-Authorship Networks in he Digital Library Research Community" by Xiaoming Liu and others (Liu, Bollen, Nelsson, and Van de Sompel, 2005) is one of the examples for how social network analysis can be used to identify the co-authorship network pattern among digital ibrary research community.

It is understood that the Web 2.0 technologies have provided many opportunities for webometrics research to be used for analyzing them. The vebometrics is an important research technique for studying emerging Web phenomena.

4.2 Altmetrics or Alternative Metrics for Measuring Research Impact

Another emerging research area as a subfield of webometrics is altmetrics or alternative metrics for measuring research impact. Altmetrics is nothing but measuring authors research footprints in social Web. Earlier, research impact was measured using citation indexing databases such as *Science Citation Index* (SCI), *Social Science Citation Index* (SSCI) and *Arts and Humanities Citation Index* (A and HCI) collectively known as Web of Science owned by Thomson Scientific (earlier nstitute of Scientific Information, ISI created by Eugene Garfield) or Scopus of Elsevier and also Google Scholar, a free online citation indexing database. But, because of some inherent limitations such as number of journals covered in these citation databases, the kind of documents indexed, time span for citing a document, language barrier in indexing a journal and other limitations of these ndexing databases researchers across the globe emphasizing for introducing new method of impact measures to measure the quality of research publications. As scholarly publishing has seen paradigm shifts with open access journals coming into he picture in a big way and authors' interest in sharing their research results more and more in social media space, altmetrics is emerging as alternative impact measure for measuring authors research footprints on the Web. (*see* Table 1) [4]

Table 1, Types of Altmetrics

Altmetrics Types	Description	Examples
Shares	Posted publicly in order to share news of research article or outputs	Twitter, Topsy, Facebook, Reddit, news articles, blog posts, Google+, YouTube, Figshare, Mendeley,
Saves	Saved on social bookmarking sites or favorited on social media and social coding websites	Mendeley, CiteULike, Delicious, Github, Twitter, Slideshare

Altmetrics Types	Description	Examples
Reviews	Discussed with additional commentary added	Faculty of 1000 (F1000), Blog posts, article comments, Facebook comments
Adaptations	Creations of derivative works using an article or other output	Github
Social usage statistics	Downloads or views on Web services and social media sites	Figshare, Slideshare, Dryad, Facebook, YouTube

Altmetrics considers all stages and products of scholarly research (from "social" literature search via Facebook to discussion of published results with readers via Twitter), including any impact a publication or an author may have on other people, e.g., retweeting a tweet, downloading or bookmarking an article, sharing a blog post in social networks, or following the author—in short, a scholar's "scientific 'streetcred'" (Cronin, 2001, Cited in Bar-Ilan, Haustein, Peters, Priem, Shema and Terliesner, 2012). As such, the altmetrics approach offers new ways to measure impact of authors and publications which may complement rather than replace traditional indicators for research evaluation. The combination of traditional and alternative metrics for research evaluation will provide more complete author or article profiles as it captures more dimensions of scientific practice (Bar-Ilan, Haustein, Peters, Priem, Shema and Terliesner, 2012). This new impact measure technique (altmetrics) which is largely dependent on social Web has expanded the scope of webometrics research.

4.3 Emergence of Big Data

Exponential increase in digital information and social Web has now provided opportunities for accessing huge cache of Web data for analysis. The availability of this "Big Data" through social Web (media) has provided opportunities for LIS professionals who have been in the forefront in identifying, organizing and providing access to large datasets. The inherent advantage of having the skills to organize and manage large cache of data librarians and scholars in library and information domain are now involving in analyzing big data.

Webometrics is one of the notable example in which large amount of data is gathered and analyzed for various purposes (Thelwall, 2009). Webometrics has also developed tools and techniques to gather big data for analysis through Web crawling tools. Webometric Analyst and SociSciBot, Web data crawling softwares are two notable examples developed by Mike Thelwall and his team at the Statistical Cybermetrics Research Group at the University of Wolverhampton, UK for gathering and analyzing large cache of Web data.

There are funding initiatives like Digging into Data now explicitly encouraging researchers to engage in studies that lead to greater understanding, use, and applications of Big Data (. As LIS domains has the wherewithal at its end to explore this domain, it is a great opportunity for LIS professionals to engage in dealing with Big Data, because big data is the future where much research will be happening and also shaping the contours of social science research.

5 CONCLUSION

Webometrics has become one of the key research methods for studying Web phenomena. This paper discussed how webometrics carved a niche for itself as an advanced method of research from bibliometrics. The advancement in Web technologies made this technique as indispensable for studying and analyzing a wide array of data emerging in online and offline world. Altmerics, a sub-domain of webometrics, would challenge traditional indexing databases metrics such as JIF (Journal Impact Factor) and also help to devise new measures to analyze research output in social Web space and make them more credible and standard measure. Webometrics would help in analyzing large amount of data emerging on the Web which is very important to social science research.

REFERENCES

1. Almind, T.C. and Ingwersen, P. (1997) Informetric analyses on the World Wide Web: Methodological
2. approaches to 'Webometrics'. *Journal of Documentation*, 53(4): 404-426.
3. Bar-Ilan, J. (2004) Use of search engines in information science research. *Annual Review of Information Science and Technology*, 38: 231-288.
4. Bar-ilan, J.; Haustein, S.; Peters, I.; Priem, J.; Shema, H. and Terliesner, J. (2012, September 5-8) Beyond citations: Scholars' visibility on the social Web. Paper presented at the *17th International Conference on Science and Technology Indicators*, Montreal, Canada. Retrieved from http://arxiv.org/pdf/1205.5611v1.pdf.
5. Björneborn, L. and Ingwersen, P. (2004) Toward a basic framework for webometrics. *Journal of the American Society for Information Science andTechnology*, 55(14): 1216-1227.
6. Hood, W.H. and Wilson, C.S. (2001) The literature of biblometrics, scientometrics, and informetrics. *Scientometrics*, 52(2): 291-314.
7. Ingwersen, P. (1998) The calculation of Web impact factors. *Journal of Documentation*, 54(2): 236-243.
8. Koehler, W. (2002) Web page change and persistence - a four-year longitudinal study. *Journal of the American Society for Information Science and Technology*, 53(2): 162-171.
9. Koelher, W. (2004) A longitudinal study of Web pages continued: A consideration of document persistence. *Information Research*, 9(2). Retrieved from http://informationr.net/ir/9-2/paper174.html

10. Konkiel, S. (2013) Altmetrics: A 21st-century solution to determining research quality. *Online Researcher*, July/August Issue. Retrieved from http://www.infotoday.com/ OnlineSearcher/Articles/ Features/Altmetrics-A-stCentury-Solution-to-Determining-Research-Quality-90551.shtml
11. Kousha, K. (2005) Webometrics and scholarly communication: An overview. Quarterly Journal *of the National Library of Iran (Faslenameh Ketab)*, 14(4): 7-16.
12. Kousha, K. and Thelwall, M. (2007) Google Scholar citations and Google Web/URL citations: A multi-discipline exploratory analysis, *Journal of the American Society for Information Science and Technology*, 58(7): 1055-1065.
13. Kousha, K., and Thelwall, M. (2008). Sources of Google Scholar citations outside the Science Citation Index: A comparison between four science disciplines. *Scientometrics*, 74(2), 273-294.
14. Kousha, K.; Thelwall, M. and Abdoli, M. (2012) The role of online videos in research communication: A content analysis of YouTube videos cited in academic publications. *Journal of the American Society for Information Science and Technology*, 63(9): 1710–1727.
15. Metayer, E. (2010) Tapping into the invisible Web for competitive intelligence. Competia. Retrieved from http://competia.com/tapping-into-the-invisible-Web-for-competitive-intelligence/
16. Pritchard, A. (1969) Statistical bibliography or bibliometrics. *Journal of documentation*, 25(4): 348-349.
17. Shema, H.; Bar-Ilan, J. and Thelwall, M. (2012) Research blogs and the discussion of scholarly information. *PLOS ONE* 7(5). Retrieved from http://www.plosone.org/article/info%3Adoi% 2F10.1371%2Fjournal.pone. 0035869
18. Tague-Sutcliffe, J. M. (1992) An introduction to informetrics. Information Processing and Management, 28: 1-3.
19. Thelwall, M. (2007) Blog searching: The first general-purpose source of retrospective public opinion in the social sciences? *Online Information Review,* 31(3): 277-289.
20. Thelwall, M. and Stuart, D. (2007) RUOK? Communication technologies blogged during a crisis. *Journal of Computer-Mediated Communication,* 12(9).
21. Thelwall, M. (2009) *Introduction to webometrics: Quantitative Web research for the social sciences*. New York: Morgan and Claypool.
22. Thelwall, M. (2012) Webometrics and social Web research methods. Retrieved from http://www.scit.wlv.ac. uk/~cm1993/mtpublications.html#Webometrics
23. Thelwall, M.; Buckley, K. and Paltoglou, G. (2012) Sentiment strength detection for the social Web. *Journal of the American Society for Information Science and Technology*, 63(1): 163-173.
24. Thelwall, M. (2010) Webometrics: Emerged or doomed? *Information Research*, 15(4). Retrieved from http://informationr.net/ir/15-4/colis713.html
25. Thelwall, M. (2012) A history of webometrics. *Bulletin of the American Society for Information Science and Technology*, 38(2). Retrieved from http:/mail.asist.org/Bulletin/Aug-12/AugSep12_Thelwall.pdf
26. Thelwall, M.; Vaughan, L. and Björneborn, L (2005) Webometrics. In Cronin, B. (ed.), *Annual Review of Information Science and Technology*. Medford, NJ: Information Today, Inc., 39: 81-135
27. Vaughan, L. and Shaw, D. (2003) Bibliographic and Web citations: What is the difference? *Journal of the American Society for Information Science and Technology*, 54(4): 1313-1324.
28. Wilkinson, D. and Thelwall, M. (2012) Trending Twitter topics in English: An international comparison. *Journal of the American Society for Information Science and Technology*, 63(8): 1631-1646.

13

Mapping of Scholarly Research in Cloud Computing: A Bibliometric Study

A. Thirumagal and ***S. Niruba Sethukumari***

Cloud computing, a popular topic in the past few years involves various technologies and provides scalable IT related services over the Internet. Much has been written about this concept and its applications in the IT and business fields. The aim of the study is to analyse the quantum literature output in the area of cloud computing from 2008 - 2012 from the Web of Knowledge. The downloaded 2207 data were analysed with the Bibexcel Tool. This objective of this article is to identify and analyse the rate and growth of scholarly publication, analyse the authorship pattern and to examine the publication type of research, application of Lotka's Law, Creating Label View, Cluster View and finding the Citation map.

KEYWORDS: Cloud computing, Bibliometric analysis, Cluster view, Lotka's Law, Bibexcel, Citation analysis

1 INTRODUCTION

The aim of libraries being to provide information services to users and for delivering the best services, librarians should be willing to take advantage of useful resources including computer technologies. In some extent, development of information technology makes a huge impact on the development of libraries. Cloud computing is delivering virtual computing resources including computer hardware (eg. Networking) equipment and software, data storage and services through the Internet to end users. Many of the top companies have been in the process of switching from company owned computing assets to cloud based services.

2 CLOUD COMPUTING

A large number of computer servers and other resources are grouped together and offer their combined capacity on demand and pay per use basis. The end users do not have any idea where the servers are positioned; they just login to their required application and start working. The two most significant components of cloud computing architecture are known as the front end and the backend. The front end is the part seen by the client i.e the computer user. This includes the client's network and the applications used to access the cloud via a user interface such as a web browser. The back end of the cloud computing architecture is the cloud itself, comprising various computers, servers and data storage devices. Cloud computing involves three basic service models in which public cloud means IT resources offered as a service and shared across multiple organisations managed by an external service provider. It provides a way to reduce customer risk and cost by providing a flexible, even temporary extension to enterprise infrastructure.

3 NEED OF THE STUDY

Cloud computing has recently attracted commercially and academically great attention. In cloud computing, we can send the networked visual server and real time image transmission. Eugene Garfield's HistCite software, linked to Thomson Scientifics' Web of Science, as made available by Garfield, for the period 1956–2004, was used as the core database for analysis in this essay. A brief comparison of *Library Quarterly* contributor citation impact and that of *College & Research Libraries* is also provided. *Library Quarterly* continues to attract a roster of highly productive, international scholars [1]. F. W. Lancaster, as the most cited author during the 1970s to early 1990s, has broad intellectual influence in many fields of research in library and information science. This bibliometric study collected citation data for Lancaster's publications from 1972 to 2006 and analyzed the data in terms of the time and space and disciplinary breadth of his intellectual influence. The result shows that Lancaster has established an extraordinary record of both productivity and citations [2]. The considerable computing resources offered by the GRID computing system made it possible to perform calculations on the entire enzyme system, consisting of six protein subunits, as highlighted in the recent literature [3]. A bibliometric analysis of 1,456 articles appearing in Indian Library and Information Science journals between 1975 and 1985 revealed that the average rate of citations per article in the field was quite low [4]. The mapping of scientific fields, based on principles established in the seventies, has recently shown a remarkable development and applications are now booming with progress in computing efficiency [5]. Supplying library users with literature by a seamless linking of media is the goal of (scientific) libraries. By the digitization of primary and secondary data and the convergence of products and providers, libraries have already come very close to achieving this ideal. A digital library is the realization of this goal [6]. Kunwar P Singh, Aarti Jain and Parveen Babbar were analysis the research productivity of DESIDOC journal publication over the period of 1992-2002. The fixed the objectives like year wise, Productivity of Authors, Institution-wise and Gender-wise and others. [7]. Bibliometric methods are frequently used in the areas of *Library and Information Science*. It has become as an important standard tool for science policy and research management for the recent decades.

4 LIMITATIONS

The study is focused on cloud computing in relation to atmospheric sciences and related fields. The peeriod cover is 2008-2012. The data is derided from the Web of Knowledge Database. The research prodused 2207 results.

5 METHODS OF DATA ANALYSIS

The data were analysed with the toolbox named **Bibexcel**. This is built up by Olle Persson, Inforsk, Umeå Univ (Sweden). This software is intended to assist a user in analysing bibliographic data or any data of a textual nature formatted in a similar manner.

6 OBJECTIVES

To find out in relation to cloud computing applies to Atmosphier Sciences from 2008 - 2012:

- research productivity;
- Authorship Pattern;
- Degree of Collaboration;
- Language-wise distribution of Research;
- Relative Growth Rate and Doubling Time;
- Publication Types;
- Ranking of Journals;
- Application of Lotka's Law; and
- Label and Cluster Analysis.

Creation of Citation Map on Cloud Computing in relation to Atmoshier Sciences.

7 AUTHORSHIP PATTERN OF CLOUD COMPUTING RESEARCH

First an authorship pattern of research publication in Cloud Computing. The year-wise distribution of contributions according to the number of authors is shown in Table 1. About 16.45% represent Single Authors contributions, 22.02% for Joint Authors and 23.47% shows three authors research.

Table 1: Authorship pattern in Cloud Computing Research

Sl. No.	Authorship Pattern	2008	2009	2010	2011	2012	Total	%
1.	Single	18	52	68	95	130	363	16.45
2.	Joint	44	59	77	137	169	486	22.02
3.	Three	43	53	88	147	187	518	23.47
4.	Four	43	41	63	93	121	361	16.36
5.	Five	18	19	34	57	78	206	9.33
6.	Six	11	17	15	14	47	104	4.71
7.	Seven	2	9	8	12	16	47	2.13
8.	More than Seven	12	19	20	37	34	122	5.53
	Total	**191**	**269**	**373**	**592**	**782**	**2207**	**100**

8 DEGREE OF COLLABORATION

The Degree of Collaboration of authors year-wise is shown in Table 2. The extent of Degree of Collaboration in Cloud Computing research has been measured with the help of the formula devised by K. Subramaniam.

The formula is: **C = Nm/Nm + Ns**

Where

C = Degree of Collaboration in a discipline

Nm = Number of multiple authored papers

Ns = Number of single authored papers

Accordingly, the Degree of Collaboration has been calculated for the year 2006 is as Likewise the Degree of Collaboration is calculated for every year and presented in Table 2. The collaborative authorship is a well recognized feature of modern science. Mallinath Kumbar and N.G. Kumbar reveal that intellectual sharing took place by two or more scientists. Multiple author's research is very familiar in the present days [8]. It is true for our study also. Single author's contribution is 363. At the same time multiple authors' research is 1844. The year-wise Degree of Collaboration falls in between 0.81 to 0.91. The Degree of Collaboration for any subject ranges from 0.01 to 0.99 and it is always below 1.

Table 2: Degree of Collaboration in cloud computing research

Sl. No.	Year	Single	Multiple	Total	Degree of Collaboration
1.	2008	18	173	191	0.91
2.	2009	52	217	269	0.81
3.	2010	68	305	373	0.82
4.	2011	95	497	592	0.84
5.	2012	130	652	782	0.83
	Total	**363**	**1844**	**2207**	**0.84**

9 DISTRIBUTION OF RESEARCH PRODUCTION BY LANGUAGE *VS.* YEAR

The distribution of Cloud Computing literature by language is shown in Table 3. The scholarly communication is through English language in almost all the countries irrespective of the native language of the country. This phenomenon is not an exception to the subject of Cloud Computing which published about 99.14% of the research output in English. This is followed by Spanish (0.27%) as to Second position.

Table 3: Languages *vs.* year of cloud computing research

Sl. No.	Language	2008	2009	2010	2011	2012	Total	Percentage
1.	English	191	268	369	588	772	2188	99.14
2.	Polish		1	1	1	1	4	0.18
3.	Chinese			2		2	4	0.18
4.	Spanish			1	3	2	6	0.27
5.	German					2	2	0.09
6.	French					2	2	0.09
7.	Portuguese					1	1	0.05
	Total	**191**	**269**	**373**	**592**	**782**	**2207**	**100**

10 RELATIVE GROWTH RATE (RGR)

One of the most obvious features of science in recent years has been its rate of growth. Scientific growth has involved not only increase in man power but also finance. Relative Growth Rate (R) over the specific period of interval can be calculated from the following equation:

$$1-2^{\bar{R}} = \frac{\text{Log}_e W_2 - \log_e W_1}{2^T - 1^T}$$

where:

$1\text{-}2\ \bar{R}$ = mean relative growth rate over the specific period of interval

$log_e\ W_1$ = log of initial number of articles/pages

$log_e\ W_2$ = log of final number of articles/pages after a specific period of interval

$_2T\ -\ _1T$ = the unit difference between the initial time and the final time

The year can be taken here as the unit of time. The RGR for both articles and pages can be calculated separately.

Therefore

$1-2^{R(aa^{-1}year^{-1})}$ can represent the mean relative growth rate per unit of articles per unit of year over a specific period of interval

and

$1-2^{R(pp^{-1}year^{-1})}$ can represent the mean relative growth rate per unit of pages per unit of year over a specific period of interval.

The analysis of data on the literary output in Cloud Computing has also been done with parameters such as Relative Growth Rate (RGR) and Doubling Time. It is seen from Table 4 that Relative Growth Rate has been decreasing from 2009 (0.856975) to 2012 (0.437462) in the span of four years.

Table 4: Relative growth rate of cloud computing research literature

Sl. No.	Year	Quantum of Output	Cumulative Total of Output	W1	W2	$1-2^{\bar{R}(aa^{-1}year^{-1})}$ RGR	Dt(a)
1.	2008	191	191		5.252273		
2.	2009	269	450	5.252273	6.109248	0.856975	0.808659
3.	2010	373	833	6.109248	6.725034	0.615786	1.125392
4.	2011	592	1425	6.725034	7.261927	0.536893	1.29076
5.	2012	782	2207	7.261927	7.699389	0.437462	1.584136

11 DOUBLING TIME (DT)

There exists a direct relationship between relative growth rate and doubling time. If the number of articles/pages of a subject doubles during a given period then the difference between the logarithms of numbers at the beginning and end of this period must be logarithms of number 2. If natural logarithm is used this difference has a value of 0.693. Thus the corresponding doubling time is for each specific period of interval. Baskaran examined the research growth, relative growth rate and doubling time of publications, institution wise and ranking of authors in research productivity of Graph Theory during 2004-2011 [9].

$$\textbf{Doubling time (Dt)} = \frac{0.693}{\bar{R}}$$

Therefore:

$$\text{Doubling Time for articles Dt(a)} = \frac{0.693}{1-2^{\bar{R}(aa^{-1}\,year^{-1})}}$$

$$\text{Doubling time for pages Dt(p)} = \frac{0.693}{1-2^{\bar{R}(pp^{-1}\,year^{-1})}}$$

The Doubling Time for cloud computing research increases from 0.80 to 1.58.

12 PUBLICATION TYPES AND YEAR WISE DISTRIBUTION OF CLOUD COMPUTING RESEARCH

Table 5 reveals the distribution of 'Cloud Computing' research output according to publication type and year of publication. It is a traditional fact that most of the scholarly message of scientific research is published in journals and sometimes offered in the conferences. In this study, about 1915 were published in journals,

105 in Editorial Materials and 88 in Proceedings volum. The literature published in other bibliographic forms in where Review, News item, Book Review and others.

Table 5: Publication type cloud computing research *vs* year

Sl. No.	Publication Type	2008	2009	2010	2011	2012	Total
1.	Article	163	219	309	522	702	1915
2.	Proceedings Paper	15	14	19	17	23	88
3.	Review	9	11	14	8	18	60
4.	Editorial Material	3	19	20	36	27	105
5.	News Item	1	3	3	1	1	9
6.	Book Review		1	3	1	7	12
7.	Others		2	5	7	4	18
	Total	**191**	**269**	**373**	**592**	**782**	**2207**

13 RANKING OF JOURNALS IN CLOUD COMPUTING RESEARCH

Ranking of the journals based on the research output on 'Cloud Computing' during the study period presented in the Table 6. This analysis is done in the Bibexcel tool.

Table 6: Ranking of journals in cloud computing research

Journal Name	No. of Records	Ranking
Astronomy & Astrophysics	93	1
Astrophysical Journal	57	2
Journal of Geophysical Research-Atmospheres	52	3
Monthly Notices of The Royal Astronomical Society	50	4
Fujitsu Scientific & Technical Journal	35	5
IEEE Internet Computing	26	6
Atmospheric Chemistry and Physics	20	7
Computer	20	8
Concurrency and Computation-Practice & Experience	18	9

Journal Name	No. of Records	Ranking
IBM Journal of Research And Development	17	10
Journal of Applied Meteorology And Climatology	15	11
Journal of Climate	15	12
China Communications	14	13
ACM Sigplan Notices	14	14
IEEE Transactions on Geoscience And Remote Sensing	13	15
Journal of Atmospheric And Oceanic Technology	13	16
Journal of Parallel And Distributed Computing	12	17
Journal of Grid Computing	12	18
Applied Optics	12	19
Computer Communication Review	11	20
Communications of the ACM	11	21
Astronomical Journal	11	22
Journal of Internet Technology	10	23
Future Generation Computer Systems-The International Journal of Grid Computing-Theory Methods and Applications	10	24
IEEE Security & Privacy	10	25
Journal of Quantitative Spectroscopy & Radioactive Transfer	10	26

The highly productive journals up to five ranks are as follows:

1. 'Astronomy and Astrophysics' with 93 contributions get First Rank.
2. 'Astrophysical Journal' with 57 contributions gets Second Rank.
3. 'Journal of Geophysical Research-Atmospheres' with 52 contributions get Third Rank.
4. Monthly Notices of the Royal Astronomical Society 50 results
5. Fujitsu Scientific and Technical Journal 35 output
6. IEEE Internet Computing 26 records

Most Astronomy researchers used cloud computing technic. They published more article in their subject journals. Computer professional journals took Fifth and Sixth rank only.

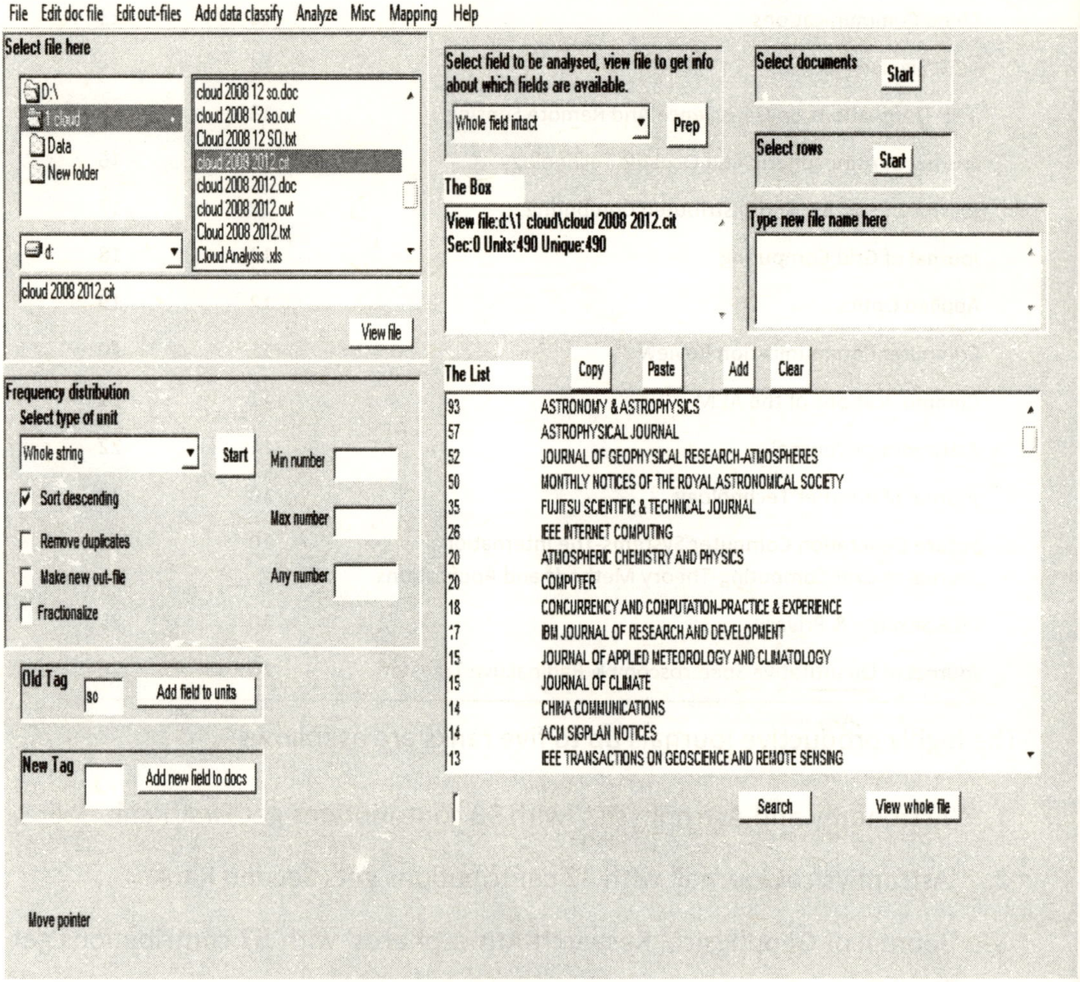

Image 1: Results of ranking of journals

From the source field "SO" of the downloaded data, ".doc" file was created as per the instruction of Bibexcel. From this ".out" we got. The ".out" file was arranged on the basis of descending order. The above screen short shows the ranking of journals result.

14 LOTKA'S LAW IN CLOUD COMPUTING RESEARCH

Table 7 shows some of the top scientists' productivity: Yang P contribute 12, Kattawar GW 8 and Minnis P and Buyya R 7. During the years 2008 to 2012 for the Cloud Computing Research 5303 authors contributed their work. This analysis is carried out with the help of Bibexcel Software. According to Lotka's Law, large number of papers published by a limited number of authors is conformed true Cloud in Computing research.

Sl. No.	Author's Name	No. of Contributions
1.	Yang P	12
2.	Kattawar GW	8
3.	Minnis P	7
4.	Buyya R	7
5.	Llorente IM	7
6.	Galli D	6
7.	Nenes A	5
8.	van Dishoeck EF	5
9.	Gallart C	5
10.	Montero RS	5
11.	Piatti AE	5
12.	Liu QH	4
13.	Qian XP	4
14.	Lee S	4
15.	Liu X	4
16.	Platnick S	4
17.	Marley MS	4
18.	Chen JJ	4
19.	Chakrabarti SK	4
20.	Dasso S	4
21.	Weng FZ	4
22.	Falgarone E	4
23.	Wang Y	4
24.	Yang Y	4
25.	Rutan DA	3
26.	Padovani M	3

15 LABEL AND CLUSTER ANALYSIS OF CLOUD COMPUTING RESEARCH

For analyzing bibliometric networks VOSviewer is primarily used. Maps are created by using the VOS mapping and the VOS clustering technique. The out file is created for the year 2012 Cloud Computing research results with the Bibexcel database. Then with the help of out file the Label view of Cloud Computing Research is displayed.

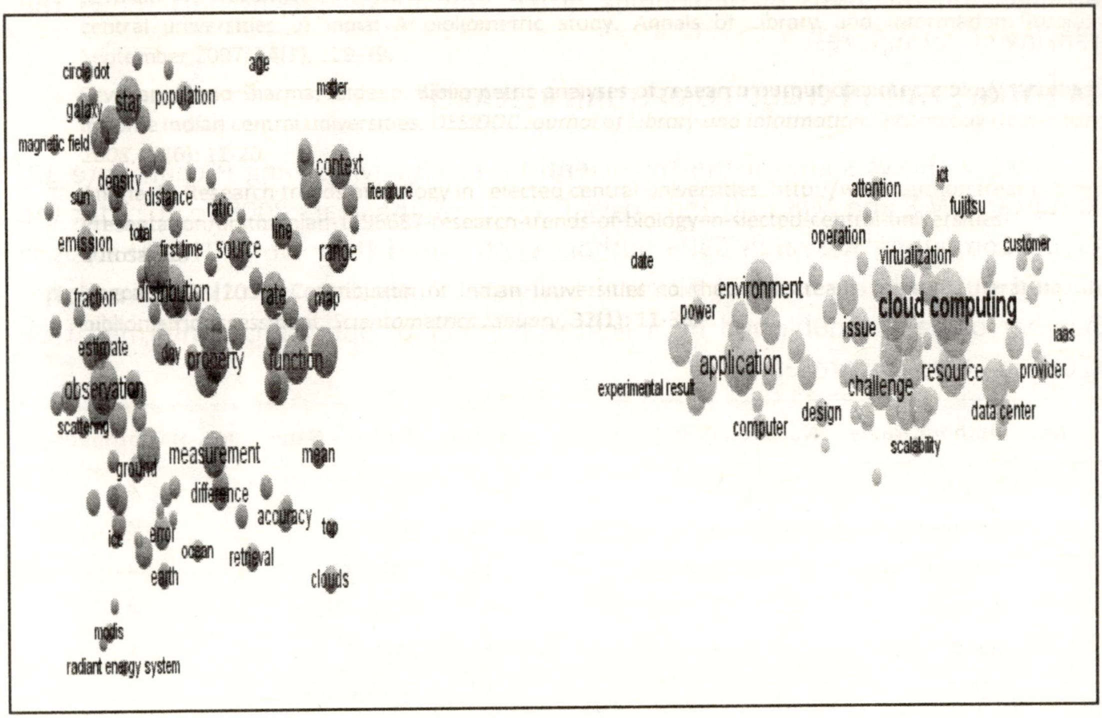

Image 2: Label view of cloud computing research

For the years 2008 - 2012, on the basis of Abstract field the ".out" is derived from the bibexcel. The result of ".out" file is called from the Vosviewer. From there we can find 198 items form cluster in 2. First cluster 117 items with cluster first with red color and in the second cluster 81 with items with green color. Here we can find out the word "distribution" occurred in 107 times. That is also shown in the diagram (Image 3).

16 CITED DOCUMENT ANALYSIS

The data Cited Document field was taken for the analysis with the help of "Any: separator text" in the Bibexcel tool. As a result ".out" file was obtained. On this basis ".net" file we created. The ".net" file was called from the Pajek. From the Pajek the highly cited map was created. That map is shown below in Image 4.

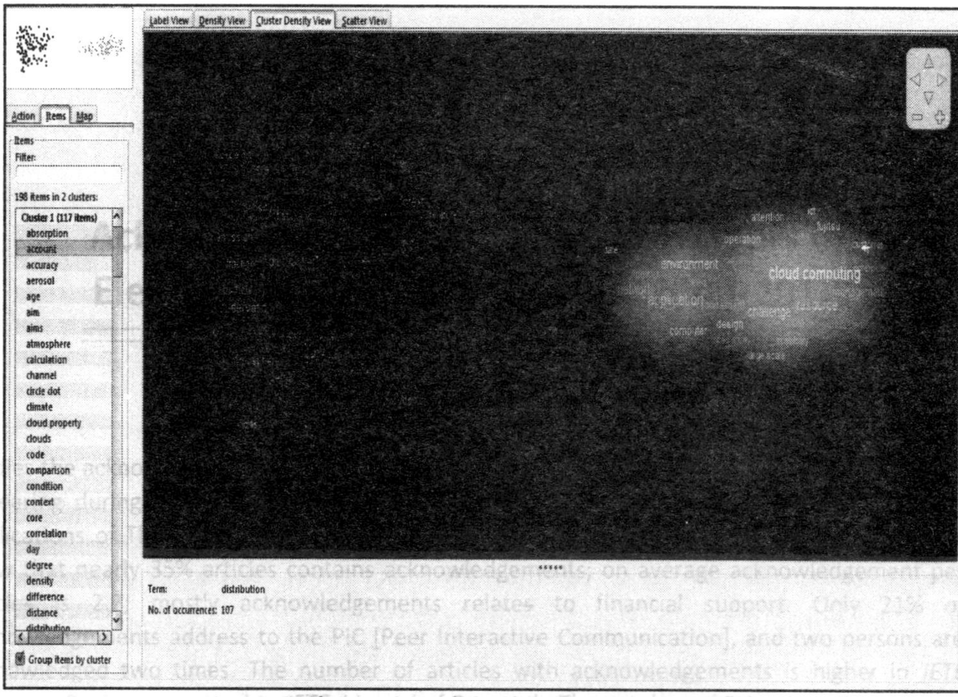

Image 3: Cluster view of cloud computing research

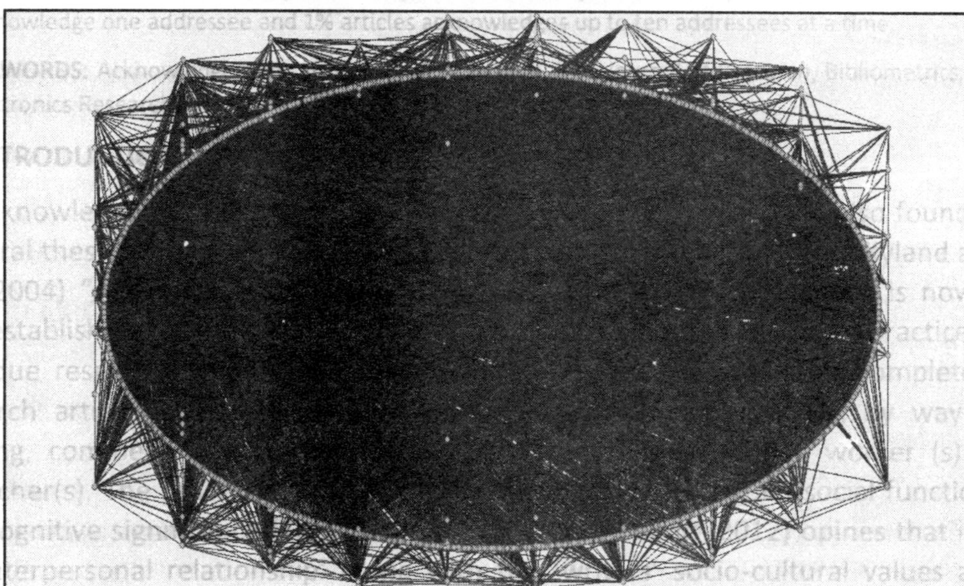

Image 4: Citation analysis of cloud computing research

17 CONCLUSION

In the field of information technology, cloud computing has been a principle from area in recent years. Cloud computing is changing the way information technology is implemented in organizations today. Total Number of Research literature published in "Cloud Computing from the Web of Knowledge for the year 2008 to 2012 was 2207. Single authorship is 363 and multiple authors are 1844. The Degree of Collaboration is at 0.84. Relative Growth Rate for Cloud Computing decreased year after year (0.85 to 0.43) for the years 2008 to 2012. The Doubling Time has increased from 0.80 to 1.58. For Cloud Computing Research, Journal article contribution 1915 followed by Editorial Methods 105. For Cloud Computing Research "Astronomy and Astrophysics" Journal got first rank with 93 contributions. According to Lotkas Law large number of papers is produced by a small number of authors. For the Cloud Computing research 5503 authors contributed for the years 2008 - 2012. 198 items are clustered in 2 times with two different colors. Cluster and Label Analysis was done with the help of VOS mapping technique. With the help of Pajek the data Cited Document Map was created for 2008 - 2012 without single citations. The private cloud IT resources are dedicated to a single organization and offered on demand. The hybrid cloud is a mix of private and public clouds managed as a single entity to extend capacity across clouds as needed.

REFERENCES

1. Arthur P. Young. (2006) An Exploratory Bibliometric Analysis 1956-2004: *Library Quarterly.* 76(1): 10-13.
2. Jian Qin (2008). F. W. Lancaster: A Bibliometric Analysis. *Library Trends,* 56(4): 954-967.
3. Librando, V and Pappalardo, M. (2012) Engineered enzyme interactions with polycyclic aromatic hydrocarbons: A theoretical approach. *Journal of Moldecular graphics and modeling,* 36: 30-35.
4. Mahapatra. (1994) Indian Library and Information Science Journals: A Bibliometric Analysis of the Rate of Citations and Their Characteristics. *Library Review,* 43(3): 41-46.
5. Michel Zitt.; Alain Lelu and Elise. (2011) Bassecoulard Hybrid citation-word Representations in Science Mapping: Portolan Charts of Research Fields. *Journal of the American Society for Information Science and Technology,* 62(1): 19-39.
6. Rafael Ball and Dirk Tunger. (2006) Bibliometric Analysis - a New Business Area for Information Professionals in Libraries? *Scientometrics,* 66(3): 561-577.
7. Kunwar P Singh; Aarti Jain and Parveen Babbar. (2011) DESIDOC Bulletin of Information Technology: A Bibliometic Study. *SRELS Journal of Information Management,* 48(1): 57-68.
8. Mallianath Kumbar and N. Gurusg Kumar. (2011) Authorship trend and collaborative research in Genetics and plant breeding. *SRELS Journal of Information Management*, 48(2): 113-122.
9. Baskaran, C. (2012) Research Productivity of Graph Theory during 2004-2011: A Bibliometic Study. *SRELS Journal of Information Management*, 49(6): 683-691.

14

World University Rankings

Aparna Basu

Performance Evaluation of Academic and Research Institutions is important from the point of several groups such as funding agencies, students, employers, etc. For some years now, rankings have been produced by different agencies around the world. Scientometric methods using research publication and citation data feature in almost all rankings of research excellence. In this article we try to summarize the criteria used by some of these agencies. In particular we note the presence of only a few Indian institutes in these rankings. The need for initiating a systematic ranking of Indian institutes at regular intervals is stressed.

KEYWORDS: Performance evaluation, Academic and Research Institutions, World University Rankings

1 INTRODUCTION

Ranking academic institutions of higher learning is a complex process as the institutions can be evaluated on different fronts such as teaching, research, faculty, students, alumni, awards and infrastructure. Although ideally all these need to be taken into consideration, in practice there may not be good bases for comparison, information may be difficult to get, qualitative and quantitative data may be difficult to combine, or there may be delays in gathering information. All these factors contribute to restricting the criteria chosen by individual agencies to an achievable set. This set may differ between agencies. Also, the relative weights of the criteria may differ. Apart from objective data, opinion surveys are also used. Here we outline some of the strategies adopted by different agencies to arrive at their own rankings.

Scientometric methods feature widely in most of the ranking exercises currently adopted. This is because research output is an important component of the activities of institutions of higher education and research. In the form of published papers, it is already captured effectively by the several databases that index publications, such as Web of Science or Science Citation Index-Expanded and Scopus apart from many subject specific databases. Citation databases also indicate the number of times the papers have been cited. Thus publications and their citations and other derived quantities form an effective basis of research performance evaluation. Most of the ranking exercises indicate on what ccriteria they have arrived at their results.

One of the older ranking exercises was done in the UK jointly by the Times Higher Education group and Quacarelli-Symonds. From 2010, the Times Higher Education has been doing a ranking exercise jointly with Thomsom Reuters, while Quacarelli Symonds has been publishing their own rankings. Apart from this there is the Leiden Ranking published from the Netherlands and the Academic Ranking of World Universities from Shanghai, China, also called the Shanghai Ranking. There is the SIR ranking published from Spain and the Web Ranking also from Spain.

More recently, there is the NTU from the National Taiwan University, Taiwan. Other performance evaluation tools at different levels of aggregation from individuals to disciplines are available, such as the Publish or Perish website from Australia and Science Watch published from the USA.

Some of the ranking criteria that have been used are:

- Peer Review;
- Awards;
- Manpower;
- Papers;
- Citations;
- Collaboration;
- Internationalization;
- Income; and
- Patents.

Both objective or data based criteria and opinion based or survey based criteria have been used.

2 QUACARELLI-SYMONDS AND TIMES HIGHER EDUCATION RANKINGS (THE-QS)

The objective of the THE-QS ranking was to recognize universities for the multi faceted organizations that they are, and to provide a global measure of their success against a notional idea of becoming or remaining world class. The four main criteria used by them are:

- Teaching Quality;
- Research Quality;
- International Outlook; and
- Graduate employability.

The information gathered was based on survey of experts and was questionnaire based. In 2009, universities ranked numbered 600, of which 300 top universities are listed at their website (www.topuniversities.com).

From 2010, Quacarelli-Symonds has been publishing its own rankings:

QS World University Rankings Results 2010

QS Rankings 2010 | Subject | Academic Criteria | Methodology 2010

Top 100 101-200 201-300 301-400 401-500 500+

Rank 2010	Rank 2009	School Name	Country	Size	Research	Focus	Score 2010
1	2	University of Cambridge	United Kingdom	L	VH	FC	100.00
2	1	Harvard University	United States	L	VH	FC	99.18
3	3	Yale University	United States	M	VH	FC	98.68
4	4	UCL (University College London)	United Kingdom	L	VH	FC	98.54
5	9	Massachusetts Institute of Technology (MIT)	United States	M	VH	CO	98.19
6	5=	University of Oxford	United Kingdom	L	VH	FC	98.16
7	5=	Imperial College London	United Kingdom	L	VH	FC	97.78
8	7	University of Chicago	United States	M	VH	FC	97.52
9	10	California Institute of Technology (Caltech)	United States	S	VH	CO	96.46
10	8	Princeton University	United States	M	VH	CO	96.03

It is seen from the website that Cambridge University is ranked at the top of the list followed by Harvard and Yale Universities. No Indian universities feature in the list and probably were not in the initial 600 taken for the exercise.

3 THE TIMES HIGHER EDUCATION WORLD UNIVERSITY RANKINGS

The most recent World University Rankings are for 2012-2013. The Times Higher Education work jointly with Thomson Reuters to produce the rankings, and claim to be the only global university ranking to assess universities across all their core missions, namely

- Teaching;
- Research;
- Knowledge transfer; and
- International outlook.

Their data is based on the Web of Science, and according to them they use 13 well calibrated performance indicators to arrive at the rankings. The top 400 universities are given by region and subject area. To minimise error, ranks are given within error bars rather than as an exact number.

The Indian institutes that feature in this list are, with corresponding ranks,

- 226-250 IIT Kharagpur;
- 251-275 IIT Bombay; and
- 351-400 IIT Roorkee.

4 THE LEIDEN RANKINGS

The most recent Leiden Ranking 2011-12 measures the performance of 500 major universities worldwide. They are published from Leiden in the Netherlands and are based mainly on scientometric indicators. They claim to be based on highly accurate measurements of scientific research in universities and their scientific collaboration. The current results for 2011-2012 are based on Thomson Reuters' Web of Science database of 2005-2009.

Indicators of scientific impact are:

Mean Citation Rate (MCR) or the average number of citations received by the publications of the university,

Mean Normalized Citation Score (MNCS) The average number of citations of the publications of a university, normalized for field differences, publication year, and document type. An MNCS value of two for instance means that the publications of a university have been cited twice above world average.

Proportion top 10% publications ($PP_{top\ 10\%}$). The proportion of the publications of a university that, compared with other similar publications, belong to the top 10% most frequently cited. Publications are considered similar if they were published in the same field and the same publication year and if they have the same document type. The $PP_{top\ 10\%}$indicator is more stable than the MNCS indicator, and therefore regarded as the most important impact indicator of the Leiden Ranking.

Indicators of collaboration are:

Proportion collaborative publications (PP_{collab}). The proportion of the publications of a university that have been co-authored with one or more other organizations.

Proportion international collaborative publications ($PP_{int\ collab}$). The proportion of the publications of a university that have been co-authored by two or more countries.

Mean geographical collaboration distance (MGCD). The average geographical collaboration distance of the publications of a university, where the geographical collaboration distance of a publication equals the largest geographical distance between two addresses mentioned in the publication's address list.

Proportion long distance collaborative publications ($PP_{>1000\ km}$). The proportion of the publications of a university that have a geographical collaboration distance of more than 1000 km.

The Leiden ranking use 'fractional counting' which means that they give fractional credit to institutions based on the number of institutions that have co-authored a paper.

The Leiden Ranking also offers regional rankings. According to that, in Asia there are several Indian institutes that are ranked. Within the top 100 in Asia are the following institutes and ranks:

33 Indian Institute of Technology, Kharagpur;

36 Indian Institute of Technology, Madras;

39 Indian Institute of Science, Bangalore; and

40 Indian Institute of Technology, Delhi.

5 SIR WORLD REPORTS 2012

The SIR World Reports claim to be the most comprehensive research assessment of the World universities, higher education institutes and other research focused institutions that have published at least 100 papers in the period 2006-2010. This amounts to 3290 institutions that account for 80% of papers published worldwide. The papers are taken from Elsevier's database Scopus.

The institutions are grouped into sectors:

Higher Education	Health System
Government Corporations	Others

The SIR rankings use six indicators that measure:

- scientific impact;
- thematic specialization;
- output size; and
- international collaboration networks of the institution

The six indicators are:

- O:: Output - Documents published in scholarly journals indexed in Scopus;
- IC:: International Collaboration - Institution's output ratio produced in collaboration with foreign institutions;
- NI:: Normalized Impact -Values (in %) showing the relationship between an institution's average scientific impact and the world average set to a score of 1;
- Q1:: High Quality Publications - Publications an institution publishes in the most influential journals those ranked in the first quartile (25%) in their categories as ordered by SCImago Journal Rank SJR indicator;
- Spec:: Specialization Index - Indicates the extent of thematic concentration / dispersion of an institution's scientific output based on the Gini Index y;
- Exc:: Excellence Rate - % of an institution's scientific output that is included in 10% of the most cited papers in their respective scientific fields; and

- Leadership:: Scientific Leadership - Indicates an institution's "output as main contributor", that is the number of papers in which the corresponding author belongs to the institution.

The following chart shows a single Indian institution that appears in the top 100 of the SIR rankings, CSIR at rank 98:

The SIR Reports also have regional rankings for the Ibero-American region.

Rank	Organization	Country	Sector	Output	CxD	Int. Coll.	Norm. SJR	Norm. Cit.
85	University of Texas, Austin	United States	Higher educ.	15670	7.84	27.61	0.99	1.65
86	Ludwig-Maximilians Universität München	Germany	Higher educ.	15625	9.73	43.15	1.06	1.57
87	Georgia Institute of Technology	United States	Higher educ.	15527	6.32	24.65	0.9	1.98
88	New York University	United States	Higher educ.	15419	11.45	28.63	1.09	1.83
89	Huazhong University of Science and Technology	China	Higher educ.	15337	1.46	11.72	0.91	0.62
90	Brigham and Women's Hospital	United States	Health	15293	19.39	31.48	1.17	2.72
91	University of New South Wales	Australia	Higher educ.	15265	6.46	38.72	0.99	1.43
92	University of Southern California	United States	Higher educ.	15243	9.05	29.27	1.01	1.8
93	Michigan State University	United States	Higher educ.	15100	7.26	31.11	1.02	1.53
94	Universita degli Studi di Bologna	Italy	Higher educ.	14942	6.85	35.24	1	1.25
95	Universidad Nacional Autonoma de Mexico	Mexico	Higher educ.	14716	4.6	43.35	1.01	0.84
96	Peking University	China	Higher educ.	14673	4.31	23.58	0.98	0.96
97	Università degli Studi di Milano	Italy	Higher educ.	14668	8.17	36.02	1.05	1.31
98	Council of Scientific and Industrial Research	India	Government	14428	5.28	15.46	1.03	0.93
99	Academy of Sciences of the Czech Republic (cas.cz)	Czech Republic	Government	14292	5.56	53.86	1.01	1
100	National Institute of Advanced Industrial Science & Technology	Japan	Government	14237	5.45	23.81	0.98	1.18

6 ACADEMIC RANKING OF WORLD UNIVERSITIES (ARWU OR SHANGHAI RANKING)

The Academic Ranking of World Universities is published from Shanghai. 1200 Universities are evaluated and finally a list of the top 500 are published on the web. The criteria used are as follows,

- Quality of Alumni NOBEL Prizes, Fields Medals
- Quality of Faculty
- Highly Cited Researchers
- Papers in Nature and Science
- Papers in SCI and SSCI
- Per capita performance

There are two Indian institutions in the Shanghai ranking.

7 THE NATIONAL TAIWAN UNIVERSITY OR NTU RANKING

The NTU is a recent ranking published by the University of Taiwan. Ranking is on the basis of publications, citations, h-index, and accounts for smaller size and recent performance. Two Indian institutes feature in the ranking at the ranks given below,

Indian Institute of Science	424
Tata Institute of Fundamental Research	457

8 RANKING OF INDIAN UNIVERSITIES AND RESEARCH INSTITUTES

It is seen from the above rankings that very few Indian institutions feature in the top 500 institutions and in particular Indian universities are missing from the lists. This means that in order to get a comparative basis for evaluation of Indian institutions, it will be necessary to separately rank Indian institutes. While world rankings give us an idea of the global rank of a few Indian institutions, an Indian ranking will give us an idea where an institution stands on a national level.

It is necessary to make an appropriate choice of parameters for a national level exercise. Each of the global rankings cited above have a different parameter set, but these parameters need not be indiscriminately taken for a national level evaluation. We can however take analogues which will be more appropriate to a national exercise. For example, the Bhatnagar award can be substituted for the Nobel prize or Fields medal in the global ranking. Other parameters could be publications, citations, highly cited papers, papers in Nature, Science or other highly cited journals. It is also preferable to rank universities and research institutes on the same footing rather than have separate rankings.

Some early efforts in evaluation were done in India based on publications. These are described below together with a recent exercise on rating Indian universities, published in 2013.

9 NATIONAL MAPPING OF SCIENCE

The National Mapping of Science was one of the earliest exercises to evaluate S&T in India based on several citations and subject linked databases. It funded by the National Information Systems on Science and Technology (NISSAT) of the Department of Scientific and Technical Research (DSIR). It was done by several groups across India in late 1990s. The Science Citation Index (SCI) was analyzed across all subjects at the National Institute of Science Technology and Development Studies (NISTADS). It was based on a quantity factor, the number of publications in SCI and a quality factor, the journal impact factor (IF) of the publications.

The top Indian institutes for 1997 and their Impact Factors are shown below. Subject specific rankings are also obtained in Basu (2000).

Table 1: Ranking on Indian Institutions based on publications in SCI (1997)

	Papers	Impact Factor
Indian Institute of Science	635	1.70
Bhaba Atomic Research Centre	413	1.38
Tata Institute of Fundamental Research	337	2.41
Banaras Hindu University	276	1.20
All India Institute of Medical Sciences	272	5.42
Indian Institute of Technology (Bombay)	254	1.21
Indian Institute of Technology (Madras)	254	0.90
National Chemical Laboratory	252	1.71
Indian Association of Cultivation of Science	241	1.54
Indian Institute of Technology (Kanpur)	230	1.55
Delhi University	230	1.48

	Papers	Impact Factor
Indian Institute of Technology (Kharagpur)	217	0.84
Indian Institute of Technology (Delhi)	204	1.16
Jadavpur University	183	1.22
Hyderabad University	157	2.30
Calcutta University	148	1.46
Madras University	148	0.92
Post Graduate Institute of Medical Education and Research	140	3.70
Saha Institute of Nuclear Physics	139	1.80
Indian Institute of Chemical Technology	136	1.84

This list evaluates the institutions along two dimensions representing quantity and quality. Although the list is dominated by the large producers, the average impact factor, IF allows us to pick out smaller actors such as the University of Hyderabad which has the highest Impact Factor in this list.

9.1 Analysis by Kademani, et. al. (2007)

A further analysis based on the Science Citation Index data 1990-2004 was undertaken by Kademani et al., in 2007. It has separate listings for universities and other institutes. It lists the following universities at the top based on data from 1990-2004.

Table 2: Universities at the top ranks based on SCI data 1990-2004

Banaras Hindu University, Varanasi
University of Delhi, Delhi
Jadavpur University, Kolkata
Panjab University, Chandigarh
University of Kolkata, Kolkata
University of Hyderabad, Hyderabad
University of Madras, Chennai
Aligarh Muslim University, Aligarh
Osmania University, Hyderabad
Anna University, Chennai
Jawaharlal Nehru University, Delhi
Christian Medical College, Vellore
University of Rajasthan, Jaipur

9.2 Analysis of 16 subject areas in Scopus (Gupta and Dhawan)

A ranking of 16 subject fields was also obtained from Scopus data 1996-2006 by Gupta and Dhawan. Based on that, we have obtained a list of universities that are in the top 30 in a majority of fields.

Table 3: Institutes which are highly productive in Top 30 in many subjects: Scopus data 1996-2006

Indian Institute Of Science	15 subjects
Delhi University	14
Banaras Hindu University	14
University of Madras	12
Jadavpur University	11
University of Mumbai	7

9.3 Indian Citation Index

It must be noted that apart from the standard citation indices such as Science Citation Index, Scopus and Google Scholar, an Indian Citation Index has also been set up for Indian journal publications.

10 RECENT RANKINGS

A recent ranking of universities in India has a scheme of rating the universities as 5 star, 4 star, etc. based on several criteria such as NAAC accreditation score, publications in WoS and Scopus in 2011, patents applied for and granted. Public and private universities are separately rated. Public universities in the North, South, East and West regions which obtained 5 stars are as follows, (not in any particular order)

Table 4: Ranking of Universities by Careers 360-'Outstanding Universities'-2013

University of Calcutta
Jadavpur University
Banaras Hindu University
University of Delhi
Panjab University
Aligarh Muslim University
Jawaharlal Nehru University
University of Hyderabad
University of Madras
Andhra University

No universities in the Western region are rated with 5 stars. For more details *see* the website (www.careers360.com/MDU-Public.pdf,www.careers360.com/MDU-Private.pdf). As can be seen, the 2011 ranking includes universities that are not very different from those in earlier assessments based on publications. Patents and NAAC score apparently do not provide sufficient discrimination.

11 WHAT PARAMETERS TO CHOOSE?

As seen above, Indian universities by and large do not feature in world rankings and the ranking of Indian universities have been done primarily on their publication output as indexed in the different citation databases. As the data is readily available, this is the most straightforward analysis that can be done. However, in order to broaden the exercise and bring in more facets of performance evaluation there is a need to re-think the parameters that are being used. As we have seen the global ranking exercises use a variety of criteria in order to arrive at their results. Clearly it is futile to use identical criteria, such as Nobel prizes or Field's medals for the Indian academia, but an analogue such as the Bhatnagar awards can be used. A few criteria that may be used in the Indian context are proposed here. There is an emphasis on research, but teaching can also be considered if some standardised method of capturing teaching quality is suggested. Although, as I have mentioned earlier the main focus of Indian institutes has traditionally been research and for universities it is teaching, it is important to do an assessment exercise for both kinds of institutions on the same footing rather than separately.

Some criteria for performance evaluation could be:

- Awards;
  - Bhatnagar awards and other awards
  - Academy Fellowships
- No. of publications by discipline;
- No. of citations by discipline;
- Ranking for each discipline;
- Highly cited papers;
- Papers in Nature, Science, etc.;

- Co-authored publications; and
- Normalization for size.

The last factor is important in order that new emerging institutions are not overshadowed by the larger sized established institutions.

12 CAUTIONARY WORDS

Before concluding, a few words of caution need to be added. Ranking exercises work with constructs which may not always reflect quality adequately. Some degree of care and calibration is required in the choice and relative weights of factors. The race to achieve high ranks can also skew the activities in the institutions, according lower priority to important factors of performance which cannot directly be measured.

In summary, scientometric evaluation forms an important part of performance evaluation of higher education and research institutes. The factors that are taken for evaluation, and their relative weights, differ in the different ranking exercises. As a consequence of this there is no single or unique ranking. Scientometric data that form the basis for evaluation, such as papers or citations, will also vary with the choice of database. There are several ranking methods that rank institutions across the globe. The contributing factors vary from awards, to research papers, citations, quality of faculty and alumni, collaboration and internationalization. Only a few Indian institutions feature in these lists that may rank up to 500 institutions although some do feature in the regional lists. There is an urgent need to do a similar exercise for India so that performance of institutions within India may be compared. It has been suggested here that research institutes and primarily teaching institutions such as universities be evaluated on the same footing. A slightly different set of factors has also been proposed here, as against the global factors, to suit the Indian context, such as the use of the Bhatnagar awards, separate ranking for different disciplines, normalization for the size of the institution, etc. Finally, there is a need to adopt caution in these exercises so that the results adequately express the accepted notions of quality and do not adversely affect the normal activities of institutions under study.

REFERENCES

1. Academic Ranking of World Universities, www.arwu.org
2. Basu, A. and P.S. Nagpaul. (1998) National Mapping of Science, NISTADS Report No. 248/98, New Delhi
3. Basu, A.; Ritu Aggarwal; Devender Kumar; Geeta Kathuria; Satyendra Jha and Taruna Rani. (2000) Scientific Productivity, where do we stand?, *Second Brief Report on Bibliometric Indicators of Indian Science*
4. Bibliometric study of India's Scientific Publication Outputs during 2001-2010, DST report 2012 (http://www.dst.gov.in/whats_new/whats_new12/report.pdf)
5. B. M. Gupta and S. M. Dhawan: Status of India in science and technology as reflected in its publication output in the Scopus international database, 1996-2006.
6. Indian Citation Index, www.indiancitationindex.com
7. Jacso, P. (2008) The pros and cons of computing the h-index using Web of Science DOI 10.1108/14684520810914043
8. Kademani, B.S.; Anil Sagar; Vijay Kumar and B.M. Gupta. (2007) Mapping of Indian Publications in S&T: A Scientometric Analysis of publications in Science Citation Index. *DESIDOC Journal of Library and Information Technology*, 27(1).
9. Outstanding Universities, http://www.careers360.com/MDU-Public.pdf
10. Outstanding Universities, http://www.careers360.com/MDU-Private.pdf
11. QS World University Rankings, http://www.topuniversities.com/university-rankings
12. THE World University Rankings, http://www.timeshighereducation.co.uk/world-university-rankings/

15

SRELS Journal of Information Management - History and Contributions: A Golden Jubilee Review

A.Y. Asundi

The *SRELS Journal of Information Management* was started in 1964 with the title *Library Science with a Slant to Documentation* under the sponsorship of the Sarada Ranganathan Endowment for Library Science (SRELS). It is now a peer reviewed periodical. With the advent of e-publishing, keeping with the trend, an online version is also available. At the beginning the papers mainly focused on the research conducted at DRTC in particular, Library Classification and Library Cataloguing, Documentation and gradually extended its coverage to new areas of interest e.g. Computer Applications, Library Management and Information Systems. During the 1970's, when CSIR/NISSAT was launched, special issues devoted to Information Systems - planning and organization, were brought out. Now the periodical is fully multidisciplinary, covering all facets of Library and Information Science (LIS). This paper attempts to map the subjects of the papers of this periodical which has spanned the last fifty years. The analysis would serve as a check list for the areas of current and traditional subject interests in the field of LIS. The paper will also highlight the important contributions this periodical has made for the progress and development of LIS during the last fifty years.

KEYWORDS: Library Science, Information Science, Library Science with a slant to Documentation, SRELS Journal of Information Management, Subject Analysis.

1 INTRODUCTION

SRELS Journal of Information Management is an organ of the Sarada Ranganathan Endowment for Library Science (SRELS). SRELS was founded in 1961 by Dr. S.R. Ranganathan. It was registered as a charitable Endowment with the Government of India in 1963 and with the Government of Karnataka in 2006. The principal aims of the Endowment are to promote and support the improvement of library and information services in India.

- Training of library and information service personnel;

- The provision of efficient library and information service; and
- The application of research results to library information studies.

As a means of fulfilling these objectives, the need to disseminate results of research in library and information science (LIS) became evident. Therefore, SRELS initiated the publication of its periodical titled *Library Science with a Slant to Documentation,* as a quarterly.

The first issue came out in February 1964. Since then the periodical has continued its unbroken publication for the past fifty years. Reflecting the changes in the LIS field, the title of the periodical was changed to *Library Science with a Slant to Documentation and Information Studies* in 1988, and again changed to the present title in 2000. Started as a quarterly the frequency changed to six issues a year from v.47 2010. Dr. Ranganathan was its first editor. The periodical is now accessible online at http://www. indianjournals.com.

This paper attempts to briefly describe the transformation of the periodical embracing the new developments in LIS, through the analysis of the papers published in the periodical during the last fifty years from volume one through volume fifty (1964-2013).

2 METHODOLOGY

The analysis is a simple quantitative measure under broad subject headings. The subject headings represent traditional and some recently emerging branches of LIS. The traditional headings have been continued to be used as, the papers integrated both traditional and upcoming subjects. To exemplify this, the "Library Cataloguing" now has evolved into "Metadata", "Online Public Access Catalogue" (OPAC). The OPAC and the traditional physical forms of catalogue have the identical objective of a Library Catalogue as proposed by Cutter way back in the 19th Century. So the entry for OPAC will appear in Library Cataloguing, Metadata and Indexing and not under "Library Automation and Networking or Digital Library".

The title of the paper represents broad subject content. Though referring to full text or abstract of papers was not impossible; but highly time consuming, hence title of the paper is considered as main identity for the subject heading. Each title's subject content is placed under its core and dependent facets. For instance the core of "UGC-INFONET Digital Library Consortium" is though considered as Digital Library, if the paper deals with the study of "User Awareness and Use Pattern of

UGC-INFONET", the core would be "Use, User Studies" and so on. But an entry under the main heading digital library for UGC-INFONET is also posted as a dependent facet. If a paper has deals only with a descriptive account of the working of Digital Library Consortium, then the core would be "Digital Library". In the quantification and compilation of the data, this methodology has been followed as a logical, consistent and uniform method of collecting data.

The main subject headings were not predetermined, but have been generated concurrently as the data collection and compilation process progressed. As far as possible the standard terminology is used, but the synonymous terms also appear in the lists which are sometimes discerning their conceptual bases. For instance again, observe, 'Electronic Sources of Information and Internet Sources of Information', in this case both the terms are used. In spite of all this some overlaps were found because during the preparation of this paper enough potentialities are embedded in its data to draw more useful inferences to conclude some interesting issues. However the methodology described above appears to be more suitable and pragmatic in compiling the data for analysis. In all thirty five broad subject Headings have been evolved and several related areas within them have also been identified. These main headings, it is hoped will be of some use in the analysis of papers of any periodical in Library and Information Science.

3 DATA COLLECTION AND ANALYSIS

The MS EXCEL spread sheet was used to post the data under each of the broad subject field name related to LIS and also related sub-fields/fringe areas. As already explained, the content ofthe paper was determined at two levels – on the level of the core content of the paper and second on the level of dependent facet of the core content. The dependent facets are spread across different subject fields, but the data is determined only under the core content of the paper, the data on dependent facets reflects on the treatment of different areas. So the total number of postings is not equal to the total number of papers published in the last 50 years of the existence of the periodical – which comes to 1249 papers including the Editorials and Book Reviews. The subject content of the latter sections revealed to be very unique and interesting that supplemented the courses of happenings in the field, and similarly the book reviews. The period covered ranges from Volume 1 Number 1, 1964 to Volume 50, Number 4, 2013.

Totally about 204 issues of 50 volumes from February 1964 through August 2013 are covered in this study. The average number of pages per paper is estimated to be around 10 pages. Roughly each paper gets on an average 3 Keywords and that comes to around 4000 postings on different subjects and their surrogate areas.

The number of broad subject areas identified is 35 including some non-LIS fields like Financial Services, Administration and Management, Education and Learning and so on. Some recent developments on the Taxation to e-resources would be a critical issue and it is expected that more papers might come from these areas. As a prelude to recent happenings in this context, an editorial has appeared in the recent issue of the periodical (Asundi, 2013) [1]. In other cases, namely, Administration and Management, topics like, e-commerce and e-governance have reflected their implications in the library and information system administration too.

4 RANKED LIST OF SUBJECT FIELDS

The 35 core subjects identified in the study are ranked by the number of postings received by each and the data is presented under Table 1 and Fig. 1.

Table 1: Ranking of subjects by number postings

Sl. No.	Ranking of Subjects by Number Postings	Postings
1	Bibliometrics, Scientometrics, Informetrics & Webometrics	150
2	Library Classification and Knowledge Organisation	136
3	Information Services	123
4	Library Science Education	81
5	User, Use, User Behaviour	80
6	Library Automation and Networking	78
7	Library Cataloguing, Metadata & Indexing	75
8	Subject Study	74
9	Library Management	69
10	Information Sources (Print, Non-print, Electronic)	64
11	Digital Libraries	50
12	Information Systems	39
13	Internet and World Wide Web	35
14	Knowledge Management	34
15	Public Libraries	33
16	Academic Libraries	30
17	Library Profession and Professionals	27

Sl. No.	Ranking of Subjects by Number Postings	Postings
18	Library and Information Science	26
19	Information Technology	25
20	Scientific Communication	12
21	Intellectual Property Rights	11
22	Education and Learning	9
23	Open Access Initiatives	9
24	Documentation	9
25	Information Analysis, Consolidation, Repackage	8
26	Five Laws of Library Science	7
27	Special Libraries	5
28	Banking and Financial Services	4
29	Information Industry	4
30	Administrative Management	3
31	Professional Communication	3
32	Archival Management	2
33	Information Society	2
34	Research Methods	2
35	Data Services	1

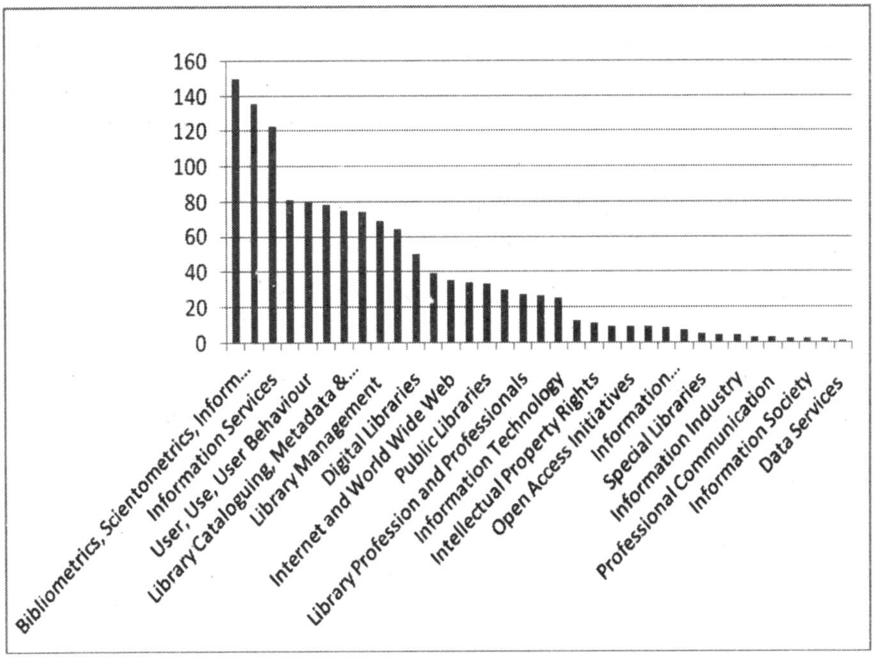

Fig. 1: List of subjects with ranks

5 ANALYSIS AND INTERPRETATION OF RANKS

The subject fields are ranked by the number postings they have received. The analysis and interpretation on the behaviour of the data is made viewing the changing profile of LIS and the new developments and computational tools available now for the researchers for the study of the subjects.

The percentages of the first ten ranks are presented in the Table 2.

Table 2: Selected of subjects - first 10 ranks

Sl. No.	Subjects field	Postings	Percentage
1.	Bibliometrics, Scientometrics, Informetrics, Webometrics etc.	150	12
2.	Library Classification & Knowledge Organisation	136	11
3.	Information Services	123	9.84
4.	LIS Education	81	6.5
5.	User, User Study and Behaviour	80	6.4
6.	Library Automation and Networking	78	6.24
7.	Library Cataloguing, Metadata and Indexing	75	6
8.	Library Management	69	5.52
9.	Information Sources	64	5.12
10.	Digital Library	50	4

The area of Bibliometrics and Scientometrics with 130 (12%) postings is in the first rank. The studies on this subject have been receiving greater attention in the recent years as the findings of the bibliometrics and scientometrics studies have a bearing on the academic research output from the Universities and higher educational institutions and it has been partially accepted by the academic community all over the world. Some of the parameters evolved from these studies like "Impact Factor" "h-Index are regularly receiving the attention of academicians and also of higher education assessment and accreditation bodies.

Until early 1980's Bibliometrics was not much in focus for research and it involved arduous and time consuming work of collecting vast number of citations and also involved lengthy statistical calculations as there were no statistical software packages relevant to compute the bibliometrics parameters. Dr. Ranganathan had introduced the concept of Librametry as early in 1940's (Ranganatha, 1995 [11]) and the methodology for estimation of library staff for a library. The formula used for estimating the professional staff for libraries, and is one such example of study of librametry. A paper on "Dispersion of documents" appeared in 1972 (Ravichandra Rao, 1972 [12]) and discussed Bradford distribution, but the term "Bibliometrics" was not used, and the periodical referred it under "Librametrics Series".The first paper on Bibliometrics was published in 1983.

The growth in the number of papers is found to be more in the recent years, and it may be due to the availability of customized databases like "SCOPUS and Web of Science" which eliminated the task of collection of citations and also resolved the complexity of statistical calculations and the paper visualizes this as the reason for its sudden growth. If the growth of number of papers on Bibliometrics and related areas is plotted into a graphical representation it can be hypothesized that it would follow a time series linear growth model. This can be tested with relevant detailed data compiled year-wise.

The second rank is for Library Classification and Knowledge Organization with 136 (11%) postings. The study of Library Classification was conceived to have only a limited scope as a tool for shelf-arrangement. Its role and concept as an active subject changed with the development of a dynamic theory of library classification by Dr. Ranganathan, and this periodical brought a close communication among researchers in Library Classification. Its role is renewed as Knowledge Organization System in the web environment and that would be receiving more significant attention in the years to come. The number of papers published in the initial years of the periodical focused on Library Classification theory and its development, methodology for the design of depth schedules, exemplified with several schedules in some very narrow specialized subjects like Fountain Pen Production. Researchers in knowledge organization from foreign countries are in the process of reinventing Ranganathan and other Classificationists and Indexing Linguistics to apply them to the digital era and in particularly in the domain of the semantic web.

It is significant that Library and Information Services occupies the third rank, after all. the library is a service organization.. The library services ranged from a basic lending to the Online Information Retrieval Services to reach of the high-tech web-based internet services. It is observed from the detailed data on services that the studies on computer-based services (Online) and User Education and Information Literacy are more compared to conventional Bibliographical and Reference Services. The entry of Information Literacy is in recent times and the number of papers are also noteworthy.

The fourth rank is for LIS Education. A distinct emphasis and importance was given on teaching methods by Dr. Ranganathan. Adoption of innovative teaching methods is focused in the papers published in the periodical.

Table 3: Examples of bibliometrics and library classification with dependent facets

Name of the Field and the Dependent Facets	No. of Postings	Name of the Field and the Dependent Facets	No. of Postings
Bibliometrics, Scientometrics, Informetrics and Webometrics.	**150**	***Library Classification (Knowledge Organisation)***	***136***
Authorship Pattern	10	Analytico-Synthetic Classification	1
Bibliometric Laws	10	Anteriorising Common Isolates	3
Circulation Transactions	4	Automatic Classification	1
Citation Analysis	9	Classification Research Groups	1
Coefficient of Dispersion	1	Classification Theory	1
Communication Pattern	1	Colon Classification	9
Core Periodicals Identification	2	Common Subdivisions	1
Doctoral Dissertations	3	Comparison of Schemes	4
Evaluation of concept	1	Component Ideas	1
Grant-in-aid study	1	Decimal Classification	2
Impact factor	5	Depth Classification – Methodology & Schedules	18
Information Literacy Research	1	Facet Structure	1
Library Management	1	Fundamental Categories	1
Linguistics	1	Glossary	1
Literature Review	1	Indian Systems	1
Mapping	3	Information Processing	2
Metrics – Conceptual Study	2	Knowledge Organisation	16
Obsolescence	5	Lateral Relations	1
Pedalogical	1	Modes of Formation	6
Research Methodology	5	Multidisciplinary Subjects	3
S & T Indicators	1	Multilingual Studies	1
Science Citation Index	1	Natural Language Processing	5
Scientific Collaboration	12	Notational System	2
SCOPUS	1	Patent Classification System	1
		Phase Relations	2
		Planes of work	1
		Postulational Approach	1
		Research	1
		Seminal Mnemonics	1
		Space Isolates	1
		Speciators	1
		Teaching	1
		Terminology	2
		Text retrieval	1
		Universal Decimal Classification	3
		Universe of Knowledge/Subjects	17
		User Interface	3

The studies on user and user needs studies are becoming a trend with the advent of Digital Library Consortia and Internet Services, otherwise the studies on library use, use of documents and information are few.

Another area of significance that has attracted LIS professionals is Library Automation and Networking which grew with the developments in ICT due to the availability of Integrated Library Management Systems (ILMS) and the cost of hardware becoming affordable to libraries. The availability of Free Open Source Software (FOSS) should have attracted more professionals to work on their use and experience. It is found that there are only a few papers in this area out of the total 78 postings. The highest number of postings is on ILMS.

In comparison with library classification, the number of postings on Library Cataloguing is less. In this category more numbers of postings are on subject cataloguing, indexing, thesaurus and other tools and techniques of indexing.

The next three areas covered are, Library Management, Information Sources, and Digital Library. The concepts under the Digital Library are spread across different disciplines hence there is a moderate number of postings under the core area and studies on digital library

6 GAPS IN THE STUDIES

On going through the 50years papers, it is observed that there is significant fall in the output of papers in some of the areas and/or no significant attention was also not perceived for the fields which have distinct professional applications. So the areas which have not been receiving research papers are discussed here.

Information Systems has almost been non significant since the advent of Online Information Systems and the World Wide Web. The components of Information Systems, as was conceived in 1970's and 1980's, such as Information Centres, Documentation Centres, Information Analysis Centre, and the most depleted "Translation Centre" and the much significant Data Centres and Data Services have not received much attention.

There is an upcoming new trend of "integrated library systems" and the compartmentalization of libraries as Public, School, and Special would alter in the coming years and this is visible in the ranks, as there are hardly any work reported on Special Libraries, Academic Libraries and School Libraries. As many as 75 different domains of study have been used as cases for the study in Bibliometrics, Information Services and Information Sources.

Another area getting into the realm of LIS is Archival Management or Document Management Systems as part of the Digital Library Systems. The papers on digital library are more or less on its conceptual basis and on the use and working of Digital Library Consortia. There are only two papers on projects and efforts on on-going on digitizing but lack on digitizing the archives, classic and rare books. The born digital scenario has no innovative inklings as most of that work is now commercialized and there is still a wider gap to Digital Archiving in India as it is revealed from the number of papers on this subject.

It is also observed that number of papers on Professional Communication that manifests, Technical Writing and other communication skills so essential for research reporting has received a very scant attention. The areas of manual of style, referencing, and styles of scientific writing are becoming more demanding as LIS professionals are endowed with techniques and skills in this regard. The areas like Web design, Content Management Systems now require good professional writing skills. So the profession has to diversify and carry out some innovative and creative work and some of these areas of distinct identity have to be nurtured. For example, "Use, User Studies, Information Seeking Behaviour" all use the same parameters, identical methodology, using questionnaires and come out with some quantitative data and present them in Tables and Graphs. So a new direction in this regard is proposed in this attempt of not just quantitative analysis of the papers but to create an inquisitive approach among LIS professionals.

In these sections an effort is made to map the areas which are consistently being studied and also some new areas which have been in the limelight obviously impacted by technology. Once again it is found that, innovating in traditional subjects has been one of the cause for increasing studies on some emerging areas like digital libraries, metadata, knowledge organization and so on. So it can be said that the papers published in the periodical are in concurrence with the changing times of the subjects in dealing with both traditional and upcoming areas and it is visible from the papers received by the periodical in recent years. In consonant with these changes the periodical has also thought of changing its title – from "Library Science with a slant to Documentation" to the present title *"SRELS Journal of Information Management"*.

7 THE PERIODICAL'S CONTRIBUTION TO THE LIS PROFESSION

The role of the periodical in the advances and development of the profession is being assessed here with the contributions in the last fifty years. The research carried out at DRTC and the papers published in the periodical since then have made a perpetual impact on the research process in LIS and its traces can be observed even to this day. It started some distinct practices of denoting each paper's core content by naming them by a series. The names of the series used in the periodical are listed below.

1. Classification Problems;
2. Design Series;
3. Computer and Logic in Documentation;
4. Bibliographical References;
5. Teaching Library Science (changed to) Education to Library and Information Science;
6. Standards Series;
7. Comparison Series;
8. Documentation Problems;
9. Non-Conventional Methods in Document Retrieval;
10. Library Organization;
11. Book Science Series;
12. Subject Headings;
13. Cataloguing Problems;
14. Development of Library Science;
15. Librametrics Series;
16. Social Sciences Series;
17. Universe of Subjects;
18. CC Ed. 7 Series;
19. Planning Series;
20. Reprography Series;
21. Administration Series;
22. Thesaurus Series;
23. Information Systems;
24. Information User Studies;
25. Communication Sciences; and
26. Information for Industry.

So this implies the areas of specialization on which the contributions have come from the periodical. The papers reflect the future vision of the professional subjects now visible is some of the developments seen in the areas of Knowledge Organisation, Information Storage and Retrieval, Mechanised and Computer-based information systems and services like "Doc-Finder", application of IT in information delivery and dissemination, Bibliometrics, and so on. Some of the contributions are highlighted in the forthcoming sections.

8 A PICTURE OF CONTRIBUTIONS

It can be observed from the key papers published from the first issue of the periodical, that a systematic and structured knowledge had inherently been accumulated in the memory of Dr. Ranganathan, begotten from his practice, teaching and research work. Library Classification being one his first desires, yet the aura of the collaboration he entered with other authors showed a team work that was carried from the DRTC. In effect the first issue of the periodical published a very detailed and comprehensive "Methodology on Design of Depth Classification (Ranganathan, 1964). This paper on "Depth Classification Methodology" written by him is unique in respect of its detailed methodology on designing depth schedules. This was successively followed with many Depth Schedules (for micro-subjects) by teachers and students of DRTC, on specialized and specific subjects, such as: Production Engineering of screw, nut, bearing, boiler, automobile, aircraft wing, missiles and rockets, etc. The in-depth facet analysis of a micro-subject, identifying its related narrower and broader subjects and other associated subjects, recognizing the strength of bond among the resulting component concepts are necessary prerequisites of the work. Even to present times the methodology holds its relevance in the conceptual elucidation of facets of knowledge organization. Evidently such work of facet analysis is precursor to domain analysis, data mining, and knowledge analytics. The generalized facet structure for embodied knowledge based on canons and principles is a useful framework for knowledge analysis and synthesis, organization and representation in the area of knowledge organization. In a recent paper on "Principles for Helpful Sequence" it was demonstrated how the Principles can be employed in the deduction of knowledge organization systems (Asundi, 2013) [2].

The studies relating to the "Universe of Knowledge: its Structure and Development" and the modes of formation of subjects are integral to the analysis of subjects and their organization consistently were part of the DRTC curriculum. Guide lines for the Study of the Subject" was prepared by Ganesh Bhattacharyya and published in the periodical and today it stands as a key benchmark for understanding the structural dynamics of a subject.

Two un-matching and distinct contributions have come from Ranganathan and Bliss – the concepts of seminal mnemonics and Gradation in Speciality. The concept of seminal mnemonics has far reaching application across different domains of knowledge and in a recent paper to demonstrate its potentiality, Neelameghan (1970) [3] (Neelameghan, 2007 [4]; Neelameghan and Raghavan, 2005 [8]) has correlated them in the terms of "leitmotif".

The second area of focus was on Library Cataloguing and Indexing. The papers though mainly focused on issues relating to Classified Catalogue Code (CCC) and Chain Indexing but also undertook several comparative studies with Anglo American Cataloguing Rules (AACR) and which resulted in the improvement of the latter. One of the intricate rules of procedure in Indexing is the "Citation Order" which amounted to intellectual and logical organization of terms in subject cataloguing. It is resolved by the Chain Indexing, which used the Class Number as a basis of generation and sequencing of terms. The conceptual basis of Chain Indexing based on facet analysis of subjects was adapted by the British National Bibliography and British Technology Index. PRECIS (the PREserved Context Indexing System) developed by Derek Austin, KWIC and KWAC indexing systems can be seen as variants derivable from the general theory of indexing languages proposed by Bhattacharyya which resulted in the design of POPSI (Postulate-based Permuted Subject Indexing) and the development of CLASSAURUS and COSSCO Relation – and the one of its kind only. SRELS's periodical was the first channel to carry and disseminate these developments.

In the design and construction of Thesaurus, the three relations – hierarchical, equivalent and associative are easily identifiable. In the human intellectual process, yet another inherent relation exists – like "Kitchen and Food". The relation between the two terms is considered to be non-hierarchical, yet associative and such relation was identified demonstrated with several real life examples which helped in the design of an information retrieval thesaurus (Neelameghan & Ravichandra Rao, 1976 [6], Neelameghan and Raghavan, 2005 & 2006 [5,7,8])

Another area in which some pioneering contributions of this periodical is computer applications to LIS domain.. The first paper per se on Library Automation appeared in 1986 and the numbers of papers on different facets of this subject have not been very substantial in the recent years. But, since 1969 the periodical has been publishing the results of computer applications in "Information organization and retrieval". Some of the distinctly termed packages like "Doc-

Finder, SPEEDS" are those pioneering works which were developed at a time when programming such tasks was, time consuming, tedious and equally an intellectual effort of human information processing skills.(Ranganathan, 1968 [10]) (Venkatraman & Neelameghan, 1968 [9]) COBOL Programming Language was used in the designing of databases and SDI Service. The area of "artificial intelligence' confined to selected disciplines where construction of inferential schema was considerably comforting, attempts were made to "Automatically Synthesise Colon Class Numbers" a work of intricate texture (Neelameghan & Venkataraman, 1968 [9], Venkataraman & Neelameghan, 1968 [13]). However, after 1986 and till the end of 1990's the number of papers on Automating Libraries started catching up and using then emerging DBMS was quite large, and papers on library housekeeping operations and on different modules on library operations were built and published at a regular sequence.

The 1970's brought a revolution on information science and saw the conceptualization of philosophy of international information systems, and saw the emergence of UNESCO/UNISIST (programme and also mission/discipline –oriented, International cooperative information systems. This influenced the member countries, e.g. of UNESCO to re-organize their national information infrastructure. This resulted in the establishment of NISSAT and Sectoral Information Systems under it in India. The periodical brought out few special issues which provided systematic guidelines for the design, planning and development of specialized Library and Information Centres and the formation of several of them such as – NICMAP (CMTI), NICFOS (CFTRI), NICLAIR (CLRI) and so on. This regenerated the application of some modeling concepts, manpower planning using a systematized 'staff formula' and design and development of several specialized information services. The DRTC in collaboration with INSDOC conducted many training programmes to train LIS professionals and as well scientists' users of the CSIR Laboratories. In turn this was the impacted due to the series of papers published in the periodical on most of the sectoral information centres and systems.

The periodical also emphasized on LIS education, teaching. It can be further emphasized in this context that the periodical created a series entitled "Teaching of Library Science" and later as "Education for Library and Information Science". This implies the importance given towards systematic delivery and dissemination of professional knowledge and also stressed on effective learning both by teachers as well as students. The teaching method was designed to be highly interactive and participative. It is a well known fact that the teaching and learning process happened during the morning walks of students of DRTC along with Dr.

Ranganathan. The ideas generated at such walks were discussed in class rooms and papers on this account appeared in the early volumes of the periodical.

The continuous professional development was considered a very serious activity and papers were published in the periodical under "Development of Library Science" and to assess the user needs several papers appeared in the periodical under the series "Information User Studies". Though the first paper on Information Literacy appeared in 2004 and it is found there awere few papers on this subject with the enhanced interest in the last decade, whereas the number of papers on User Education and Training are comparatively more, and a series of papers were published during the 1970's.

The exposure to the subject Bibliometrics to the profession was made through this periodical with a paper that appeared late in the 1980's. It is well known that Dr. Ranganathan introduced the concept of "Librametry" as early as in 1948 at the International Conference on Scientific Information held in 1948 organised by Royal Society, London (Ranganatha, 1995) [11]. Many papers were published on Bibliometrics under the series "Librametry Series". Thus the periodical has initiated several concepts which are also being contemplated even in the present times and it is evident from the fact that the periodical has very successfully completed 50 years of its fruitful existence and promisingly it is going to serve the cause of the profession for many more years to come. In the meantime it has also changed with times and has been publishing papers in emergent fields of LIS. In the initial years, the periodical was publishing only full length articles and no book reviews or editorials appeared. In the last decade the journal has introduced a Guest Editorial and the Book Reviews for the books received at SRELS. But surprisingly, no Book Review has appeared so far for the books and monographs generated from the "Endowment Lecture Series".

9 CONCLUSION

This analysis initially desired just to present a quantitative map of the papers published in the last fifty years of SRELS Journal of Information Management (formerly Library Science with a slant to documentation) by counting and quantifying them by heads of broad subjects of LIS. In a gradual process of examining their idea content, to the present, a distinct and diverse view of the papers was conceived as useful to incite and identify new areas of research by the visualization of gaps in the papers appeared in the last 50 years. In the historical method of research, two distinct paths are conceptualized – one a chronological presentation of the happenings and the second a conceptual development of a phenomena or event or an organization. In this context the second method is adopted here for presenting the periodical's more enduring features.

10 ACKNOWLEDGEMENTS

The author expresses his gratitude to Sarada Ranganathan Endowment for Library Science for giving him the opportunity to prepare this paper and present his views, and hopes it would be helpful for furthering the research work.

REFERENCES

1. Asundi, AY. (2013). Taxation and other Regulatory norms on e-Scholarly Communication. (Editorial). *SRELS Journal of Information Management*, 50(4): 357-358.
2. Asundi, A.Y. (2013). Principles for Helpful Sequence and Deduction of knowledge organization systems – An exploratory study. *Journal of Information Science Theory and Practice,* 1(2): 6-15.
3. Neelameghan, A. (1970) Seminal mnemonics as a pattern for systems analysis. *Library Science with a slant to Documentation,* 7(4): 353-364.
4. Neelameghan A. (2007) Seminal mnemonic and leitmotif. *Information Studies*, 13(4): 185-186.
5. Neelameghan, A. and Raghavan, K.S. (2006) Seminal Mnemonics in Knowledge Organization: Ancient Traditions and Modern Practices. *Information Studies,* 12(1): 5-26.
6. Neelameghan, A. and Ravichandra Rao, I.K. (1976) Non-hierarchical associative relationships and computer-generation of RT links. *Library Science with a slant to Documentation,* 13(1): 24-42.
7. Neelameghan, A. and Raghavan, K.S. (2006) Semantics of Relationships in Knowledge Organization - Lateral Relationships: Update 1. *Information Studies,* 12(2): 115-122.
8. Neelameghan A. and Raghavan, K.S. (2005) Semantics of Relationships in Knowledge Organization: Lateral Relationships. SRELS *Journal of Information Management,* 42(4): 361- 382.
9. Neelameghan, A. and Venkataraman, S. (1968) Use of computer for the synthesis of class numbers: A case study with a freely faceted version of Colon Classification. *Library Science with a slant to Documentation,* 5(4): 359-388.
10. Ranganathan, S.R. (1968) Doc-Finder. *Library Science with a slant to Documentation,* 5(4): 289-302.
11. Ranganathan, S.R. (1995) Librametry and its scope (Reprinted). *JISSI: The International Journal of Scientometrics and Informetrics,* 1(1): 15-21.
12. Ravichandra Rao, I.K. (1972) Dispersion of documents on survey analysis: Bradford and Pareto distributions. *Library Science with a slant to Documentation*, 9(3): 396-403.
13. Venkataraman, S. and Neelameghan, A. (1968) Document finding. *Library Science with a slant to Documentation,* 5(4): 331-358.

List of Contributors

Asundi, A.Y.

Professor and Chairman (Ret.), Dept. of Library and Information Science, Officer-in-charge, IT Centre, Bangalore University, Bangalore -560 079, INDIA.

E-mail: ashok_asundi@yahoo.com

Bala, Adarsh

Government Medical College & Hospital, Sector 32, Chandigarh, INDIA.

E-mail: adarshbindu@rediffmail.com

Basu, Aparna

National Institute of Science Technology and Development Studies (CSIR-NISTADS), Dr. K.S. Krishnan Marg, Pusa Gate, New Delhi 110012, INDIA.

E-mail: aparnabasu.dr@gmail.com

Dutta, Bidyarthi

Asst. Professor, Department of Library & Information Science, Vidyasagar University, Midnapore 721 102, West Bengal, INDIA.

E-mail: bidyarthi.bhaswati@gmail.com

Dwivedi, Sandhya

H.C. P.G. College, Varanasi, Uttar Pradesh, INDIA.

E-mail: sandhpandey79@gmail.com

Garg, K.C.

Ex-Chief Scientist, National Institute of Science Technology and Development Studies (CSIR-NISTADS), Dr. K.S. Krishnan Marg, Pusa Gate, New Delhi 110012.

E-mail: gargkc022@gmail.com

Gun, Raf

Institute for Education and Information Sciences, IBW, University of Antwerp, Venusstraat 35, Antwerp, B-2000 BELGIUM. E-mail: raf.guns@ua.ac.be

Gupta, B.M.

National Institute of Science Technology and Development Studies (CSIR-NISTADS), Dr. K.S. Krishnan Marg, Pusa Gate, New Delhi 110012, INDIA. E-mail: bmgupta1@gmail.com

Harinarayana, N.S.

Associate Professor, Department of Library and Information Science, University of Mysore, Mysore 570 006, INDIA. E-mail: ns.harinarayana@gmail.com

Koley, Susanta

Librarian, Durgapur Institute of Advanced Technology & Management, G.T. Road Rajbandh, Durgapur, Burdwan, West Bengal, INDIA. E-mail: shayanikoley.2013@gmail.com

Kretschmer, Hildrun

National Institute of Science Technology and Development Studies (CSIR-NISTADS), Dr. K.S. Krishnan Marg, Pusa Gate, New Delhi 110012, INDIA. E-mail: bmgupta1@gmail.com

Kumar, S.

National Institute of Science Technology and Development Studies (CSIR-NISTADS), Dr. K.S. Krishnan Marg, Pusa Gate, New Delhi 110012, INDIA. E-mail: sureshkr@nistads.res.in

Kumbar, B.D.

Karnatak University, Department of Library & Information Science, Dharwad 580 003, Karnataka, INDIA. E-Mail: bdkumbar@yahoo.com

Liu, Yuxian

Library of Tongji University, Tongji University, Siping Street 1239, Shanghai, 200092, CHINA. E-mail: yxliu@lib.tongji.edu.cn

Raju, N. Vasantha

Librarian, Government First Grade College, Periyapatna. INDIA.
E-mail: vasanthrz@gmail.com

Rath, Durga Sankar

Professor, Department of Library & Information Science, Vidyasagar University, Midnapore 721 102, West Bengal, INDIA

Ravichandra Rao, I.K.

Visiting Scientist, Knowledge Analytics and Ontology Engineering Centre (KAnOE), PES Institute of Technology, Bangalore-560085, INDIA.

Former Professor and Head, Documentation Research and Training Centre, Indian Statistical Institute, Bangalore-560059, INDIA.
E-mail: ikrrao@hotmail.com

Rousseau, Ronald

Institute for Education and Information Sciences, IBW, University of Antwerp, Venusstraat 35, Antwerp, B-2000 BELGIUM. E-mail: ronald.rousseau@ua.ac.be

Faculty of Engineering Technology, VIVES-KHBO (Association KU Leuven), Zeedijk 101, Oostende, B-8400, BELGIUM, KU Leuven, Leuven B-3000, BELGIUM

Sangam, S.L.

Former Professor & Chairman, Department of Library and Information Science, Karnatak University, Dharwad 580003, INDIA. E-mail: slsangam@gmail.com

Santosh Kumari

Government Medical College & Hospital, Sector 32, Chandigarh, INDIA.
E-mail: parjapattisantosh@gmail.com

Saxena, Anurag

Indira Gandhi National Open University (IGNOU), New Delhi, INDIA.
E-mail: anurags@ignou.ac.in

Sen, B.K.

Project Investigator, Indian National Science Academy, 80, Shivalik Apartments, Alaknanda, New Delhi-110019, INDIA. E-mail: bksen1938@gmail.com

Sethukumari, S. Niruba

Research Scholar, Manonmaniam Sundaranar University Library, Tirunelveli 627 012, INDIA. E-mail: nirubasathish@gmail.com

Shivaranjini, S. Mogali

Research Scholar, Department of Library and Information Science, Karnatak University, Dharwad 580003. INDIA. E-mail: mogali.ranju@gmail.com

Stegmann, Johannes

Karnatak University, Department of Library and Information Science, Dharwad 580 003, Karnataka, INDIA. E-Mail: bdkumbar@yahoo.com

Thirumagal, A.

Librarian, Manonmaniam Sundaranar University, Tirunelveli 627 012, INDIA.
E-mail: librarian@msuuniv.ac.in; athirumagala@yahoo.co.in

Visakhi, P.

Indian Institute of Science Education and Research (IISER) Mohali, S.A.S. Nagar, Mohali 140306, Punjab, INDIA. E-mail: visakhi @iisermohali.ac.in

INDEX